Emerging Issues in Global Marketing

James Agarwal • Terry Wu

Editors

Emerging Issues in Global Marketing

A Shifting Paradigm

 Springer

Editors
James Agarwal
Haskayne Research Professor & Full
Professor of Marketing at the Haskayne
School of Business
University of Calgary
Calgary, AB, Canada

Terry Wu
Faculty of Business and Information
Technology
University of Ontario Institute of
Technology
Oshawa, ON, Canada

ISBN 978-3-319-74128-4   ISBN 978-3-319-74129-1   (eBook)
https://doi.org/10.1007/978-3-319-74129-1

Library of Congress Control Number: 2018933598

Printed on acid-free paper

This Springer imprint is published by the registered company Springer International Publishing AG part of Springer Nature.
The registered company address is: Gewerbestrasse 11, 6330 Cham, Switzerland

Foreword

This world has become a global marketplace and Professors Agarwal and Wu did an outstanding job of editing a book that presents the paradigm shift in global marketing. Inside the covers of this book, you will find a wide range of topics that are pertinent to consumers, businesses, institutional thinkers, and policy makers in navigating the current dynamics of the global world. The topics examined include trends in political risk across the globe and their impact on global marketing, the influence of cultural values in shaping consumer behavior, cross-border e-commerce (CBEC) as a new driver of international trade in the global economy, global brand positioning, and the role of social media that allows for real-time interaction among business-to-business (B2B), peer-to-peer (P2P), and consumer-to-consumer (C2C) markets, as well as between business-to-customer (B2C) markets. Of course, markets are different and you will find insights on differences across emerging markets with special reference to entry mode strategies of MNEs (multinational enterprises) and e-commerce firms. Finally, you will be intrigued by thought-provoking ideas on global CSR, sustainability, and macromarketing issues.

This book has been put together in a way that crystallizes the cohesiveness of the topics covered by different authors so as to present a unified picture of the global marketplace. This book is recommended reading for every serious student, scholar, practitioner, and administrator concerned with issues of a global economy.

Georgia Institute of Technology (Georgia Tech),   Naresh K. Malhotra
Scheller College of Business   ,
Atlanta, GA, USA

Contents

Part I   Introduction

**1   The Changing Nature of Global Marketing:
A New Perspective**   3
James Agarwal and Terry Wu

Part II   Emerging Trends in Global Markets

**2   A Thematic Exploration of the Changing Trends
in Political Risk and Global Marketing Scholarship
in the Last Three Decades (1986–2015): Implications
and Future Research**   15
James Agarwal, Tatiana Vaschilko, and Elena Loukoianova

**3   Does Country or Culture Matter in Global Marketing?
An Empirical Investigation of Service Quality
and Satisfaction Model with Moderators in Three Countries**   61
Naresh K. Malhotra, James Agarwal, and G. Shainesh

4   Cross-Border E-Commerce: A New Driver of Global Trade   93
Yanbin Tu and Joe Z. Shangguan

Part III   Global Marketing Strategies

5   Standardized Global Brand Management Using C-D Maps   121
Charan K. Bagga and Niraj Dawar

**6   Social Network Brand Visibility (SNBV):
Conceptualization and Empirical Evidence**   149
Aijaz A. Shaikh, Richard Glavee-Geo, Adina-Gabriela Tudor,
Chen Zheng, and Heikki Karjaluoto

7 **Reconfiguring the Marketing Mix to Counter
   the Counterfeits in the Global Arena** 179
   Karminder Ghuman and Hemant Merchant

8 **Bridging Institutional Distance: An Emerging
   Market Entry Strategy for Multinational Enterprises** 205
   Ogechi Adeola, Nathaniel Boso, and James Adeniji

9 **E-Commerce in Emerging Economies: A Multi-theoretical
   and Multilevel Framework and Global Firm Strategies** 231
   James Agarwal and Terry Wu

Part IV   Global CSR, Sustainability, and Macromarketing Issues

10 **CSR-Driven Entrepreneurial Internationalization:
    Evidence of Firm-Specific Advantages
    in International Performance of SMEs** 257
    Maria Uzhegova, Lasse Torkkeli, Hanna Salojärvi,
    and Sami Saarenketo

11 **Case Study of Corporate Social Responsibility
    in Japanese Pharmaceutical Companies: A Comparison
    with Western Firms** 291
    Terry Wu and Yuko Kimura

12 **How Do Western Luxury Consumers Relate
    with Virtual Rarity and Sustainable Consumption?** 311
    Anne-Flore Maman Larraufie and Lucy Sze-Hang Lui

13 **Putting African Country Development
    into Macromarketing Perspective** 333
    Mark Peterson and Saman Zehra

Index 369

List of Figures

Fig. 2.1   EFA path diagram for Russia, 2001–2005 22
Fig. 2.2   Scree plot for Russia, 2001–2005... 23
Fig. 2.3   Change in factor scores for Russia, 2001–2005 25
Fig. 2.4   Factor loadings for the first two factors for BRICS
           and MINT countries 26
Fig. 2.5   Temporal changes in the EFA-based index of political
           risk of BRICS and MINT countries for 1986–2015.................... 28
Fig. 2.6   EFA-based index and ICRG political risk rating: geographic
           maps 1986–2015.. 30
Fig. 2.7   Total number of publications per journal per year, 1986–2015.... 32
Fig. 2.8   Distribution of the percentages of cases for each automatically
           identified topic, 1986–2015... 34
Fig. 2.9   Preliminary clusters of broad areas of global marketing
           scholarship based on automated content analysis 35
Fig. 2.10 (**a, b**) Distribution of number of cases on global marketing
           (Dictionary Approach), 1986–2015. Distribution of number
           of cases on ICRG political risk categories (Dictionary Approach),
           1986–2015 37
Fig. 2.11 The word cloud of keywords and key phrases in the entire
           corpus of scholarly articles, 1986–2015..................................... 39
Fig. 2.12 Number of published papers per topic per journal, 1986–2015.
           Note: the category "world economic system" includes
           mention of all the countries 40
Fig. 2.13 The number of publications per major topic for each time
           period: 1986–1995, 1996–2005, 2006–2015.............................. 41
Fig. 2.14 Subcategories of the world economic system, for 1986–2015..... 41
Fig. 2.15 Research topics in global marketing scholarship, 1986–2015 42
Fig. 2.16 Co-occurrence of research topics in global marketing
           and research on BRICS and MINT, 1986–2015.......................... 43
Fig. 2.17 Distribution of global marketing topics per journal,
           1986–2015 44

Fig. 2.18	Distribution of ICRG topics per journal, 1986–2015	45
Fig. 2.19	Temporal changes in the number of published papers per ICRG political risk topic, 1986–2015	46
Fig. 2.20	Co-occurrence of major research topics with research on BRICS, MINT, and the rest of the world	46
Fig. 2.21	The number of papers on BRICS and MINT per journal, 1986–2015	47
Fig. 2.22	The temporal changes in the number of papers on BRICS and MINT, 1986–2015	48
Fig. 2.23	The co-occurrences of ICRG political risk categories with research on BRICS and MINT, 1986–2015	49
Fig. 2.24	Research across BRICS and MINT countries, 1986–2015	49
Fig. 2.25	Research on BRICS and MINT countries across journals, 1986–2015	50
Fig. 2.26	Changes in global marketing scholarship across three time periods: 1986–1995, 1996–2005, 2006–2015	52
Fig. 3.1	Second-order service quality→satisfaction model with moderators: cross-national vs. cross-cultural analysis	71
Fig. 4.1	Export CBEC in China (Data Source: CECRC 2016)	99
Fig. 4.2	Bonded warehousing vs. direct import (Source: Ng 2015)	100
Fig. 4.3	Infrastructure and environment of China's CBEC (Source: Revisions on Lee 2015)	101
Fig. 4.4	Trading center service in CBEC pilot cities (Source: CFTA 2015)	104
Fig. 4.5	Abandoned products by DaiGou at Airport	106
Fig. 5.1	C-D map of US passenger car market (Map reproduced from Dawar and Bagga 2015a)	124
Fig. 5.2	Flow chart detailing C-D mapping implementation in international markets	134
Fig. 5.3	Details of alpha and its competition in all seven markets	137
Fig. 5.4	C-D maps of Italy and France. C-D map of Italy, dashed orange circle represents competitive set, dashed blue circle represents cognitive neighbors. C-D map of France, dashed orange circle represents competitive set, dashed blue circle represents cognitive neighbors	139
Fig. 5.5	Alpha's cognitive neighbors and competition in Spain. *Dashed orange circle* represents competitive set. Dashed blue circle represents cognitive neighbors	140
Fig. 5.6	Distance of Alpha from Beta in each of the seven countries	141
Fig. 5.7	Alpha's performance along the consumer's decision-making journey. Dashed red circles represent where Alpha is weak along the customer decision journey	141
Fig. 5.8	Budgetary implications for Alpha in each market	143
Fig. 5.9	Which positioning dimension makes more sense?	144

Fig. 6.1	Four-dimensional conceptualization of SNBV............................	155
Fig. 6.2	SNBV-relationship variables framework....................................	155
Fig. 6.3	Conceptual model (A)	158
Fig. 6.4	Conceptual model (B)	161
Fig. 6.5	Results of structural model with second-order loadings (model A)...	166
Fig. 6.6	Results of path analysis (structural model B)............................	167
Fig. 7.1	Counterfeiting issues affecting the brand owners......................	184
Fig. 7.2	Institutional context affecting trade in counterfeits....................	187
Fig. 7.3	Conventional marketing mix	188
Fig. 7.4	Extended marketing mix constituents to counter the counterfeits	189
Fig. 7.5	Extended marketing mix..	190
Fig. 8.1	FDI inflows into Africa ($ Millions) (Data source: UNCTAD: World Investment Report 2015)	212
Fig. 8.2	Using stakeholder engagement to bridge institutional distance ...	217
Fig. 9.1	E-commerce in emerging economies: a multilevel framework	237
Fig. 10.1	A research framework	269
Fig. 10.2	Distribution of sample by industry, % from total sample............	270
Fig. 10.3	A primary international entry mode	270
Fig. 10.4	A mediating model	275
Fig. 10.5	Indirect effect of market-sensing capability through social responsibility on international performance (Note: $*p < 0.05$, $**p < 0.01$, $***p < 0.001$)	275
Fig. 10.6	Indirect effect of environmental responsibility through social responsibility on international performance (Note: $*p < 0.05$, $**p < 0.01$, $***p < 0.001$)	276
Fig. 11.1	Product donations-performance matrix	304
Fig. 12.1	Conceptual framework	325
Fig. 13.1	The SSI's 3 dimensions, 7 categories, and 21 dimensions (Source: Sustainable Society Foundation http://www.ssfindex.com/ssi/framework/)..................................	335
Fig. 13.2	Africa and the rest of the world on the 21 dimensions of the SSI in 2016..	338
Fig. 13.3	Africa and the other developing countries on the 21 dimensions of the SSI in 2016. * = group means are statistically the same (others are statistically different at $p = 0.05$)...............................	339
Fig. 13.4	Africa, other developing countries, and developed countries on averages for well-being	340
Fig. 13.5	Political map of Africa (GeoCurrents 2017)	342

Fig. 13.6   United Nations Statistics Division's geoscheme
               for Africa's five regions 354
Fig. 13.7   2006–2016 change in 21 SSI dimensions for the 5 regions
               of Africa 355
Fig. 13.8   2016 SSI ratings on three dimensions of well-being
               for UN regions of the world 356
Fig. 13.9   Average of three well-being dimensions for UN regions
               of the world 357
Fig. 13.10 Overall sustainability scores for Africa, other developing
               countries, and developed countries 358

List of Tables

Table 2.1	Rotated factor loadings for Russia, 2001–2005	22
Table 3.1	Psychometric properties of measurement model and correlation matrix	75
Table 3.2	Service quality structural model: cross-national vs. cross-cultural analysis...	77
Table 3.3	Moderating role of individualism: cross-national analysis vs. cross-cultural analysis....................................	79
Table 3.4	Moderating role of uncertainty avoidance: cross-national analysis vs. cross-cultural analysis.............................	81
Table 4.1	Global online retail sales	94
Table 4.2	CBEC vs. traditional international trade	94
Table 4.3	Trade volume of China's CBEC......................................	95
Table 4.4	Fitted i-based N-OLI framework for CBEC.....................	97
Table 4.5	The structure of China's CBEC......................................	98
Table 4.6	Traditional international trade vs. cross-border e-commerce	99
Table 4.7	Ten pilot cities for CBEC	103
Table 4.8	Key support and promotion policies for China's CBEC	105
Table 5.1	Comparison of the C-D mapping method vis-à-vis other global brand management methodologies..................................	126
Table 6.1	Summary of past literature on SNBV...............................	153
Table 6.2	Six-dimensional social network brand visibility conceptualization..	154
Table 6.3	Measures and items	162
Table 6.4	Demographic characteristics of respondents...................	163
Table 6.5	Correlation matrix	164
Table 6.6	Three-dimensional SNBV, with first- and second-order loadings...	166
Table 6.7	Results of hypothesis testing (model A)........................	167
Table 6.8	Results of hypothesis testing (model B)........................	168

Table 7.1 Profile of different groups of counterfeit producers 181
Table 7.2 Mapping extended marketing mix to counterfeit issues.............. 198

Table 8.1 Major Nigerian oil production joint ventures
(slightly amended to reflect parent name of the companies)........ 215

Table 10.1 Differences in CSR between MNCs and SME............................ 261
Table 10.2 A typology of responsible business practice orientation.............. 266
Table 10.3 Descriptive statistics and correlations of key variables................ 274
Table 10.4 Results of hypotheses test... 274

Table 11.1 Overall ranking and rating (2016) 302
Table 11.2 Product donations and philanthropic activities index (2016) 302
Table 11.3 Company financial information for fiscal year 2016.................... 303

Table 12.1 List of participants.. 316

Table 13.1 SSI dimensions, measures, and source of measures.................... 336
Table 13.2 The dimensions of the SSI and corresponding dimensions
of the UN's sustainable development goals................................. 337
Table 13.3 Typology of progress-prone and progress-resistant cultures
(Grondona 2000) 360

List of Appendices

Appendix 6.1 Six-dimensional conceptualization of SNBV 172
Appendix 6.2 Standardized parameter estimates
(second-order loadings) 173
Appendix 6.3 Single-phase data collection procedure
for developing measures (Source: Adapted
from Churchill 1979:66) 173

Appendix 10.1 International performance, market-sensing capability,
social responsibility, and environmental responsibility 282

List of Contributors

James Adeniji Leeds University Business School, University of Leeds, Leeds, UK

Ogechi Adeola Lagos Business School, Pan-Atlantic University, Lekki, Nigeria

James Agarwal Haskayne Research Professor & Full Professor of Marketing at the Haskayne School of Business, University of Calgary, Calgary, AB, Canada

Charan K. Bagga Haskayne School of Business, University of Calgary, Calgary, Alberta, Canada

Nathaniel Boso KNUST School of Business, Kwame Nkrumah University of Science and Technology, Kumasi, Ghana

Niraj Dawar Ivey Business School, Western University, London, ON, Canada

Karminder Ghuman LM Thapar School of Management, Thapar University, Patiala, India

Richard Glavee-Geo Department of International Business, NTNU-Norwegian University of Science and Technology, Aalesund, Norway

Heikki Karjaluoto Jyväskylä University School of Business and Economics, University of Jyväskylä, Jyväskylä, Finland

Yuko Kimura School of Business, University of Leicester, Leicester, UK

Anne-Flore Maman Larraufie SémioConsult® & ESSEC Business School, Paris, France

Elena Loukoianova Asia and Pacific Department of the International Monetary Fund (IMF), Washington, DC, USA

Lucy Sze-Hang Lui Fendi, Paris, France

Naresh K. Malhotra Georgia Tech CIBER and Regents' Professor Emeritus, Scheller College of Business, Georgia Institute of Technology, Atlanta, GA, USA

Hemant Merchant University of South Florida in St. Petersburg, St. Petersburg, FL, USA

Mark Peterson College of Business, University of Wyoming, Laramie, WY, USA

Sami Saarenketo School of Business and Management, Lappeenranta University of Technology, Lappeenranta, Finland

Hanna Salojärvi School of Business and Management, Lappeenranta University of Technology, Lappeenranta, Finland

Aijaz A. Shaikh Jyväskylä University School of Business and Economics, University of Jyväskylä, Jyväskylä, Finland

G. Shainesh Indian Institute of Management (IIM), Bangalore, India

Joe Z. Shangguan School of Business, Robert Morris University, Moon Township, PA, USA

Lasse Torkkeli School of Business and Management, Lappeenranta University of Technology, Lappeenranta, Finland

Yanbin Tu School of Business, Robert Morris University, Moon Township, PA, USA

Adina-Gabriela Tudor Department of International Business, NTNU-Norwegian University of Science and Technology, Aalesund, Norway

Maria Uzhegova School of Business and Management, Lappeenranta University of Technology, Lappeenranta, Finland

Tatiana Vaschilko Haskayne School of Business, University of Calgary, Calgary, AB, Canada

Terry Wu Faculty of Business and Information Technology, University of Ontario Institute of Technology, Oshawa, ON, Canada

Saman Zehra College of Business, University of Wyoming, Laramie, WY, USA

Chen Zheng Department of International Business, NTNU-Norwegian University of Science and Technology, Aalesund, Norway

About the Authors

James Adeniji is a doctoral researcher in the Marketing Division of Leeds University Business School. His research seeks to understand motivations for employees seeking customer feedback and the effects of this behavior on relational assets such as trust and commitment, as well as employee performance measures. Prior to doctoral studies, James earned a first degree in accounting from the University of Oklahoma and an MSc in international accounting and finance from the University of Strathclyde.

Ogechi Adeola teaches marketing management at the Lagos Business School (Pan-Atlantic University), Nigeria. Her research interests include tourism and hospitality marketing, strategic marketing, digital marketing strategies, branding management, and export marketing strategies in developing economies, particularly sub-Saharan Africa. She has published academic papers in top scholarly journals. Her coauthored papers had won best paper awards in conference in 2016 and 2017. She is a fellow of the Institute of Strategic Management (ISMN), Nigeria, and the National Institute of Marketing of Nigeria (NIMN). She holds a doctorate in business administration (DBA) from Manchester Business School, UK, and started her career at Citibank Nigeria, spending approximately 14 years in the financial sector before moving into academia.

James Agarwal (PhD, Georgia Tech) holds the Haskayne research professorship and is full professor of marketing at the Haskayne School of Business (HSB), University of Calgary. He served as chair and research director of the Marketing Area at HSB from 2002 to 2005 and 2013–2015, respectively. He is listed in *Canadian Who's Who*, University of Toronto Press, and *Marquis Who's Who in America*. In 2017, he received the Albert Nelson Marquis *Lifetime Achievement Award* from Marquis Who's Who. He has published over 50 research papers in major refereed journals, proceedings, and book chapters and has presented his work in major national and international conferences in 20 countries. In 2005, he was listed in *Most Prolific Scholars in International Business Research* compiled by Cavusgil et al. (2005), authored articles published in *International Marketing*

Review in 1996–2006, and coauthored Xu et al.'s (2008) article published in *Asia Pacific Journal of Management*. He has received several best paper awards from the American Marketing Association and the Academy of Marketing Science. He is a member of the editorial review board of the *Journal of International Marketing* and *International Marketing Review*, among others. In his spare time, he is passionate about studying and teaching the Bible and is a member of Centre Street Church in Calgary, Alberta. He has been married to Pritam for 22 years and they have four children, Joel, Joshua, Johanan, and Joseph.

Charan K. Bagga is an assistant professor of marketing at the Haskayne School of Business. Charan has a PhD in marketing from the Ivey Business School, Canada, and was formerly a visiting professor at Tulane University (2015–2016). He does research in the areas of brand positioning, cognitive representations of competition and innovation, and consumer decision making in alternate market exchange settings. His research has been published in the *Harvard Business Review*, *MIT Sloan Management Review*, and the *Journal of Consumer Psychology*. Charan has also worked as a senior manager in sales and consulting at global corporations (CSC, Standard Chartered, and HCL) in the USA and India.

Nathaniel Boso is an associate professor of marketing and executive dean at KNUST School of Business, Kwame Nkrumah University of Science and Technology, Ghana. His research interests lie in international entrepreneurship and marketing and supply chain management from a developing economy perspective. His research has been published in leading journals including the *Journal of Business Venturing*, *Journal of Business Ethics*, *Journal of International Marketing*, *Journal of Product Innovation Management*, and *Industrial Marketing Management*, among many others. He received his PhD in international entrepreneurship and marketing from Loughborough University, UK.

Niraj Dawar is professor of marketing at the Ivey Business School, Canada. His research on marketing strategy and global consumer behavior has appeared in the *Journal of Marketing*, *Journal of Marketing Research*, *Journal of International Business Studies*, *Harvard Business Review*, and other outlets. He works with PhD and MBA students as well as with executives of leading companies around the world.

Karminder Ghuman has been the area chair in marketing and entrepreneurship and an associate professor at LM Thapar School of Management, Thapar University, Patiala, India, since July 2013. He was the PGP chair from May 2014 to February 2015 and possesses professional experience of 20 years in teaching and in corporate sector. He also heads the Venture Lab – Thapar, an incubation center of Thapar University, and is the coordinator for the Centre for Indian Management, Thapar University. With a PhD (rural marketing) and MBA from Himachal Pradesh University, Shimla, India, he did his MSc (sustainable development) from the Indian Institute of Ecology and Environment, New Delhi, India. He has attended numerous competency development programs at prestigious institutions like the University of Groningen, the Netherlands; the University of Twente, Holland; Indian School of Business (ISB), Hyderabad; CIIE, Indian Institute of Management, Ahmedabad; Indian Institute of Technology (IIT), Delhi; and Indian Institute of Management (IIM), Kozhikode. Dr. Ghuman's books titled *Rural Marketing* (2007) and *Management: Concept, Practice, and Cases* (2010) have been published by McGraw-Hill. His recent book *Effective Mentoring* has been published by Ane Books. He also coedited a book *Indian Management*, which was published by Bloomsbury in 2016.

Richard Glavee-Geo graduated with MSc and PhD in business logistics from Molde University College, Norway. He also has a postgraduate diploma in marketing (CIM-UK) and advanced marketing diploma from Harstad University College (now the Arctic University of Norway). He is associate professor of marketing/logistics and supply chain management (SCM) at the Department of International Business, Faculty of Economics and Management, Norwegian University of Science and Technology (NTNU), Norway. His teaching experience is in consumer behavior, marketing research, international marketing, logistics and SCM and export management at the undergraduate level, and international marketing at the master level. His research interest includes global logistics and SCM, country of origin, social media, bank marketing, interorganizational relationships, and consumer and organizational buying behavior. Richard is particularly interested in the use of second-generation structural equation modeling techniques (e.g., PLS) and CB-SEM application in the broader areas of business and management research. His publications include book chapters published by Palgrave Macmillan and IGI Global and articles published in *International Journal of Export Marketing*, *Research in International Business and Finance*, and *International Journal of Bank Marketing*.

Heikki Karjaluoto is a professor of marketing at the University of Jyväskylä, Finland. His research interests include electronic and mobile business, customer value, and financial services marketing. Previous publications have appeared in the *Computers in Human Behavior*, *Industrial Marketing Management*, *Internet Research*, and *Telecommunications Policy*, among others.

Yuko Kimura is currently a PhD candidate of social science in the School of Business at the University of Leicester, UK. She graduated with an MBA with merit from the University of Leicester. She obtained her bachelor's degree in pharmaceutical science from Meiji Pharmaceutical University. She has been a registered pharmacist with a national pharmacist certificate in Japan. She has worked in several divisions (medical affairs, global marketing, corporate social responsibility, corporate strategy, and research and development) of a Japanese pharmaceutical company in both Japan and the USA. Her research focuses on organizational behavior, cross-regional and functional collaboration, workplace learning, and lifelong learning. She has published in the *Journal of Business Research*.

Elena Loukoianova has worked at the IMF since 2002, and currently she is a deputy division chief at the Asia and Pacific Department of the International Monetary Fund (IMF). In the IMF, she has been working on country surveillance issues, financial inclusion, financial surveillance issues, financial soundness indicators (FSIs) methodology and use for surveillance, methodological and analytical issues of balance sheet analysis, macroprudential policies, and analytical tools to assess and monitor systemic risks. In 2008–2010, she worked as a senior economist (Russia and CIS) in Emerging Market Research for Emerging Europe and Middle East and Central Asia in Barclays Capital, London, as well as a senior economist at the European Bank for Reconstruction and Development (EBRD), where she evaluated policy dialogue and program implementation in different countries. Apart from political risk area, her current research focuses on global liquidity, monetary aggregates, and systemic risks, and she recently published a paper on these issues in the *Economic Policy*. Her work also appeared in the *European Economic Review* and the *Journal of Derivatives*. She holds a PhD in economics from the University of Cambridge, England, and a PhD in mathematics from Ulyanovsk State University, Russia.

Lucy Sze-Hang Lui graduated with an MBA in luxury business degree jointly at ISC Paris School of Management and Mod'Art International School of Fashion Design. She is trilingual in English, Cantonese, and Mandarin with an advanced proficiency in French. SzeHang is currently working as a sales associate at Fendi Paris. She previously worked as a sales associate in Loewe for her internship. She was also a property officer in a luxury residential estate in Hong Kong. In her position as a flight attendant for Cathay Pacific Airways, she demonstrated her abilities in providing customer service to VIPs and first-class passengers.

Naresh K. Malhotra is a senior fellow of Georgia Tech CIBER and a regent's professor emeritus at Scheller College of Business, Georgia Institute of Technology, USA. In 2010, he was selected as a marketing legend, and his refereed journal articles were published in nine volumes by SAGE with tributes by other leading scholars in the field. He has been listed in Marquis *Who's Who in America* continuously since the 51st edition in 1997 and in *Who's Who in the World* since 2000. In 2017, he received the Albert Nelson Marquis Lifetime Achievement Award from Marquis Who's Who. In 2015, he received the Lifetime Achievement Award from the Prestige Institute of Management, Gwalior, India. He received the prestigious Academy of Marketing Science CUTCO/Vector Distinguished Marketing Educator Award in 2005. In 2011, he received the Best Professor in Marketing Management, Asia Best B-School Award. He has several top (number one) research rankings that have been published. His marketing research books are global leaders. He is an ordained minister of the Gospel, a member and Deacon, First Baptist Church, Atlanta, and president of Global Evangelistic Ministries, Inc. This ministry has documented in independent reports more than 1.7 million people praying to receive Jesus Christ as personal Savior and Lord. He has been married to Veena for more than 36 years, and they have two grown children Ruth and Paul.

Anne-Flore Maman Larraufie graduated from the Military Academy of Saint-Cyr as an engineer, got an advanced master in strategy and management of international business (SMIB) from ESSEC Business School (France) and a Certificate in Advanced Studies at Thunderbird Business School (USA), and finally completed her PhD in business administration at ESSEC. After several working experiences in various companies including EADS and LVMH (Guerlain), she decided to set up her own consulting agency SémioConsult® while teaching in prestigious business schools and universities all around the world (ESSEC, HEC, Ca' Foscari, Shanghai Normal University, etc.). She also became a delegate of INPI (the French IP-regulating body) for the European Union and an expert on Made in France and Luxury for the French Ministry of Economy. She is an expert in luxury, consumer behavior, branding, and counterfeiting. She still pursues academic research and publishes in top-tier journals. She got recently the best paper award for her article on the e-semiotics of luxury, published in the *Journal of Global Fashion Marketing*. She is also the academic director of the Advanced Master in Strategy and Management of International Business at ESSEC, for the three campuses (two in Paris and one in Singapore), and as such manages yearly more than 300 students and works with an administrative team of 6 people, all spread around the world. She is also the academic director of Master in Management in the Perfume Industry in partnership with ISIPCA.

Hemant Merchant (PhD, Purdue University) is professor of global business at the University of South Florida in St. Petersburg, USA (USFSP). Prior to joining USFSP, he was a professor of international strategy and the dean's endowed research fellow at Simon Fraser University (Vancouver, Canada); his most recent position was at Florida Atlantic University (FAU). He currently is ranked as the tenth most prolific international management scholar in the world. His work has been published in several leading refereed journals, including the *Canadian Journal of Administrative Sciences*, *Global Strategy Journal*, *International Business Review*, *Journal of Management*, *Journal of World Business*, *Management International Review*, *Multinational Business Review*, *Strategic Management Journal*, and *Thunderbird International Business Review*. He has authored *Competing in Emerging Markets* (2008; Routledge) and coedited the *Handbook of Research on International Strategic Management* (2012; Elgar). His most recent edited volume is the *Handbook of Contemporary Research on Emerging Markets* (2016; Elgar). His research endeavors have earned him approximately $225,000 in various types of grants as well as six research accolades conferred by the *Academy of International Business* (AIB) and *Administrative Sciences Association of Canada* (ASAC). In 2006, Dr. Merchant won the Douglas Mackay Outstanding Paper Award – a coveted prize that he also won in 2005. In 1990, he earned AOM's Best Paper Award. He currently is the editor-in-chief of the *Journal of Asia Business Studies* and also a consulting editor at the *Journal of International Business Studies*, the top-ranked journal in international business. Until recently, he served as the "strategy" editor at the *International Journal of Emerging Markets* and the "strategic management and international business" editor at *Canadian Journal of Administrative Sciences*.

Mark Peterson received his PhD in marketing from Georgia Tech in 1994 and joined the University of Wyoming faculty in fall 2007 where he teaches doctoral, MBA (online and on-campus), as well as undergraduate students. His research interests include international marketing, marketing and society issues, as well as research methods. His research has been published in such outlets as *Journal of the Academy of Marketing Science*, *Entrepreneurship Theory and Practice*, *and the Journal of Macromarketing* (where he is ranked as the top author in terms of number of articles and number of citations). He was a Fulbright scholar at Bilkent University in Ankara, Turkey, in 2006. Mark's SAGE Publications book *Sustainable Enterprise: A Macromarketing Approach* in 2013 received three extensive reviews by authors including Shelby Hunt in the December 2012 issue of the *Journal of Macromarketing*. It is in use around the world on campuses, such as Virginia Tech and WU-Vienna. He worked for 11 years at the University of Texas at Arlington where he taught qualitative research to grad students in the specialty masters' program in marketing research. He received the Outstanding Senior Research Award from the College of Business at the University of Wyoming in 2016.

Sami Saarenketo is a professor of international marketing at the School of Business and Management, at Lappeenranta University of Technology, Finland. His primary areas of research interest are international marketing and entrepreneurship in technology-based small firms. He has published on these issues in the *Journal of World Business*, *International Business Review*, *Management International Review*, *European Journal of Marketing*, and *Journal of International Entrepreneurship*, among others.

Hanna Salojärvi is an associate professor at the School of Business and Management at Lappeenranta University of Technology. Her main research interests include customer relationships, customer knowledge management, and strategic orientations. She has published on these issues, for example, in *Industrial Marketing Management* and *European Journal of Marketing*, among others.

Aijaz A. Shaikh is a university lecturer (in marketing) at the Jyväskylä University School of Business and Economics in Finland. He earned his PhD (with a major in marketing) from the Jyväskylä University School of Business and Economics in Finland. Prior to that, he earned his MSc from the AACSB-accredited Hanken School of Economics in Finland, and he has more than 15 years of professional (mostly banking), teaching, and research experience. His primary research interests include both qualitative and quantitative studies in the broader areas of consumer behavior, mobile banking, branchless banking, Internet banking, payment systems, and social media. He has published in *Computers in Human Behavior*, *Telematics and Informatics*, and other refereed journals, such as the *Journal of Financial Services Marketing*, the *International Journal of E-Business Research*, and the *International Journal of Bank Marketing*.

G. Shainesh is professor of marketing, Indian Institute of Management (IIM) Bangalore. He has over two decades of research and teaching experience in India and abroad, including the Goteborg University (Sweden), University of St. Gallen (Switzerland), Audencia Nantes and IESEG (France), Vienna University and MCI Innsbruck (Austria), Bocconi University (Milan), and Curtin University of Technology (Perth). His research and teaching focus on CRM, brand management, services marketing, and innovations. He leads the cross-functional research initiative on consumer insights. His case study "Narayana Nethralaya: Expanding Affordable Eye Care" was the second place winner in the GlobaLens 2014 NextBillion Case Writing Competition. The "Best Professor in Marketing" Award was conferred on Shainesh by the CMO Asia Council during the "Best B-Schools in Asia" Awards, July 2011, Singapore. Shainesh is the editor-in-chief of the *Journal of Indian Business Research* (JIBR), an Emerald (UK) publication. His papers on services and relationship marketing have been published in the *MIS Quarterly*, *Journal of Service Research*, *Journal of International Marketing*, *International Journal of Bank Marketing*, *International Journal of Retail & Distribution Management*, *International Journal of Technology Management*, *Journal of Relationship Marketing, and International Marketing Review.* His books include *Customer Relationship Management: A Strategic Perspective* (Laxmi Publications) and *Customer Relationship Management: Emerging Concepts, Tools and Applications* (20th Reprint 2017, McGraw-Hill).

Joe Z. Shangguan is an associate professor of accounting at the School of Business, Robert Morris University. He holds a doctorate in accounting from the University of Connecticut. He conducts research on corporate financial reporting, the capital market implications of accounting information, and other interdisciplinary topics. He has published in the *Journal of Corporate Finance*, *Review of Quantitative Finance and Accounting, International Journal of Banking, Accounting and Finance, International Journal of Accounting and Finance,* and *Eurasia Economic Review.*

Lasse Torkkeli is an associate professor at the School of Business and Management at Lappeenranta University of Technology, Finland. His research interests include SME internationalization, business networks, organizational capabilities and competencies, and business-to-business interaction. He has previously published in the *Journal of International Entrepreneurship* and in the *European Management Journal,* among others.

Yanbin Tu is a professor of marketing at the School of Business, Robert Morris University, Pennsylvania. He is also a summer visiting professor and Chutian scholar at the School of Business, Jianghan University, China. He obtained his doctorate degree from the University of Connecticut. His research interests cover e-commerce, interactive marketing, database marketing, and customer relationship management. His work has appeared in *International Journal of Electronic Commerce, Applied Economics, Decision Support Systems, Journal of Electronic*

Commerce Research, *International Journal of Internet Marketing and Advertising*, *International Journal of Electronic Business*, and *Communications of the ACM*.

Adina-Gabriela Tudor is a graduate student at the Department of International Business Faculty of Economics and Management, Norwegian University of Science and Technology (NTNU), Norway.

Maria Uzhegova is a junior researcher at Lappeenranta University of Technology (LUT) School of Business and Management. Her research focuses on the international business relationships of firms, with specific emphasis on the role of corporate social responsibility and sustainability in internationalization of SMEs. She has previously published in the *International Journal of Multinational Corporation Strategy*.

Tatiana Lukoianova Vashchilko is an assistant professor in strategy and global management at Haskayne School of Business at the University of Calgary. After receiving her PhD in political science and MA in economics from the Pennsylvania State University, she worked as a visiting assistant professor in international business at the Sellinger School of Business at Loyola University Maryland (2015–2016), at the Max M. Fisher College of Business at the Ohio State University (2013–2015), and as a sessional instructor at the DeGroote School of Business at McMaster University (2013). Her main research centers on the strategic responses of multinational enterprises (MNEs) to new challenges and opportunities in international business environment. Specifically, her research focuses on the conditions under which international politics, international institutions, and political risks influence strategies and performance of MNEs. Her work has appeared in the *Journal of International Business Studies (JIBS)*, *International Business Review (IBR)*, and *Journal of the Association for Information Science and Technology (JASIST)*. Dr. Vashchilko was a finalist of the International Management (IM) Division Fundação Dom Cabral Best Paper in Strategy/International Business (IB) Theory Award and a finalist of the William H. Newman Dissertation Award at the 2013 AOM Annual Meeting.

Terry Wu is professor of business at the University of Ontario Institute of Technology (UOIT), Canada. His research focuses on international marketing, marketing of higher education, globalization, and trade policy. His research has been published in academic journals including *Management International Review*, *Columbia Journal of World Business*, *Journal of Marketing Management*, *International Marketing Review*, *Journal of Business and Industrial Marketing*, *Journal of International Communication*, and *Thunderbird International Business Review*, among others.

Saman Zehra is a marketing doctoral student at the University of Wyoming. She has an undergraduate degree in chemistry and a master's degree in business administration (MBA) with a concentration in marketing and human resource management from Aligarh Muslim University (A.M.U.), India. She was awarded two university gold medals for her academic performance at the master's level in business, as well as in management. She was also awarded the university merit scholarship at the undergraduate as well as at the master's level. After completing her MBA, she worked in the packaging films industry in India for 19 months as a senior executive in the marketing of exports to Europe and Canada. Her research interests include topics in consumer behavior, specifically the influence of religion, spirituality, and culture on the consumption of goods and services. In her spare time, she enjoys reading, cooking, and traveling.

Chen Zheng is a graduate student at the Department of International Business Faculty of Economics and Management, Norwegian University of Science and Technology (NTNU), Norway.

Endorsements

1. This well-crafted research volume is an excellent addition to the growing literature on new trends in international marketing. The authors present the latest insight on the impact of phenomena such as crossborder e-commerce and digital markets, and they discuss new tools for political risk assessment, international branding and more broadly the reconfiguring of marketing-mix strategies – A powerful reminder that the new global market remains a rugged landscape.

   – **Alain Verbeke** is McCaig Research Chair in Management and Editor-in-Chief Journal of International Business Studies, University of Calgary, Canada.

2. Emerging trends in institutions, markets, and societies, accompanied by new technological advances, are redefining the scope and strategy in global marketing. Professors Agarwal and Wu have assembled a remarkable collection of cutting-edge topics and issues that captures the shifting paradigm in global marketing. This book is very timely and makes a valuable contribution, useful for both scholars and practitioners of global marketing.

   – **Constantine S. Katsikeas** is Arnold Ziff endowed research chair in marketing and international management and editor-in-chief of the *Journal of International Marketing*, University of Leeds, UK.

3. This book presents new and cutting-edge thinking at a time when the traditional views of international marketing need to be scrapped. Convergence forces are creating new opportunities as well as threats on a daily basis, and marketing practitioners as well as scholars must be forewarned as well as forearmed on how to deal with these changes. The real growth is coming from the emerging nations, and the theories that provided sufficient insights 10 years ago have been completely outmoded by the ever-accelerating rate of innovation and technological

change as well as the pressures to address the needs of all of the firm's relevant stakeholders. The strategic insights provided here are absolutely invaluable. Don't miss an opportunity to read this book!

- **John B. Ford** is professor of marketing and international business, eminent scholar and Haislip-Rohrer fellow, and editor-in-chief of the *Journal of Advertising Research*, Old Dominion University, USA.

Part I
Introduction

Chapter 1
The Changing Nature of Global Marketing: A New Perspective

James Agarwal and Terry Wu

Abstract There have been significant changes in the global marketing landscape that is presenting contemporary threats and opportunities in markets, institutions, and technology for global marketers. Much of the mainstream research on global marketing has focused on the traditional marketing strategy combined with the traditional paradigms to analyze international markets. Global companies need to challenge traditional assumptions in global marketing in an era of shifting political, cultural, economic, and technological changes. Given scant research attention on the emerging issues in global marketing for the twenty-first century, there is a critical need for a new research direction to shed new insights into emerging and cutting-edge issues in global marketing. This book examines emerging theories and frameworks of global marketing and discusses how global marketing strategies are evolving and being re-calibrated in a globalized and digital economy that is fast changing.

Introduction

There have been significant changes in the global marketing landscape due to growing economic integration, declining trade barriers, and new global markets. As an outcome of globalization, there has been a rapid increase in international business transactions taking place since the beginning of the twenty-first century (Jormanainen and Koveshnikov 2012). Nowadays, companies are able to gain unprecedented access to a global market for consumers worldwide. At the same time, they are able to produce goods and services in other countries or source suppliers globally, achieving efficiency and reducing the cost of production (Trent and Monczka 2002).

J. Agarwal (✉)
Haskayne Research Professor & Full Professor of Marketing at the Haskayne
School of Business, University of Calgary, Calgary, AB, Canada
e-mail: james.agarwal@haskayne.ucalgary.ca

T. Wu
Faculty of Business and Information Technology, University of Ontario Institute of
Technology, Oshawa, ON, Canada

© Springer International Publishing AG, part of Springer Nature 2018
J. Agarwal, T. Wu (eds.), *Emerging Issues in Global Marketing*,
https://doi.org/10.1007/978-3-319-74129-1_1

While globalization of markets and production creates new market opportunities, it also brings in newer challenges and complexities for marketers in a globally competitive environment. In addition to the changing world economy, the global market is further transformed by major advances in information and communication technologies (ICT). Thus, the traditional approach to global marketing is no longer sufficient to address emerging issues in global markets for the twenty-first century. Global companies need to take a new look at the contemporary threats and opportunities in markets, institutions, and technology and how they affect entry and expansion strategies through careful recalibration of the marketing mix. They are likely to apply approaches different from those implemented in the past, reflecting a paradigm shift in global marketing.

Emerging Trends in Global Marketing

Global companies must deal with the new reality of global marketplace for global consumers in the twenty-first century. Several emerging trends are developing that present both opportunities and challenges for global marketers.

1. The world has witnessed increasing economic integration and gradual reduction of trade barriers over the last two decades, primarily as a result of the World Trade Organization (WTO) (Agarwal and Wu 2004). On the positive side, tariff and nontariff barriers, in general, are on the decline, leveling the playing field for global competitors. Several developing economies have deregulated erstwhile protected industries and have liberalized trade and investment policies. Signs of new market potential with authoritarian regimes are promising as embargoes are lifted. For example, after the normalization of US-Cuba relations, US companies are permitted to enter the Cuban market, raising hopes that Cuba is at last ending its more than 60 years of isolation. Similarly, Myanmar has undergone substantial economic and political reforms since 2010, allowing the US and other Western countries to lift their economic sanctions. On the negative side, there are some indications that globalization is facing strong headwinds across countries. Emerging political risks and security concerns are changing the global game plan as economies falter under populist leadership (e.g., Venezuela) and countries begin to weaken their commitment to regional trading blocs. The political climate has significantly changed after the US withdrawal from Trans-Pacific Partnership (TPP) in 2016 and the impending exit of the United Kingdom from the European Union (i.e., Brexit) scheduled for March 2019.
2. The increasing global competition for goods and services has led many business firms to develop international marketing strategies as part of their corporate mandate and corporate strategy. While previously the focus of international marketing was largely focused on the cultural differences at the country level, there is a call for challenging traditional assumptions underlying cultural distance and improving the quality of cross-cultural research in an era of global crossvergence (Merchant et al. 2012; Tung 2008). This has implications for global companies

with respect to market segmentation, i.e., vertical versus horizontal global market segmentation (Agarwal et al. 2010). Further, the role of institutional distance especially in the context of emerging markets is of particular interest for global marketers. Current research in institutional distance needs to make a careful theoretical and empirical distinction between institutional profile and institutional distance in the research context of emerging economies (Meyer and Peng 2016; Van Hoorn and Maseland 2016; Yang et al. 2012).

3. The spread of innovation and technology has enabled countries to produce new products and services across national boundaries. There has been an exponential growth in innovation and technological advances (Agnihotri et al. 2016) especially in emerging markets that is impacting the approach to global marketing as firms reach out to potential customers globally. The explosive growth of the Internet has transformed the global marketplace into a borderless world where goods, services, and information can be exchanged freely across national boundaries. Electronic commerce is replacing not only traditional retailing in the home country, but it is also transforming the pattern and speed of internationalization of online retailers in the global marketplace (Schu et al. 2016). At the same time, firms are using sophisticated data-capturing technologies, customer relationship management, big data, and social media to identify market needs, to build prototypes, to develop positioning and segmentation strategies, and ultimately to develop marketing mix strategies. These positive developments call for global marketers to incorporate newer methodologies to better understand brand positioning and brand management strategies using data from multiple sources. However, the downside risk of innovation and e-commerce has also resulted in the proliferation of the counterfeit market globally across multiple industries, a growing problem that needs to be effectively managed by deploying anti-counterfeit marketing strategies.

4. As growth has picked up in emerging markets and slowed down in advanced economies, firms have had to rethink their global strategies in exporting, contractual agreements, and foreign direct investments (Ramamurti 2012). With the recent growth of emerging economies, e.g., the BRICS countries (Brazil, Russia, India, China, and South Africa) as well as the MINT countries (Mexico, Indonesia, Nigeria, and Turkey), there is a critical need for scholars to redefine and reconceptualize new theories and conceptual frameworks that highlight the rapid globalization of firms, especially in the domain of e-commerce. E-commerce has not only revolutionized the global marketplace, but it has also brought about a paradigm shift in the way business is conducted in emerging economies, particularly in China and India (Agarwal and Wu 2015). However, one of the greatest challenges for global companies still prevalent in many emerging economies is the seemingly insurmountable "institutional distance" and "institutional voids" (Van Hoorn and Maseland 2016) compared to home markets. With economic development, global marketers are increasingly cognizant of rising stakeholder expectations of their company's CSR activities, i.e., triple bottom line, especially in emerging and bottom-of-pyramid (BOP) markets (Prahalad and Hammond 2002; Berman 2013). Stakeholders in general, and customers in particular, are increasingly demanding ethical products and consumption, ethical sourcing,

ethical value chains, social and environmental responsibility of companies, sustainable consumption, and marketing's positive role in society.

Despite the growing importance of global markets in the global economy, research is still limited to old research themes. Much of the mainstream research on global marketing has focused on the traditional marketing strategy combined with the traditional paradigms to analyze international markets. There is scant research attention on emerging issues in global marketing with little focus on emerging contemporary challenges and opportunities facing global marketers in the twenty-first century. Hence, there is an urgent need for a new research direction to shed new insights into emerging and cutting-edge issues in global marketing and highlight how global marketing strategies are changing in a globalized and digital economy that is fast changing. Against this background, this book aims to address the paucity of research that currently exists in this area. Drawing from many areas of expertise, this book presents emerging issues and shifting paradigms in global marketing. This book is organized as follows. The next section summarizes the 13 chapters presented in this book. The last section is devoted to a summary and conclusion.

Organization of the Book

This book is organized into 13 chapters. Part 1 (Chap. 1) is the introduction to the book in which the editors reflect on the paradigm shift in global marketing and summarize the key contributions made in each chapter. Part 2 (Chaps. 2, 3, and 4) discusses emerging trends in global marketing; Part 3 (Chaps. 5, 6, 7, 8, and 9) discusses global marketing strategies; and Part 4 (Chaps. 10, 11, 12, and 13) discusses global corporate social responsibility, sustainability, and macromarketing issues. Chapter 2 examines the trends in political risk across the globe and its impact on global marketing research in the past 30 years (1986–2015). To compare the political risk across countries, a novel measure of political risk index is derived from the exploratory factor analysis (EFA). This EFA-based index is then used to identify global, regional, and country-specific dimensions of political risk. Monthly data were collected from Political Risk Services' International Country Risk Guide (ICRG) political risk index's 12 components for each of 140 countries in three time periods, 1986–1995, 1996–2005, and 2006–2015. Each country's 5-year time series of 12 ICRG observations of political risk is analyzed using exploratory factor analysis. The purpose is to ascertain the latent factor structure of a country's political risk by identifying factors (i.e., factor loading plots) that contribute to intercorrelations of ICRG components. The second part of the chapter focuses on whether and how the scholarship in global marketing has captured the changing nature of the political risk landscape since the last 30 years. The scholarly evidence on political risk research can be demonstrated by publication records in the academic literature. Using a sample of seven top international business and marketing journals (*Journal of International Business Studies, Journal of World Business, Management*

International Review, International Business Review, Journal of Marketing, Journal of International Marketing, and *International Marketing Review*), an automated content analysis is conducted to ascertain publication frequencies, followed by the cluster analysis to group research areas. The results reveal the evolution of various research areas within global marketing (entry modality – FDI and contractual agreements, brand positioning, start-up innovation and global diffusion, and political risk and corruption) and identify existing gaps in research on political risk and global marketing.

Chapter 3 examines the influence of cultural values in shaping consumers' perception of service quality and satisfaction through cross-national vs. cross-cultural analysis. Prior research in global marketing has assumed cultural homogeneity within countries, and as a result, country and culture have been assumed to be synonymous. The objective of this study is to analyze the moderating role of the cultural values of individualism/collectivism and uncertainty avoidance on service quality dimensions and the relationship between perceived service quality (modeled as a second-order reflective construct) and satisfaction. A conceptual framework of service quality, customer satisfaction, and cultural values is developed to test several hypotheses. Survey data ($N = 1059$) were collected from bank customers in three countries – the United States, India, and Philippines – and the model tested using structural equations modeling (LISREL). This study provides a new and interesting perspective on international service quality. Despite globalization, cross-national research (i.e., country effect) continues to have important meaning and significance for global marketers. Yet, at the same time, findings also validate the need for cross-cultural research that recognizes within-country heterogeneity on cultural values, thus pointing to the right etic-emic balance. This study presents a number of theoretical, methodological, and managerial contributions that highlight the shifting paradigm in global marketing.

Chapter 4 explores cross-border e-commerce (CBEC) as a new driver of international trade in the global economy. The study adopts a modified version of i-based N-OLI framework (Agarwal and Wu 2015) for CBEC. Using China as a case study, the study examines the rapid growth, structure, export/import models, as well as infrastructure and environment of China's CBEC. It is found that China's CBEC success is attributed, both directly and indirectly, to several key factors: e-commerce giants such as Alibaba.com and JD.com, the designation of CBEC pilot cities, supportive governmental policies, and big capital inflows. The evidence presented in this study is a confirmation that strong government support, growing middle class, improved technologies, and increasing e-commerce adoptions by SMEs are in fact instrumental to the success of CBEC in China. This study also shows that cultural differences, customer trust, logistics, payment, and legal and regulatory barriers are among the biggest challenges facing CBEC. This chapter therefore brings a more nuanced understanding to CBEC with policy implications for foreign firms entering the Chinese market via e-commerce.

The third part of this book is devoted to global marketing strategies. Chapter 5 proposes the centrality-distinctiveness mapping (C-D mapping) methodology in global brand positioning. The C-D map methodology is explained with detailed guidelines for implementation and is applied to a large European company operating in seven European countries: France, Poland, Spain, Italy, the Netherlands, Sweden, and Germany. This approach allows marketers to detect differences in consumer perceptions of brands across markets. The distinct advantage of this methodology is that it sets consistent positioning and performance goals for a global brand across geographical markets, enabling global brand managers with brand standardization versus localization decisions. While the traditional globalization paradigm has shifted toward digital markets (Lund et al. 2016), e.g., Internet and social media that are fast converging in brand perceptions, country-specific competitive contexts still require local branding and positioning strategies. In addition to providing information on actual brand performance across countries, the C-D map methodology supplies a means and a vocabulary for strategic conversations about global brand positioning between headquarters and local managers.

Chapter 6 investigates social media that allows for real-time interaction among business-to-business (B2B), peer-to-peer (P2P), consumer-to-consumer (C2C), as well as between business-to-customer (B2C) markets. It is argued that customers are increasingly accessing and using social networking sites (SNS). For this reason, it is important for businesses and organizations to ensure a presence on these platforms to enhance corporate visibility. The objective of this chapter is to conceptualize and operationalize social network brand visibility (SNBV) in an exploratory study. A conceptual model is developed with six dimensions: social media presence, brand awareness, value equity, knowledge, social media marketing, and information exchange. Data were collected from an online survey in Norway, with a sample size of 122. Using structuring equation modeling (AMOS), two competing models were run to test the validity of testable hypotheses. Results showed validity for a three-dimensional SNBV model (i.e., brand awareness, value equity, and product knowledge). The findings reveal that social media plays an important role in promoting e-commerce.

Chapter 7 proposes different strategies to counter the global trade in counterfeit goods. The majority of efforts by governments to curb the trade in counterfeits have been largely ineffective. Despite rapid growth of global counterfeit trade, there is very little research in this area, especially a conceptual framework that can be used to explain anti-counterfeit interventions. Using a holistic framework, this study extends marketing mix variables to include anti-counterfeiting strategies for specific counterfeiting issues. The authors argue that reconfiguring the traditional marketing mix is a desirable solution for significantly stamping out counterfeit goods as part of the marketing program design.

In Chapter 8, the authors argue that there are significant differences across emerging markets with special reference to entry mode strategies of MNEs (multinational enterprises) to these markets. The focus of this study is on market entry strategy that would narrow the "institutional distance" (i.e., regulatory, cognitive, and normative) between MNEs' home and host markets, using Nigeria as an example. In terms of market entry strategies, this study identifies several key issues for MNEs to consider when entering the Nigerian market in order to build legitimacy: corporate social responsibility, social media engagement, governmental relations, and informal relational ties. The study reveals that cognitive and normative institutional distance is in fact a greater challenge for MNE to succeed in Nigeria than the regulatory institutional distance.

Chapter 9 develops a multi-theoretical and multi-level framework for analyzing growth potential of e-commerce in emerging economies. In developed economies, Internet usage and e-commerce have expanded rapidly in the last two decades. Recognizing the market potential of information technology, emerging economies are quickly embracing e-commerce as an engine of economic growth. Using a multi-theoretical and multi-level framework, this study examines determinants and deterrents of e-commerce growth potential in emerging economies. Understanding key factors influencing the development of e-commerce is of critical importance to the economic development of emerging economies. As expected, there are significant differences between developed and emerging economies in e-commerce growth. The first part of the study presents a multi-theoretical framework to explain growth of e-commerce in emerging economies. A combination of multiple theories on transaction cost economies, resource-based view, network theory, network-based ownership-location-internalization (N-OLI) paradigm, institutional theory, and entrepreneurship theory provides a theoretical framework in explaining e-commerce in emerging economies. To complement the multi-theoretical framework, this chapter also identifies the global (trade agreements, technological innovations, and strategic behavior of firms), national (institutional environment, infrastructure, and culture), and transactional (integrity of transactions, online intermediaries, and network externalities) level factors. Based on the conceptual framework, the study highlights implications for MNEs, both from developed markets and emerging markets, operating in emerging economies.

The fourth part of this book is devoted to global CSR, sustainability, and macro-marketing issues. Chapter 10 examines the role of corporate social responsibility (CSR) and market-sensing capability in firm performance in foreign markets. Previous studies on CSR focus primarily on large multinational enterprises (MNEs). This study attempts to fill the research gap by focusing on the impact of CSR on international performance of small- and medium-sized enterprises (SMEs). A conceptual model is developed to include three key variables: market-sensing capability, social responsibility, and environmental responsibility. The data used in this study was based on a sample of 85 CEOs from Finnish SMEs covering a variety of industries collected through an online survey. The findings based on regression and mediation analysis suggest that market-sensing capability improves socially responsible behavior which then contributes to international performance of SMEs. However, environmentally responsible behavior pays off and improves international performance only through social responsibility.

Chapter 11 examines corporate social responsibility (CSR) in the pharmaceutical industry comparing Japanese firms and Western firms. However, Japanese pharmaceutical companies have started late on CSR activities in comparison to their Western counterparts. The study is based on a sample of eight pharmaceutical companies: four Japanese-based firms and four Western-based firms. The samples consisting of Japanese firms are Eisai, Takeda, Astellas Pharma, and Daiichi Sankyo.

For comparison, the samples consisting of four non-Japanese Western firms are GlaxoSmithKline (GSK), Johnson and Johnson (J & J), Novartis, and Merck. The results suggest that there are differences between Japanese and Western firms in terms of the level of CSR.

Chapter 12 explores the relationship between virtual rarity and sustainable development in the luxury industry from Western consumers' perspective. In general, luxury goods are characterized by limited supply (rarity), high quality, premium value, and exorbitant price. Purchasing luxury products is to enhance one's self-image and to distinguish oneself from other groups. In contrast, sustainability focuses on environmental issues and social responsibility. In order to ascertain the relationship between virtual rarity and sustainable luxury goods, an interpretive qualitative interview was conducted in order to understand the beliefs and experiences of luxury consumers. The data used in this study is based on a sample of 20 respondents who are regular luxury customers from Europe, North America, and Latin America. In addition to basic demographic information, the respondents were asked to indicate their attitudes toward rarity and sustainable luxury in separate interviews. Content analysis was then used to analyze the interview data. The research found that quality and design are still the two key variables influencing purchase intention of luxury goods. Although consumers are generally aware of sustainability, they are reluctant to purchase luxury goods on the basis of sustainability only.

Chapter 13 focuses on macromarketing to understand the interactions among markets, marketing, and society at large. This study uses Sustainable Society Index to analyze country and regional developments in Africa. The purpose is to compare the indicators for human, environmental, and economic well-being for societies across the African continent. Specifically, comparisons are made with respect to (i) the rest of the world, (ii) other developing countries, and (iii) regions of the world. The results reveal that Africa does well on the planet (environmental) dimension. However, Africa lags in the people and profit dimensions (human and economic development). In the African context, these results have huge relevance for both African-based and non-African multinational firm strategies as marketing and society intersect each other in clear ways.

Conclusion

The chapters in this book form a collection of scholarly analyses that cover both emerging trends, theories, strategies, and applications relevant for global marketing in the twenty-first century. Emerging trends in the political, cultural, and economic landscape of countries and markets, accompanied by new developments in technological advances, e-commerce, and networked economies, are redefining the scope and strategy of global marketing. Global marketers are harnessing the power of e-commerce to enter new markets and reconfiguring their marketing mix, both online and offline, to better address the complex issues surrounding standardization vs. customization decisions in global markets. The challenge for global marketers is to think outside the "marketing mix" box in the bigger context of institutions, markets, and society at large. The book provides an impressive state-of-the-art overview of the "shifting paradigm" of global marketing that will be of relevance to both academic scholars and reflective managers and policymakers. It is hoped that the core insights found in this book will be of interest to current and future scholars and practicing managers to rethink global marketing strategies for a world market that is fast changing.

References

Agarwal, J., and T. Wu. 2004. China's entry to WTO: Global marketing issues, impact, and implications. *International Marketing Review* 21 (3): 279–300.

———. 2015. Factors influencing growth potential of E-commerce in emerging economies: An institution-based N-OLI framework. *Thunderbird International Business Review* 57 (3): 197–215.

Agarwal, J., N.K. Malhotra, and R.N. Bolton. 2010. A cross-national and cross-cultural approach to global market segmentation: An application using consumers' perceived service quality. *Journal of International Marketing* 18 (3): 18–40.

Agnihotri, R., R. Dingus, M.Y. Hu, and M.T. Krush. 2016. Social media: Influencing customer satisfaction in B2B sales. *Industrial Marketing Management* 53: 172–180.

Berman, J.E. 2013. *Success in Africa: CEO insights from a continent on the rise*. Brookline: Bibliomotion.

Jormanainen, I., and P.C.A. Koveshnikov. 2012. International activities of emerging market firms. *Management International Review* 52: 691–725.

Lund, S., J. Manyika, and J. Bughin. 2016. Globalization is becoming more about data and less about stuff. *Harvard Business Review* 94 (3):2–5.

Merchant, H., R.L. Tung, and A. Verbeke. 2012. The tenuous link between cultural distance and international strategy: Navigating the assumptions of cross-cultural research. In *Handbook of research on international strategic management*, ed. Alain Verbeke and Hemant Merchant. Edward Elgar: UK.

Meyer, K.E., and M.W. Peng. 2016. Theoretical foundations of emerging economy business research. *Journal of International Business Studies* 47: 3–22.

Prahalad, C.K., and A. Hammond. 2002. Serving the world's poor, profitably. *Harvard Business Review* 80 (9): 48–57.

Ramamurti, R. 2012. What is really different about emerging market multi-nationals? *Global Strategy Journal* 2: 41–47.

Schu, M., D. Morschett, and B. Swoboda. 2016. Internationalization speed of online retailers: A resource-based perspective on the influence factors. *Management International Review* 56: 733–757.

Trent, R.J., and R.M. Monczka. 2002. Pursuing competitive advantage through integrated global sourcing. *Academy of Management Executive* 16 (2): 66–80.

Tung, R.L. 2008. The cross-cultural research imperative: The need to balance cross national and intra-national diversity. *Journal of International Business Studies* 39 (1): 41–46.

Van Hoorn, A., and R. Maseland. 2016. How institutions matter for international business: Institutional distance effects vs. institutional profile effects. *Journal of International Business Studies* 47: 374–381.

Van Hoorn, A., and R. Maseland. 2016. How institutions matter for international business: Institutional distance effects vs. institutional profile effects. *Journal of International Business Studies* 47: 374–381.

Yang, Z., C. Su, and K.S. Fam. 2012. Dealing with institutional distances in international marketing channels: Governance strategies that engender legitimacy and efficiency. *Journal of Marketing* 76 (3): 41–55.

Part II
Emerging Trends in Global Markets

Chapter 2
A Thematic Exploration of the Changing Trends in Political Risk and Global Marketing Scholarship in the Last Three Decades (1986–2015): Implications and Future Research

James Agarwal, Tatiana Vaschilko, and Elena Loukoianova

Abstract This chapter analyzes temporal patterns in political risk across the globe and in global marketing scholarship in 1986–2015 to offer perspectives on emerging political risk issues for current and future research. We offer a novel measure of political risk based on exploratory factor analysis (EFA) to identify the most influential sources of political risk and its latent structure within a country in three time periods, 1986–1995, 1996–2005, and 2006–2015. This EFA-based measure provides a more nuanced way of analyzing global-, regional-, and country-level political risk dynamics compared to the existing indices based on the observable characteristics of political environment. We synthesize global marketing scholarship to examine the evolution of various research topics/themes within global marketing and identify potential future research directions on the impact of political risk on global marketing activities abroad.

The views expressed in this paper are those of the author(s) and do not necessarily represent the views of the IMF, its Executive Board, or IMF management.

J. Agarwal (✉)
Haskayne Research Professor & Full Professor of Marketing at the Haskayne School of Business, University of Calgary, Calgary, AB, Canada
e-mail: james.agarwal@haskayne.ucalgary.ca

T. Vaschilko
Haskayne School of Business, University of Calgary, Calgary, AB, Canada

E. Loukoianova
Asia and Pacific Department of the International Monetary Fund (IMF), Washington, DC, USA

© Springer International Publishing AG, part of Springer Nature 2018   15
J. Agarwal, T. Wu (eds.), *Emerging Issues in Global Marketing*,
https://doi.org/10.1007/978-3-319-74129-1_2

Introduction

As the world enters "a period of political recession" (Bremmer and Kupchan 2017) combined with the information overflow rather than the lack thereof, the nature and dynamics of political risks[1] have been shifting and inadvertently affecting international business in unpredictable ways. For example, the recent terrorist attacks in Paris, Beirut, Brussels, Berlin, and Barcelona demonstrate that "we are talking about a new qualitative threat, because we have arrived at the intersection of terrorism and globalization" (Melhem 2015) and the "traditional intelligence exchange is not enough anymore" to identify the potential of new terrorist threats (Walt 2016). In contrast to even a few years ago, most companies today have little doubt in the value of assessment of political risks, which can tell not just, for example, "whether a particular country *can* pay its debt," but also "whether that country *will* pay its debt" (Bremmer 2005, p. 3). As a matter of fact, reduction in exposure to political risks has taken unprecedented urgency in global markets and has emerged as "a key aspect of doing business globally today" (Export Development Canada 2012).

The scholarly examination of political risk has been continuously evolving in different disciplines, including political science (e.g., Baccini et al. 2014; Ballard-Rosa 2016; Barry and Kleinberg 2015; Jensen et al. 2012, 2013; Li 2009; Paine 2016), international business (e.g., Li and Vashchilko 2010; Henisz et al. 2010; Oh and Oetzel 2011; Darendeli and Hill 2016, Bekaert et al. 2016), and global marketing (Welch and Wilkinson 2004; Agarwal and Feils 2007; Czinkota et al. 2010; Laufs et al. 2016). Scholarship in political risk has undisputedly demonstrated that 30 years ago, if the typical response of many multinational enterprises (MNEs) to political risk was avoidance (Kobrin 1979), today, this is not an option for any global company including domestic firms competing with MNEs from other countries. The contemporary fundamental response of the firms today consists of building resilience to political risks (Sheffi 2007; Van der Vegt et al. 2015), which are risks of uncertain political events or conditions that, if and when they occur, can cause significant negative multi-country or multi-industry impact for prolonged periods of time (World Economic Forum (WEF) 2015). Building such resilience (or buffer), however, depends on the types of political risks prevalent in the firm's business environment, the potential degree of the firm's exposure to those risks, and the firm's capabilities to mitigate and diminish their adverse impact (Bremmer and Kupchan 2017).

The goal of this chapter is to track the changing political landscape globally in the last three decades with a focus on political risk and its impact on international marketing activities of companies. To do this, the chapter identifies the most influential sources of political risk within a country and offers a novel measure of political risk to analyze the changing political landscape across the world, with a sharper

---

[1] Political risk deals with uncertainty originating in political actions of governmental and nongovernmental actors (e.g., NGOs, terrorist groups, MNEs) that lead to adverse consequences for business.

focus on BRICS[2] and MINT countries. Furthermore, this chapter synthesizes the evolution of global marketing scholarship and its main research areas including the accumulated scholarly knowledge on influences of politics on international marketing. The main goal is to identify (1) global, regional, and country levels of political risk during the last 30-year period, 1986–2015; (2) whether and how the scholarship of global marketing has studied and captured the changing nature of political landscape and its influence on global marketing, i.e., the evolution of various research areas within global marketing; and (3) existing gaps in research in global marketing and potential future research directions on the impact of political risk on global marketing.

To trace the 30-year political risk dynamics and its multiple country-specific dimensions, we use International Country Risk Guide (ICRG) monthly political risk index and its components for the 1986–2015 period. This index has the longest running time-series data since 1984 and the broadest coverage of different facets of political risk, i.e., 12 components for about 140 countries. To outline global marketing scholarship, we chose seven top journals in the 1986–2015 period: *Journal of Marketing* (JM), *International Marketing Review* (IMR), *Journal of International Marketing* (JIM), *Journals of International Business Studies* (JIBS), *Management International Review* (MIR), *Journal of World Business* (JWB), and *International Business Review* (IBR). Altogether, temporal trends in political risk across the globe and in global marketing scholarship should provide a comprehensive picture of the past research retrospectively and offer perspectives and contexts on the changing landscape of political risks for current and future research. This will set the stage for understanding why some research topics in the confluence of political risk and global marketing were overstudied and others understudied and how they might have shaped global marketing activities of MNEs. Going forward, these understudied areas will serve as the basis for identifying gaps in the scholarship at the intersection of global marketing and political risk.

To analyze trends in political risk across countries in the past 30 years (1986–2015) and to accurately assess country levels of political risk, we need to understand the underlying processes that generate various observable components, i.e., dimensions of political risk. Such understanding seems to be lacking, as there seems to be no scholarly or practitioner publication attempting to study how to (a) describe the "structure of political risk" among its various observable components within a country and (b) what this structure could look like if one uses ICRG components of political risk. The answer to both of these questions depends on the identification of the underlying latent structure that produce changes in political environment within a country. Since only ICRG components are observable, factor analysis of ICRG components of political risk index allows us to investigate the latent structure of political risk within a country and across time. The value of this approach for scholarly and practitioner communities is that our chapter will provide a more systematic

---

[2] BRICS stands for Brazil, Russia, India, China, and South Africa. MINT stands for Mexico, Indonesia, Nigeria, and Turkey.

approach for using accumulated quantitative information on political risk in the past 30 years.

To analyze the research trends in global marketing scholarship, our chapter uses content analysis of the abstracts and titles of all published papers in seven journals specified above in the 1986–2015 time period and each of the three time periods separately, 1986–1995, 1996–2005, and 2006–2015, to examine the temporal changes across research areas. The main premise of the content analysis is to identify and examine the changes in research domains within global marketing across 30 years based on the weighted frequencies of the main theoretical concepts. Thus, the use of the content analysis allows us to trace the historically persistent and emergent intellectual foundations of global marketing and subareas of research as political risk's impact on international marketing.

The chapter proceeds as follows. The first section will focus on the analysis of the 30-year political environment in BRICS, MINT, and the worldwide trends based on ICRG political risk index including a brief overview of the exploratory factor analysis and its use for identifying the underlying country-specific dimensions of political risk. The second section will briefly outline the methodological foundations of content analysis to map research areas and trends in global marketing and political risk across the entire global marketing scholarship in each decade of the entire 30-year period, 1986–1995, 1996–2005, and 2006–2015. Once the key 30-year global marketing scholarship and political risk trends are analyzed, the third section will focus on the identification of potential gaps and future research directions in global marketing scholarship.

Section 1: Country, Cluster and Global-Level Trends in Political Risk in 1986–2015

In this section, we focus on the identification and analysis of the prevalent sources of political risks across countries in the past 30 years by utilizing existing observable indicators of various dimensions of political risk and subjecting them to exploratory factor analysis. Novel empirical measures have been developed by public and private institutions to measure political risk. The main goal of the majority of these measures is to inform investors and other stakeholders about the emergent political challenges in different parts of the world based on the qualitative subjective assessments of political risk by experts combined with the quantitative economic, financial, and political information.

Economist Intelligence Unit (EIU) developed the operational risk model to quantify the risks to business profitability (EIU 2017). In 2007, Eurasia Group in collaboration with Citi Private Bank developed political risk index that intended to synthesize the investment process research and political risk analysis to develop a unique indicator providing better understanding of the trade-offs between financial rewards and political risk, especially in frontier and emerging countries (Eurasia

2007). Now, this political risk index provides the basis for the annual Eurasia's flagship publication, "Global Risks," that offers past political trends and future scenarios of the geopolitical developments around the world (Eurasia 2017). Maplecroft (2017) offers one of the broadest set of indicators (over 150) including political risk index to benchmark inherent risk in any country, city, or specific types of assets. Relying on over 30 individual data sources to assess different dimensions of governance[3] in a country, Worldwide Governance Indicators (WGI) developed a survey-based aggregate indicators to quantify political stability, government effectiveness, regulatory quality, rule of law, control of corruption, and government accountability (WGI 2017). In 1995, Transparency International developed Corruption Perception Index (CPI) to evaluate the extent of corruption[4] across countries based on about 13 different data sources from 12 different institutions that could perform regular and credible assessments of corruption perceptions from country experts and business people (Transparency International 2017b).

Political Risk Services (PRS)'s International Country Risk Guide (ICRG) is one of the oldest indicators of political risk developed in 1984, and, therefore, it provides one of the longest time-series data for political risk for about 140 countries (PRS 2017a). The main goal of ICRG index since its inception has been to assess different types of risks to international business operations that currently include 22 components split into three main categories, economic, financial, and political risk. Political risk index has 12 main components: government stability, socioeconomic conditions, investment profile, internal conflict, external conflict, corruption, military in politics, religious tensions, law and order, ethnic tensions, democratic accountability, and bureaucratic quality, which when combined measures the total political risk at the country level on a monthly or annual basis.

Each of these measures boasts important information about changes in political environment at the global, regional, and country levels. Many of these measures are used in scholarly research and company reports to assess past trends and forecast the emergence of new ones. In an increasingly interconnected world, these multiple efforts result in companies having no dearth of information about international and domestic politics in different countries supplied by multiple private and public organizations specializing in political risk analytics, risk management, and/or political risk insurance (e.g., Eurasia Group, EDC). Yet, abundant information might not imply specific knowledge about political dynamics and its impact on competition in particular markets where the firm operates and on its required strategic responses. The evidence pertaining to the continued and new losses of many companies due to political risks demonstrates apparent deficiencies in internal capabilities of

---

[3] "Governance consists of the traditions and institutions by which authority in a country is exercised. This includes the process by which governments are selected, monitored, and replaced; the capacity of the government to effectively formulate and implement sound policies; and the respect of citizens and the state for the institutions that govern economic and social interactions among them" (WGI 2017).

[4] "Corruption is the abuse of entrusted power for private gain. It can be classified as grand, petty and political depending on the amounts of money lost and the sector where it occurs" (Transparency International 2017a).

companies to systematically incorporate information on country-specific latent structures of political risk into the formulation of their strategies. To overcome this gap, this section offers an overview of the political dynamics in the past 30 years and a novel measure of political risk using the ICRG data, i.e., EFA-based political risk index, to capture the most influential forces shaping a country's political risk structure.

Data and Methodology

Among different measures of political risk, we chose the PRS's ICRG political risk index's 12 components because it has the broadest coverage of temporal, country, and phenomenon-based dimensions that are required to draw conclusions about the underlying latent structure of political risk within a country. The data consist of monthly observations of 12 ICRG variables for each of 140 countries for the period of 1986–2015. Each of these ICRG components is supposed to measure an extent of the presence of a particular feature of a country's political environment. For example, an ICRG component "corruption" quantifies the level of corruption within the political system of a country (PRS 2017b).

Our objective is to identify the latent factor structure of a country's political risk by uncovering groups of highly interconnected ICRG components that are explained by fewer underlying factors. To achieve this data reduction objective, we employ exploratory factor analysis (EFA). We analyze the within-country variability of political risk structure by estimating the relationships among the 12 observable ICRG components across time for every country. These components have relatively high correlations for every country as many of the ICRG components are conceptually related. For example, high levels of corruption within a country imply a great extent of various illegal activities (e.g., extortions, a black market, racketeering) and in general are associated with the lack of contract enforceability according to the rule of law, problems with government effectiveness, government instability, democratic accountability, and bureaucracy quality (Cuervo-Cazurra 2016; Jiang and Nie 2014; Sequeira and Djankov 2014; Luiz and Stewart 2013; Langbein and Knack 2010).

To compare the political risk across countries and over time, we develop a novel EFA-based index of political risk (EFA-based index). Our EFA-based index uses the orthogonality assumption of the extracted latent factors (i.e., factor scores) which implies that we can treat them as separate dimensions that form a corresponding coordinate system, an N-dimensional real space.[5] Within this coordinate system (and in general, in any N-dimensional real space), every point can be considered a vector, the length of which represents the magnitude of the corresponding metric defined on that space and thereby associated with that vector. Therefore, this metric

---

[5] N is indicating the number of the factors satisfying the Kaiser's criterion and each country's space dimensionality depends on the EFA results.

should capture the extent of a country-level political risk across country-specific dimensions of political risk in a particular 5-year time period. We employ a common approach to measure a vector's length from the origin of the coordinate system, i.e., the Euclidian distance.

We run EFA separately for each country's 5-year time series of 12 ICRG observable components of political risk with 60 observations (12 months*5 years= 60). Thus, the columns in this EFA are 12 ICRG variables, and the rows are the monthly observations of those 12 variables for one country. We assume that the error terms are uncorrelated.[6] Such EFAs allow us to make inferences about the relationships among the 12 ICRG components for every country for every 5-year period, 1986–1990, 1991–1995, 1996–2000, 2001–2005, 2006–2010, and 2011–2015. As a result, we derive a comprehensive picture of changes in a country's underlying political risk structure based on the historical time-series trends of each of the ICRG variable and the overall political environment based on the relationships among those ICRG variables.

Country-Level Political Risk Trend: An Illustrative Example

EFA for Russia in 2001–2005

To illustrate, Fig. 2.1 schematically demonstrates the three underlying factors of Russia's political risk structure in 2001–2005, F1, F2, and F3. Table 2.1 provides rotated factor loading matrix and unique variance estimates for Russia in 2001–2005, from which we extracted the appropriate number of factors based on Cattell's scree test (Cattell 1966) and Kaiser's criterion of eigenvalues greater than unity.

Figure 2.2 contains the scree plot with eigenvalues on the y-axis and the number of factors on the x-axis. Table 2.1 and Fig. 2.2 demonstrate that the three factors have a large eigenvalue compared to other factors and explain a predominant part of the variance in the data on Russia's political risk structure for 2001–2005. The interpretation of the factors is subjective and in general depends on the values of the factor loadings, which are the correlations between a factor and a variable and thereby demonstrate the extent to which each of the variables contributes to the meaning of the factor.

Factor 1 correlates most with corruption (0.91), religious tensions (0.81), and ethnic tensions (0.92) as well as describes the largest amount of variance in the data (31%).[7] Since corruption, ethnic, and religious tensions explain about 31% of varia-

---

[6] We recognize that the data structure implies that we have 60 repeated monthly observations for every ICRG component. However, we make an assumption that during the 60-month period for which we run EFA, there are stronger exogenous forces that drive each of the monthly ICRG components making the repeated observations relatively independent. The p-factor analysis could be a way to relax the independence assumption of the repeated observations; however, we leave it for future research.

[7] The amount of variance that is explained by a factor is calculated as the sum of the squared factor

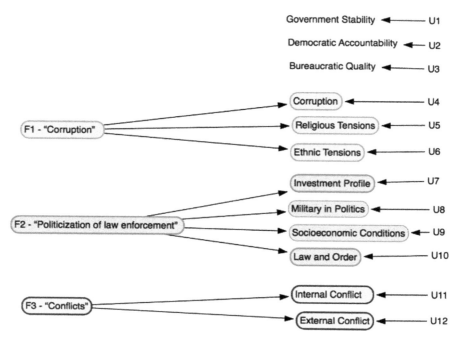

Fig. 2.1 EFA path diagram for Russia, 2001–2005

Table 2.1 Rotated factor loadings for Russia, 2001–2005

Variable	Factor1	Factor2	Factor3	Factor4	Factor5	Factor6	Factor7	Uniqueness	Communality
government stability	-0.5332	0.0721	0.3245	0.0217	0.5215	-0.0015	0.0002	0.3329	0.6671
socioeconomic conditions	0.5539	**0.7765**	-0.096	0.2629	0.0337	-0.0789	-0.0041	0.0045	0.9955
investment profile	0.1825	**0.9359**	0.0157	0.0464	-0.1131	-0.0887	-0.0039	0.0677	0.9323
external conflict	-0.1921	-0.2611	**0.7982**	-0.0519	0.0248	-0.0384	-0.0014	0.2531	0.7469
internal conflict	-0.4632	-0.1477	**0.6726**	-0.2261	0.2295	0.0864	0.002	0.2	0.8
corruption	**0.9051**	0.3284	-0.1876	0.1681	-0.045	0.023	-0.0013	0.007	0.993
law and order	0.3106	0.7622	-0.4531	0.1956	0.1776	0.1084	0.0007	0.0358	0.9642
religious tensions	**0.8119**	0.3441	-0.1974	0.3629	0.0317	-0.1421	0.0066	0.0306	0.9694
ethnic tensions	**0.9218**	0.2537	-0.1778	-0.1166	-0.1251	0.0762	-0.0016	0.0193	0.9807
democratic accountability	0.1716	0.4275	-0.1904	0.677	0.0055	0.0121	-0.0003	0.293	0.707
military in politics	0.2642	**0.825**	-0.3363	0.1436	0.0507	0.1281	0.0099	0.0968	0.9032
Notes: Factor loadings areestimated using Maximum Likelihood method with varimax rotation									
12 ICRG components are used. The factor loadings larger than 0.6 are in bold.									

tions in political risk in Russia in 2001–2005, we name this factor as "corruption," because many of the religious and ethnic tensions in a multinational Russian Federation seems to be connected (or even driven) by the distribution of political power, "administrative resources controlled illicitly by governors," and the degree of influence exerted by various government officials in the regions with "pervasive"

loadings of that factor and then divided by the number of the variables (and multiplied by 100%).

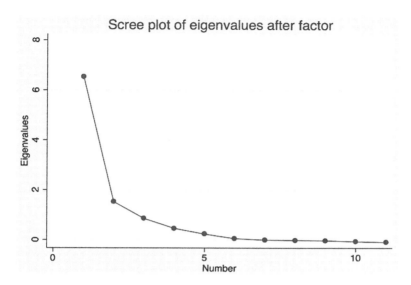

Fig. 2.2 Scree plot for Russia, 2001–2005

corruption at the "regional level" (Slider 2010, p. 186). The link between corruption, ethnic, and religious tensions could become especially apparent once we examine media freedom across different regions as free media, in general, is associated with higher levels of transparency and greater accountability of government (Brunetti and Weder 2003; Dininio and Orttung 2005). For example, when assessing whether a region in Russia has a "free" media, the Glasnost Reform Foundation (GDF) found in its 2007–2008 survey that 17 out of 81 regions that had "unfree" media included many of the non-Russian regions (e.g., Basjkortostan, Ingushetia, Kalmykia, Karachai-Cherkessia, Mari El, Mordovia, Tatarstan, and Chechnya) (Slider 2010).[8] Moreover, other evidences demonstrate that the greatest barrier to foreign direct investment (FDI) in Russia is corruption (Baranov et al. 2015), whereas the quality of the subnational governance is influenced by norms and values of the population (Grosfeld et al. 2013; Knack and Keefer 1997; and Menyashev and Polishchuk 2011). Additional events, starting with 1999 second Chechen war and the inauguration of Vladimir Putin as President in 2000 led to the increased tolerance in Chechen Republic and other North Caucasus Republics (Dagestan, Ingushetia, North Ossetia, and Kabardino-Balkaria) of "generalized corruption, clan hegemony, and nepotism." Thus, not surprisingly the first factor loads most highly on corruption, ethnic, and religious tensions.

---

[8]According to the survey of the Russian journal *Ekspert* ("Expert") conducted in 2007 on the degree of influence of various officials or other persons in regions, local religious leaders were ranked fourth in their influence within the region after the Governor, Region Legislature Chair, and the Mayor of Capital (Slider 2010).

Factor 2 correlates most with socioeconomic conditions (0.78), investment profile (0.94), law and order (0.76), and military in politics (0.825) as well as describes the second largest amount of variance in the data (30%) on political risk. President Putin appointed *siloviki*, "those with the background in the armed forces or security services," to many important positions in Russian politics, which led to "the growing power of the military" (Mathers 2010, p. 253) not only in politics but also in the economy as political and economic areas have become tightly interwoven in Russia since 2000. The presence of siloviki in Russia's higher echelons of political power and in the key positions of the largest state-owned enterprises has led to further politicization and selective enforcement of law (Smith 2010; Draguiev 2015) which in turn contributed to additional challenges of contract enforcement (one of the main components of ICRG Investment Profile) (Frye 2004). Thus, we named this factor as "politicization of law enforcement."

Factor 3 correlates most with external conflict (0.8) and internal conflict (0.67) accounting for about 15% of the variance in the political risk data. Russia's counter-terrorism operation in the republic of Chechnya ended only in 2009 according to official Kremlin's declaration with the end of military phase in Chechnya only in 2002 (O'Loughlin et al. 2011). Unfortunately, conflict in North Caucasus region fueled terrorist attacks in other Russian regions.[9] ICRG external conflict component is defined as anything from any non-violent external pressure such as diplomatic pressure, sanctions, trade restrictions, and the like to violent external pressure from cross-border conflicts to all-out war. During Putin's first two terms as president (2000–2008), Russia returned "as a major international player," while witnessing a "worsening of relations with the West" (Mankoff 2009, p. 23). Thus, we name Factor 3 as "Conflicts."

The values of these three factors can be considered as the three underlying dimensions of political risk structure in Russia in 2001–2005.[10] Table 2.1 also provides the measurement errors of the ICRG components or, in other words, "Uniqueness," a unique variance of an ICRG component that cannot be explained by any of the factors. No single ICRG component contains more than 33% (government stability) of the variance that we cannot attribute to at least one newly derived three dimensions of political risk structure in Russia in 2001–2005. That is, individually, these ICRG components do not explain much of the variance of the latent structure of political risk in Russia.

---

[9] During this time several high profile cases include October 2002's hostage takings at the Dubrovka Theater in Moscow leading to over 170 deaths; June 2004 attack on Nazran town in Ingushetia targeting 15 government buildings and leaving 88 dead; August 2004's hijacking of two domestic airlines; September 2004's attack on a secondary school in Beslan, North Ossetia, leading to over 380 deaths including many children; and October 2005's massive attack on the capital of Kabardino-Balkaria, Nal'chik, leaving 100 dead including 14 civilians (O'Loughlin et al. 2011).

[10] To check the fit of the three-factor model, we performed a likelihood ratio (LR) test, which compares the three-factor model to the alternative one. The LR statistics is 930.45 (p-value 0.00) implying that the LR test rejects the null hypothesis that the estimates of the two models are equal in favor of the three-factor model.

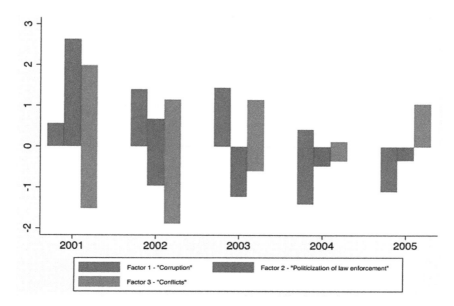

Fig. 2.3 Change in factor scores for Russia, 2001–2005

EFA-Based Index for Russia in 2001–2005

We next use the corresponding factor scores to construct our new measure of the country's political risk, EFA-based index that accounts for the country's underlying political risk structure. Each of the three factors that we calculated in the Russia example represents a unique unobservable political force that is formed from the interactions among related sources of political risk. Figure 2.3 demonstrates the changes in the factor scores for Russia for each year during 2001–2005. We imposed orthogonality restriction on the factors as part of the EFA modeling, which implies that F1, F2, and F3 on Fig. 2.1 are orthogonal to each other. This orthogonality of the three factors implies that we could mathematically define a new 3D space that represents the latent political structure of Russia in 2001–2005. The estimated factor scores represent the extent of the presence or magnitude of each of the three dimensions and correspond to a point or a vector drawn from the origin of the coordinate system in this new three-dimensional space. Thus, to calculate the EFA-index, we employ the Euclidian distance to measure the length of the vector in the 3D space representing the *extent of political risk* that accounts for the underlying latent political risk structure.

	1986-1995	1996-2005	2006-2015
Brazil			
Russia			
India			
China			
South Africa			

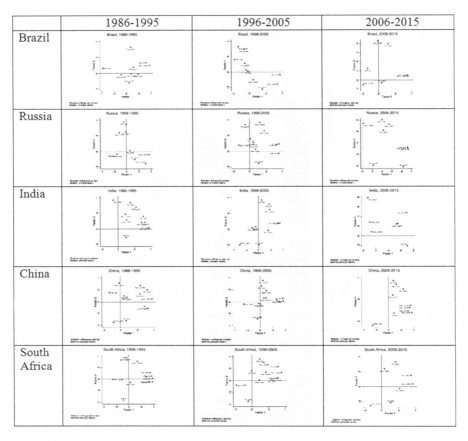

Fig. 2.4 Factor loadings for the first two factors for BRICS and MINT countries

Cluster-Level Political Risk Trends: BRICS and MINT

Following the same procedure, we identified the underlying latent factors of political risk for the BRICS and MINT countries. Figure 2.4 depicts the loadings of the first two factors for these countries in three time periods: 1986–1995, 1996–2005, and 2006–2015. Figure 2.4 demonstrates the clusters of the variables with similar factor loadings. For example, the first leading factor of Indonesia in 1986–1995 correlated most with external conflict, bureaucratic quality, law and order, internal conflict, corruption, ethnic tensions, military in politics, and government stability, whereas the second leading factor has most correlation with socioeconomic conditions and investment profile. By 2006–2015, the underlying political structure in Indonesia had changed with the leading latent factor influencing most democratic accountability, external conflict, and law and order, whereas the second leading factor influencing investment profile, internal conflict, and government stability.

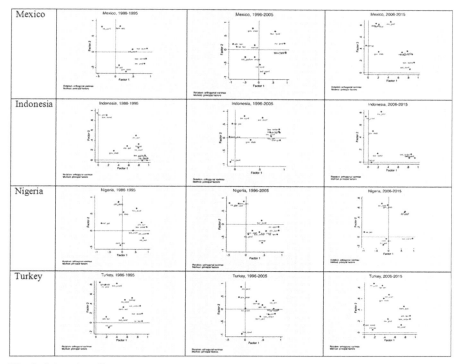

Fig. 2. 4 (continued)

Figure 2.5 shows the year-to-year temporal changes in the EFA-based index, i.e., vector employing Euclidean distance for BRICS and MINT countries for 30 years.

Global-Level Political Risk Trends: Geographic Map

For an overview of the changing nature of political risk structures manifested by EFA-based index, we calculated the EFA-based index for every country for which ICRG index is available and created a geographic map for each time period (Fig. 2.6). To place countries in different groups of political risk, we used natural breaks (Jenks) in combinations with quantile classification and manual intervals to identify the groupings of countries based on the similarities of the observations (ArcGIS 2017). In addition, we also provide geographic maps for each time period using ICRG index based on the sum of the 12 components.

Our proposed EFA-based index using orthogonal factors (i.e., factor scores) allows us to project the political risk in an N-dimensional real space onto a point, wherein every point can be considered a vector. This metric offers the advantage of comparing political risk across countries and time periods using a common denominator. The plot of EFA-based index for each country reveals changes in the overall

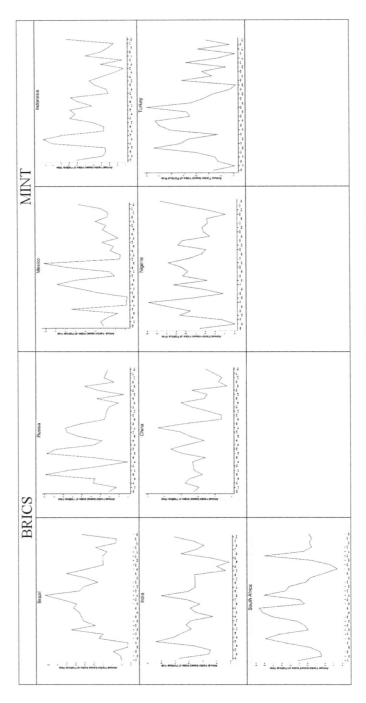

Fig. 2.5 Temporal changes in the EFA-based index of political risk of BRICS and MINT countries for 1986–2015

potency of political risk across time. This index works relatively fine when we need to identify the most influential political risk drivers and the underlying structure of political risk for a short time period which is especially evident when we interpret factor loading plots (see Fig. 2.5). However, our index might be sensitive when we average it across 10 years. For example, some of the Sierra Leone's EFA-based index values for some of the years were the largest compared to the rest of the countries, as Sierra Leone had a civil war in 1991–2002. However, when we averaged across 10 years, for some reason, in 1986–1995 the country with the largest value of EFA-based index (and thereby the largest political risk) was Germany (or East Germany prior to 1989). One explanation is that when the values of political components do not change over time, those components are dropped out of the factor analysis model. That is, what EFA-based index might be also capturing is more of the changes in political risk, rather than just the level of political risk. By contrast, ICRG-constructed political risk rating captures the levels of political risk (based on the original 100-point ICRG political risk index). One supporting evidence to this effect is found in 1996–2005, when the ICRG index rating demonstrated declining political risk in many countries, whereas our EFA-based index showed an increase. In general, we would expect that after September 11, 2001, the overall terrorism threat level in many advanced countries would increase, plus, there were other changes in the world politico-economic system (Iraq war in 2003 that involved not only Iraq but also some of the NATO countries), which would imply that the overall risk level in many countries should be higher in the second decade (1996–2005) compared to that in the first decade (1986–1995).

Section 2: Research Trends in Global Marketing and Political Risk in 1986–2015

In this section, our goal is to identify whether and how the scholarship of global marketing has captured the changing nature of the political risk landscape, vis-à-vis changing political risk and its influence on global marketing scholarship, i.e., the evolution of various research themes/topics in global marketing. The scholarly work in global marketing and political risk provides the elements of the main definitional theoretical concepts that gave rise to additional neologisms as the scholarly area on the study of nonmarket risks associated with political actions of government and nongovernment actors has been developing in the past 30 years. These neologisms are a natural way for scholarship to expand as global marketing phenomena itself has been changing requiring novel and more nuanced explanations.

The identification of the research trends in global marketing and its connection to the trends in political risk research in international business (IB) and international marketing (IM) literature since the last 30 years, 1986–2015, consists of content analysis of the topics studied in IB/IM journals based on the abstracts/titles. First we identified the top journals that publish papers in global marketing and political risk

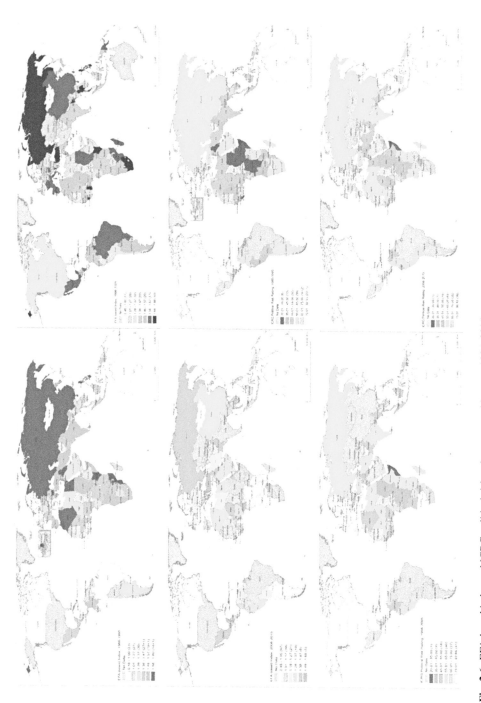

Fig. 2.6 EFA-based index and ICRG political risk rating: geographic maps 1986–2015

in international business based on the 5-year journal impact factors (IF) as of 2016 (Thomson Reuters 2016). The final list included seven journals: *International Business Review* (IBR) (IF = 3.095), *International Marketing Review* (IMR) (IF = 3.450), *Journal of International Business Studies* (JIBS) (IF = 7.433), *Journal of International Marketing* (JIM) (IF = 4.910), *Journal of Marketing* (JM) (IF = 8.971), *Journal of World Business* (JWB) (IF = 4.541), and *Management International Review* (MIR) (IF = 2.732). The number of articles for each journal for the entire time period is IBR, 1030; IMR, 853; JIBS,1311; JIM, 460; JM, 1085; JWB, 1094; and MIR, 896. The total number of publications in these seven journals was 6729. The number of articles for all journals (combined) for each year from 1986–2015 is in Fig. 2.7.

Data and Methodology

The data for the content analysis part consists of all abstracts and titles from the seven journals in the period 1986–2015. We assume that the main thrust of any scholarly article is captured in both the title and the abstract of the article. For the rest of the chapter, we herein refer to the combination, i.e., title and abstract of a scholarly article, as a document. We decided not to rely on author-provided keywords to identify the main research trends as the metadata on keywords might not be consistent across the seven journals for the entire 30-year period. To conduct content analysis of the documents for the purpose of identifying the main research trends in global marketing and political risk, we used the automated and dictionary approaches. For both approaches we used WordStat 7.1.17 from QDA Miner 5.0 software (Provalis Research 2017).

Automated Content Analysis Approach

Automated content analysis approach uses exploratory factor analysis (EFA) with words and their frequencies as the data for identification of the main topics for each of the documents and the entire collection. To identify discriminative and unique keywords for the entire corpus of the documents based on the calculated TF*IDF[11] score, we used WordStat's "topic modeling" feature. TF*IDF increases with the number of occurrences of the word within a document and therefore indicates that the word is important to characterize that document. TF*IDF also increases with the rarity of the word within the collection of the documents and therefore captures how discriminative the word is within the entire collection. In the EFA analysis, each document is represented by a vector of TF*IDF scores assigned to each word of that document.

---

[11] TF*IDF stands for term frequency–inverse document frequency.

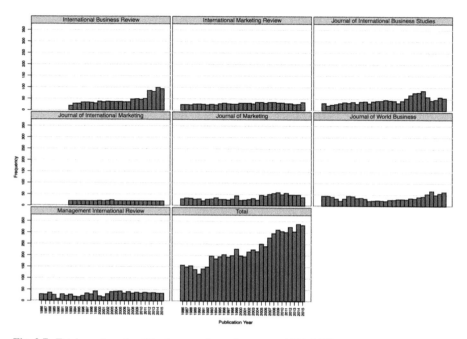

Fig. 2.7 Total number of publications per journal per year, 1986–2015

For the first and subsequent rounds of the EFA, we set the number of topics to 30 and the minimum factor loading to 0.3 to ensure keeping only the words that characterize most of the topics with the rest of the words being cutoff (0.3 is the factor loading that a word needs to reach to be left in the solution). We excluded the words that appear in 95% of the cases as these top 5% most frequent words in the corpus are the nondiscriminate common ones such as, for example, "international" or "marketing" in addition to a general "exclusion dictionary" of the WordStat that includes the words such as, for example, articles ("the," "an," "a") and alike. For over 6000 documents in our collection, the top 300 words with the highest TF*IDF scores out of the total number of just over 18,551 unique words (948,950 total words) in the entire corpus of documents should provide relatively valid results for the automated identification of the main topics (Provalis Research 2017).

After the first run of the automated content analysis, the identified topics with the corresponding eigenvalues and the list of words that correspond to each topic reflected to some degree the major areas of these top seven IB/IM journals that tend to publish the articles on global marketing. Some of the topics included "capabilities," "MNE," and "Alliance." However, one cycle of the automated content analysis is not enough as words cannot really characterize the topic and can be misleading at times if the same concept has two different meanings such as MNCs and MNEs, which are placed in two different categories. To improve the results of the automated content analysis, we ran a few rounds of EFA utilizing the "topic modeling" feature in WordStat with each round excluding nondiscriminative and out-of-topic words based on the top TF*IDF scores calculated for the words. The resulting categories included the main global marketing and political risk-related categories. Figure 2.8 lists the percent of the cases per year for some of these preliminary topics that emerged from the EFA analysis of the word frequencies.

To understand the preliminary relationships between the topics from the automated content analysis, we run the co-occurrence and clustering analysis based on the occurrences of the topics associated with the most frequent keywords in the same sentence. The clustering on the same sentence helped to identify potential phrases from more narrow clusters and the potential broader topics from more extensive clusters. Figure 2.9 demonstrates some of the main topics appearing during the entire 30-year period and some of the preliminary clusters of those topics. We see, for example, that intellectual property rights often appear in the same sentence as corruption and officials, some of which in turn appear in the same sentences as enforcement and barriers. Political risk appears more often in the same sentence as government regulation, which appear more often (compared to co-occurrence with other topics) with import and export topic.

However, even though automated content analysis gives us a glance at some of the predominant topics in the collection of published articles, we cannot fully rely on it to identify the main research topics because some of the words might have different meaning depending on the context, while others do not have a particular meaning if not used as part of a phrase. For example, if we include the keyword "war" to potentially capture those papers that deal with different types of internal or external military conflicts, then the set of abstracts containing "war" would also include those scholarly articles that are written on "war for customers," which is a completely unrelated concept to a civil or an interstate warfare.

Since the automated topic modeling is more of an inductive approach for having a general idea about various potential topics in the collection of the documents, this approach did not allow us to identify more specific topics such as the ones associated with the 12 ICRG political risk components or more specific global marketing research topics. Thus, we turn to the second content analysis approach, a dictionary approach, to identify the key research trends in global marketing and the impact of political risk on international marketing.

Dictionary Approach

Dictionary approach relies on the construction of a dictionary that categorizes the discriminative phrases by their associations with particular research categories and subcategories. We followed seven steps to build the dictionary to identify the main research trends and key research areas in global marketing and political risk. Relying on the main theories in global marketing, international business, and political science as well as the co-occurrences and cluster analysis results of the automated

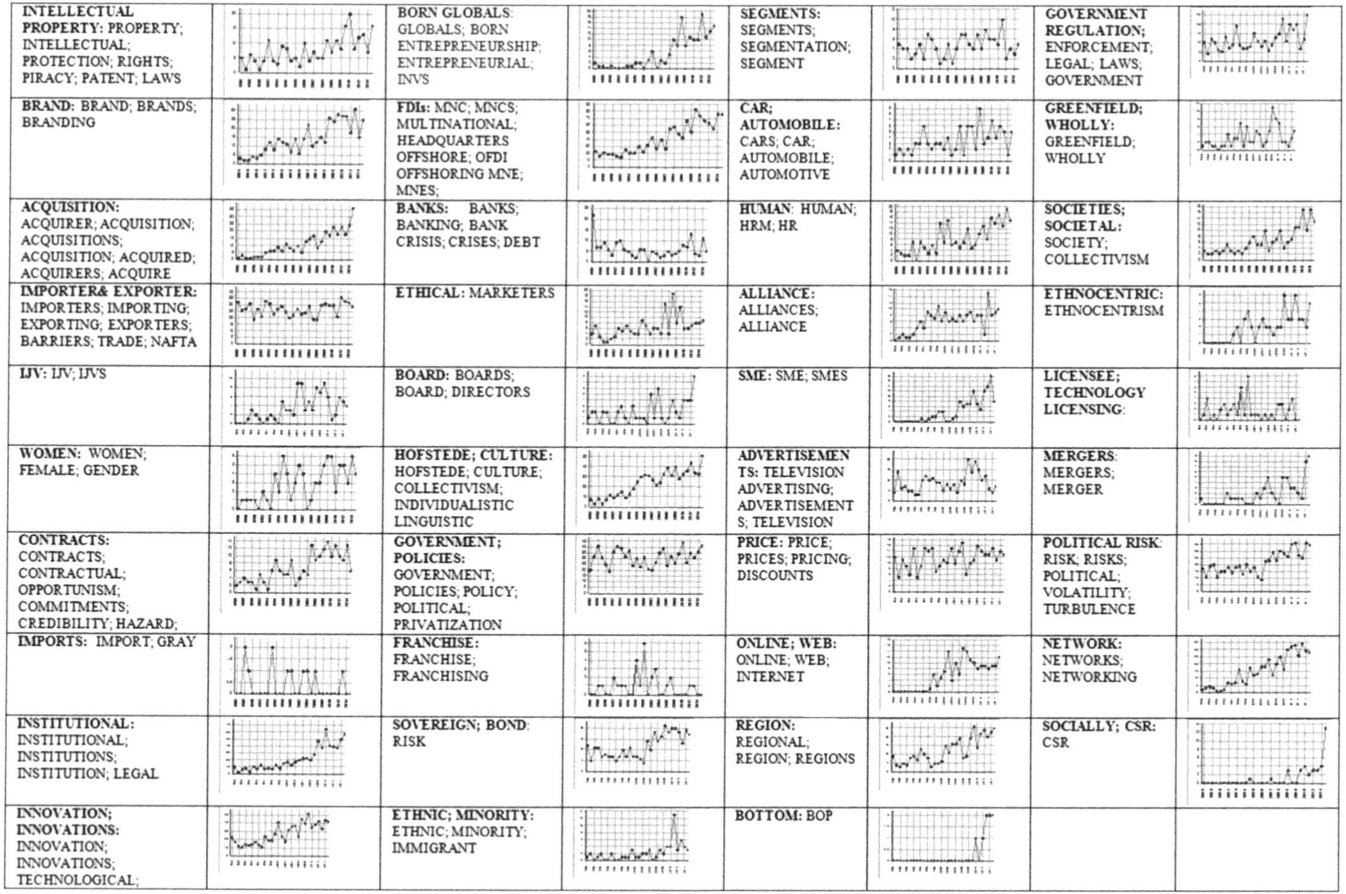

INTELLECTUAL PROPERTY: PROPERTY; INTELLECTUAL; PROTECTION; RIGHTS; PIRACY; PATENT; LAWS

BRAND: BRAND; BRANDS; BRANDING

ACQUISITION: ACQUIRER; ACQUISITION; ACQUISITIONS; ACQUISITION; ACQUIRED; ACQUIRERS; ACQUIRE

IMPORTER& EXPORTER: IMPORTERS; IMPORTING; EXPORTING; EXPORTERS; BARRIERS; TRADE; NAFTA

LIV: LIV; LIVS

WOMEN: WOMEN; FEMALE; GENDER

CONTRACTS: CONTRACTS; CONTRACTUAL; OPPORTUNISM; COMMITMENTS; CREDIBILITY; HAZARD;

IMPORTS: IMPORT; GRAY

INSTITUTIONAL: INSTITUTIONAL; INSTITUTIONS; INSTITUTION; LEGAL

INNOVATION: INNOVATIONS; INNOVATION; INNOVATIONS; TECHNOLOGICAL;

BORN GLOBALS: GLOBALS; BORN ENTREPRENEURSHIP; ENTREPRENEURIAL; INVS

FDI: MNC; MNCS; MULTINATIONAL; HEADQUARTERS; OFFSHORE; OFDI; OFFSHORING MNE; MNES;

BANKS: BANKS; BANKING; BANK; CRISIS; CRISES; DEBT

ETHICAL: MARKETERS

BOARD: BOARDS; BOARD; DIRECTORS

HOFSTEDE; CULTURE: HOFSTEDE; CULTURE; COLLECTIVISM; INDIVIDUALISTIC; LINGUISTIC

GOVERNMENT; POLICIES: GOVERNMENT; POLICIES; POLICY; POLITICAL; PRIVATIZATION

FRANCHISE: FRANCHISE; FRANCHISING

SOVEREIGN; BOND: RISK

ETHNIC; MINORITY: ETHNIC; MINORITY; IMMIGRANT

SEGMENTS: SEGMENTS; SEGMENTATION; SEGMENT

CAR: AUTOMOBILE; CARS; CAR; AUTOMOBILE; AUTOMOTIVE

HUMAN: HUMAN; HRM; HR

ALLIANCE: ALLIANCES; ALLIANCE

SME: SME; SMES

ADVERTISEMENTS: TELEVISION; ADVERTISING; ADVERTISEMENT; TELEVISION

PRICE: PRICE; PRICES; PRICING; DISCOUNTS

ONLINE; WEB: ONLINE; WEB; INTERNET

REGION: REGIONAL; REGION; REGIONS

BOTTOM: BOP

GOVERNMENT REGULATION: ENFORCEMENT; LEGAL; LAWS; GOVERNMENT

GREENFIELD: WHOLLY; GREENFIELD; WHOLLY

SOCIETIES: SOCIETAL; SOCIETY; COLLECTIVISM

ETHNOCENTRIC: ETHNOCENTRISM

LICENSEE: TECHNOLOGY LICENSING

MERGERS: MERGERS; MERGER

POLITICAL RISK: RISK; RISKS; POLITICAL; VOLATILITY; TURBULENCE

NETWORK: NETWORKS; NETWORKING

SOCIALLY; CSR: CSR

Fig. 2.8 Distribution of the percentages of cases for each automatically identified topic, 1986–2015

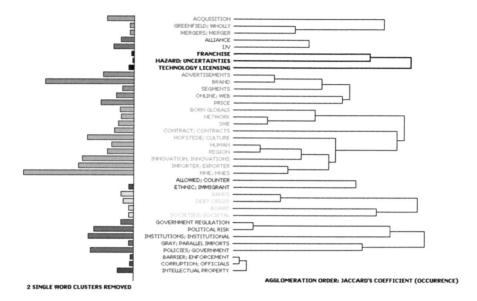

2 SINGLE WORD CLUSTERS REMOVED

AGGLOMERATION ORDER: JACCARD'S COEFFICIENT (OCCURRENCE)

Fig. 2.9 Preliminary clusters of broad areas of global marketing scholarship based on automated content analysis

content analysis, we build the categorization dictionaries for global marketing scholarship. We followed the following main steps to building the dictionary:

1. Identify the main keywords based on the most frequent phrases and keywords from the automated approach.
2. Find the synonyms within the corpus for the identified keywords and overlapping phrases in which the most frequent phrases appear combined with synonyms and different abbreviations of the same concepts and terms into larger categories (e.g., various ways to describe "FDI," "foreign direct investment," "foreign investments" were combined in a large category called "FDI").
3. Create the categories of the main research themes for global marketing, for which we coded the phrases associated with the global marketing theories based on the key theoretical concepts and the results of the automated analysis.
4. Utilize ICRG categorization to classify political risks by assigning the keywords and key phrases to each of the 12 components of political risk that ICRG defines. To identify research themes on political risk, we coded the extracted unique phrases and words according to the 12 dimensions of ICRG index (PRS 2017). By definition of ICRG index, each dimension captures a particular aspect of any country's political environment. Thus, by applying this differentiation to the analysis of the research trends in the top marketing journals, we are able to identify the number of papers that studied each of the 12 ICRG components. These frequencies allowed us to understand the extent of the scholarship on each political risk dimension in top international business and global marketing journals.

5. Add the identified phrases to the appropriate categories of global marketing and political risk to make sure that a phrase does not carry multiple meanings within the context.
6. Validate the dictionary making sure that every phrase included in the corresponding category measures only with reference to specific phenomena or concept (e.g., we had to exclude the word "war," and, instead, in the "external conflict" category, we included more specific phrases characterizing conflictual relationships between countries such as "Cold War," "Gulf War," "war/military animosity," etc.).
7. Reapply the dictionary to the collection of the documents to identify those documents that are not categorized and search the uncategorized documents for the additional phrases that might be used to study various research questions in global marketing or that might be used to define the ICRG types of political risks.

Once the dictionary achieved a good coverage (over 60% of all papers from the top seven journals were jointly covered by global marketing and ICRG dictionaries), we applied the dictionary to the entire corpus of abstracts and titles to examine the research trends in global marketing. Figure 2.10a, b demonstrates the changes in the dictionary-based research areas of global marketing and ICRG political risk for the entire 30-year period (similar to Fig. 2.8).

To better understand the dynamics of the global marketing scholarship, we compared the frequencies of papers that were published on global marketing and political risk (against research topics on world economic system and international business) across seven journals and three different time periods, 1986–1995, 1996–2005, and 2006–2015. We also compared joint occurrences of the research themes from both global marketing and political risk, which allowed us to understand the extent of joint scholarship on different aspects of political risk and global marketing. Country and region coverage have been very extensive across all time periods; however, we were especially interested in the research on BRICS and MINT countries.[12]

We identified four broad research themes: global marketing, international business, political risk, and world economic system, each of which has a number of categories and subcategories.[13] The word cloud (Fig. 2.11) demonstrates the extent of research in the entire corpus of articles on every subcategory and geographic region with the sizes of the words and phrases reflecting the number of scholarly articles written on those topics. The total number of all identified key phrases and

---

[12] For robustness checks, we also conducted the analysis of the keywords that authors assigned to their articles following the approach taken by Lamberton and Stephen (2016). Results are available upon request. However, we believe that the content analysis based on the keywords is somewhat narrow as the number of keywords is not discriminative enough and very limited resulting in their inability to capture the essence of the entire paper. In this regard, relying on the content of abstracts and titles produces a more comprehensive and thorough analysis of the research trends.

[13] All categories and subcategories for keywords are available upon request.

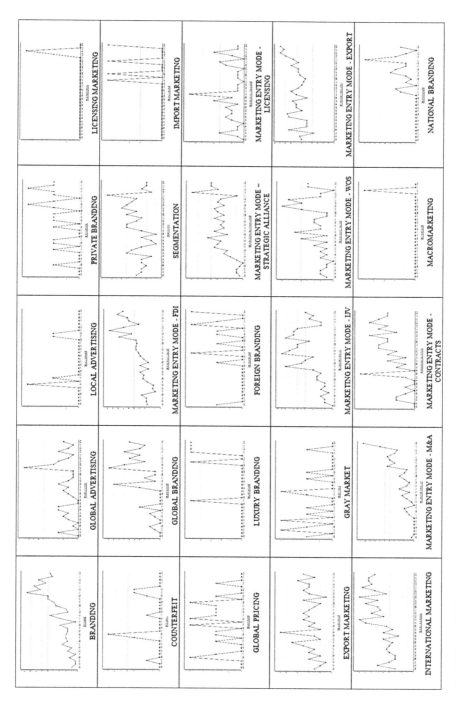

Fig. 2.10 (a, b) Distribution of number of cases on global marketing (Dictionary Approach), 1986–2015. Distribution of number of cases on ICRG political risk categories (Dictionary Approach), 1986–2015

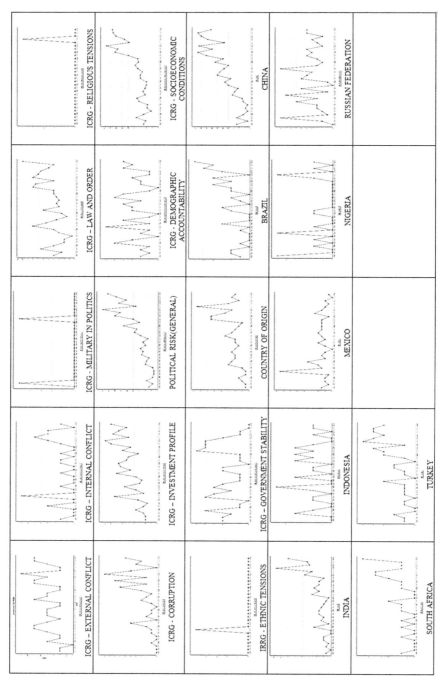

Fig. 2.10 (continued)

ABSORPTIVE CAPACITY   ACQUISITION   AFRICA   ASIA   AUSTRALIA AND NEW ZEALAND   BRANDING   BRIC CARIBBEAN
CENTRAL AMERICA   CENTRAL ASIA   CLOSED_ECONOMY COMPANY   CONTRACT_VIABILITY/EXPROPRIATION
COUNTERFEIT COUNTRY OF ORIGIN   CULTURE   EASTERN AFRICA
EASTERN ASIA   EASTERN EUROPE   ECONOMIC RISK   ECONOMIC_DEVELOPMENT
EMERGING ECONOMIES   EMPLOYMENT_AND_UNEMPLOYMENT   ETHICS   EUROPE   EXPORT MARKETING
FINANCIAL RISK   FOREIGN BRANDING   FOREIGN ECONOMIC POLICY   FRANCHISING GLOBAL ADVERTISING   GLOBAL BRANDING
GLOBAL PRICING GRAY MARKET GREENFIELD   HOST COUNTRY   ICRG - BUREAUCRACY QUALITY   ICRG - CORRUPTION
ICRG - DEMOCRATIC ACCOUNTABILITY   ICRG - ETHNIC TENSIONS   ICRG - EXTERNAL CONFLICT   ICRG - GOVERNMENT STABILITY
ICRG - INTERNAL CONFLICT   ICRG - LAW AND ORDER   ICRG - MILITARY IN POLITICS ICRG - RELIGIOUS TENSIONS
ICRG - SOCIOECONOMIC CONDITIONS IFDI   IMPORT IMPORT MARKETING   INTERNATIONAL ENTERPRENERSIP AND BORN GLOBALS
INTERNATIONAL INSTITUTIONS   INTERNATIONAL TRADE   INTERNATIONAL_MARKETING LICENSING MARKETING
LICENSING TECHNOLOGY LOCAL ADVERTISING LUXURY BRANDING M&A MACROECONOMY MACROMARKETING
MARKETING ENTRY MODE - CONTRACTS   MARKETING ENTRY MODE - EXPORT
MARKETING ENTRY MODE - FDI   MARKETING ENTRY MODE - IJV
MARKETING ENTRY MODE - LICENSING   MARKETING ENTRY MODE - STRATEGIC ALLIANCE MARKETING ENTRY MODE - WOS
MNE
MELANESIA MIDDLE AFRICA MIDDLE EAST   MIDDLE EAST AND NORTH AFRICA   NATIONAL BRANDING
NEWLY INDUSTRIALIZED COUNTRIES   NEWLY INDUSTRIALIZED ECONOMIES   NORTHERN AFRICA
NORTHERN AMERICA NORTHERN EUROPE   OECD OFDI PACIFIC
POLITICAL RISK [GENERAL] POVERTY PRIVATE BRANDING PROFIT_REPATRIATION REGIONAL BRANDING   SEGMENTATION
SMALL ECONOMIES SMES SOCIAL_DEVELOPMENT   SOUTH AMERICA SOUTH-EASTERN ASIA   SOUTHERN AFRICA SOUTHERN ASIA
SOUTHERN EUROPE WESTERN AFRICA   WESTERN ASIA WESTERN EUROPE WORLD_ECONOMIC_TRENDS

Fig. 2.11 The word cloud of keywords and key phrases in the entire corpus of scholarly articles, 1986–2015

words in the final dictionary for global marketing is 906, for ICRG political risk is 881, for international business is 184, and for world economic systems is 175.

After applying the WordStat exclusion dictionary on the entire 30-year collection of articles, the total number of unique words in 6729 abstracts and titles is 17,453 out of 929,967 total words. 82.9% of the entire collection of abstracts was written on any of the four major topics, global marketing, political risk, international business, or world economic system (which also includes BRICS, MINT, and the rest of the countries), whereas the rest of just over 17% of articles was written on other topics. Over the 30-year period, JIBS published most articles on IB (704) and political risk (494), whereas JWB published the largest number of articles on world economic system (716),[14] and IMR was the leader in the number of published articles on global marketing (521) (Fig. 2.12). JM has the least number of publications in almost all four categories. The topics on global marketing and IB co-occur more often in the same paper than the pair of topics on political risk and world economic system.

Over time, the number of articles on each broad topic in IB and global marketing has increased with a noticeable jump after 2006 and after 2007 for political risk. The topic of world economic systems (which also includes all countries) has been researched most extensively during the entire 30-year period, though after 2008 the

---

[14] Note that the category "world economic system" includes the mentioning of all the countries.

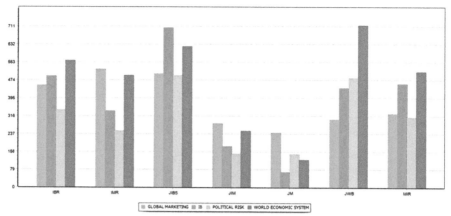

Note: The category "World Economic System" includes mention of all the countries.

Fig. 2.12 Number of published papers per topic per journal, 1986–2015. Note: the category "world economic system" includes mention of all the countries

relative number of articles on world economic system has declined compared to the number of articles on global marketing and international business.

In each of the three time periods, 1986–1995, 1996–2005, and 2006–2015, we can see the steady increase in the number of publications on each of the topics (Fig. 2.13), although the topics pertaining to MINT countries have not increased substantially over the entire time period, whereas research on BRICS countries has been steadily increasing (Fig. 2.14). Research on different regions and countries has been the largest in 1996–2005 time period followed by the research on marketing and international business, whereas research on global marketing and political risk exceeded the one on international business in 1986–1995. In the last decade, 2006–2015, research on IB had the largest number of published papers followed by research on regions and countries, global marketing, and political risk. Research on various aspects of the world economic system, such as international institutions, global economic trends, foreign economic policy, and host countries, has been increasing over time with substantial jump in research on host countries and world economic trends in the last decade (Fig. 2.14).

Research Trends in Global Marketing in 1986–2015

In 1986–2015, 39.2% of the papers published in the seven journals are on global marketing, and if we add research on BRICS and MINT countries, then the total coverage is 48.4%. The largest number of papers is written on marketing entry modes, export, FDI, international joint ventures (IJVs), and strategic alliances (SAs) as well as branding and international marketing (Fig. 2.15). The predominant global marketing topics on BRICS included FDI, IJVs, export, international marketing,

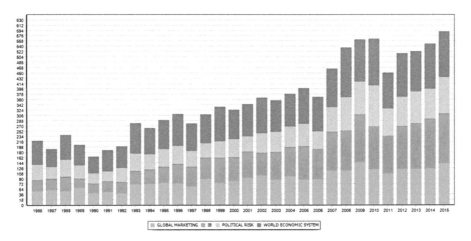

Fig. 2.13 The number of publications per major topic for each time period: 1986–1995, 1996–2005, 2006–2015

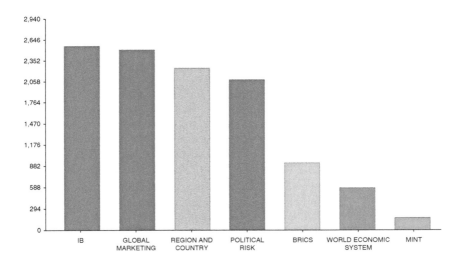

Fig. 2.14 Subcategories of the world economic system, for 1986–2015

mergers and acquisitions (M&As), and branding; for MINT these were wholly owned subsidiary (WOS), country of origin, FDI, IJVs, SAs, and export marketing. The least researched topics on global marketing for both BRICS and MINT are macro marketing, luxury branding, local advertising, import marketing, counterfeit, and global pricing (Fig. 2.16).

If JIBS, IBR, MIR, and to some degree JWB predominantly publish research on various market entry modes as well as global pricing, country of origin, and local advertising, JIM and IMR's publications centered on global advertising, global branding, regional branding, international marketing, export marketing, and to a

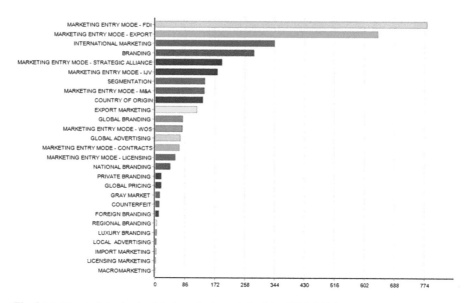

Fig. 2.15 Research topics in global marketing scholarship, 1986–2015

lesser degree import marketing, gray market, national branding, counterfeit market, segmentation, and foreign branding. JM is sort of an outlier with main research topics in global marketing related to private branding, branding, and to a lesser extent luxury branding and licensing (Fig. 2.17).

Temporal distribution of global marketing topics across the three time periods demonstrates that research on market entry modes has been steadily increasing across all three time periods; however, specifically, research on FDI has significantly increased only in the last decade, 2006–2015. If in the first two decades, research in international marketing exceeded the volume of research in branding; in the last decade research in branding has exceeded the one in international marketing. Research in M&A in 2006–2015 exceeded the one in IJVs which was the largest in 1996–2005. The amount of research in the country of origin, global branding, global advertising, and national branding has also jumped in the last decade, whereas research in licensing has declined compared to the decade before.

Research Trends in ICRG Political Risk in Global Marketing Scholarship in 1986–2015

In 1986–2015, 31.3% of the papers were published on political risk, and if we add BRICS and MINT countries, the coverage increases to 39.9%. The largest number of papers was written on socioeconomic conditions, investment profile, bureaucracy quality, and law and order. JWB published the largest number of papers on

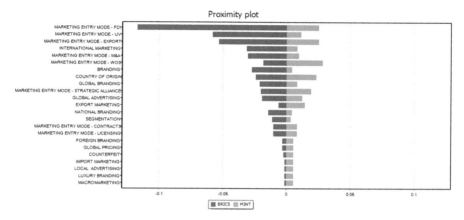

Fig. 2.16 Co-occurrence of research topics in global marketing and research on BRICS and MINT, 1986–2015

socioeconomic conditions associated with political risk (270), law and order (78), government stability (20), democratic accountability (29), and internal conflict (8). JIBS published the largest number of papers on investment profile component of political risk (128), bureaucracy quality (102), corruption (22), and external conflict (13), whereas MIR published 12 papers on issues related to external conflict. Most research on aggregate level of political risk (keyword "political risk") is published by JIBS (52) (Fig. 2.18). Only one paper was published on ethnic tensions and religious tensions, both in JWB, and two papers on military in politics, one in JWB and IMR each. The publications on ICRG financial and economic risks are mainly found in JIBS (54), JWB (53), and MIR (37).

Over time, the volume of research on socioeconomic type of political risk jumped in the last decade, 2006–2015 (Fig. 2.19). If research on political risks within the ICRG category of investment profile was the second largest in the first two decades (1986–2005) and almost no research on bureaucracy quality in the first decade (1986–1995), research on bureaucracy quality became the second largest in the last decade (2006–2015). Research on corruption, internal conflict, as well as law and order has also significantly increased in the last decade compared to the ones in the first two decades. Only research on economic and financial risks as well as the one on democratic accountability decreased in the last decade.

Research on BRICS and MINT in 1986–2015

The research on various regions and countries (including the cultural groups) was very extensive in 1986–2015 period with the number of papers on BRICS (969) substantially exceeding the ones on MINT (179). Most research were conducted on BRICS and political risk and least on BRICS and world economic system, whereas

Case Occurrence for JOUR

Fig. 2.17 Distribution of global marketing topics per journal, 1986–2015

Case Occurrence for JOUR

	IBR	IMR	JIBS	JIM	JM	JWB	MIR
ICRG - SOCIOECONOMIC CONDITIONS	⬤	⬤	⬤	◯	◦	⬤	⬤
ICRG - INVESTMENT PROFILE	◯	◯	◯	◦	◦	◯	◯
ICRG - BUREAUCRACY QUALITY	◯	∘	◯	∘	◦	◦	◯
ICRG - LAW AND ORDER	◯	◦	◯	∘	◦	◯	◯
POLITICAL RISK [GENERAL]	◯	◦	◯	∘	∘	◦	◯
ICRG ECONOMIC AND FINANCIAL RISKS	◯	◦	◯	·	∘	◯	◯
ICRG - GOVERNMENT STABILITY	∘	∘	◯		∘	◦	∘
ICRG - DEMOCRATIC ACCOUNTABILITY	∘	∘	∘		·	◯	∘
ICRG - CORRUPTION	∘	∘	◯	·	·	∘	∘
ICRG - EXTERNAL CONFLICT	∘	∘	∘	∘	·	∘	∘
ICRG - INTERNAL CONFLICT	·		∘	·		∘	·
ICRG - MILITARY IN POLITICS							
ICRG - ETHNIC TENSIONS							
ICRG - RELIGIOUS TENSIONS							

Fig. 2.18 Distribution of ICRG topics per journal, 1986–2015

MINT countries were most featured in the research on world economic system followed by political risk with the rest of the world being featured most in the research on IB and global marketing (Fig. 2.20).

JWB published the largest number of papers on both BRICS and MINT countries, whereas JM published the least number of articles on them (Fig. 2.21). The number of publications on BRICS countries has been steadily increasing, whereas the number of publications on MINT has been more or less within the same range per year during the entire 30-year period (Fig. 2.22). If we look at each of the time periods, the number of papers on BRICS has been steadily increasing from one period to another, whereas the number of papers on MINT has been more or less the same in each of the time periods. The number of papers for each of the categories of

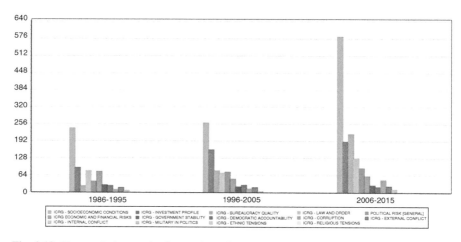

Fig. 2.19 Temporal changes in the number of published papers per ICRG political risk topic, 1986–2015

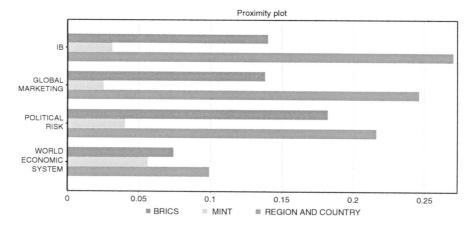

Fig. 2.20 Co-occurrence of major research topics with research on BRICS, MINT, and the rest of the world

political risk was larger for both groupings of countries, BRICS and MINT (Fig. 2.23).

Among the nine countries in MINT and BRICS, nor surprisingly, China has been researched the most (691 papers), followed by India (160), Russia (118), Mexico (89), Turkey (54), Brazil (52), South Africa (28), Indonesia (28), and Nigeria (18) (Fig. 2.24). China was featured most in JWB (150), JIBS (142), and IBR (139). India had the largest number of publication in JWB (46), followed by MIR (25),

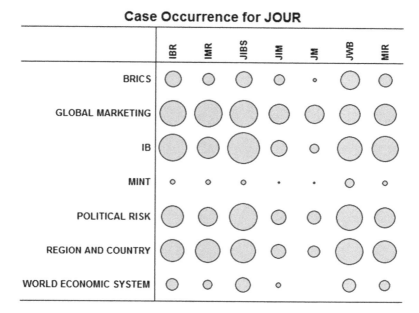

Fig. 2.21 The number of papers on BRICS and MINT per journal, 1986–2015

JIBS (24), and IBR (23). Research on Russia has also mostly published in JWB (52), followed by JIBS (17), IBR (16), and IMR (13). Research on Brazil has the largest number of publications in JWB (17) followed by IBR (13), IMR (8), and MIR (5). Research on Turkey was mainly featured in JWB (15), IMR (12), IBR (10), and MIR (8). Research on Mexico was predominantly published by JWB (36), MIR (15), JIBS (13), and IMR (9). No research on South Africa and Nigeria appeared in either JIM or JM. JM also did not publish any research on Indonesia. South Africa, Indonesia, and Nigeria seem to be the least researched countries in all seven journals with the largest number of publication on each of the three countries published in JWB (nine, eight, and six papers correspondingly) (Fig. 2.25).

We use the Jaccard coefficient to examine the extent of research on each of the ICRG political risk topics and each of the nine countries. Of all documents containing either of the four ICRG categories (internal conflict, external conflict, corruption, and religious tensions) and either of nine countries, less than 2% of those articles (Jaccard is less than 0.02) contained both. Slightly more than 4% of all articles containing either Russia or key phrases associated with ICRG democratic accountability contained both Russia and ICRG democratic accountability key phrases. Just under 3% of all articles on either India or key phrases associated with bureaucratic quality featured both India and bureaucratic quality key phrases.

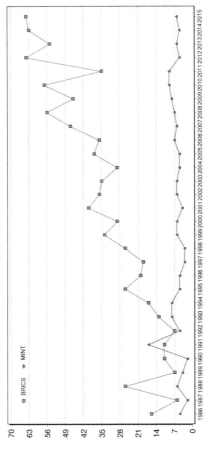

Fig. 2.22 The temporal changes in the number of papers on BRICS and MINT, 1986–2015

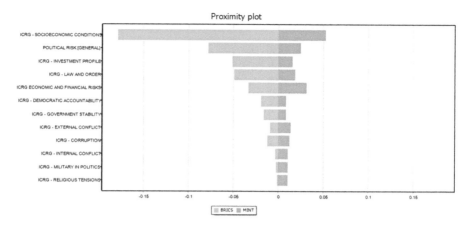

Fig. 2.23 The co-occurrences of ICRG political risk categories with research on BRICS and MINT, 1986–2015

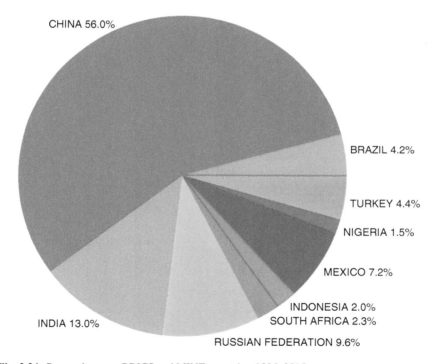

Fig. 2.24 Research across BRICS and MINT countries, 1986–2015

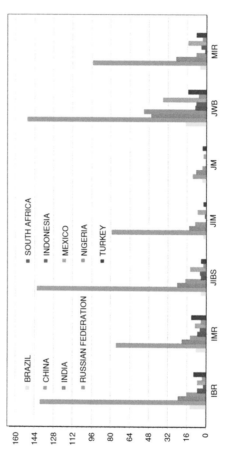

Fig. 2.25 Research on BRICS and MINT countries across journals, 1986–2015

Content Analysis of Research Trends in 1986–2015

In 1986–1995, the total number of unique words in 1577 abstracts and titles is 7924 out of 178,688 total words. Percentage of words excluded based on the exclusion dictionary is 65.8%, and the total number of words that we used to build the global marketing and ICRG political risk dictionary is 34.2%. In 1996–2005, the total number of unique words in 2121 abstracts and titles is 9719 out of 286,522 total words. Percentage of words excluded based on the exclusion dictionary is 66.2%, and the total number of words that we used to build the global marketing and ICRG political risk dictionary is 33.8%. In 2006–2015 period, the total number of unique words in 3031 abstracts and titles is 12,181 out of 483,740 total words. Percentage of words excluded based on the exclusion dictionary is 66.1%, and the total number of words that we used to build the global marketing and ICRG political risk dictionary is 33.9%.The exclusion dictionary is supplied by the WordStat and includes such words as pronouns, etc.

1986–1995: Our dictionary coverage of the papers for each time period is very comprehensive. 30.8% of the papers are related to any of the topics on global marketing; 28.7% of the papers are related to any topic political risk (these numbers are derived after we applied the corresponding Global Marketing and ICRG Political Risk Dictionary). When we apply both dictionaries simultaneously, the number of scholarly articles that are included in the analysis increases to 51.8%. If we add a category "world economic system," which captures such broad economic global trends (e.g., "international financial crises") and international institutions (e.g., "IMF," "FTA"), the coverage increases to 58.5%. If we also add the category "International Business," then the coverage increases to 80.2% in this time period, which means that the rest of the papers published in these seven journals are on other topics.

The most research during this time period was done on various regions/countries and global marketing followed by political risk, IB, and world economic system (see Fig. 2.26). Proximity plot indicates that of all papers published on different countries or global marketing, over 25% of research featured both; of all papers on IB or global marketing, over 20% of papers features both; and of all papers on global marketing or political risk, about 18% of papers were done on both global marketing and political risk.

In this time period, the largest number of papers on global marketing was published by IMR (154), followed by JIBS (107); the largest number of papers on political risk was published by JWB (203), followed by MIR (76) and JIBS (74); the largest number of papers on IB was published by JIBS(127), MIR (84), and JWB (75); and the largest number of papers on the world economic system was published by JWB (58), JIBS (28), and MIR (24). The research on most of the topics has declined by 1990 and then intensified again.

1996–2005 36.5% of the papers are related to any of the topics on global marketing; 28.5% of the papers are related to any topic on political risk (these numbers are derived after we applied the corresponding Global Marketing and ICRG Political

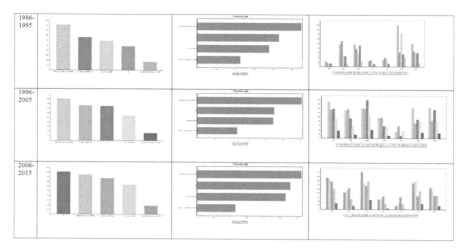

Fig. 2.26 Changes in global marketing scholarship across three time periods: 1986–1995, 1996–2005, 2006–2015

Risk Dictionary). When we apply both dictionaries simultaneously, the number of scholarly articles that are included in the analysis increases to 54%. If we add a category "world economic system," which captures such broad economic global trends (e.g., "international financial crises") and international institutions (e.g., "IMF," "FTA"), the coverage increases to 61.2%. If we also add the category "International Business," then the coverage increases to 84.6% in this time period, which means that the rest of the papers published in these seven journals are on other topics.

The most research during this time period was done on various regions/countries and global marketing followed by IB, political risk, and world economic system (see Fig. 2.26). Proximity plot indicates that of all papers published on different countries or global marketing, over 30% of research featured both; of all papers on IB or global marketing, about 22% of papers features both; and of all papers on global marketing or political risk, about 21% of papers were done on both global marketing and political risk. In this time period, the largest number of papers on global marketing was published by JIBS (164), followed by IMR (163), and IBR (159); the largest number of papers on political risk was published by JIBS (129), followed by IBR (108), JWB (97), and MIR (93); the largest number of papers on IB was published by JIBS(214), IBR (164), MIR (161), and JWB (105); and the largest number of papers on the world economic system was published by JIBS (47), IBR (42), and JWB (32). The research on most of the topics has been steadily increasing over time during thistle period.

2006–2015 37.5% of the papers are related to any of the topics on global marketing; 34% of the papers are related to any topic political risk (these numbers are derived after we applied the corresponding Global Marketing and ICRG Political

Risk Dictionary). When we apply both dictionaries simultaneously, the number of scholarly articles that are included in the analysis increases to 56.8%. If we add a category "world economic system," which captures such broad economic global trends (e.g., "international financial crises") and international institutions (e.g., "IMF," "FTA"), the coverage increases to 62.4%. If we also add the category "International Business," then the coverage increases to 83.8% in this time period, which means that the rest of the papers published in these seven journals are on other topics.

The most research during this time period was done on IB, various regions/countries, and global marketing followed by political risk and world economic system (see Fig. 2.26). Proximity plot indicates that of all papers published on different countries or global marketing, over 32% of research featured both; of all papers on IB or global marketing, about 28% of papers featured both; and of all papers on global marketing or political risk, about 26% of papers were done on both global marketing and political risk. In this time period, the largest number of papers on global marketing was published by IBR (269) and JIBS (230), followed by IMR (204) and MIR (134); the largest number of papers on political risk was published by JIBS (273), followed by IBR (200), JWB (180), and MIR (136); the largest number of papers on IB was published by JIBS (363), IBR (307), JWB (258), and MIR (211); and the largest number of papers on the world economic system was published by JIBS (92), IBR (60), and JWB (56). The research on most of the topics has been fluctuating during this time period with the least amount of research on almost all topics in 2006 and 2011. Not surprisingly, the amount of research on world economic systems and political risks was the largest in 2010.

Section 3: Political Risk and Global Marketing – Implications and Future Research

1. While research on political risk using multiple country-specific dimensions (i.e., ICRG index) draws the attention of companies operating globally, these fixed components ignore complexities associated with underlying latent structures that are actually driving the phenomena. This latent structure exists as real entity apart from and independent of its measurements but which influences scores on their associated measures. At the same time, each dimension also has unique variance with distinctive characteristics, and eliminating any one of them would compromise the conceptual domain of political risk. In this chapter, we have empirically demonstrated country- and time-specific variations of political risk structure that are useful for academics, practitioners, and policy makers.

Indeed, in reality the multidimensionality of political risk phenomenon is unique to every country and every time period due to the complexities of internal politico-economic processes of that country combined with unique dyadic and multilateral international relations. For example, political regime changes could increase direct and indirect expropriations (Li 2009). The ICRG index captures only the increase in expropriation (which is part of the Investment Profile component of ICRG index) and the decline in democratic accountability, a separate component of ICRG index. If one would employ ICRG index to calculate the total level of political risk in that country, the interactive effect of both expropriation and political regime would be missed. Moreover, the strength of association between different ICRG components varies across countries and over time mainly due to each country's distinctive histories, which is also absent from all the existing measures of political risk. For example, more politically constrained governments expropriate less; however, these political constraints are more effective in restraining governments from expropriation than in imposing transfer restrictions on foreign investors (Graham et al. 2017).

2. The EFA factor loading plots help researchers/analysts to identify the most potent underlying drivers of political risk with its concomitant observable dimensions. Comparison of plots for the same country across time reveals changes in the configuration of these drivers (Fig. 2.4). Factor loading plots are extremely helpful in understanding similarities and differences in the underlying latent political risk structures of countries. Countries with similar political risk structures in the same time period should have comparable levels of political risks and thereby pose similar nonmarket challenges to foreign investors. For example, in 1986–1995, law and order correlated most with the first factor for Brazil, India, South Africa, Indonesia, Nigeria, and Turkey, whereas corruption correlated most with the first factor only for Turkey, Indonesia, and Brazil. This would imply that some of the most influential components of political risk in Turkey, Indonesia, and Brazil in 1986–1995 were corruption and related inefficiencies with the legal systems in those countries. On the other hand, in India, South Africa, Nigeria, Turkey, and Indonesia, inefficiencies in legal system were associated with ethnic tensions, internal conflict, religious tensions, and external conflict in the same time period. By contrast, in China and Russia, government stability, socioeconomic conditions, and investment profile correlated most with the leading factor and thereby introduced the greatest challenge to foreign investors in 1986–1995.[15] In 2006–2015, law and order variable continued to correlated most with the first factor in Brazil, South Africa, Indonesia, Turkey, and now also in Russia, China, and Mexico, whereas in India inefficiencies in legal system became less important consideration of political risk in 2006–2015. Surprisingly, corruption continued to play an important role in political risk calculations only in India and Russia in 2006–2015 implying that either the rest of the MINT and BRICS countries (whether via domestic or international legal

---

[15] Ethnic tensions in China were also contributing most to higher levels of political risk in that time period.

means) were able to decrease corruption or foreign investors learned[16] to deal with it using various domestic and international legal tools or both.[17]

3. Using automated content analysis and based on co-occurrence and cluster analysis (see Fig. 2.8), we find the emergence of the following five broad clusters of research topics in global marketing published in the top seven journals in IB/IM in the last 30 years. These are (i) entry mode FDI consisting of acquisitions, Greenfields, wholly owned subsidiaries (WOS), M&As, alliances, and IJVs; (ii) entry mode contractual agreements consisting of franchises, hazards, uncertainties, and technology licensing; (iii) brand positioning and communication consisting of advertisement, branding, segmentation, online (Web), and pricing; (iv) startup innovation and global diffusion consisting of born global, networks, SMEs, contracts, culture, human, region, innovation, importer, exporter, and MNE; and (v) political risk and corruption consisting of government regulation, political risk, institutions, gray and parallel imports, policies, government barrier, enforcement, corruption, officials, and intellectual property. Automated content analysis also reveals the following published research topics that have been on a steady rise in the last 30 years: intellectual property rights, branding, acquisition, born global, FDI, Hofstede culture, SMEs, and societal issues. Interestingly, very recently the following topics/themes have been published in rapid succession: bottom of pyramid (BOP) markets and CSR. Global marketers are beginning to realize the hidden business potential locked in this vast market and are correcting their erstwhile mistaken assumptions of the BOP market (Prahalad and Hammond 2002; Karamchandani et al. 2011). Further, global firms are ramping up their CSR activities to get a share of the increasing pie in both BOP markets and emerging economies.

4. The marketing journal, IMR, published the most articles in global marketing closely followed by JIBS and IBR. JIBS published the most articles on political risk closely followed by JWB. IMR was in the middle of the pack, and JIM had the least articles published in political risk (see Fig. 2.12). While the increase in the total number of articles in the four topics (Global Marketing/IB/Political Risk/World Economic System) was gradual in 1986–2006, we see a sharp increase from 2007 to 2015 (Fig. 2.13). Fortunately, such increase has come from scholarship in global marketing and IB, albeit a greater proportion is driven by scholarship in IB. This presents opportunities for scholars in global marketing to push the research agenda to new frontiers in the coming years. Where are some under-researched areas that global marketing scholars can pursue? A breakdown of the research areas in global marketing published in the top seven journals in IB/IM in the last 30 years, 1986–2015 (Fig. 2.15), indicates that the largest number of papers is written on (a) entry modes, namely, exports, FDIs,

---

[16] We can make this conclusion because corruption component of ICRG is assessed from a foreign investor perspective.

[17] Furthermore, the number of international and domestic initiatives to improve international and domestic anti-corruption law has improved dramatically in the last decade (Arnone and Leonardo 2014).

IJVs, M&As, and SAs (see 30 years of meta-analytic review by Zhao et al. 2017) and (b) international marketing, branding, segmentation, and country of origin (see 29 years of review of publications in IMR by Malhotra et al. 2011). These results are consistent with preliminary cluster analysis reported earlier. To a limited extent, some other research topics include WOS, contractual agreements, and global advertising. In the past, JIM and IMR publications have generally centered on international marketing, export marketing, global branding, country of origin, and global advertising and to a lesser degree import marketing, gray marketing, national branding, counterfeit markets, segmentation, and foreign branding (see Fig. 2.17). However, we see very little scholarship and publication in the domain of national, regional, private, and luxury branding. Similarly, very limited research has been published in global pricing, gray markets, counterfeit markets, imports, and macro marketing (see Fig. 2.15). With the establishment of WTO and regional trading blocs and the exponential growth of e-commerce, issues related to global pricing, gray markets, counterfeit markets, and imports will become more significant in the future.

5. At the country cluster level, the topics that frequently co-occur with BRICS include market entry modes, namely, FDI, IJV, export, M&A, WOS, SAs, international marketing, country of origin, and branding and advertising. For MINT countries, these include FDI, export, WOS, SAs, and country of origin. It is interesting to note that for MINT countries, IJV has not been studied as much, perhaps as a reflection of reality of the level of difficulty in finding a compatible JV partner from this cluster. Similarly, country of origin is still relevant for both BRIC and MINT clusters even though global branding seems to have trumped the COO effect (Holt et al. 2004; Magnusson et al. 2011). Country of origin literature has a long tradition in global marketing, and it seemed that global branding may have partially replaced it; however, in the BRIC and MINT context, it is well and alive. The least researched topics in global marketing for BRICS and MINT are macro marketing, luxury branding, local advertising, imports, counterfeits, and global pricing (Fig. 2.16). Scholars in global marketing should develop systematic research agendas in these identified under-researched areas pertaining to BRICS and MINT economies, as they occupy 27% of the world's GNI share (2015 data) with projected increasing levels of growth going forward (World Development Indicators 2017). South Africa, Indonesia, and Nigeria seem to be least researched countries in all seven journals with the largest number of publication on each of the three countries published in JWB. On the ICRG political risk components, while IMR had a disproportionately high number of publications in socioeconomic conditions compared with JIM, they both had a balanced, albeit lower, representation among topics including investment profile, bureaucracy quality, and law and order. The least researched topics for both IMR and JIM include government stability, democratic accountability, corruption, and conflict. Global marketing scholars are encouraged to address these political risk components as we enter into an era of global political uncertainty marked with populism, political instability, trade protectionism, and de-globalization.

References

Agarwal, J., and D. Feils. 2007. Political risk and the internationalization of firms: An empirical study of Canadian-based export and FDI firms. *Canadian Journal of Administrative Sciences* 24 (3): 165–181.

ArcGIS. 2017. Data classification methods. http://pro.arcgis.com/en/pro-app/help/mapping/symbols-and-styles/data-classification-methods.htm.

Arnone, Marco, and Leonardo S. Borlini. 2014. *Corruption – Economic analysis and international law*. Cheltenham: Edward Elgar Publishing.

Baccini, L., Q. Li, and I. Mirkina. 2014. Corporate tax cuts and foreign direct investment. *Journal of Policy Analysis and Management* 33 (4): 977–1006.

Ballard-Rosa, C. 2016. Hungry for change: Urban bias and autocratic sovereign default. *International Organization* 70 (2): 313–346.

Baranov, A., E. Malkov, L. Polishchuk, M. Rochlitz, and G. Syunyaev. 2015. How (not) to measure Russian regional institutions. *Russian Journal of Economics* 1 (2): 154–181.

Barry, C.M., and K.B. Kleinberg. 2015. Profiting from sanctions: Economic coercion and US foreign direct investment in third-party states. *International Organization* 69 (4): 881–912.

Bekaert, Geert, Campbell R. Harvey, Christian T. Lundblad, and Stephan Siegel. 2016. Political risk and international valuation. *Journal of Corporate Finance* 37: 1–23.

Bremmer, I. 2005. Managing risk in an unstable world. *Harvard Business Review* 83 (6): 2–9.

Bremmer, I., and C. Kupchan 2017. Top risks 2017: The geopolitical recession. *Eurasia Group Politics First Report*: 1–25. https://www.eurasiagroup.net/files/upload/Top_Risks_2017_Report.pdf.

Brunetti, A., and B. Weder. 2003. A free press is bad news for corruption. *Journal of Public Economics* 87: 1801–1824.

Cattell, R.B. 1966. The scree test for the number of factors. *Multivariate Behavioral Research* 1: 245–276.

Cuervo-Cazurra, A. 2016. Corruption in international business. *Journal of World Business* 51 (1): 35–49.

Czinkota, M.R., G. Knight, P.W. Liesch, and J. Steen. 2010. Terrorism and international business: A research agenda. *Journal of International Business Studies* 41: 826–843.

Darendeli, I.S., and T.L. Hill. 2016. Uncovering the complex relationships between political risk and MNE firm legitimacy: Insights from Libya. *Journal of International Business Studies* 47 (1): 68–92.

Dininio, P., and R. Orttung. 2005. Explaining patterns of corruption in the Russian regions. *World Politics* 57 (4): 500–529.

Draguiev, D. 2015. How Russia really works. *World Arbitration Mediation Review* 8 (4): 577–618.

Economist Intelligence Unit (EIU). 2017. World risk: Alert – guide to risk briefing methodology. http://viewswire.eiu.com/index.asp?layout=RKArticleVW3&article_id=855339669&country_id=1510000351&refm=rkCtry&page_title=Latest%2520alerts.

Eurasia. 2007. Citi private bank to provide its clients Eurasia Group's "Global Political Risk Index" for economic and political risk analysis. https://www.eurasiagroup.net/media/citi-private-bank-to-provide-its-clients-eurasia-groups-global-political-risk-index-for-economic-and-political-risk-analysis.

———. 2017. Global top risks 2017: The geopolitical recession. https://www.eurasiagroup.net/files/upload/Top_Risks_2017_Report.pdf.

Export Development Canada 2016. Political risk insurance for companies with overseas assets. http://www.edc.ca/EN/Our-Solutions/Insurance/Documents/brochure-political-risk-insurance-assets.pdf.

Frye, T. 2004. Credible commitment and property rights: Evidence from Russia. *American Journal of Political Science* 98 (3): 453–466.

Graham, B.A.T., N.P. Johnston, and A.F. Kingsley. 2017. Even constrained governments take. *Journal of Conflict Resolution* 59 (4): 002200271770118–002200271770130.

Grosfeld, I., A. Rodnyansky, and E. Zhuravskaya. 2013. Persistent anti-market culture: A legacy of the pale of settlement after the holocaust. *American Economic Journal: Economic Policy* 5 (3): 189–226. http://info.worldbank.org/governance/wgi/#home.

Henisz, W.J., E.D. Mansfield, and M.A. Von Glinow. 2010. Conflict, security, and political risk: International business in challenging times. *Journal of International Business Studies* 41: 759–764.

Holt, D.B., J.A. Quelch, and E.L. Taylor. 2004. How global brands compete. *Harvard Business Review* 82 (9): 68–75.

Jensen, N., G. Biglaiser, Q. Li, and E. Malesky. 2012. *Politics and foreign direct investment*. Ann Arbor: University of Michigan Press.

Jensen, N.M., E. Malesky, and S. Weymouth. 2013. Unbundling the relationship between authoritarian legislatures and political risk. *British Journal of Political Science* 44 (03): 655–684.

Jiang, T., and H. Nie. 2014. The stained China miracle: Corruption, regulation, and firm performance. *Economics Letters* 123 (3): 366–369.

Karamchandani, A., M. Kubzansky, and N. Lalwani 2011. Is the bottom of the pyramid really for you? *Harvard Business Review*. March.

Knack, S., and P. Keefer. 1997. Does social capital have an economic payoff? A cross-country investigation. *The Quarterly Journal of Economics* 62: 1251–1288.

Kobrin, S.J. 1979. Political risk: A review and reconsideration. *Journal of International Business Studies* 10 (1): 67–80.

Lamberton, C., and A.T. Stephen. 2016. A thematic exploration of digital, social media, and mobile marketing: Research evolution from 2000 to 2015 and an agenda for future inquiry. *Journal of Marketing* 80: 146–172.

Langbein, L., and S. Knack. 2010. The worldwide governance indicators: Six, one, or none? *Journal of Development Studies* 46 (2): 350–370.

Laufs, K., M. Bembom, and C. Schwens. 2016. CEO characteristics and SME foreign market entry mode choice. The moderating effect of firm's geographic experience and host-country political risk. *International Marketing Review* 33 (2): 246–275.

Li, Q. 2009. Democracy, autocracy, and expropriation of foreign direct investment. *Comparative Political Studies* 42 (8): 1098–1127.

Li, Q., and T. Vashchilko. 2010. Dyadic military conflict, security alliances, and bilateral FDI flows. *Journal of International Business Studies* 41 (5): 765–782.

Luiz, J.M., and C. Stewart. 2013. Corruption, South African multinational enterprises and institutions in Africa. *Journal of Business Ethics* 124 (3): 383–398.

Magnusson, P., S.A. Westjohn, and S. Zdravkovic. 2011. Further clarification on how perceived brand origin affects brand attitude: A reply to Samiee and Usunier. *International Marketing Review* 28 (5): 497–507.

Malhotra, M.K., L. Wu, and J. Whitelock. 2011. An updated overview of research published in the international marketing review: 1983–2011. *International Marketing Review* 30 (1): 7–20.

Mankoff, Jeffrey. 2009. *Russian foreign policy: The return of great power politics*. New York: Rowman & Littlefield Publishers.

Maplecroft. 2017. Risk indices. https://maplecroft.com/human-rights-political-environmental-economic-risk-indices.

Mathers, Jennifer. 2010. The military, security, and the politics. In *Developments in Russian politics*, ed. S. White, R. Sakwa, and H. Hale, 245–262. Durham: Duke University Press.

Melhem, H. 2015. Apocalyptic terror visits Paris. *Al Arabiya English News*. http://english.alarabiya.net/en/views/news/middle-east/2015/11/14/Apocalyptic-terror-visits-Paris.html, Nov 16, 2015.

Menyashev, R., and L. Polishchuk. 2011. Does social capital have economic payoff in Russia? *Higher School of Economics Working Paper Series WP10/2011/01.*

O'Loughlin, J., E.C. Holland, and F.D.W. Witmer. 2011. The changing geography of violence in Russia's North Caucasus, 1999–2011: Regional trends and local dynamics in Dagestan, Ingushetia, and Kabardino-Balkaria. *Eurasian Geography and Economics* 52 (5): 596–630.
Oh, C.H., and J. Oetzel. 2011. Multinationals' response to major disasters: How does subsidiary investment vary in response to the type of disaster and the quality of country governance? *Strategic Management Journal* 32 (6): 658–681.
Paine, J. 2016. Rethinking the conflict "Resource Curse": How oil wealth prevents center-seeking civil wars. *International Organization* 70 (4): 727–761.
Political Risk Services (PRS). 2017a. International country risk guide (ICRG). https://www.prs-group.com/about-us/our-two-methodologies/icrg.
————. 2017b. ICRG methodology. https://www.prsgroup.com/wp-content/uploads/2012/11/icrgmethodology.pdf.
Prahalad, C.K., and A. Hammond. 2002. Serving the world's poor, profitably. *Harvard Business Review* 80: 48–57.
Provalis Research. 2017. WordStat 7.1.17 for QDA Miner 5.0.
Sequeira, S., and S. Djankov. 2014. Corruption and firm behavior: Evidence from African ports. *Journal of International Economics* 94 (2): 277–294.
Sheffi, Y. 2007. *The resilient enterprise*. Cambridge, MA: MIT Press.
Slider, Darrell. 2010. Politics in the regions. In *Developments in Russian politics*, ed. S. White, R. Sakwa, and H. Hale, 171–187. Durham: Duke University Press.
Smith, Gordon. 2010. Legal reform and the dilemma of rule of law. In *Developments in Russian politics*, ed. S. White, R. Sakwa, and H. Hale, 135–151. Durham: Duke University Press.
Thomson Reuters. 2016. https://annual-report.thomsonreuters.com/downloads/annual-report-2016-thomson-reuters.pdf.
Transparency International (TI). 2017a. Corruption perception index. https://www.transparency.org/research/cpi/overview.
————. 2017b. Corruption perception index 2016: Short methodology note. http://files.transparency.org/content/download/2054/13228/file/CPI_2016_ShortMethodologyNote_EN.pdf.
Van der Vegt, G.S., P. Essens, M. Wahlstrom, and G. George. 2015. Managing risk and resilience. *Academy of Management Journal* 58 (4): 971–980.
Walt, V. 2016. Europe's top cop: It's "Almost Certain" terrorists will try to strike again. *Time.com.* http://time.com/4336919/europol-terrorist-paris-brussels-rob-wainright/, Jan 29, 2017.
Welch, C., and I. Wilkinson. 2004. The political embeddedness of international business networks. *International Marketing Review* 21 (2): 216–231.
World Economic Forum. 2015. Global risk report 2016. https://www.weforum.org/reports/the-global-risks-report-2016.
Worldwide Governance Indicators (WGI). 2017. http://info.worldbank.org/governance/wgi/#home.
Zhao, H., J. Ma, and J. Yang. 2017. 30 years of research on entry mode and performance relationship: A meta-analytic review. *Management International Review* 57: 653–682.

Chapter 3
Does Country or Culture Matter in Global Marketing? An Empirical Investigation of Service Quality and Satisfaction Model with Moderators in Three Countries

Naresh K. Malhotra, James Agarwal, and G. Shainesh

Abstract The increased importance and acceleration of service globalization during the first decade and a half of the twenty-first century has resulted in multinational firms serving customers with divergent needs and expectations shaped by different cultural background and values. This divergence in consumer perceptions across countries may be attributed to cultural differences. Yet, several cross-cultural studies in services marketing have assumed cultural homogeneity within countries, i.e., country and culture are assumed to be synonymous. In this study, we investigate the influence of cultural values in shaping consumers' perception of service quality and satisfaction through cross-national vs. cross-cultural analysis. We also analyze the moderating role of the cultural values of individualism/collectivism and uncertainty avoidance on service quality dimensions and the relationship between perceived service quality and satisfaction. We present the conceptual background on service quality, customer satisfaction, and cultural values and develop our hypotheses by integrating these domains. Both cross-national vs. cross-cultural models are empirically tested using customer survey data in three countries. We discuss our SEM-based methodology, present our results, and discuss research implications. Our study makes a number of theoretical, methodological, and managerial contributions that highlight the shifting paradigm in global marketing.

N. K. Malhotra
Georgia Tech CIBER and Regents' Professor Emeritus, Scheller College of Business, Georgia Institute of Technology, Atlanta, GA, USA

J. Agarwal (✉)
Haskayne Research Professor & Full Professor of Marketing at the Haskayne School of Business, University of Calgary, Calgary, AB, Canada
e-mail: james.agarwal@haskayne.ucalgary.ca

G. Shainesh
Indian Institute of Management (IIM) Bangalore, Bangalore, India

© Springer International Publishing AG, part of Springer Nature 2018
J. Agarwal, T. Wu (eds.), *Emerging Issues in Global Marketing*,
https://doi.org/10.1007/978-3-319-74129-1_3

61

Introduction

During the 1990s, the growth of services in international markets was driven by declining trade barriers, globalization of businesses and markets, and the emergence of modern information technologies which facilitated cost-effective international services operations (Knight 1999). The acceleration of service globalization during the first decade of the twenty-first century has resulted in multinational firms serving customers with divergent needs and expectations shaped by different cultural background and values (Wong 2004). The growth of global firms across services including banking, insurance, retailing, hospitality, healthcare, telecom, transportation, consulting, etc. with presence in several countries also catalyzed research focusing on how consumers in different countries and cultures form attitudes, assess performance, and perceive the quality of service offerings. Research on consumer perceptions of service quality, satisfaction, and behavioral intentions indicate great divergence in perceptions of service quality among consumers belonging to different nations and cultures (Malhotra et al. 1994; Winsted 1997; Donthu and Yoo 1998; Mattila 1999; Furrer et al. 2000; Brady and Robertson 2001; Van Birgelen et al. 2002; Raajpoot 2004; Voss et al. 2004; Malhotra et al. 2005; Agarwal et al. 2010). This divergence in consumer perceptions across countries may be an artifact of their cultural differences. As the importance of service quality in improving customer satisfaction is very well established in extant literature (Parasuraman et al. 1985, 1988; Brady et al. 2005), the impact of culture on consumer perceptions assumes relevance for theory as well as practice.

Several cross-cultural studies in services marketing have assumed cultural homogeneity within countries, i.e., country and culture are assumed to be synonymous (Leung et al. 2005). But culture refers to any form of social environment which shares common values and does not automatically correspond to country borders or ethnic groups (Steenkamp 2001). Emerging evidence points to the spread of global culture facilitated by globalization, growth of transnational firms, and homogenization of global consumption (Ger and Belk 1996; Agarwal et al. 2010). As a result of this global culture permeating down to the individual cognitive level, cultural convergence is taking place at the external layer of behavior (Erez and Gati 2004; Leung et al. 2005) thus underscoring the need to explore the homogeneity of cultural values across countries while simultaneously recognizing the heterogeneity across consumers belonging to a country.

A related issue is the specific role played by culture in influencing consumer perceptions, attitudes, and behavioral intentions. Van Birgelen et al. (2002) stated that the theoretical and empirical foundations of culture's consequences for services are fluid and advocated for further research on the interaction between culture and consumers' perceptions of service performance. Similarly, Liu et al. (2001) had called for research to be directed toward empirically testing the indirect and moderating effects of cultural factors to aid theoretical development in cross-cultural services marketing. However, the moderating role of cultural values in the relationship between service quality and customer satisfaction is not fully understood as limited studies have analyzed culture as a moderator (Van Birgelen et al. 2002; Reimann et al. 2008; Schumann et al. 2010). Our research aims to fill this void and contribute to a greater understanding of the moderating role of cultural values in influencing consumer perceptions.

The objectives of this study are twofold. First, we investigate the influence of cultural values in shaping consumers' perceptions of service performance through cross-national and cross-cultural analysis. Second, we analyze the moderating role of individualism/collectivism and uncertainty avoidance on service quality dimensions and the relationship between perceived service quality and satisfaction. This fits in with the growing need for understanding systematic variations in service quality and satisfaction across nations and cultures (Liu et al. 2001). The article is organized as follows: in the next section, we present the conceptual background on service quality, customer satisfaction, and cultural values and develop our hypotheses by integrating these domains. We discuss our methodology, present our results, and discuss research implications. Finally, our study makes a number of theoretical, methodological, and managerial contributions that are identified.

Conceptual Background

Service Quality and Satisfaction

Service quality plays a key role in satisfying and retaining customers (Parasuraman et al. 1985, 1988). Perceived service quality is defined as the degree and direction of discrepancy between consumers' perceptions and expectations (Parasuraman et al. 1988). It is conceptualized and operationalized as a multidimensional construct comprising of the dimensions of reliability, responsiveness, assurance, empathy, and tangibles.[1] Service quality is an overall evaluation similar to attitude, while satisfaction is a global affective construct based on feelings and emotions related to the buying and consumption experience over time. Prior research showed that the cognitively oriented service quality is an antecedent to the affective-oriented satisfaction which in turn precedes behavior (Cronin Jr. et al. 2000; Spreng and Mackoy 1996). This cognitive-affective-behavioral sequence is consistent with Bagozzi's (1992) appraisal → emotional response → coping framework, drawn from Lazarus (1991). Applying this framework, service quality, a cognitive and appraisal-oriented construct (Bolton and Drew 1991), leads to both an evaluative state (attitude) and an

---

[1] Reliability means performing the service dependably, consistently, and accurately. Responsiveness refers to prompt and substantive service offered to customers by frontline employees. Empathy refers to caring and individualized attention provided to customers. Assurance refers to the knowledge and courtesy of frontline employees and their ability to inspire trust and confidence on customers. Finally, tangibility refers to the physical evidence of the service including physical facilities, technology, and appearance of personnel, tools, or equipment, as well as physical presentation of the service.

affective state (satisfaction) (Oliver 1997). When affective states are not favorable, problem-solving or emotional coping is undertaken at the behavioral intentions stage to reduce conflict (Bagozzi 1992). However, when affective states are favorable, behavioral intentions are positively reinforced through future patronage. Service quality and customer satisfaction determine the long-term success of service businesses (Parasuraman et al. 1994).

Cultural Values

Culture is defined as "the collective programming of the mind, which distinguishes the members of one group or category of people from another" (Hofstede 2001). The cultural context is often expressed in shared norms and value systems as highlighted by Hill (1997, p. 67) who defined culture as "a system of values and norms that are shared among a group of people and that when taken together constitute a design for living." These shared cultural values influence individual cognitions. This influence on the underlying cognitive constructs (Triandis 1972) and cognitive processing (McCort and Malhotra 1993) often results in shared behavioral patterns among people belonging to a culture or subculture.

Hofstede (1980) identified values as the basic manifestations of culture and defined them as "broad tendencies to prefer a certain state of affair over others." Based on his seminal work on cultural differences in values, Hofstede (1980/1991) identified five dimensions of culture on which people belonging to different countries diverge in their orientations. These dimensions are power distance, individualism/collectivism, masculinity/femininity, long-term orientation, and uncertainty avoidance. Values are programmed early in people's lives, and these values shape subjective attitudes and preferences and form the basis for comparisons used by customers to evaluate a service experience (Lovelock and Yip 1996; Van Birgelen et al. 2002).

Culture, Service Quality, and Satisfaction

The cultural context, often expressed in shared norm and value systems (Hofstede 1980), is known to influence consumer cognitions and behavior (McCort and Malhotra 1993). Empirical studies have explored the impact of culture on consumer expectations, perceptions, and satisfaction based on the service quality (SERVQUAL) framework (Parasuraman et al. 1985, 1988) and dimensions of cultural values (Hofstede 2001, 2011). Despite several years of research in cross-cultural differences in the evaluation of services, several issues elude complete understanding, so there is increased research interest in cross-cultural studies (Zhang et al. 2008). Many of the earlier studies focused on relationship between dimensions of cultural values and service quality (Furrer et al. 2000) and differences in the perception of service quality dimensions between developed and developing economies (Malhotra et al. 2005). Recent studies have started examining the moderating role of culture on consumer's beliefs and attitudes. Reimann et al. (2008) analyzed the moderating role of uncertainty avoidance in the relationship between perceived service quality and customer satisfaction. Schumann et al. (2010) tested a model of the moderating effects of cultural values on trustworthiness beliefs about service providers' ability, benevolence, predictability, and integrity which drive consumer trust. Similarly, Agarwal et al. (2010) investigated the application of cross-national versus cross-cultural approaches to segmenting markets by estimating a country-based model and cluster-based model of consumers' perceived service quality. Their research identified distinctive differences between cross-national and cross-cultural models of perceived service quality, thus reinforcing the relevance for more cross-cultural research.

In our research, we focus on the relative importance of the dimensions of perceived service quality vis-à-vis reliability, responsiveness, assurance, empathy, and tangibles and the impact of perceived service quality on satisfaction across (a) three countries, i.e., USA, India, and Philippines, and (b) across segments of customers who belong to similar clusters based on their similarities in cultural values. We also explore the moderating role of individualism/collectivism and uncertainty avoidance on service quality dimensions and in the relationship between perceived service quality and satisfaction. Our research follows in the spirit of the earlier studies and extends recent research on service quality and satisfaction through a cross-national and cross-cultural empirical study.

Hypotheses Development

Cross-National Versus Cross-Cultural Models

Hofstede (2001) argued that as the mental programs of people do not change rapidly, so culture changes slowly, endures over time, and is consistent within countries. Thus national culture is seen as a relatively stable construct reflecting a shared knowledge within a country. In line with this thinking, many research in international services marketing focused on cross-national research wherein national culture is used as a grouping variable to study cultural divergence across countries (Adams and Markus 2004). Even in culturally diverse countries, people share a common cultural foundation, and thus, nationality is adopted as a viable proxy for culture in cross-national research (Beaudreau 2006; Dawar and Parker 1994). One major argument in favor of cultural stability is that traditional values, such as group solidarity, interpersonal harmony, paternalism, and familism, can coexist with modern values of individual achievement and competition (Smith and Bond 1998). For example, Chang et al. (2003) find that the Chinese in Singapore endorsed traditional values of moderation and social power denoting deference to authority and face-saving along with modern values such as prudence, industry, civic harmony, and moral development.

However, assumptions about the stability of national cultural values become a bit tenuous during rapid changes in the environment leading to adaptation and cultural change. Despite the backlash of globalization in recent years (e.g., Brexit, populism in nation-states), globalization in the last quarter century has given birth to free market economies, democracy, and freedom of choice, individual rights, acceptance and tolerance of diversity, and openness to change (Leung et al. 2005). Hence, the assumption of absence of change in cultural dimensions across nations, and therefore, stability of cultural distance measures between countries across time is unrealistic. For example, Heuer et al. (1999) found that continuous economic development over a period of 30 years in Indonesia resulted in an unprecedented socio-cultural transformation. The authors found a narrowing over time of the differences between Indonesian and American managers in terms of individualism/collectivism and power distance, thus suggesting crossvergence (Ralston 2008). Drawing from dialectical thinking and the yin-yang principle, Fang (2005–2006) uses the "ocean" metaphor to explain the "paradoxical nature" of culture, the "moment" of culture, and the "new identity" of national culture in the era of globalization.

Erez and Gati (2004) view culture as a dynamic construct. Culture and individual psychological processing are seen as evolving and adapting to ecological and sociological influences (Kitayama 2002). Erez and Gati (2004) using the "onion" metaphor view culture as a multilevel, multilayered construct in which global culture shapes national culture, i.e., macro level, which in turn shapes nested cultural units at the organizational and group levels, i.e., meso level, which then permeates to the individual level, i.e., micro level. As cultural values are transmitted from national culture to the individual, a set of core common values at each level are retained, while unique values are introduced that reflect heterogeneity (Leung et al. 2005). In addition to top-down processes, bottom-up processes also take place that emerge at the individual level and then permeate the group and organizational levels, and over time new cultural norms become national-level culture. Gould and Grein (2009) interpret culture to be distinct from national culture and as a holistic and pivotal construct whose formation and evolution involves a social construction of practices and experiences highlighting meaning, context, practices and process. The transfer and construction of meaning involves processes like glocalization, hybridization, and identity formation.

Drawing on the concepts of poly-contextualization (Von Glinow et al. 2004), culture as a multilevel, multilayer dynamic construct (Erez and Gati 2004; Leung et al. 2005), and multicultural status of nation-states (Naylor 1996), it is clear that there is considerable within-country variation on cultural values because the ever-growing hegemony of global culture influences the "elective identity" of customers within nation-states to yield significant heterogeneity (Au 1999; Arnett 2002; Cornwell and Drennan 2004; Kirkman et al. 2006). In comparing several countries, Au (1999) found that intra-cultural variation on certain variables was greater than intercultural variation. These variables ranged from demographics, rigidity of rules and social structures, cultural tightness and looseness, moral discipline, and government policies that reinforce the dominant behavior. Emerging evidence also shows considerable within-country variation on cultural values and the existence of significant cultural differences between regions or subcultures within a country (Kirkman et al. 2006; Tung 2008).

On the other hand, there is growing support for cultural homogeneity across countries, driven by global culture's continual influence which alters and influences individuals' personal cultures (Broderick et al. 2007; Eckhardt and Houston 2007; Kjeldgaard and Askegaard 2006). Cultural differences across countries are declining, and a convergence of cultures and values is taking place (Ralston 2008). By identifying culture-based segments which transcend national boundaries and share more commonalities than differences, we expect cross-cultural research to detect more homogeneity. Thus, culture-based segments will show greater homogeneity in consumers' perceptions and attitudes as compared to cross-national groupings that will reveal greater differences (Agarwal et al. 2010). Based on these discussions, we propose:

H1 *Cross-national model will reveal greater differences than cross-cultural model in the importance of service quality dimensions assigned by customers and the impact of service quality on satisfaction.*

Moderating Effects in Cross-National and Cross-Cultural Analysis

Individualism/Collectivism

Individualism/collectivism reflects a culture's relation to individual goals and accomplishments (Hofstede 2001). The ties between individuals are loose in individualistic societies, and everyone is expected to look after him-/herself and his/her immediate family. Individualists are characterized by a strong "I" consciousness, and their identity is independent from institutions and organizations. Collectivists are characterized by a "we" consciousness, and their identity is based on the social system in which they are embedded. Thus the self is always defined in the context of social networks. Hofstede's individualism/collectivism scales were originally designed for country-level analysis, and yet cross-national researchers have utilized them at the individual level of analysis. Consequently, such disparity between the theoretical and methodological underpinnings of Hofstede's conceptualization inherent in the two levels of analysis has resulted in equivocal findings slowing down the accumulation of research findings into a generalizability template and hence the advancement of the field (Kirkman et al. 2006; Oyserman et al. 2002).

To alleviate this limitation, we borrow from the work of Markus and Kitayama (1991, 1994) who proposed the concept of independent versus interdependent self-construal which is seen as an alternative explanation for individualism/collectivism. Markus and Kitayama (1991, 1994) and others (e.g., Triandis 1995) have argued that individuals possess both independent and interdependent self-construal and that cultural contexts typically promote the development of one or the other self-construal more strongly. Self-construal refers to how individuals define and make meaning of the self and is conceptualized as a constellation of thoughts, feelings, and actions concerning one's relationship to *others* and the degree to which the self is distinct or *separate* from others or *connected* with others. That is, self-construal is typically defined as how individuals see the self in relation to others.

Independent self-construal is defined as a "bounded, unitary, stable" self that is separate from social context. The constellation of elements includes an emphasis on (a) internal attributes, thoughts, and feelings, (b) being unique and expressing the self, (c) realizing internal attributes and promoting one's own goals, and (d) being direct in communication (Markus and Kitayama 1991; Singelis 1994). Individuals with highly developed independent self-construal consider their own (or others') attributes and characteristics as referents when thinking about themselves (or others) rather than relational or contextual factors. On the other hand, interdependent self-construal is defined as a "flexible, variable" self that emphasizes (a) external roles and relationships, (b) belongingness to a group, (c) engaging in appropriate action, and (d) being indirect in communication and "reading others' minds" (Markus and Kitayama 1991; Singelis 1994).

Independent self-construal and interdependent self-construal are typically identified as corresponding to individualism and collectivism, although the latter is used to describe national cultures whereas self-construal refers to at the individual level (Gudykunst et al. 1996; Oyserman et al. 2002). Individualists, with independent self-construal, strive to know and validate their unique real self by behaving autonomously and resisting the influence of others (Markus and Kitayama 1991). Individuals with independent self-construal view themselves consistently across situations and display beliefs and value judgments that are consistent with past personal commitments (Petrova et al. 2007). Individual consistency is therefore reflective of maturity and self-integrity in individualistic societies and a lack of consistency poses a threat to the core authentic self (Cross et al. 2003). Individualists are more independent and self-centered and, due to their drive and self-responsibility ethic, will demand others to be efficient and are more demanding than people in more collectivistic cultures. Because they are promotion focused and strive for goal attainment and efficiency (Higgins 1998), individualists want prompt service, and these services must be provided right the first time. Individualists base their perceptions of competence and trust on a person's reliability and courtesy with respect to rights, attitudes, and privacy (Hofstede 1991). Thus individualists are expected to differ from collectivists on the service quality dimensions of reliability and responsiveness, i.e., individualists give higher importance to reliability and responsiveness than collectivists (Furrer et al. 2000; Agarwal et al. 2010).

During a service interaction, individualists will also prefer to maintain a distance between themselves and the service provider. Tangibles are a mean to maintain this distance and offers autonomy allowing one to freely enter and leave social relations (Furrer et al. 2000; Kwan et al. 1997). Therefore, individualists give higher importance to tangibility. Further, due to self-confidence, an individualist is expected to seek more assurance (i.e., knowledge and courtesy) from individual frontline service employees and less from service providers and hence likely to assign lower importance to assurance from service providers. Also, individualists have greater self-knowledge that are more distinctive and elaborate in memory and fewer others-knowledge; as a result, accessibility of others-knowledge is reduced in a decontextualized schema resulting in lack of sensitivity and empathy. Thus individualists assign lower importance to empathy. Finally, for the service quality-satisfaction link, individualists express true feelings of satisfaction/dissatisfaction without reservation, allowing people to freely enter and leave relationships. Expression of feelings of satisfaction is not shaped by a consideration of the reaction of others, and hence it is candidly expressed to safeguard the authentic self (Markus and Kitayama 1991). Based on these discussions, we propose:

H2a *Customer perceptions of the importance of service quality dimensions and the impact of service quality on satisfaction are moderated by individualism/collectivism in both cross-national model and cross-cultural model.*

H2b *However, based on the arguments presented in H1, cross-national model will reveal greater differences than cross-cultural model in the importance of service quality dimensions assigned by customers and the impact of service quality on satisfaction.*

Uncertainty Avoidance

Uncertainty avoidance (UA) refers to the tolerance for unstructured, ambiguous, or unpredictable future events (Hofstede 2001). The degree of UA can be used to distinguish societal norms related to beliefs, attitudes, and behavior (Hofstede 1980, 2001). A high UA indicates higher anxiety, greater stress levels, more propensity to display emotions, and a tendency for aggressive behavior when challenged. There is less tolerance and acceptance of unclear situations, less acceptance of dissent, and a strong need for consensus, clarity, and structure. There is a strong belief in expertise and knowledge for problem-solving, commitments are long-lasting, and there is a strong need for adherence to rules and regulations to make behavior predictable (Reimann et al. 2008). In contrast, a low UA refers to low levels of stress and anxiety, weaker superegos and less showing of emotions, greater tolerance and acceptance of diversity and uncertain situations, and a general approach and common sense to problem-solving. Commitments are less binding, rules and regulations are adaptive and changed if they don't work, there is greater acceptability of dissent, and a willingness to take unknown risks (Reimann et al. 2008).

In a service context, customers of high UA culture have a much lower tolerance for ambiguity as they find it difficult to accept unclear situations and deviations from norms. High UA cultures are characterized by a need to reduce ambiguity and risk through strict rules and regulations (Kale and Barns 1992) and by seeking to minimize service defect potentials (Wong 2004). People high on UA perceive life more as a threat and experience higher levels of anxiety. They would be motivated to reduce the perceived ambiguity and uncertainty of life to lower this anxiety (Doney et al. 1998). Seeking advice or assurance from others is one way to lower this anxiety. People reduce their inherent uncertainty by technology, law, and general rituals (Hofstede 2001). Thus, tangibles will be used as a surrogate for service quality as they are visible evidence of service quality in high UA cultures (Donthu and Yoo 1998). Uncertainty and ambiguity from unknown situations can also be reduced through close relationships with a service provider who is responsive and empathetic and by seeking advice or assurance from trusted others. However, a caveat is worth noting in that when a frontline employee engages in employee interaction, there is a good chance that high uncertainty avoidance (i.e., narrow tolerance zone) may lead to significant service defect. Providing clear structure and accuracy in the service process, i.e., reliable service, may help ease customers from high UA cultures. Furrer et al. (2000) proposed that the uncertainties are higher in infrequent service situations, and therefore all dimensions of service quality are important in cultures with higher UA, i.e., individuals from higher UA cultures give greater importance to all dimensions of service quality than individuals from lower UA cultures. Finally, for the service quality-satisfaction link, because of the narrow tolerance zone of high UA individuals, the higher the degree of uncertainty avoidance, the less satisfied the customer will be when a service is defective (Reimann et al. 2008). Based on these discussions, we propose:

H3a *Customer perceptions of the importance of service quality dimensions and the impact of service quality on satisfaction are moderated by uncertainty avoidance in both cross-national model and cross-cultural model.*

H3b *However, based on the arguments presented in H1, cross-national model will reveal greater differences than cross-cultural model in the importance of service quality dimensions assigned by customers and the impact of service quality on satisfaction.*

The research model, incorporating our hypotheses, is shown in Fig. 3.1.

Methodology

We chose banking services for our study context because they are widely available in all three countries, namely, the USA, India, and the Philippines, and the banking sector is an important part of the service economy in each nation. A structured questionnaire was prepared and administered in English to bank customers by marketing research professionals. The questionnaire was pretested in each country using personal interviews to identify and eliminate potential problems in question content, wording, difficulty, and instructions. The survey data were obtained from major metropolitan areas, and the respondents in each of the countries were fluent in English, thereby avoiding the need for questionnaire translation. A total of 1069

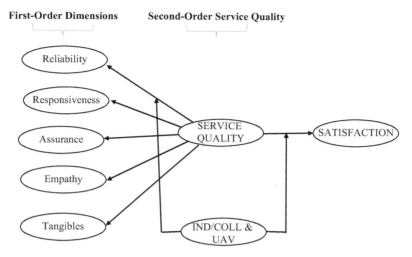

Fig. 3.1 Second-order service quality→satisfaction model with moderators: cross-national vs. cross-cultural analysis

interviews were completed: 455 in the USA, 314 in India, and 300 in the Philippines. We used the 21-item SERVQUAL 9-point scale (Parasuraman et al. 1988, 1994) tapping performance perception measures along the five dimensions of perceived service quality following recent research (Dabholkar et al. 2000). To measure overall satisfaction, we used both evaluative and emotion-based measures derived and adapted from the work of Oliver (1997). Finally, we used Hofstede's 7-point Likert-type scale to measure the cultural dimensions of individualism/collectivism and uncertainty avoidance with four items for each cultural dimension (adapted from Hofstede 1991; Furrer et al. 2000).

Results and Analysis

Modeling of Service Quality

We developed and estimated a second-order reflective model of perceived service quality. Service quality has typically been conceptualized as a first-order factor, antecedent, one-factor model, and/or multi-item summary construct (e.g., Brady and Cronin 2001). For example, Brady and Cronin (2001) include three primary dimensions and nine subdimensions in a hierarchical structure. Their three primary dimensions – interaction quality, physical environment quality, and outcome quality are modeled as antecedents to SQ (measured as a two-item global construct) rather than dimensions reflecting higher-order SQ. However, theoretical work predicts that SQ is a higher-order, multidimensional, and multilevel construct.

We tested for alternative conceptualizations of service quality: Rindskopf and Rose (1988) proposed a hierarchy of models for factor structure comparisons specifically when testing for a second-order factor model. The least restricted model is a bi-factor model consisting of one general factor plus group factors. The next nested model is the group factor model which is equivalent to first-order correlated factor model without the general factor (i.e., loadings for the general factor are set to zero). Next in the hierarchy of nested models is the second-order model which is a special case of group factor model. The second-order reflective model puts a structure on the pattern of correlations among the first-order group factors. Finally, the one-factor model is a special case of the second-order model where the unique variances of the first-order factors are set equal to zero. The one-factor model is the most restrictive model in the hierarchy. Based on factor structure models and nomological net comparison, model fit results confirmed that service quality is best conceptualized as a second-order reflective construct, with five dimensions with reflective constructs at the first-order level. Details of the development of measurement equivalence procedures are not presented due to space constraints but are available from the authors upon request.

Based on psychometric theory, a reflective model is appropriate because its indicators share a common theme, are expected to covary with each other, and are manifestations of the construct (Jarvis et al. 2003). Prior research is consistent with this notion; Dabholkar et al. (1996) report high internal consistency reliability of service quality factors and high intercorrelations across first-order factors – implying a high degree of shared variance. From a causal perspective, the association between the first-order dimensions (as reflective indicators) and second-order service quality is fairly stable over time. Such association tends to generally remain stable in reflective models as opposed to formative models where the association between the measures and the construct depends upon the composite that best predicts the dependent variable (Edwards and Bagozzi 2000). Further, an important advantage of modeling service quality as a second-order reflective construct is that it is possible to determine the measurement error (or reliability) at both the individual item level as well as the first-order factor level – thereby allowing for prescriptive measures for scale improvement (Bagozzi and Heatherton 1994). The full model was tested using cross-national and cross-cultural analysis as in Fig. 3.1.

Measurement Model

We performed confirmatory factor analysis (using LISREL) by running measurement models separately on each sample – the USA, India, and the Philippines. Initially our measurement model included six latent factors, i.e., tangibility (TANG), reliability (REL), responsiveness (RESP), assurance (ASSU), empathy (EMP), and satisfaction (SAT) and 25 indicators. However, two items (TANG 5 – convenience of operating hours) and (REL 2 – sincere interest in solving customer problem) had loadings less than 0.60, and the overall model results were less than the recommended minimum requirement. Given that the loadings were low for these items and that they lacked convergent validity with their respective constructs (cross-loadings were high), we deleted these two items and ran a modified measurement model with the same six latent factors and 23 indicators – TANG (four items), REL (four items), RESP (three items), ASSU (four items), EMP (four items), and SAT (four items). The results were as follows: *USA sample* χ^2 (215) = 565.13, RMSEA = 0.061, SRMR = 0.034, CFI = 0.96, NNFI = 0.95, and CAIC = 983.15; *India sample* χ^2 (215) = 392.21, RMSEA = 0.053, SRMR = 0.044, CFI = 0.96, NNFI = 0.95, and CAIC = 804.17; and *Philippines sample* χ^2 (215) = 546.98, RMSEA = 0.075, SRMR = 0.030, CFI = 0.96, NNFI = 0.95, and CAIC = 956.66.

CMV and Measurement Equivalence Test

We also tested for common method variance (CMV), i.e., the mount of spurious covariance shared among variables because of common method used in collecting data. We utilized the marker variable test by estimating the marker variable post hoc to acquire a reliable estimate of CMV by selecting the second smallest positive correlation (Lindell and Whitney 2001; Malhotra et al. 2006) among the manifest variables – rM of 0.23, 0.17, and 0.14 for the USA, India, and Philippines samples, respectively. Assuming that a method factor has a constant correlation with all measured items, we computed CMV-adjusted correlations [rA = (rU − rM)/(1 − rM)], where rA is the adjusted correlation and rU is the unadjusted correlation and their corresponding t-statistics denoted by $t(a/2), n-3 = \left(rA / \sqrt{(1-rA^2)}\right)/(n-3)$ where n is the sample size. We did not find such effects to be problematic. Therefore using the preceding measurement model results, we worked with the observed correlations to test for their psychometric properties. In addition, we also performed a series of measurement equivalence tests at different levels of invariance following the procedure suggested by Steenkamp and Baumgartner (1998). We examined configural, metric, scalar, and variance-covariance equivalence (Malhotra et al. 1996). These equivalence tests were conducted separately and measurement equivalence was established. Details of the development of measurement equivalence procedures are not presented due to space constraints but are available from the authors upon request.

Reliability and Validity

We further tested for reliability and convergent and discriminant validity of the measurement model, and the results were found acceptable. Both the construct reliability (CR) and average variance extracted (AVE) values for the three samples were above the recommended minimum levels of 0.70 and 0.50, respectively (Hair et al. 2010; Malhotra 2010). This established the reliability of the measurement scales.

We next tested for convergent and discriminant validity. Convergent validity is established if all item loadings are equal to or above the recommended cutoff level of 0.60. Of a combined total of 69 loadings in three samples, only one item had a loading less than 0.70, and the rest were above 0.70. The distribution of all loadings was 25 items (0.70 – <0.80), 25 items (0.80 – <0.90), and 18 items (≥0.90) with one loading equaling 0.69, thus confirming convergent validity. Table 3.1 contains the psychometric properties of the measurement model and the correlation matrices of for each of the three samples.

Discriminant validity is achieved if the square root of the AVE is larger than correlation coefficient. In the *USA sample*, we found all of the correlation estimates met the criterion except in 3 out of the 15 cases. These involved the dimensions of RESP, ASSU, and EMP. In the *India sample*, 10 out of the 15 cases involving five dimensions of TANG, REL, RESP, ASSU, and EMP were found to have high correlations. In the *Philippines sample*, all correlation estimates met the criterion except for 1 out of the 15 cases (REL and ASSU). Given the size of the correlation matrix while some violations can occur through chance, these results confirm earlier reports of high intercorrelations found across service quality dimensions (Dabholkar et al. 1996). First, theoretical work predicts that perceived service quality is a higher-order, multidimensional, and multilevel construct (Brady and Cronin 2001; Carman 1990; Dabholkar et al. 1996). Because our study models perceived service quality as a second-order reflective construct, significant intercorrelations at the first-order level are conceivable. In order to further test the robustness of our findings on discriminant validity, we checked for it by examining whether a correlation between two constructs is significantly different from unity. The correlation of the two constructs was freely estimated in the first model but set to one in the second model. A chi-square difference was examined to determine whether the two constructs were significantly different. Results of the 15 pairs in all three samples indicate that all pairs of constructs had significant difference at $p < 0.001$, thus supporting discriminant validity. In summary, the scale items were both reliable and valid for model testing.

Hypothesis 1   Cross-National Versus Cross-Cultural Models

First, we tested for the fit of the service quality structural model in all three countries by running a three-group simultaneous cross-national analysis. The model fit for each sample was satisfactory and above the recommended level. These were as follows: *USA sample* χ^2 (224) = 611.44, RMSEA = 0.063, SRMR = 0.041, CFI = 0.95, NNFI = 0.95, and CAIC = 970.01; *India sample* χ^2 (224) = 410.97, RMSEA = 0.054, SRMR = 0.045, CFI = 0.95, NNFI = 0.95, and CAIC = 766.84; and *Philippines sample* χ^2 (224) = 613.44, RMSEA = 0.079, SRMR = 0.043, CFI = 0.95, NNFI = 0.94, and CAIC = 956.74. Further, we found significant difference between the unrestricted model and the fully restricted model in the three-group analysis at $p < 0.05$. Results were unrestricted model χ^2 (672) = 1635.85, RMSEA = 0.065, SRMR = 0.043, CFI = 0.95, NNFI = 0.95, and CAIC = 2867.81 and fully restricted model χ^2 (776) = 3363.01, RMSEA = 0.093, SRMR = 0.14, CFI = 0.87, NNFI = 0.88, and CAIC = 3425.44.

Table 3.1 Psychometric properties of measurement model and correlation matrix

Constructs	USA sample									
					Correlation matrix					
	Mean	SD	CR	AVE	1	2	3	4	5	6
1. TANG	6.85	1.22	0.85	0.59	0.77					
2. REL	7.10	1.41	0.90	0.70	0.77	0.84				
3. RESP	6.90	1.36	0.86	0.68	0.65	0.81	0.83			
4. ASSU	7.08	1.32	0.92	0.64	0.70	0.83	0.92	0.80		
5. EMP	6.83	1.45	0.91	0.72	0.67	0.81	0.87	0.93	0.85	
6. SAT	6.69	1.67	0.95	0.82	0.52	0.61	0.68	0.71	0.70	0.91
Constructs	India sample									
					Correlation matrix					
	Mean	SD	CR	AVE	1	2	3	4	5	6
1. TANG	5.48	1.09	0.84	0.56	0.75					
2. REL	5.37	1.04	0.83	0.55	0.83	0.74				
3. RESP	5.45	1.09	0.79	0.55	0.87	0.94	0.74			
4. ASSU	5.33	1.00	0.83	0.54	0.80	0.92	0.91	0.73		
5. EMP	5.41	1.08	0.85	0.59	0.80	0.91	0.92	0.95	0.77	
6. SAT	6.61	1.32	0.88	0.65	0.45	0.61	0.63	0.57	0.57	0.81
Constructs	Philippines sample									
					Correlation matrix					
	Mean	SD	CR	AVE	1	2	3	4	5	6
1. TANG	7.03	1.14	0.93	0.76	0.87					
2. REL	6.99	1.21	0.95	0.82	0.81	0.91				
3. RESP	7.17	1.19	0.93	0.82	0.77	0.83	0.91			
4. ASSU	7.12	1.22	0.95	0.82	0.71	0.76	0.93	0.91		
5. EMP	7.13	1.20	0.96	0.86	0.74	0.79	0.85	0.83	0.93	
6. SAT	7.13	1.29	0.96	0.85	0.24	0.21	0.17	0.24	0.21	0.92

Value on the diagonal of the correlation matrix is the square root of AVE
TANG tangibles, *REL* reliability, *RESP* responsiveness, *ASSU* assurance, *EMP* empathy, *SAT* satisfaction, *SD* standard deviation, *CR* composite reliability, *AVE* average variance extracted

The mean (standard deviation) of cultural dimensions for each country is *power distance* [USA(1) 3.45 (0.94), India(2) 3.90 (0.46), Philippines(3) 3.01 (0.96). Scheffe's multiple range comparison: (1)–(2) = −0.449*, (1)–(3) = 0.433*, and (2)–(3) = 0.883*], *individualism* [USA(1) 3.79 (0.68), India(2) 4.10 (0.44), Philippines(3) 3.95 (0.65). Scheffe's multiple range comparison: (1)–(2) = −0.316*, (1)–(3) = −0.159*, and (2)–(3) = 0.156*], *masculinity* [USA(1) 3.68 (0.80), India(2) 3.96 (0.48), Philippines(3) 3.60 (0.78). Scheffe's multiple range comparison: (1)–(2) = −0.278*, (1)–(3) = 0.080, and (2)–(3) = 0.359*]; *uncertainty avoidance* [USA(1) 4.56 (0.67), India(2) 3.96 (0.48), Philippines(3) 4.39 (0.60). Scheffe's multiple range comparison: (1)–(2) = 0.607*, (1)–(3) = 0.172*, and (2)–(3) = −0.435*], and *long-term orientation* [USA(1) 4.13 (0.68), India(2) 3.86 (0.47), Philippines(3) 4.07 (0.54). Scheffe's multiple range comparison: (1)–(2) = 0.273*, (1)–(3) = 0.057, and (2)–(3) = −0.216*].

To identify specific differences in the structural links, we also compared three pair-wise differences (i.e., USA versus India, USA versus Philippines, and India versus Philippines) across each structural link in the first-order dimensions of service quality and the service quality→satisfaction link. The top portion of Table 3.2 contains the structural coefficients and the differences in structural links between each pair of countries. As is evident, except for tangibility and responsiveness, each of the dimensions of service quality is structurally different in terms of second-order factor loadings in at least one paired comparison with all three comparisons significantly different for the service quality→satisfaction link. On the service quality→satisfaction link, it is also interesting to find that the impact of second-order service quality was the strongest in the USA sample (0.84), followed by India sample (0.46), and the lowest in the Philippines sample (0.22).

To test hypothesis 1, we compared the cross-national findings with that of cross-cultural analysis. We performed cluster analysis using Ward's method on the aggregate sample (i.e., all three country samples) using Hofstede's cultural dimensions and generated a 3-cluster solution with the best fit. Based on F-values and group sizes, a three-cluster solution gave us the best fit (with $n_1 = 370$, $n_2 = 394$, and $n_3 = 291$). The mean (standard deviation) of cultural dimensions for each cluster is *power distance* [Cluster(1) 3.53 (0.79), Cluster(2) 3.30 (0.98), Cluster(3) 3.58 (0.89). Scheffe's multiple range comparison: (1)–(2) = 0.229*, (1)–(3) = −0.050, and (2)–(3) = −0.281*], *individualism* [Cluster(1) 3.92 (0.59), Cluster(2) 4.01 (0.62), Cluster(3) 3.82 (0.64). Scheffe's multiple range comparison: (1)–(2) = −0.092, (1)–(3) = 0.0.98, and (2)–(3) = 0.191*], *masculinity* [Cluster(1) 3.82 (0.64), Cluster(2) 3.63 (0.77), Cluster(3) 3.79 (0.75). Scheffe's multiple range comparison: (1)–(2) = 0.198*, (1)–(3) = 0.034, and (2)–(3) = −0.164*], *uncertainty avoidance* [Cluster(1) 4.29 (0.62), Cluster(2) 4.32 (0.67), Cluster(3) 4.40 (0.65). Scheffe's multiple range comparison: (1)–(2) = −0.037, (1)–(3) = −0.114, and (2)–(3) = −0.076], and *long-term orientation* [Cluster(1) 4.04 (0.62), Cluster(2) 4.03 (0.57), Cluster(3) 4.00 (0.61). Scheffe's multiple range comparison: (1)–(2) = 0.007, (1)–(3) = 0.037, and (2)–(3) = 0.029].

Subsequently, we ran the SQ structural model across these three clusters by using a three-group simultaneous LISREL. Here again, the model fit for each cluster was satisfactory and above the recommended level. These were as follows: *Cluster1* χ^2 (224) = 474.76, RMSEA = 0.059, SRMR = 0.043, CFI = 0.97, NNFI = 0.96, and CAIC = 856.85; *Cluster2* χ^2 (224) = 475.96, RMSEA = 0.057, SRMR = 0.030, CFI = 0.97, NNFI = 0.97, and CAIC = 847.61; and *Cluster3* χ^2 (224) = 602.71, RMSEA = 0.079, SRMR = 0.051, CFI = 0.94, NNFI = 0.93, and CAIC = 951.83. Similar to country analysis, we also compared three-way cluster differences across each structural link in the first-order dimensions of perceived service quality and the service quality-satisfaction link. Results for the unrestricted model were χ^2 (672) = 1553.43, RMSEA = 0.065, SRMR = 0.051, CFI = 0.96, NNFI = 0.96, and CAIC = 2828.99 and for the fully restricted model χ^2 (776) = 1860.00, RMSEA = 0.069, SRMR = 0.087, CFI = 0.95, NNFI = 0.95, and CAIC = 2419.32. The bottom portion of Table 3.2 contains the structural coefficients and the differences in structural links between each pair of countries. Results

Table 3.2 Service quality structural model: cross-national vs. cross-cultural analysis

Dimensions of second-order SQ		3G cross-national analysis			3G cross-national analysis		
		Second-order loading estimates					
		USA(1)	India(2)	Philippines (3)	(1)–(2)	(1)–(3)	(2)–(3)
TANG	γ_{11}	0.75	0.73	0.89	$[\Delta\chi^2$ (1) = 0.08] NSD	$[\Delta\chi^2$ (1) = 2.62] NSD	$[\Delta\chi^2$ (1) = 3.60] NSD
REL	γ_{21}	1.01	0.70	0.84	$[\Delta\chi^2$ (1) = 16.48] **SD**	$[\Delta\chi^2$ (1) = 4.16] **SD**	$[\Delta\chi^2$ (1) = 3.66] NSD
RESP	γ_{31}	0.99	0.88	0.97	$[\Delta\chi^2$ (1) = 1.72] NSD	$[\Delta\chi^2$ (1) = 0.03] NSD	$[\Delta\chi^2$ (1) = 1.39] NSD
ASSU	γ_{41}	1.06	0.79	0.97	$[\Delta\chi^2$ (1) = 12.21] **SD**	$[\Delta\chi^2$ (1) = 1.19] NSD	$[\Delta\chi^2$ (1) = 5.75] **SD**
EMP	γ_{51}	1.01	0.82	0.91	$[\Delta\chi^2$ (1) = 6.40] **SD**	$[\Delta\chi^2$ (1) = 1.66] NSD	$[\Delta\chi^2$ (1) = 1.57] NSD
SQ→SAT	γ_{61}	0.84	0.46	0.22	$[\Delta\chi^2$ (1) = 25.91] **SD**	$[\Delta\chi^2$ (1) = 53.92] **SD**	$[\Delta\chi^2$ (1) = 9.46] **SD**
Dimensions of second-order SQ		3G cross-cultural analysis			3G cross-national analysis		
		Second-order loading estimates					
		CLUS(1)	CLUS(2)	CLUS(3)	(1)–(2)	(1)–(3)	(2)–(3)
TANG	γ_{11}	0.89	0.84	0.79	$[\Delta\chi^2$ (1) = 0.38] NSD	$[\Delta\chi^2$ (1) = 1.25] NSD	$[\Delta\chi^2$ (1) = 0.36] NSD
REL	γ_{21}	0.93	0.92	0.89	$[\Delta\chi^2$ (1) = 0.01] NSD	$[\Delta\chi^2$ (1) = 0.23] NSD	$[\Delta\chi^2$ (1) = 0.14] NSD
RESP	γ_{31}	0.93	0.99	0.97	$[\Delta\chi^2$ (1) = 0.72] NSD	$[\Delta\chi^2$ (1) = 0.22] NSD	$[\Delta\chi^2$ (1) = 0.09] NSD
ASSU	γ_{41}	0.92	0.99	1.00	$[\Delta\chi^2$ (1) = 1.05] NSD	$[\Delta\chi^2$ (1) = 1.23] NSD	$[\Delta\chi^2$ (1) = 0.04] NSD
EMP	γ_{51}	0.92	0.97	0.95	$[\Delta\chi^2$ (1) = 0.52] NSD	$[\Delta\chi^2$ (1) = 0.13] NSD	$[\Delta\chi^2$ (1) = 0.07] NSD
SQ→SAT	γ_{61}	0.49	0.44	0.71	$[\Delta\chi^2$ (1) = 0.36] NSD	$[\Delta\chi^2$ (1) = 6.72] **SD**	$[\Delta\chi^2$ (1) = 10.76] **SD**

3G three-group simultaneous estimation. *SD* significantly different at $p < 0.05$, *NSD* not significantly different i.e., $p > 0.05$, *SQ* service quality, *TANG* tangibles, *REL* reliability, *RESP* responsiveness, *ASSU* assurance, *EMP* empathy, *SAT* satisfaction

indicate that with the exception of two pairs in the service quality→satisfaction link, all of the second-order loadings were *not* significantly different across the three clusters. These findings suggest that cross-cultural model across segments exhibit more similarities than cross-national model across countries, thus supporting hypothesis H1.

Hypothesis 2 Individualism/Collectivism as Moderator of Service Quality in Both Cross-National and Cross-Cultural Models

To test for the moderating role of individualism (high versus low), we ran a two-group analysis in each of the three countries (cross-national) and three clusters (cross-cultural). For the *country-level analysis*, the results were as follows: *USA* χ^2 (448) = 1049.19, RMSEA = 0.078, SRMR = 0.073, CFI = 0.93, NNFI = 0.92, and CAIC = 1754.90; *India* χ^2 (448) = 709.94, RMSEA = 0.059, SRMR = 0.067, CFI = 0.94, NNFI = 0.93, and CAIC = 1379.32; and *Philippines* χ^2 (448) = 1003.42, RMSEA = 0.088, SRMR = 0.049, CFI = 0.93, NNFI = 0.92, and CAIC = 1600.96. Empathy was significantly different between low and high individualism in all the three samples. Further, assurance was significantly different in the USA sample (low IND 1.04, high IND 0.81), and tangibility was significantly different in the India sample (low IND 0.97, high IND 0.69). For the *culture-level analysis*, the results were as follows: *Cluster1* χ^2 (448) = 820.06, RMSEA = 0.070, SRMR = 0.067, CFI = 0.95, NNFI = 0.95, and CAIC = 1544.07; *Cluster2* χ^2 (448) = 815.74, RMSEA = 0.066, SRMR = 0.052, CFI = 0.96, NNFI = 0.95, and CAIC = 1511.45; and *Cluster3* χ^2 (448) = 1038.97, RMSEA = 0.097, SRMR = 0.089, CFI = 0.91, NNFI = 0.90, and CAIC = 1698.39. Here also, empathy was significantly different between low and high individualism in two clusters (2 and 3), while assurance was significantly different in cluster 3. Respondents low in individualism (or high collectivism) attached greater importance to empathy and assurance than respondents high in individualism. In clusters 1 and 3 the SQ-SAT link was found significant implying that perceived service quality has a greater impact in collectivists than individualists. Table 3.3 contains the results for the moderating role of individualism in both cross-national and cross-cultural analyses.

Hypothesis 3 Uncertainty Avoidance as Moderator of Service Quality in Both Cross-National and Cross-Cultural Models

Similarly, to test for the moderating role of uncertainty avoidance (high versus low), we ran a two-group analysis in each of the three countries (cross-national) and three clusters (cross-cultural). The results for the *country-level analysis* were as follows: *USA* χ^2 (448) = 926.50, RMSEA = 0.069, SRMR = 0.051, CFI = 0.94, NNFI = 0.94, and CAIC = 1628.22; *India* χ^2 (448) = 704.45, RMSEA = 0.060, SRMR = 0.058, CFI = 0.94, NNFI = 0.93, and CAIC = 1385.57; and *Philippines* χ^2 (448) = 933.89, RMSEA = 0.083, SRMR = 0.050, CFI = 0.94, NNFI = 0.93, and CAIC = 1561.01. Tangibility emerged significantly different between low and high uncertainty avoidance only in the USA sample (low UA 1.03, high UA 0.61) but not in India and the Philippines sample. For the *culture-level analysis*, the results were as follows: *Cluster1* χ^2 (448) = 770.98, RMSEA = 0.064, SRMR = 0.052, CFI = 0.96, NNFI = 0.95, and CAIC = 1475.13; *Cluster2* χ^2 (448) = 765.44, RMSEA = 0.063, SRMR = 0.031, CFI = 0.96, NNFI = 0.96, and CAIC = 1490.32; and *Cluster3* χ^2 (448) = 927.30, RMSEA = 0.087, SRMR = 0.072, CFI = 0.93, NNFI = 0.92, and CAIC = 1594.14. While there were no significant differences in cluster 1 and cluster 2, four dimensions were found to significantly differ in cluster 3. These were

Table 3.3 Moderating role of individualism: cross-national analysis vs. cross-cultural analysis

Dimensions of second-order SQ		2G cross-national analysis — Second-order loading estimates — USA(1) — Individualism			2G cross-national analysis — Second-order loading estimates — India(2) — Individualism			2G cross-national analysis — Second-order loading estimates — Philippines(3) — Individualism		
		Low	High	Low–high	Low	High	Low–high	Low	High	Low–high
TANG	γ_{11}	0.72	0.80	[$\Delta\chi^2$(1) = 0.43] NSD	0.97	0.69	[$\Delta\chi^2$(1) = 4.24] SD	0.86	0.70	[$\Delta\chi^2$(1) = 1.77] NSD
REL	γ_{21}	0.89	0.81	[$\Delta\chi^2$(1) = 0.61] NSD	1.05	0.86	[$\Delta\chi^2$(1) = 1.86] NSD	0.87	0.84	[$\Delta\chi^2$(1) = 0.04] NSD
RESP	γ_{31}	0.96	0.85	[$\Delta\chi^2$(1) = 0.95] NSD	1.06	0.86	[$\Delta\chi^2$(1) = 2.63] NSD	0.99	0.92	[$\Delta\chi^2$(1) = 0.29] NSD
ASSU	γ_{41}	1.04	0.81	[$\Delta\chi^2$(1) = 4.03] SD	1.02	0.88	[$\Delta\chi^2$(1) = 1.15] NSD	1.00	0.78	[$\Delta\chi^2$(1) = 3.35] NSD
EMP	γ_{51}	1.04	0.65	[$\Delta\chi^2$(1) = 13.45] SD	1.08	0.79	[$\Delta\chi^2$(1) = 5.17] SD	0.96	0.71	[$\Delta\chi^2$(1) = 5.23] SD
SQ→SAT	γ_{61}	0.80	0.51	[$\Delta\chi^2$(1) = 7.23] SD	0.68	0.48	[$\Delta\chi^2$(1) = 2.50] NSD	0.22	0.23	[$\Delta\chi^2$(1) = 0.01] NSD

Dimensions of second-order SQ		2G cross-cultural analysis — Second-order loading estimates — CLUS(1) — Individualism			2G cross-cultural analysis — Second-order loading estimates — CLUS(2) — Individualism			2G cross-cultural analysis — Second-order loading estimates — CLUS(3) — Individualism		
		Low	High	Low–high	Low	High	Low–high	Low	High	Low–high
TANG	γ_{11}	0.80	0.93	[$\Delta\chi^2$(1) = 1.30] NSD	0.94	H0.75	[$\Delta\chi^2$(1) = 3.39] NSD	0.85	H0.74	[$\Delta\chi^2$(1) = 0.66] NSD
REL	γ_{21}	0.95	0.88	[$\Delta\chi^2$(1) = 0.47] NSD	1.00	0.87	[$\Delta\chi^2$(1) = 1.58] NSD	0.87	0.88	[$\Delta\chi^2$(1) = 0.01] NSD
RESP	γ_{31}	0.94	0.97	[$\Delta\chi^2$(1) = 0.04] NSD	1.01	0.90	[$\Delta\chi^2$(1) = 1.48] NSD	1.01	0.85	[$\Delta\chi^2$(1) = 1.58] NSD
ASSU	γ_{41}	0.97	1.01	[$\Delta\chi^2$(1) = 0.11] NSD	1.02	0.88	[$\Delta\chi^2$(1) = 1.99] NSD	1.06	0.67	[$\Delta\chi^2$(1) = 8.32] SD
EMP	γ_{51}	0.97	0.87	[$\Delta\chi^2$(1) = 0.79] NSD	1.05	0.83	[$\Delta\chi^2$(1) = 5.75] SD	1.02	0.70	[$\Delta\chi^2$(1) = 5.71] SD
SQ→SAT	γ_{61}	0.58	0.36	[$\Delta\chi^2$(1) = 3.98] SD	0.60	0.42	[$\Delta\chi^2$(1) = 2.98] NSD	0.68	0.32	[$\Delta\chi^2$(1) = 7.25] SD

2G two-group simultaneous estimation. *SD* significantly different at $p < 0.05$, *NSD* not significantly different i.e., $p > 0.05$, *SQ* service quality, *TANG* tangibles, *REL* reliability, *RESP* responsiveness, *ASSU* assurance, *EMP* empathy, *SAT* satisfaction *tangibility* (low UA 1.04, high UA 0.62), *reliability* (low UA 1.03, high UA 0.73), *responsiveness* (low UA 1.15, high UA 0.82), and *empathy* (low UA 1.11, high UA 0.82). These results indicate that high UA respondents in cluster 3 tend to assign lower importance to SQ dimensions than low UA respondents. Table 3.4 contains the results for the moderating role of uncertainty avoidance in both cross-national and cross-cultural analyses.

Discussion and Implications

Cross-National Research

With regard to hypothesis 1, our study suggests that there are distinctive differences between cross-national and cross-cultural models of perceived service quality. In the cross-national study, *reliability*, *assurance*, and *empathy* were distinctive dimensions with significant differences in at least one paired comparison among the three countries (USA, India, and Philippines). Similarly, perceived service quality linkage with satisfaction was significantly different across all three pairs of comparisons in cross-national analysis. These findings indicate that significant cross-national differences in the study of service quality and satisfaction emerge pointing to a need for an emic-centered research methodology whereby the assumption of more differences than similarities becomes the default standard (Malhotra et al. 1996). That is, in cross-national research, national culture is a relatively stable construct (i.e., static entity) that reflects a shared knowledge structure within a nation-state and that attenuates variability in values, behavioral norms, and patterns of behaviors (Erez and Earley 1993). Hofstede (2001) has been a strong proponent of cultural stability in that national culture, particularly individualism/collectivism, endures over time and is consistent within countries. Even when countries are culturally diverse, members share the same cultural foundation and thus according to cross-national research nationality may be considered a viable proxy for culture (Beaudreau 2006; Dawar and Parker 1994).

However, *tangibility* and *responsiveness* dimensions showed nonsignificant difference in all three countries. One plausible explanation is that customers across countries may tend to use tangibility as a substitute for evaluating service outcomes as opposed to service delivery. That is, given the impact of globalization and rising consumer expectations of services worldwide, technical quality of services as exemplified by technology and tangible servicescape (Brady and Cronin 2001) becomes the "differentiating" factor rather than functional quality of services which has reached competitive parity. This is quite pronounced in India and the Philippines where customers have historically been utilitarian driven but now are aspiring for better service quality and delivery. Both economies, in particular India, have undergone substantial economic transformation in the last 25 years as a result of the liberalization of trade and foreign direct investment policies. The influence of global

Table 3.4 Moderating role of uncertainty avoidance: cross-national analysis vs. cross-cultural analysis

Dimensions of second-order SQ		2G cross-national analysis Second-order loading estimates USA(1) Uncertainty avoidance			2G cross-national analysis Second-order loading estimates India(2) Uncertainty avoidance			2G cross-national analysis Second-order loading estimates Philippines (3) Uncertainty avoidance		
		Low	High	Low–high	Low	High	Low–high	Low	High	Low–high
TANG	γ_{11}	1.03	0.61	$[\Delta\chi^2$ (1) = 10.33] **SD**	0.93	H0.74	$[\Delta\chi^2$ (1) = 1.75] NSD	0.90	0.74	$[\Delta\chi^2$ (1) = 1.90] NSD
REL	γ_{21}	0.97	0.81	$[\Delta\chi^2$ (1) = 2.08] NSD	1.04	0.80	$[\Delta\chi^2$ (1) = 2.87] NSD	0.96	0.79	$[\Delta\chi^2$ (1) = 2.03] NSD
RESP	γ_{31}	1.03	0.90	$[\Delta\chi^2$ (1) = 1.37] NSD	0.99	0.95	$[\Delta\chi^2$ (1) = 0.10] NSD	1.00	0.94	$[\Delta\chi^2$ (1) = 0.34] NSD
ASSU	γ_{41}	0.98	0.98	$[\Delta\chi^2$ (1) = 0.00] NSD	0.98	0.91	$[\Delta\chi^2$ (1) = 0.27] NSD	1.01	0.87	$[\Delta\chi^2$ (1) = 1.59] NSD
EMP	γ_{51}	1.04	0.90	$[\Delta\chi^2$ (1) = 1.57] NSD	1.01	0.85	$[\Delta\chi^2$ (1) = 1.52] NSD	0.97	0.84	$[\Delta\chi^2$ (1) = 1.57] NSD
SQ→SAT	γ_{61}	0.66	0.74	$[\Delta\chi^2$ (1) = 0.53] NSD	0.65	0.54	$[\Delta\chi^2$ (1) = 0.63] NSD	0.35	0.15	$[\Delta\chi^2$ (1) = 2.59] NSD

Dimensions of second-order SQ		2G cross-cultural analysis Second-order loading estimates CLUS(1) Uncertainty avoidance			2G cross-cultural analysis Second-order loading estimates CLUS(2) Uncertainty avoidance			2G cross-national analysis Second-order loading estimates CLUS (3) Uncertainty avoidance		
		Low	High	Low–high	Low	High	Low–high	Low	High	Low–high
TANG	γ_{11}	0.93	0.76	$[\Delta\chi^2$ (1) = 2.40] NSD	0.88	H0.84	$[\Delta\chi^2$ (1) = 0.15] NSD	1.04	0.62	$[\Delta\chi^2$ (1) = 10.09] **SD**
REL	γ_{21}	0.95	0.91	$[\Delta\chi^2$ (1) = 0.20] NSD	0.85	1.00	$[\Delta\chi^2$ (1) = 2.34] NSD	1.03	0.73	$[\Delta\chi^2$ (1) = 5.87] **SD**
RESP	γ_{31}	0.96	0.94	$[\Delta\chi^2$ (1) = 0.04] NSD	0.98	0.95	$[\Delta\chi^2$ (1) = 0.12] NSD	1.15	0.82	$[\Delta\chi^2$ (1) = 7.54] **SD**

(continued)

Table 3.4 (continued)

Dimensions of second-order SQ		2G cross-cultural analysis			2G cross-cultural analysis			2G cross-national analysis		
		Second-order loading estimates			Second-order loading estimates			Second-order loading estimates		
		CLUS(1)			CLUS(2)			CLUS (3)		
		Uncertainty avoidance			Uncertainty avoidance			Uncertainty avoidance		
		Low	High	Low–high	Low	High	Low–high	Low	High	Low–high
ASSU	γ_{41}	0.98	0.99	$[\Delta\chi^2$ (1) = 0.01] NSD	0.96	0.97	$[\Delta\chi^2$ (1) = 0.02] NSD	1.05	0.89	$[\Delta\chi^2$ (1) = 1.75] NSD
EMP	γ_{51}	0.93	0.93	$[\Delta\chi^2$ (1) = 0.00] NSD	1.00	0.94	$[\Delta\chi^2$ (1) = 0.33] NSD	1.11	0.82	$[\Delta\chi^2$ (1) = 6.21] **SD**
SQ→SAT	γ_{61}	0.44	0.51	$[\Delta\chi^2$ (1) = 0.43] NSD	0.49	0.49	$[\Delta\chi^2$ (1) = 0.00] NSD	0.59	0.6	$[\Delta\chi^2$ (1) = 0.06] NS

2G two-group simultaneous estimation. *SD* significantly different at $p < 0.05$, *NSD* not significantly different i.e., $p > 0.05$, *SQ* service quality, *TANG* tangibles, *REL* reliability, *RESP* responsiveness, *ASSU* assurance, *EMP* empathy, *SAT* satisfaction

culture has accentuated the global-national dialectic (Kjeldgaard and Askegaard 2006) shaping the definition of self and national identity. Customers, particularly in urban centers, are giving more importance to the tangible aspects of services (i.e., physical facilities, technology, appearance of personnel, etc.) and are becoming more demanding with regard to substantive and timely delivery of services. Some research has validated that economic development creates a shift toward the individualistic material-cultural environment and away from the collectivist and social obligations (Heuer et al. 1999; Inglehart and Baker 2000). For instance, the link between sustained affluence and the development of individualistic culture can be seen in countries like Japan and Singapore, where there is fear that the younger generation is losing work ethic and the sense of collective obligation (Ahuvia 2002). With continued progress in economic development, the requirement of social conformity declines and post-modernization values of self-expression and individualism emerges (Tang and Koveos 2008).

In summary, results from cross-national research suggest that despite globalization, national borders continue to have important meaning although not in the way cross-national research or values-based research tradition might suggest. An argument can be made based on Gelfand et al. (2011) study that found country-level factor, namely, degree of "cultural tightness," i.e., countries that have strong social norms and enforcement and low tolerance for deviant behavior, may influence "country effect." Thus, rather than abandoning country-level research, both country-level and intra-country-level cultural values research must be integrated for fine-grained analysis (Beugelsdijk et al. 2017). Although, culture resides at different levels, e.g., organizations, teams, professional associations, and nation-states, Beugelsdijk et al. (2017) argue that to abandon country as the unit of analysis may be too farfetched as suggested by Kirkman et al. (2017), similar in spirit to throwing the baby with the bath water. Having said that, Taras et al. (2016) found that every possible container of culture (e.g., socioeconomic status, globalization index, economic freedom, etc., to name a few) outperformed country as a criterion for setting boundaries for cultural entities. They found that only a maximum of 20% of variance in cultural values resides between countries, which of course means that 80% resides within countries, indicating wide intra-country variability. There is a need to explore other containers of culture and break out of the dominant "country equals culture" paradigm.

Cross-Cultural Research

In contrast, in cross-cultural research, no service quality dimension was significantly different across the three clusters, that is, tangibility, reliability, responsiveness, assurance, and empathy were all common dimensions of service quality. Our findings empirically validate what cross-cultural and international business scholars have maintained regarding the within-country heterogeneity on cultural values and the growing hegemony of global culture in bringing some convergence of global markets (Au 1999; Kirkman et al. 2006; Ralston 2008; Tung 2008). In contrast to cross-national research, cross-cultural research views culture as a distinct web of significance or meaning that involves sense making, meaning making or production that goes beyond the constraints of group membership (Adams and Markus 2004). Gould and Grein (2009) construe culture as a pivotal and holistic construct, distinct from national culture, and position culture-centric research as a constructivist process of meanings and patterns of practices that are rooted on the processes of culture itself. Unlike national culture, the formation and evolution of culture involves a social construction of practices and experiences which puts emphasis on meaning, context, and process. Our study provides evidence of cultural convergence at the most external layer of behavior as a result of global culture permeating down to the individual cognitive level (Erez and Gati 2004; Leung et al. 2005). However, it should be noted that culture as a multilayer construct (Schein 1992) is most easily influenced at the external layer of artifacts and behavior and gets progressively difficult to penetrate at the deeper levels of values and basic assumptions reflecting convictions about reality and human nature.

For international marketing scholars, these findings indicate a need for an etic-centered research methodology (albeit in combination with emic-centered methodology) which assumes more similarities than differences in perceived service quality and satisfaction (Malhotra and McCort 2001). This has implications for global market segmentation in that segmentation based on individual-level cultural values as opposed to nation-states detects more similarities in the dimensions of perceived service quality and satisfaction. While researchers have found empirical support for the existence of horizontal market segments for consumer products and services (Bolton and Myers 2003; Hofstede et al. 1999), we believe this study offers managerial insights on the efficacy of international market segmentation based on common segments that transcend national boundaries. Service delivery systems should be simultaneously customized to meet unique perceptions across segments and standardized on common service dimensions to meet organizational cost-effectiveness (see Agarwal et al. 2010).

Individualism/Collectivism as Moderator

With regard to hypothesis 2a, there are two implications. *First*, assurance and empathy emerged as the two most critical service quality dimensions which were significantly moderated by individualism/collectivism in both cross-national and cross-cultural models. Assurance refers to the knowledge and courtesy of employees and their abilities to inspire trust and confidence, and empathy refers to the caring and individualized attention and understanding a firm provides to its customers. Collectivists assign greater weights to assurance and empathy than individualists. This is because collectivists generally have interdependent self-construal, as opposed to independent self-construal, in which knowledge about others are relatively more elaborate and distinctive than knowledge about the self and as such they seek assurances from people rather than from technology, and are more sensitive and empathetic toward others (Gudykunst et al. 1996; Markus and Kitayama 1991, 1994; Oyserman et al. 2002). *Second*, we also find that collectivists draw greater service satisfaction arising from perceived service quality than do individualists. This finding is rather curious as one might have expected that individualists prefer open expression of emotions as a validation of their authentic self and that satisfaction and dissatisfaction can be expressed candidly. In contrast, for collectivists, one might expect that the expression of emotions is significantly shaped by a consideration of the reaction of others, and thus true feelings of dissatisfaction are often suppressed for the preservation of long-term relationship. Perhaps, one plausible explanation to this aberration is the apparent asymmetry between satisfaction and dissatisfaction and that collectivists voice their satisfaction for a high perceived service quality as a signal to reinforce their long-term relationship. This however may not be the case for voicing dissatisfaction. More research is warranted here.

Uncertainty Avoidance as Moderator

With regard to hypothesis 2b, there are two implications. *First*, tangibility emerged as the only service quality dimension which was significantly moderated by uncertainty avoidance (UAV) in both cross-national (i.e., USA sample) and cross-cultural analyses (i.e., cluster 3). Tangibility refers to the physical evidence of the service, consisting of physical facilities and technology, appearance of personnel, tools or equipment, and physical presentation of the service, which can influence consumers at physiological, sociological, cognitive, and emotional levels (Parasuraman et al. 1985). Research on uncertainty avoidance suggests that people reduce their uncertainty by technology, law, and rituals and people who are high on UAV tend to display less tolerance for unclear situations and greater proclivity toward consensus, structure, reliability, and long-term relationships (Hofstede 2001; Reimann et al. 2008). While technology and tangibility (i.e., high tech) can address the inherent narrow zone of tolerance of high UAV customers through efficiency, our study shows that customers that are high on UAV tend to assign less importance to tangibility. This is perhaps because a high-tech environment can also generate anxiety and stress especially when social interactions and personal connectivity (i.e., high touch) are compromised. Therefore, global marketers need to strike the right balance between "high tech" and "high touch" especially in cross-cultural market segments, as evidenced in our cross-cultural findings. *Second*, we also find that, in general, UAV with the exception of tangibility, does not significantly moderate dimensions of SQ in cross-national analysis. In contrast, the role of UAV as a moderator is pronounced in cross-cultural analysis in one of the clusters (cluster 3) in which it significantly moderates tangibility, reliability, responsiveness, and empathy. This implies that in international marketing studies, a cross-cultural analysis which yields more homogeneity within segments is a better unit of analysis to detect the influence of moderators when the moderator is relevant for a given segment with an expected effect size (Kirkman et al. 2006; Beugelsdijk et al. 2017). The impact of moderators gets more refined and pronounced in cross-cultural analysis as extraneous noise is eliminated and greater homogeneity is attained. Thus a better way to capture the effects of moderators in international business research is to model its influence on global segments that transcend national boundaries (i.e., cross-cultural research) rather than on nation-states (i.e., cross-national research) as conducted historically.

Contributions and Conclusion

In conclusion, our study makes a number of theoretical, methodological, and managerial contributions. Theoretically, our research contributes to the international marketing literature by demonstrating differences between cross-national and cross-cultural research and empirically validating the growing relevance of culture-based approach to global market segmentation. Until recently, most international business research has focused on cross-national research where national culture, based on group membership in a nation state, has been used as a grouping variable to study cultural variation among countries. We also investigate the moderating role of individualism/collectivism and uncertainty avoidance in the relationship between perceived service quality and satisfaction and find some insightful results in both sets of analyses. Cross-cultural analysis yields more homogeneity within segments and is a better unit of analysis to detect the refined influence of moderators for a relevant segment.

In terms of methodological contributions, we (1) collect data from large and representative samples from three countries; (2) we test for common method variance bias using the recent methodology proposed by Malhotra et al. (2006); (3) we estimate measurement models and establish the reliability, convergent, and discriminant validity of all our measures; (4) we examine configural, metric, scalar, and variance-covariance equivalence (Malhotra et al. 1996; Steenkamp and Baumgartner 1998); and (5) we employ structural equation modeling to test our hypotheses.

Our hypotheses and the resulting findings also have useful managerial implications. With regard to hypothesis 1, there are implications for global market segmentation in that segmentation based on culture as opposed to nation-states detects more similarities in the dimensions of perceived service quality and satisfaction. Thus, our study offers managerial insights on the efficacy of global market segmentation based on common segments that transcend national boundaries. Service delivery systems should be customized to meet "emic" peculiarities by adopting vertical segmentation strategies and simultaneously standardized to meet "etic" universals by adopting horizontal segmentation strategies on common service dimensions to meet organizational cost-effectiveness. In terms of hypothesis 2a, collectivists assign greater weights to assurance and empathy than individualists. Thus, marketers should emphasize assurance and empathy-based strategies and mechanisms in collectivist cultures. With regard to hypothesis 2b, global marketers need to strike the right balance between "high tech" and "high touch" to alleviate concerns related with uncertainty avoidance especially in cross-cultural market segments, as evidenced in our cross-cultural findings.

In conclusion, this research is not without limitations. Because service quality is a malleable construct contingent on personal, cultural, and institutional factors, a longitudinal study tracking its evolving nature would better detect convergence over time. Further, in this study, we only used the Hofstede framework; future studies test our model using alternative frameworks such as the GLOBE project. Notwithstanding these limitations, we believe our preliminary empirical results shed new light to an old debate that was first sparked by Levitt in 1983 in his classic published article that appeared in *Harvard Business Review*. While the debate between convergence and divergence of cultural values will continue into the future, we believe our research provides sufficient evidence for more cross-cultural research by international marketing researchers and the need for using culture both as a grouping variable and a moderating variable.

References

Adams, G., and H.R. Markus. 2004. Toward a conception of culture suitable for a social psychology of culture. In *The psychological foundations of culture*, ed. M. Schaller and C.S. Crandall, 335–360. Mahwah: Lawrence Erlbaum.

Agarwal, J., N.K. Malhotra, and R. Bolton. 2010. A cross-national and cross-cultural approach to global market segmentation: An application using consumers' perceived service quality. *Journal of International Marketing* 18 (3): 18–40.

Ahuvia, A. 2002. Individualism/collectivism and cultures of happiness: A theoretical conjecture on the relationship between consumption, cultures and subjective well-being at the national level. *Journal of Happiness Studies* 3: 23–36.

Arnett, J.J. 2002. The psychology of globalization. *American Psychologist* 57 (10): 774–783.

Au, K.Y. 1999. Intra-cultural variation: Evidence and implications for international business. *Journal of International Business Studies* 30 (4): 799–812.

Bagozzi, R.P. 1992. The self-regulation of attitudes, intentions, and behavior. *Social Psychology Quarterly* 55: 178–204.

Bagozzi, R.P., and Todd F. Heatherton. 1994. A general approach to representing multifaceted personality constructs: Application to state self-esteem. *Structural Equation Modeling* 1 (1): 35–67.

Beaudreau, B.C. 2006. Identity, entropy, and culture. *Journal of Economic Psychology* 27 (2): 205–223.

Beugelsdijk, S., T. Kostova, and K. Roth. 2017. An overview of Hofstede-inspired country-level culture research in international business since 2006. *Journal of International Business Studies* 48: 30–47.

Bolton, R.N., and J.H. Drew. 1991. A multistage model of customers' assessments of service quality and value. *Journal of Consumer Research* 17 (March): 375–384.

Bolton, R.N., and M.B. Myers. 2003. Price-based global market segmentation for services. *Journal of Marketing* 67 (July): 108–128.

Brady, M.K., and J. Cronin. 2001. Some new thoughts on conceptualizing perceived service quality: A hierarchical approach. *Journal of Marketing* 65 (July): 34–49.

Brady, M.K., and Christopher J. Robertson. 2001. Searching for a consensus on the antecedent role of service quality and satisfaction: An exploratory cross-national study. *Journal of Business Research* 51 (1), January: 53–60.

Brady, M.K., Gary A. Knight, J. Joseph Cronin Jr., G. Tomas, M. Hult, and Bruce D. Keillor. 2005. Removing the contextual lens: A multinational, multi-setting comparison of service evaluation models. *Journal of Retailing* 81 (3): 215–230.

Broderick, A.J., G.E. Greenley, and R.D. Mueller. 2007. The behavioral homogeneity evaluation framework: Multi-level evaluations of consumer involvement in international segmentation. *Journal of International Business Studies* 38 (5): 746–763.

Carman, J.M. 1990. Consumer perceptions of service quality: An assessment of the SERVQUAL dimensions. *Journal of Retailing* 66 (1): 33–55.

Chang, W.C., W.K. Wong, and J.B.K. Koh. 2003. Chinese values in Singapore: Traditional and modern. *Asian Journal of Social Psychology* 6: 5–29.

Cornwell, B.T., and J. Drennan. 2004. Cross-cultural consumer/consumption research: Dealing with issues emerging from globalization and fragmentation. *Journal of Macromarketing* 24 (2): 108–121.

Cronin, J.J., Jr., Michael K. Brady, G. Tomas, and M. Hult. 2000. Assessing the effects of quality, value, and customer satisfaction on consumer behavioral intentions in service environments. *Journal of Retailing* 76 (2), Summer: 193–218.

Cross, S.E., J.S. Gore, and M.L. Morris. 2003. The relational-interdependent self-construal, self-concept consistency, and well-being. *Journal of Personality and Social Psychology* 85 (5): 933–944.

Dabholkar, P.A., D.I. Thorpe, and J.O. Rentz. 1996. A measure of service quality for retail stores: Scale development and validation. *Journal of the Academy of Marketing Science* 24 (1): 3–16.

Dabholkar, P.A., D.C. Shepherd, and D.I. Thorpe. 2000. A comprehensive framework for service quality: An investigation of critical conceptual and measurement issues through a longitudinal study. *Journal of Retailing* 76 (2): 139–173.

Dawar, N., and P. Parker. 1994. Marketing universals: Consumers' use of brand name, price, physical appearance, and retailer reputation as signals of product quality. *Journal of Marketing* 58 (2): 81–95.

Doney, P.M., Joseph P. Cannon, and Michel P. Mullen. 1998. Understanding the influence of National Culture on the Development of Trust. *Academy of Management Review* 23 (July): 601–620.

Donthu, N., and B. Yoo. 1998. Cultural influences on service quality expectations. *Journal of Service Research* 1 (2): 178–186.

Eckhardt, G.M., and M.J. Houston. 2007. On the distinction between cultural and cross-cultural psychological approaches and its significance for consumer psychology. In *Review of marketing research*, ed. N.K. Malhotra, 81–108. Armonk: M.E. Sharpe.

Edwards, J.R., and R.P. Bagozzi. 2000. On the nature and direction of relationships between constructs and measures. *Psychological Methods* 5 (2): 155–174.

Erez, M., and E. Gati. 2004. A dynamic multi-level model of culture: From the micro level of the individual to the macro level of a global culture. *Applied Psychology: An International Review* 53 (4): 583–598.

Erez, M., and P.C. Earley. 1993. *Culture, self-identity, and work*. Oxford: Oxford University Press.

Fang, T. 2005–2006. From 'onion' to 'ocean': Paradox and change in National Cultures. *International Studies of Management and Organization* 35 (4): 71–90.

Furrer, O., B.S.-C. Liu, and D. Sudharshan. 2000. The relationships between culture and service quality perception: Basis for cross-cultural market segmentation and resource allocation. *Journal of Service Research* 2 (4): 355–371.

Gelfand, M., et al. 2011. Differences between tight and loose cultures: A 33 nation study. *Science* 332: 1100–1104.

Ger, G., and R.W. Belk. 1996. Cross-cultural differences in materialism. *Journal of Economic Psychology* 17 (1): 55–77.

Gould, S.J., and A.F. Grein. 2009. Think glocally, act glocally: A culture-centric comment on Leung, Bhagat, Buchan, Erez and Gibson (2005). *Journal of International Business Studies* 40: 237–254.

Gudykunst, W.B., Y. Matsumoto, S. Ting-Toomey, T. Nishida, K. Kim, and S. Heyman. 1996. The influence of cultural individualism-collectivism, self-construals, and individual values on communication styles across cultures. *Human Communication Research* 22: 510–543.

Hair, Joseph F., Jr., William C. Black, Barry J. Babin, and Rolph E. Anderson. 2010. *Multivariate data analysis*. 7th ed. Upper Saddle River: Pearson Prentice Hall.

Heuer, M., J.L. Cummings, and W. Hutabarat. 1999. Cultural stability or change among managers in Indonesia. *Journal of International Business Studies* 30 (3): 599–610.

Higgins, T.E. 1998. Promotion and prevention: Regulatory focus as a motivational principle. In *Advances in experimental social psychology*, ed. M.P. Zanna, vol. 30, 1–46. San Diego: Academic.

Hill, Charles W. 1997. *International business: Competing in the global market place*. Chicago: Richard D. Irwin.

Hofstede, F.T., J.B.E.M. Steenkamp, and M. Wedel. 1999. International market segmentation based on consumer-product relations. *Journal of Marketing Research* 36 (February): 1–17.

Hofstede, G. 1980. *Culture's consequences: International differences in work-related values*. Beverly Hills: Sage Publications.

———. 1991. *Cultures and organizations: Software of the mind*. London: McGraw-Hill.

———. 2001. *Culture's consequence: Comparing values, behavior, institutions, and organizations across nations*. Thousand Oaks: Sage.

———. 2011. Cultural dimensions, http://www.geerthofstede.com. Accessed 15 August 2011.

Inglehart, R., and W. Baker. 2000. Modernization, cultural change and the persistence of traditional values. *American Sociological Review* 65: 19–51.

Jarvis, C.B., S.B. Mackenzie, and P.M. Podsakoff. 2003. A critical review of construct indicators and measurement model misspecification in marketing and consumer research. *Journal of Consumer Research* 30 (2): 199–218.

Kale, Sudhir H., and John B. Barns. 1992. Understanding the domain of cross-cultural buyer-seller interactions. *Journal of International Business Studies* 23 (winter): 101–132.

Kirkman, B.L., K.B. Lowe, and C.B. Gibson. 2006. A quarter century of culture's consequences: A review of empirical research incorporating Hofstede's cultural values framework. *Journal of International Business Studies* 37: 285–320.

———. 2017. A retrospective on culture's consequences: The 35-year journey. *Journal of International Business Studies* 48: 12–29.

Kitayama, S. 2002. Culture and basic psychological processes—toward a system view of culture: Comment on Oyserman et al. (2002). *Psychological Bulletin* 128 (1): 89–96.

Kjeldgaard, D., and S. Askegaard. 2006. The glocalization of youth culture: The global youth segment as structures of common difference. *Journal of Consumer Research* 33 (2): 231–247.

Knight, Gary A. 1999. International services marketing: Review of research, 1980–1998. *Journal of Services Marketing* 13 (45): 347–360.

Kwan, V.S.Y., M.H. Bond, and T.M. Singelis. 1997. Pan-cultural explanations for life satisfaction: Adding relationship harmony to self-esteem. *Journal of Personality and Social Psychology* 73 (5): 1038–1051.

Lazarus, R.S. 1991. *Emotion and adaptation*. New York: Oxford University Press.

Leung, K., R.S. Bhagat, N.R. Buchan, M. Erez, and C.B. Gibson. 2005. Culture and international business: Recent advances and their implications for future research. *Journal of International Business Studies* 36 (4): 357–378.

Levitt, T. 1983. The globalization of markets. *Harvard Business Review* 61 (May–June): 92–102.

Lindell, M.K., and D.J. Whitney. 2001. Accounting for common method variance in cross-sectional research design. *Journal of Applied Psychology* 86 (February): 114–121.

Liu, B.S.-C., Olivier Furrer, and D. Sudharshan. 2001. The relationships between culture and behavioral intentions toward services. *Journal of Service Research*, November, 4 (2): 118–129.

Lovelock, C., and G. Yip. 1996. Developing global strategies for service businesses. *California Management Review* 38: 64–86.

Malhotra, N.K., and D.J. McCort. 2001. A cross-cultural comparison of behavioral intention models: Theoretical consideration and an empirical investigation. *International Marketing Review* 18 (3): 235–269.

Malhotra, N.K., J. Agarwal, and M. Peterson. 1996. Cross-cultural marketing research: Methodological issues and guidelines. *International Marketing Review* 13 (5): 7–43.

Malhotra, N.K., S. Kim, and A. Patil. 2006. Common method variance in IS research: A comparison of alternative approaches and a reanalysis of past research. *Management Science* 12 (December) 52 (12): 1865–1883.

Malhotra, N.K. 2010. *Marketing research: An applied orientation*. 6th ed. Upper Saddle River: Prentice Hall.

Malhotra, N.K., F.M. Ulgado, J. Agarwal, and I.B. Baalbaki. 1994. International services marketing: A comparative evaluation of the dimensions of service quality between developed and developing countries. *International Marketing Review* 11 (2): 5–15.

Malhotra, N.K., F.M. Ulgado, J. Agarwal, G. Shainesh, and L. Wu. 2005. Dimensions of service quality in developed and developing economies: Multi-country cross-cultural comparisons. *International Marketing Review* 22 (3): 256–278.

Markus, H.R., and S. Kitayama. 1991. Culture and the self: Implications for cognition, emotion, and motivation. *Psychological Review* 98: 224–253.

———. 1994. The cultural construction of self and emotion: Implications for social behavior. In *Emotion and culture: Empirical studies of mutual influence*, ed. S. Kitayama and H.R. Markus, 89–130. Washington, DC: American Psychological Association.

Mattila, A.S. 1999. The role of culture in the service evaluation process. *Journal of Service Research* 1 (3): 250–261.

McCort, D.J., and Naresh K. Malhotra. 1993. Culture and consumer behavior: Toward an understanding of cross-cultural consumer behavior in international marketing. *Journal of International Consumer Marketing* 6 (2): 91–127.

Naylor, L.L. 1996. *Culture and change: An introduction*. Portsmouth: Greenwood.

Oliver, R.L. 1997. *Satisfaction: A behavioral perspective on the consumer*. New York: McGraw Hill.

Oyserman, D., H.M. Coon, and M. Kemmelmeier. 2002. Rethinking individualism and collectivism: Evaluation of theoretical assumptions and meta-analyses. *Psychological Bulletin* 128 (1): 3–72.

Parasuraman, A., V.A. Zeithaml, and L.L. Berry. 1994. Reassessment of expectations as a comparison standard in measuring service quality: Implications for future research. *Journal of Marketing* 58 (February): 201–230.

———. 1985. A conceptual model of service quality and its implications for future research. *Journal of Marketing* 49 (4): 41–50.

———. 1988. SERVQUAL: A multiple-item scale for measuring consumer perceptions of service quality. *Journal of Retailing* 64 (1): 12–40.

Petrova, P.K., R.B. Cialdini, and S.J. Sills. 2007. Consistency-based compliance across cultures. *Journal of Experimental Social Psychology* 43: 104–111.

Raajpoot, Nusser. 2004. Reconceptualizing service encounter quality in a non-western context. *Journal of Service Research* 7 (2): 181–201.

Ralston, D.A. 2008. The Crossvergence perspective: Reflections and projections. *Journal of International Business Studies* 39 (1): 27–40.

Reimann, M., U.F. Lünemann, and R.B. Chase. 2008. Uncertainty avoidance as a moderator of the relationship between perceived service quality and customer satisfaction. *Journal of Service Research*, August, 11 (1): 63–73.

Rindskopf, D., and T. Rose. 1988. Some theory and applications of confirmatory second-order factor analysis. *Multivariate Behavioral Research* 23 (1): 51–67.

Schein, E.H. 1992. *Organizational culture and leadership*. San Francisco: Jossey-Bass.

Schumann, J.H., F.V. Wangenhei, A. Stringfellow, Z.L. Yang, S. Praxmarer, F.R. Jiménez, V. Blazevic, R.M. Shannon, G. Shainesh, and M. Komor. 2010. Drivers of trust in relational service exchange: Understanding the importance of cross-cultural differences. *Journal of Service Research*, November 13 (4): 453–468.

Singelis, T.M. 1994. The measurement of independent and interdependent self-construals. *Personality and Social Psychology Bulletin* 20 (5): 580–591.

Smith, P.B., and M.H. Bond. 1998. *Social psychology across cultures*. 2nd ed. Boston: Allyn and Bacon.

Spreng, R.A., and R.D. Mackoy. 1996. An empirical examination of a model of perceived service quality and satisfaction. *Journal of Retailing* 72 (2): 201–214.

Steenkamp, J.E.M. 2001. The role of national culture in international marketing research. *International Marketing Review* 18 (1): 30–44.

Steenkamp, J.E.M., and H. Baumgartner. 1998. Assessing measurement invariance in cross-national consumer research. *Journal of Consumer Research* 25 (June): 78–90.

Tang, L., and P.E. Koveos. 2008. A framework to update Hofstede's cultural value indices: Economic dynamics and institutional stability. *Journal of International Business Studies* 39: 1045–1063.

Taras, V., P. Steel, and B.L. Kirkman. 2016. Does country equal culture? Beyond geography in the search for cultural boundaries. *Management International Review* 56 (4): 455–487.

Triandis, H.C. 1995. *Individualism and collectivism*. Boulder: Westview.

Triandis, Harry C. 1972. *The analysis of subjective culture*. New York: Wiley.

Tung, R.L. 2008. The cross-cultural research imperative: The need to balance cross national and intra-national diversity. *Journal of International Business Studies* 39 (1): 41–46.

Birgelen, Van, Ko de Ruyter Marcel, Ad de Jong, and Martin Wetzels. 2002. Customer evaluations of after-sales service contact modes: An empirical analysis of national culture's consequences. *International Journal of Research in Marketing* 19 (1): 43–64.

Von Glinow, M.A., D.L. Shapiro, and J.M. Brett. 2004. Can we talk, and should we? Managing emotional conflict in multicultural teams. *Academy of Management Review* 29 (4): 578–592.

Voss, Christopher A., Aleda V. Roth, Eve D. Rosenzweig, Kate Blackmon, and Richard B. Chase. 2004. A tale of two countries' conservatism, service quality, and feedback on customer. *Journal of Service Research* 6 (3): 213–230.

Winsted, K.F. 1997. The service experience in two cultures: A behavioral perspective. *Journal of Retailing* 73 (3) (fall): 337–360.

Wong, N.Y. 2004. The role of culture in the perception of service recovery. *Journal of Business Research* 57 (9) September: 957–963.

Zhang, J., Sharon E. Beatty, and Gianfranco Walsh. 2008. Review and future directions of cross-cultural consumer services research. *Journal of Business Research* 61 (March): 211–224.

Chapter 4
Cross-Border E-Commerce: A New Driver of Global Trade

Yanbin Tu and Joe Z. Shangguan

Abstract In this chapter, we explore cross-border e-commerce (CBEC) as a new driver of international trade. We adopt a revised i-based N-OLI framework for CBEC. Using China as a case study, we discuss the rapid growth, structure, export/import models, and infrastructure and environment of China's CBEC. We attribute China's CBEC success to the important role of e-commerce giants such as Alibaba.com and JD.com, the designation of CBEC pilot cities, supportive governmental policies, and big capital inflows. Four factors are seen to create future opportunities for all stakeholders of global CBEC, especially for merchants: the push from governments, the rise of middle class in developing countries, technological improvements, and more SMEs adopting CBEC. On the other hand, cultural differences, customer trust, logistics, payment, and legal and regulatory barriers are among the biggest challenges facing CBEC. Lastly, we outline several recommendations for foreign firms planning on entering into China's market by means of CBEC.

Introduction

We are in an information age with a dynamic business environment. While traditional retailers struggle to keep up with market changes, with well-known names like Sears in the USA and Wanda Shopping Mall in China closing their stores, e-tailers are prospering in both developed and developing countries. As Table 4.1 shows, online retail sales in world's major economies are projected to grow at enviable rates from 2014 to 2018, with China, India, and Argentina all exceeding 100%.

Y. Tu (✉) • J. Z. Shangguan
School of Business, Robert Morris University,
Moon Township, PA 15108, USA
e-mail: tu@rmu.edu

© Springer International Publishing AG, part of Springer Nature 2018
J. Agarwal, T. Wu (eds.), *Emerging Issues in Global Marketing*,
https://doi.org/10.1007/978-3-319-74129-1_4

93

Table 4.1 Global online retail sales

#	Country	2014 $B	2018 $B	Projected increase %
1	USA	294	414	41
2	UK	70	98	40
3	China	440	990	125
4	Germany	49	75	53
5	France	41	65	59
6	Japan	63	93	48
7	Australia	25	35	40
8	India	4	24	500
9	Brazil	19	35	84
10	Mexico	2.8	5.5	96
11	Argentina	3.3	6.8	106

Data Source: Forrester (2014)

Table 4.2 CBEC vs. traditional international trade

	Advantages	Disadvantages
CBEC	Shorter channels between sellers and buyers; lower prices and wider choices for consumers; easier for SMEs to use to access foreign markets	Relatively new practice; subject to rapid changes in technology; barriers in global logistics, customer services, payment, and taxation. Prone to frauds
Traditional international trade	Long history and tradition; import/export practices well established and regulated	Longer channels, longer process time, and higher costs; more regulatory procedures and compliances (e.g., CIQ compliance checks, product registrations, etc.)

A significant portion of online sales involve sellers and buyers from different countries. This business practice is now coined as cross-border e-commerce (CBEC). CBEC can be defined in two ways. In a narrow sense, CBEC refers to cross-border retailing: sellers in one country accept orders through the Internet and deliver products to customers in another country via cross-border logistics. In a broad sense, CBEC refers to any electronic foreign trade, as products are exported from one country and imported to another through display, negotiation, and transaction on the Internet (iResearch 2014). However defined, CBEC differs from traditional foreign trade in many ways. For example, traditional import/export usually does not involve consumers, whereas in CBEC consumers are directly involved, who might pay tariffs/taxes and track shipments on their own.

CBEC has several advantages over traditional international trade. As an Internet-based business model, CBEC helps small- and medium-sized enterprises (SMEs) enter into foreign markets. CBEC allows merchants to bypass the middlemen and deal with individual wholesalers, retailers, and even end users directly. In CBEC, sellers may be able to quickly adapt to the changes in market as they actively interact with end users. In addition, CBEC is generally less regulated and taxed by governments, which often translates into lower costs for both sellers and buyers and

Table 4.3 Trade volume of China's CBEC

Year	2011	2012	2013	2014	2015	2016
Volume (in b. RMB)	1550	1860	2700	3570	4500	5400
Annual growth		20%	45%	32%	26%	20%

Data Source: CECRC (2016)

more room for this market to expand. Table 4.2 lists the advantages and disadvantages of CBEC vs. traditional international trade.

In recent years, traditional global trade has shown some growth fatigue. Four factors contribute to the slowdown: (1) slow global economic recovery after the 2008 financial crisis. Global demands for products and services have been sluggish. (2) Competition. CBEC is replacing certain parts of traditional global trade. (3) Rising trade protectionism from certain countries. (4) Digitalization of many goods and services, which are delivered via the Internet.

While traditional global trade appears to have slowed down, CBEC is rapidly growing and becoming a new driver of global trade. Global e-commerce will become a $661.66 billion market by 2017, with mobile commerce expected to grow 30% from 2016, according to PayPal and IPSOS. CBEC in China, for example, has been growing by double digits in each of the past 5 years. Table 4.3 shows the trade volume and growth rates between 2011 and 2016.

Two factors have contributed to the rapid growth of global CBEC. The first is globalization. Countries nowadays are more integrated with each other than before. Particularly, the two largest economies, the USA and China, are bonded with close economic and trade relationships. The second is information technology innovations. Infrastructures and platforms conducive to CBEC have been significantly improved, international logistics are more efficient, and international payment has become more secure.

The rapid growth of CBEC, however, is not without its roadblocks. In fact, there have been many barriers and challenges in such areas as logistics, customs clearance, international payment, customer services, and product frauds. Common problems reported by CBEC buyers are product frauds and counterfeits, limitation of delivery methods, failed deliveries, contract termination, unauthorized charges, defective products, and inconvenient returns. Solving these problems is not easy because more than one country is involved and international cooperation is often required.

Our goal in this chapter is to provide readers with a broad and deep understanding of CBEC. We use China as a case study because of its prominent role in global CBEC and relative success it has had. The remainder of the chapter is organized as follows: first, we review current literature and provide a theoretical framework for CBEC; next, we provide an overview of China's CBEC and discuss China's experience on promoting CBEC; we then discuss the opportunities and challenges in global CBEC; finally, we outline some strategies for small- and medium-sized foreign firms that are planning to enter into China's market via CBEC. Conclusion follows at the end.

Literature Review

To understand cross-border e-commerce, one needs to first understand e-commerce in general. Agarwal and Wu (2015) provide a comprehensive conceptual framework for understanding e-commerce in the global marketplace. Building upon Dunning (1995, 1998, 2000) and Singh and Kundu (2002), they propose an institution-based network-ownership, location, and internationalization (i.e., i-based N-OLI) framework due to the significant role of institutions. From this multi-theoretical perspective, they examine the factors impacting the growth potential of e-commerce in emerging economies at the global, national, and transactional levels. These factors are also applicable in the context of CBEC as it can be viewed as the globalization/internationalization of e-commerce.

Malhotra et al. (2003) synthesize several foundational theories on modes of global entry and offer a conceptual framework of the internationalization process. They discuss global strategic factors, government-imposed factors, market factors, and transaction-specific factors which jointly drive internationalization or globalization. Cross-border e-commerce is seen as the new format of international trade in the information age, with features different from traditional international trade. Yousefi (2015) investigates whether growing CBEC boosts traditional international trade or simply substitutes it. He finds that electronic delivery of digital products in CBEC helps developing countries gain deeper access to international markets. Terzi (2011) studies the impact of e-commerce on international trade and employment and finds that electronic commerce brings economy-wide benefits to all countries. The author further points out that the gains are likely to be concentrated in developed countries in the short run, but more gains will switch to developing countries in the long run.

Some studies focus on the challenges facing cross-border e-commerce and potential solutions. Xue et al. (2016) analyze the business model and ecosystem of cross-border e-commerce in China. Zhang et al. (2016) point out that, with the rapid development of CBEC in recent years, many problems have emerged including shortage of relevant professionals and lack of innovation on business model. Gomez-Herrera et al. (2014) point out that, although distance-related trade costs are greatly reduced compared to offline trade, a strong increase in trade costs related to crossing linguistic borders is observed. Pei et al. (2016) find that the most weighted factors that satisfy foreign buyers are commodity quality, relative price, delivery speed, and payment methods. Deng and Wang (2016) find that early-mover advantages may diminish beyond a critical length of tenure because of free-riding costs, resolution of technological or market uncertainty, as well as the incumbent inertia of early movers. Tao and Zhang (2016) propose a credit evaluation model for CBEC that makes use of big data, along with the application of advanced machine learning tool for training and forecast.

As Agarwal and Wu (2015) and Malhotra et al. (2003) point out, government policies play an important role in promoting the growth of both e-commerce and global trade. Several researchers have empirically explored this aspect of CBEC. Gessner and Snodgrass (2015) study the joint programs sponsored by the US and Canada federal governments to facilitate cross-border business and explore the effectiveness of participation in such programs for small- and medium-sized firms in overcoming the barriers to cross-border e-commerce transactions. Chen and Yang (2017) find that cross-border e-commerce plays a mediating role between government's pro-innovation supportive policy and firm performance. Sun et al. (2017) analyze the Sino-Russian cross-border e-commerce port city Manzhouli and discuss the opportunities and challenges for various stakeholders.

Conceptual Framework for CBEC

Though originally proposed to understand the factors influencing the growth potential of e-commerce in emerging economies, we believe that Agarwal and Wu's (2015) i-based N-OLI framework, along with the framework of internationalization process by Malhotra et al. (2003), also effectively explains CBEC in general as well as the development of CBEC in China. In Table 4.4, we identify the factors impacting China's CBEC that fit into Agarwal and Wu's three-level model. We keep the original impact factors identified by Agarwal and Wu (2015) and add a few (in

Table 4.4 Fitted i-based N-OLI framework for CBEC

#	Impact factor level	Impact factor	Example
1	Global-level	Multilateral agreements	WTO
		Strategic behavior of firms	Convergence in industry standards
		Technological innovations	Fast and secure internet
		Global logistics	Fast and economical global logistics
		International online payment	Payment platforms: PayPal, AliPay
2	National-level	Institutional environment	
		Government policies and regulations	China's CBCE pilot cities
		Legal environment	Law enforcement against Frauds
		Infrastructure	
		Physical infrastructure	Airports and seaports
		Financial and market infrastructure	Market efficiency
		Social infrastructure	Rising middle class in emerging countries
		Economy	
		Price advantage	Lower prices in emerging country
		Manufacturing advantage	Economies of scale
		Culture	Fostering online trust
3	Transactional-level	Integrity of transactions	Customer privacy, data security
		Online intermediaries	Product review, trust booster
		Network externalities and value clustering	Strategic alliances, value co-creators
		CBEC platform and venture capital	One-stop CBEC platforms, huge investment in platforms

boldface) that we think are either new or unique to CBEC and CBEC in China in particular. In the right column, we provide specific examples related to the impact factors.

Here we mainly explain the added impact factors. Readers can refer to Agarwal and Wu (2015) for details of the i-based N-OLI framework and the original factors. For the significance of China's entry into WTO, please refer to the analysis by Agarwal and Wu (2004) on its global impact, issues, and implications. At global level, global logistics and international online payment support the high growth of CBEC. At national level, rapid economic growth and cheap labor in certain emerging countries give them manufacturing and pricing advantages over other countries, which, in turn, boost export via CBEC. At transactional level, multifunctional, one-stop CBEC platforms facilitate transactions between sellers and buyers in different countries. Overall, we believe that all the factors listed in Table 4.4 contribute to the success of China's CBEC, as will be discussed in the following sections.

China's Cross-Border E-Commerce: An Overview

Current Picture, Structure, Shopping Channels, and Import Models

As mentioned earlier total transaction volume of CBEC in China reached RMB 5400 billion in 2015, up 20% from the previous year. The structure of China's CBEC can be illustrated on three dimensions: key provinces involved in export CBEC, main product categories, and main trade partners. Table 4.5 lists the rankings for the three dimensions: (1) The top CBEC provinces are Guangdong, Zhejiang, Jiangsu, Fujian, Shanghai, Beijing, Hubei, and Shandong. Not surprisingly, these provinces are located on the east coast, which represents the more developed economy than other regions in China. (2) The main product categories are 3C (computer, communication, and consumer) Electronics, Clothing, Outdoors, Health and Cosmetics, Jewelry, Gardening, Shoes and Case, and Toys. These products are suitable for international shipment at fairly low costs. (3) The main trade

Table 4.5 The structure of China's CBEC

#	CBEC province	%	Product category	%	Trade partner	%
1	Guangdong	24.7	3C Electronics	37.7	USA	16.5
2	Zhejiang	16.5	Clothing	10.2	European Union	15.8
3	Jiangsu	12.4	Outdoors	7.5	ASEAN	11.4
4	Fujian	9.4	Health and cosmetics	7.4	Japan	6.6
5	Shanghai	7.1	Jewelry	6	Russia	4.2
6	Beijing	5.2	Gardening	4.7	S. Korea	3.5
7	Hubei	4.1	Shoes and case	4.5	Brazil	2.2
8	Shandong	3.2	Toys	3.6	India	1.4

Data Source: CECRC (2016)

partners of China's CBEC are the USA, European Union, ASEAN, Japan, Russia, S. Korean, Brazil, and India.

Of the RMB 5.4 trillion total volume of CBEC, RMB 4.48 trillion are for export, and RMB 920 billion are for import. As a result, China has a super surplus in CBEC trade. Furthermore, the main component of China's CBEC is B2B commerce. The share of B2C commerce is relatively small. Figure 4.1 below shows the breakdown of total CBEC export by B2B and B2C. We can see that B2B CBEC is dominant over B2C CBEC even though B2C CBEC gains more shares in recent years. The reason for this B2C dominance is that China's CBEC started with the B2B model led by Alibaba.com 10 years ago. Only more recently are e-commerce companies putting more efforts on B2C CBEC model.

Why has CBEC in China kept growing fast over the last 10 years? One reason is that CBEC has many advantages over traditional international trade. Table 4.6 lays out some of them: First, trade procedures for CBEC are simpler. Second, overall tax rates for CBEC are lower. Third, CBEC customers have more choices

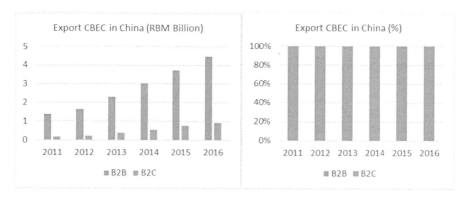

Fig. 4.1 Export CBEC in China (Data Source: CECRC 2016)

Table 4.6 Traditional international trade vs. cross-border e-commerce

#	Traditional international trade	E-commerce cross-border trade
1	Requires multiple import documents Uncertainty about compliance with China's standards Higher importation standards and involving multiple departments Longer time to go through the import procedure	Unified registration system Only need to meet standards of country of origin Unified monitoring system Goods can be sold immediately after registration Goods can be sold without labels in Chinese
2	Tariff: 10% ~30%; value-added tax: 17%	Personal postal articles tax: 10%、 20%、 30%、 50%
3	Customer chooses after imports	Customer can choose before imports

Data Source: Various news and polices

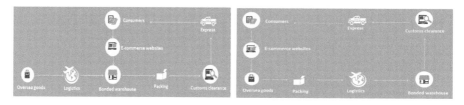

Fig. 4.2 Bonded warehousing vs. direct import (Source: Ng 2015)

of goods. Because of these advantages, the share of CBEC in China's total foreign trade has steadily increased in the past few years, from 4.4% in 2008 to 14.8% in 2014 (Lee 2015).

Chinese online shoppers mostly buy foreign products either directly from overseas websites or from domestic CBEC platforms, replacing the once-popular channel of purchasing agents (USDC 2015). Buying from CBEC platforms is the predominant method because of its relative ease and trustworthiness. Regarding CBEC imports, foreign products can find their way into China by either bonded warehousing or direct import. With the bonded warehousing model, products are imported in bulk and temporarily stored in bonded areas located in pilot cities before being ordered by consumers on CBEC platforms. After purchase orders are received, products will be delivered from bonded areas to consumers directly via local express. With the direct import model, products are ordered from overseas and shipped to China by international transportation. Although customs clearance is required for both models, China Inspection and Quarantine (CIQ) is only required of the bonded warehousing model (see Fig. 4.2).

Infrastructure and Environment of China's CBEC

CBEC cannot be run efficiently without effective infrastructure and environment. We discuss five aspects of China's CBEC infrastructure and environment: (1) platforms, (2) payment, (3) logistics, (4) regulation, and (5) third-party services.

E-commerce platforms have been the strong force behind the rapid growth of China's CBEC, both B2B and B2C models. There are two types of B2B platforms: B2B information and service platform and B2B transaction platform (Mansfield 2015). The information and service platform provides members with bid ranking, value-added service, and online advertising service. Its revenues mainly come from membership fees. Representative B2B platforms include Alibaba.com, Made-in-China.com, Toocle.com, and Globalsources.com. The transaction platform provides market-making service, product display, transaction data, and online payment. Its revenues mainly include commissions and display fees paid by sellers. Representative platforms are Dhgate.com, Aliexpress.com, Osell.com, and Tradetang.com. There are also two types of platforms on the B2C side: Open to 3rd Party platform and

Fig. 4.3 Infrastructure and environment of China's CBEC (Source: Revisions on Lee 2015)

Self-Business platform. The Open to 3rd Party B2C platform offers open platform, ecosystem, data sharing, warehousing, logistics, marketing, and promotion. Example platforms include eBay.com, Amazon.com, Wd.cm, and Wish.com. The Self-Business B2C platform has its own procurement, online transaction, branding, logistics, and post-sale services. The well-known ones are Lightinbox.com, Milanoo.com, Globalegrow.com, and Dx.com (see Fig. 4.3).

Payment is critical to CBEC. Two key elements are trusted online payment options and the availability of payment services. Secure, convenient, and preferable payment methods increase consumers' confidence in buying from overseas sellers. In recent years, Chinese companies have made heavy investments to greatly enhance their online payment processing capabilities. Alibaba's AliPay and Tencent's TenPay have established dominance in the online payment market, especially on the mobile end. The two platforms together processed RMB 12.8 trillion of payment in the fourth quarter of 2016 alone, accounting for 91.1% of market share. In addition to payment infrastructure, other financial services provided by Chinese financial institutions and even the government also play an important role in CBEC. For example, some banks and insurance companies provide credit guarantee to the CBEC exporters.

International e-commerce logistics are more expensive, complex, and time consuming than domestic logistics. China has a quite impressive logistical system, with CBEC platforms working closely with domestic shipping firms such as Shunfeng Express and international logistics firms such as UPS and FedEx. In 2016, about 30 billion deliveries were handled, averaging over 80 million per day. The amount of daily shipment is expected to grow by 50% annually to 1 billion in 7–8 years of time!

Every country has its laws and rules on trade. However, China's regulations on CBEC are generally lax compared to those on traditional international trade. China's policies on CBEC have also evolved over time, especially since 2012, to keep up with the development of the CBEC market. These policies tend to be supportive rather than restrictive. The most relevant CBEC regulatory bodies are the Ministry of Commerce, General Administration of Customs, Bureau of Foreign Exchanges, and General Administration of Quality Supervision, Inspection and Quarantine. These agencies work in coordination to maintain a conducive CBEC environment.

Finally, numerous third-party service providers have emerged in China to support CBEC. These service providers, mostly small- and medium-sized firms, play an indispensable role in the overall CBEC ecosystem. Their services range from consulting, education, and training to transaction enhancing. China E-Commerce Research Center (www.100ec.cn) estimates that there were 2.7 million people directly working in the e-commerce service industry as of December 2015.

Promoting Cross-Border E-Commerce: China's Experience

China has rich experiences on promoting cross-border e-commerce. We summarize its experiences in four aspects: (1) roles played by e-commerce giants such as Alibaba.com and JD.com, (2) government-designated CBEC pilot cities, (3) favorable governmental CBEC policies, and (4) capital inflows into the CBEC industry.

Alibaba.com and JD.com: Key CBEC Players

Alibaba started in 1999 as a B2B online marketplace (Alibaba.com) connecting Chinese manufacturers with overseas buyers. Alibaba launched Taobao (Taobao.com), a C2C online marketplace in 2003. Taobao is similar to eBay in the USA, which offers Alibaba.com rich and successful practices on electronic commerce. In 2004, Alibaba launched Alipay, an escrow-based online payment platform. Escrow allows buyers to pay securely online without exposing their credit card details. Alipay is the preferred payment solution for transactions on Taobao. In 2013, Alipay reported 300 million registered users and 12.5 billion transactions. Alipay eventually overtook PayPal as the largest mobile payment platform in the world with 100 million mobile registered users and over 2.78 billion transactions. Alibaba launched Tmall in April 2008 for the B2C market. On Tmall, brands and retailers sell products directly to end consumers. Tmall is currently selling more than 70,000 brands from over 50,000 stores. Over 4000 global brands such as Apple, Burberry, Estee Lauder, and Costco have set up stores on Tmall. Tmall, as an online platform, provides a number of services to retailers from design, operation, marketing, and payment to order fulfillment and logistics (Liang et al. 2016).

To promote its CBEC business, Alibaba.com launched AliExpress.com in 2010. AliExpress.com provides a platform to serve small Chinese businesses, offering products to international online buyers. Alibaba also uses Tmall Global to provide a solution for overseas companies to sell products directly to Chinese consumers. Orders can be fulfilled and shipped from outside of or within China. Overall, in 2016 Tmall has a market share of 24%, and AliExpress.com has a market share of 18.7% of China's import CBEC (CECRC 2017).

JD.com, formerly 360Buy, is the largest online direct sales company and the second largest online B2Ccompany in China. In 2013, JD reached a market share of 46.5% in the online direct sales market and a market share of around 20% in the online B2C market (iResearch 2014). The number of products JD offers through its online direct sales and marketplace has grown from approximately 1.5 million stock keeping units, or SKUs, as of December 31, 2011, to approximately 40.2 million as of March 31, 2014 (Liang et al. 2016).

JD started its CBEC business relatively late. It launched its CBEC platform, JD Worldwide (JD.HK) in April 2015. JD sells its own products and provides a platform for other vendors. It has a partnership with eBay, the biggest American auction house. To facilitate CBEC imports and exports, JD supports sales, marketing, and logistics services to its platform users. JD Worldwide has a market share of 9.9% of China's import CBEC (CECRC 2017).

Ten Pilot Cities on CBEC

Ten Chinese cities have been designated as pilot zones for cross-border e-commerce by the end of 2016. They include Shanghai, Hangzhou, Zhengzhou, Ningbo, Hangzhou, Chongqing, Guangzhou, Tianjin, Fuzhou, and Pingtan (see Table 4.7). Chinese central government offers favorable policies to these cities, and local governments of the cities make efforts to conduct pilot programs in terms of technical standards, business process, regulatory mode, information construction, and other

Table 4.7 Ten pilot cities for CBEC

#	Pilot city	Year est.	Operation area
1	Shanghai	2012	China (Shanghai) Pilot Free-Trade Zone
2	Hangzhou	2012	Hangzhou Bonded Logistics Center
3	Guangzhou	2013	Guangzhou Baiyun Airport Bonded Zone
4	Ningbo	2012	Ningbo Free-Trade Zone
5	Zhengzhou	2012	Henan Bonded Logistics Center
6	Chongqing	2012	Chongqing Xiyong Integrated Free-Trade Zone
7	Shenzhen	2014	Qianhai Free-Trade Port Zone
8	Tianjin	2014	China (Tianjin) Pilot Free-Trade Zone
9	Fuzhou	2016	China (Fuzhou) Pilot Free-Trade Zone
10	Pingtan	2016	China (Pingtan) Pilot Free-Trade Zone

Custom Declaration	The trading center has maintained close cooperation with customs, national inspection authority and other government units in this area, and equipped with professional service team, thus can better solve practical problems for enterprises.
Order operation	The trading center built in the first cross-border special sorting lines of southwest, and introduced the automated order processing procedure, effectively improved the orders operation processing capacity of tally, packing, sorting and etc..

Warehousing services	The trading center has built large cross-border bounded warehouses in both water port and airport, and is equipped with excellent service team and logistics equipment to meet all kinds of warehousing needs.
Logistics service	The trading Center has been building good relations with a number of large-scale logistics enterprises, thus can provide professional international freight agency service, and provide one-step solution such as overseas warehousing service and international logistics service to enterprises.

Fig. 4.4 Trading center service in CBEC pilot cities (Source: CFTA 2015)

aspects relating to cross-border e-commerce. These CBEC pilot areas also have established their own e-commerce platforms either for online sale or combing with other e-commerce services like parcel tracking, customs clearance, and products filing. Companies are allowed to store goods tax-free in bonded warehouses in the free-trade zone of a pilot city. The retailer does not pay tax until the product leaves the free-trade zone. This business model helps resolve issues related to language barrier, after-sales service, potential difficulty with Customs, and long delivery time. In return, it guarantees that the customs will collect a 10% import tax on products that might have otherwise been sent as personal parcels and not paid tax at all (Collier International 2015). There are trading centers set up in the pilot cities to facilitate CBEC processes. They provide one-stop services for vendors as described in Fig. 4.4.

Favorable CBEC Policies

Chinese governments at various levels fully support and promote CBEC. Since 2012, a number of favorable policies have been promulgated that cover the designation of pilot cities, duties and taxes, international payment, foreign currency exchanges, imported goods inspection, etc. The timeline of these policies and their implications to CBEC are listed in Table 4.8.

Venture Capital Inflows

Another driver for China's CBEC growth is venture capital inflows. The rapid growth of CBEC markets encourages venture capital to invest in start-ups and new e-commerce firms for CBEC. In 2016, the total venture capital inflows into B2B

Table 4.8 Key support and promotion policies for China's CBEC

#	Policy topics	Significance to CBEC	Time
1	The central government designates Shanghai, Zhengzhou, Ningbo, Hangzhou, and Chongqing as pilot cities for cross-border e-commerce development	The first group of CBEC pilot cities with specialized support from the central and local governments	12/2012
2	The State Council issues a policy to support export CBEC	CBEC exporters can get finance, tax return, and other supports	08/2013
3	Guangzhou designated pilot city	Guangdong is the largest exporting province in China. Guangzhou pilot zone will boost the provincial exports via CBEC	09/2013
4	The Customs Bureau allows an existing tax known as "xing you shui" (行邮税) to be applied to goods stored in or transferred through the bonded areas of the six pilot cities	Help CBEC importers save costs and simplify the importing process	03/2014
5	Companies involved in e-commerce import in Shanghai (via sales, payment, logistics, or warehousing) must register with Shanghai Customs, via the Shanghai Oriental Electronic Payment System	Integrated online payment system sponsored by the government would help speed up CBEC importing procedure	04/2014
6	China's Customs Bureau requires customs clearance for all cross-border e-commerce. Shenzhen designated pilot city	Help clear up market disorders and regulate the CBEC market. Apply successful CBEC pilot city experience to more cities	07/2014
7	The Central Government calls for faster issuance of new guidelines to support the development of cross-border e-commerce	Push local governments and administrations to supervise and support the CBEC practices	11/2014
8	Ministry of Industry and Information Technology allows overseas investors to wholly own an online transaction or data processing company in Shanghai's FTZ	Encourage foreign investors and entrepreneurs to build CBEC platforms	01/2015
9	Zhejiang Province issues a 3-year plan for the development of cross-border e-commerce (2015–2017)	Offer solid supports from local governments	01/2015
10	State Administration of Foreign Exchange provides guidance on cross-border payment	Offer favorable foreign exchange policy for CBEC importers and exporters	01/2015
11	The State Council approves the setup of the cross-border e-commerce pilot zones in Hangzhou, Tianjin, Fuzhou, and Pingtan	Apply successful CBEC pilot city experience to more cities	03/2015–01/2016
12	The State Council issues the guidance for fostering economy by CBEC	Raise status of CBEC as a vehicle to grow economy	05/2015
13	General Administration of Quality Supervision, Inspection and Quarantine issues a policy on inspection and quarantine to promote CBEC	Simplify the importing and exporting process to enhance the CBEC efficiency	05/2015

Source: Collier International (2015) and various news

Fig. 4.5 Abandoned products by DaiGou at Airport

electronic commerce platforms was over RMB 15.3 billion (CCECR 2017). These capital investments not only enhance the operation of CBEC platforms but also help integrate various services in the supply chain into one-stop services.

Government Intervention Missteps

On April 8, 2016, the General Administration of Customs started to impose a high duty on personal imported goods ("DaiGou"). Chinese travelers must pay a duty for purchases valued more that RMB 2000 per entry or more than RMB 20,000 for 1 year. The policy also adjusts the categories of customs duties from four to three, while raising tax rates accordingly. The main purpose of the new policy is to encourage Chinese to buy more domestic products. However, the hasty implementation of the new policy caused chaos in some Chinese international airports. Many Chinese abandoned their goods to avoid paying heavy duties at the airport (see Fig. 4.5). This new policy negatively affected the China's import CBEC and triggered strong protests from both Chinese consumers and CBEC vendors. Just 3 months later, the General Administration of Customs had to call for a suspension of the policy for 1 year.

Cross-Border E-commerce: Opportunities and Challenges

Opportunities

Despite its rapid expansion in recent years, it is widely held that cross-border e-commerce is still in a nascent stage and that there are even greater opportunities ahead for merchants from every corner of the world. One of the biggest benefits of the development of CBEC thus far, in our view, may be the increased awareness and desire for all parties, including merchants, consumers, service providers, as well as governments, to participate in CBEC activities. Below we discuss the opportunities for each of these critical stakeholders in the CBEC ecosystem, with an in-depth look at the opportunities for CBEC merchants in particular.

Opportunities for Merchants

From the e-commerce merchants' perspective, the opportunities to enter and grow in the CBEC space come particularly from the following areas:

1. *The push for CBEC at the government level has been stronger than ever.* In the past year or so, the world has witnessed a surge of populism and protectionism among certain populations in some countries, as evidenced in the most recent election cycles in the USA, France, Austria, and the Netherlands. At least in the political arena, there seems to be head winds against global trade. For example, the G20 meeting held in Germany in March 2017 failed to reaffirm free-trade agreement and pledge against protectionism due to the US resistance. Fortunately, a great deal of other countries remain as the proponents of globalization and free trade. Realizing that CBEC could be an important engine of economic growth, many national governments have incorporated CBEC into their strategic economic planning.

   The country that is leading the drumbeat is China. In 2013, the Chinese government proposed the "Belt and Road Initiative" as a grand scheme to promote economic development and cultural ties among the countries along the ancient Silk Road and the seaway connecting the Far East, Africa and Europe. More than 130 countries and 70 international organizations have since joined forces, signing dozens of cooperation agreements with China. In November 2016, all the 193 members of The United Nations Assembly unanimously passed the document A/71/9 to hail the initiative and called upon all parties to participate. Of all the projects undertaken under the Belt and Road Initiative such as the Silk Road Fund and the Asia Infrastructure Investment Bank (AIIB), CBEC is considered as another key element. For example, the official G20 Hangzhou, China Summit in September 2016 included a proposal of creating a global e-commerce platform, referred to as the Electronic World Trade Platform (eWTP), to strengthen cross-border digital trade (G20 2016). Besides, as mentioned before, the Chinese government has launched several CBEC pilot zones.

2. *The rise of the middle class and the e-consumer generation.* Decades of economic development has created large middle-class populations worldwide, especially in developing countries such as China, India, and Brazil. Even with the financial crisis of 2007–2008 and the ensuing slow recovery of world economies, the wealth of households in many countries has still steadily increased, albeit unevenly. A study by the Brookings Institute shows that the global middle class exceeded three billion people in 2015, nearly half of which lived in Asia. Further, the middle class are projected to increase by 160 million people per year on average through 2030. The total consumption by the middle class totaled $35 trillion in 2015, about $12,000 per person. The amount is estimated to increase by 4% per year to $10 trillion more in 2022 and $29 trillion more in 2030 (The Brookings Institute 2017).

   Besides the tremendous size of consumption by the middle class, today's consumers are increasingly shopping online, both domestically and globally. This change in shopping behavior is even more encouraging and much to the benefit of CBEC merchants. A 2016 Pitney Bowes Inc. Global Shopping Survey found that 94% of consumers frequently made domestic online purchases, about two-thirds (66%) of which also made at least one cross-border online purchase during the previous year. Singapore (89%), Australia (86%) and Hong Kong (85%) had the highest number of cross-border shoppers. In China, over two-thirds of consumers said they made online purchases on a daily or weekly basis (Pitney Bowes 2016). A study by Accenture Plc. estimates that, by 2020, over two billion e-shoppers would be transacting 13% of their overall retail consumptions online, equivalent to a market value of $3.4 trillion (Accenture 2016).

3. *Technological improvements and digital infrastructure have greatly enabled CBEC.* Innovations in technologies and ambitions of businesses are fueling the rapid growth of CBEC by lowering barriers and increasing accessibility. Several trends are particularly noteworthy:

   (a) Some of the biggest players in e-commerce have been making heavy investments to global online platforms. Alibaba Group, as mentioned before, is working with governments around the world to build a digital free-trade zone through its eWTP. The company has signed agreements with the governments of Canada, Australia, Italy, France, and Malaysia, to name a few. Meanwhile, Amazon.com has expanded its operations into more than a dozen countries, and China's JD.com has launched JD Worldwide and is partnering with EBay to pursue international expansion. To support their global ambitions, these companies are also building up massive cross-border logistical systems.

   (b) The improvement of the Internet infrastructure in the once less-developed countries and regions, along with the wide use of sophisticated end-user devices, especially mobile devices, has made cross-border online shopping easier. In addition, the application of cloud computing and big data analytics has made possible the processing of virtually unlimited volume of transactions. Some popular social media platforms such as WeChat, Weibo, and Facebook, with their hundreds of millions of users around the world, also play a key role as both providers of information and facilitators of interaction between merchants and consumers. Finally, in the near future, virtual reality (VR) and augmented reality (AR) technologies will greatly enhance online shopping experience.

(c) Online payment is emerging as one of the central issues in CBEC. Although it remains a major challenge, as will be discussed later in this chapter, there have been important advancements in payment technologies as many companies race to the competition. More payment options are available now. In addition to traditional credit card companies such as Visa and MasterCard extending their footprint, others are offering alternative, arguably more streamlined and more secured, payment solutions. PayPal, for example, has operations in more than 200 major markets and offers integrated yet flexible payment systems. AliPay and TenPay, on the other hand, offer convenient yet secure in-app payment solutions embedded in their trading and messaging platforms. Although the final competitive landscape of the global payment industry has yet to take shape, CBEC is already benefiting from the current technological advances.

4. *Small- and medium-sized businesses (SMEs) have as good chances at CBEC as big players.* One of the most promising aspects of cross-border e-commerce, compared to traditional import-export trade, is that merchants of any size and anywhere can participate due to lower barriers. In collaboration with World Trade Organization (WHO) and many national governments, Alibaba Group is leading the effort to create a level playing field for foreign SMEs through its eWTP. The company's ultimate goal is to recruit ten million retailers and vendors onto its platforms, the majority of which will be small SMEs. In fact, when it comes to consumer products, SMEs may even have an edge over the large competitors because of the variety of specialized goods only they are able to sell. SMEs sometimes may be nimbler to find their niche markets. A dairy products merchant in the Netherlands or New Zealand, for instance, can quickly find the appeal of its merchandises when a scandal breaks out about the quality of powdered milk sold in the Chinese domestic market.

Opportunities for Governments

Traditionally, the role of government relating to cross-border e-commerce has focused on regulations. For example, governments are always interested in enforcing safety standards for imported goods or adequate taxation of e-commerce activities. However, many governments seem to have evolved from passive regulators to proactive advocates of CBEC. They have embraced e-commerce, domestic or cross-border, as an important driver of economic growth. As discussed earlier, China has enacted a number of supportive laws and policies since 2012 to foster CBEC as part of the broader strategy under the Belt and Road Initiative. The government of India recently has also taken several e-commerce initiatives including opening up several government e-commerce platforms and raising the limit of FDI in Indian e-commerce marketplaces.

In Europe, the European Commission adopted the Digital Single Market strategy in 2015, which "aims to open up digital opportunities for people and business and enhance Europe's position as a world leader in the digital economy" (European Commission 2017). The European Commission has identified the completion of the Digital Single Market as one of its ten political priorities. On May 25, 2017, the Commission adopted a package of legislative proposals to boost e-commerce among the EU members. The proposals focus on three specific areas: stopping unjustified geo-blocking and other forms of discrimination, making cross-border parcel delivery more affordable and efficient, and strengthening the enforcement of consumers' rights.

Opportunities for Third-Party Providers

Third-party service providers are both enablers and beneficiaries of CBEC. The rapid growth of global CBEC also presents huge growth potential for third-party service providers in industries such as shipping and logistics, payment, financial services, and trade services. For example, the major international shipping companies have all seen steady revenue growth between 2010 and 2016, with UPS of America from $49.5 billion to $60.9 billion, FedEx Corp from $34.7 billion to $64.3 billion, and Deutsche DHL Group from €51.4 billion to €57.3 billion, all against a backdrop of slow recovery from the global economic recession during the same period. DHL specifically attributes its recent success to CBEC: "Thanks to our targeted approach to e-commerce, the entire Group is benefiting increasingly from the dynamic international development in this segment" (DHL Group 2016b). Similarly, major international payment companies such as Visa, MasterCard, and PayPal have also enjoyed significant increases in both transaction volume and revenues. Furthermore, a new class of businesses that provide either specialized services or integrated solutions to CBEC merchants have emerged in recent years.

Opportunities for Consumers

While the booming of CBEC may have created uneven opportunities for other stakeholders, consumers around the world are the clear winners. CBEC has brought about at least the following dividends to consumers:

1. Access to more foreign products and brands and hence more consumption choices. Alibaba Group's Tmall International, for instance, has a listing of 14,500 brands from 63 countries as of April 2017.

2. More savings due to wider choices and increased competition among merchants. An EU Commission study found that online shoppers could save about €11.7 billion a year from lower prices and wider choices. If e-commerce were to grow to 15% of the total retail sector and Digital Single Market barriers were eliminated, total consumer welfare gains would reach around €204 billion (EU Commission 2011).
3. More convenient and safer payment options, thanks to integrated payment solutions (such as AliPay and TenPay) offered by the major CBEC platforms as well as the international expansion of third-party payment companies (such as PayPal and Visa).
4. Better shopping experience including faster delivery and improved post-sale services. The former is made possible by the buildup of powerful logistics networks, and the latter is made possible by the nearly ubiquitous use of such social media platforms as Facebook, WhatsApp, and WeChat.

Challenges

While CBEC presents seemingly unlimited growth potential for merchants, they also face plenty of challenges and must overcome many obstacles in order to capitalize on the new e-retailing trend. Besides the obvious cultural and language obstacles and the difficulty of winning the trust of local customers, we discuss three other major challenges with regard to B2C cross-border e-commerce below.

1. *Logistics.* While the buyer and the seller could meet directly online and it may feel as if there is no distance between them, this is certainly not the case when it comes to delivering ordered goods to the customer across borders. Logistics could be the most deterring factor in CBEC. Though large merchants such as Costco or Nike with more resources and options may be able to build a well-streamlined logistics procedure, it may still put a strain on their profitability. For small merchants, challenges relating to logistics range from getting goods ready (e.g., proper labeling and packaging), high shipping costs, long shipping time, customs duties and documentation, sales allowances for defects or product returns, and post-sale customer services. Any of these steps, if not planned thoughtfully or handled well, could result in the following negative outcomes: (a) buyer's cart abandonment at the checkout, (b) bad customer experience and hence poor customer retention, (c) poor brand image and reputation, and (d) hurt profit margin or straight financial loss. Several survey studies have found that high shipping cost, long shipping time, and concerns over product return are among the most significant factors causing the abandonment of a filled shopping cart, while a good delivery experience would encourage over 80% of German, French, and British customers to choose a retailer over others (Pitney Bowes 2014; ComScore 2015; iMedia Research 2017).

2. *Payment*. This is another top hurdle to CBEC recognized by both consumers and merchants, due to the complex nature of international payment. While credit cards issued with the backing of Visa, MasterCard, and American Express are the predominant payment method in the USA, payment methods and habits in other countries could be widely different. From the consumers' perspective, lack of preferred payment method and concerns over fraudulent use of personal information can often cause shopping cart abandonment. For the merchants, the challenges go well beyond providing more payment options and security measures. They also include:

- Processing foreign cards and improving acceptance rate while battling fraud
- Settling and reconciling payments
- Handling multiple currencies
- Dealing with exchange rates and bearing the exchange rate risks
- Choosing and working with local partners (called acquirers)
- Dealing with changes or upgrades of payment system
- Dealing with cross-border remittance and related regulatory and tax issues
- Managing costs on payment to protect profit margin

    In recent years, there has been a boom of digital payment solutions such as PayPal, Google Wallet, Apple Pay, Square, AliPay, TenPay, and Paytm, just to name a few. However, the reality is that the payment market still remains highly fragmented. The payment methods are either restricted to certain geographic areas, embedded as part of the sponsoring company's ecosystem (e.g., TenPay in WeChat), or simply have not gained meaningful acceptance by consumers in a certain country.

3. *Legal and tax regulations*. Every country has its unique laws and rules. Regulations for foreign business entities could often be more stringent. Negligence of them may bring a merchant significant risks. So even with the relatively low physical barriers to entering into an overseas market, it is fair to say that CBEC is not about just putting up goods for sale on a website. At the minimum, a CBEC merchant should make clear of the following issues:

- What goods can or cannot be sold in the targeted market?
- What are the customs requirements and procedures of the country?
- To what extent should information on products be disclosed to consumers?
- What are the seller's rights and obligations in a dispute? What are the channels to resolve disputes?
- How does the foreign country's judicial process work should a dispute be turned to the court? What enforcement outcome can be realistically expected after a judgment is rendered?
- Are there any different legal and regulatory requirements for CBEC at the local government level?
- How strong is the country's legal system to protect intellectual property rights?

With respect to taxation, each country also has its own tax system applicable to CBEC. The European Union (EU), for example, has a unique value-added tax (VAT) system, with individual members of the group allowed slight adjustments (European Union 2017). This is very different from the US sales tax system, which, in its own right, could be widely different across states when it comes to implementation. China, on the other hand, has a tax system consisting of VAT, consumption tax, and tariffs. The type of tax and the tax rate also differ by product type and value of sales (GAC 2017). Adding to the complexity is that the tax rules in virtually all jurisdictions keep evolving as the governments adapt their goals to the development of CBEC. For example, some countries want to collect more tax revenues by increasing tax rates or broadening tax collection base or cracking down transfer pricing, while others may want to incentivize CBEC by lowering rates or even offering exemptions. It is a big challenge for a CBEC merchant to keep abreast of all the regulatory developments.

Cross-Border E-Commerce: China as a Destination

In this section, we shift our discussion to how foreign merchants can succeed in China's CBEC market from a B2C merchant's perspective. For a typical small- or medium-sized merchant in North America who desires to venture into the Chinese retail market via e-commerce, what can it do to succeed as to achieving sales growth and attaining profitability?

First, it is worth noting that there are already many North American brands that have had various degrees of success in China's e-retail market such as Costco, Coach, Calvin Klein, Sketchers, Victoria's Secret, Canadian Goose, etc. A prospective, less-known entrant can study these brands and benchmark the best practices. We believe a small- or medium-sized merchant should consider the following issues and strategies:

- *Conduct prelaunch market research.* Before launching sales, a merchant should conduct careful marketing research to understand the demands in the Chinese market and consumers' consumption preferences and behaviors. Some preferences and behaviors are rooted in the culture; others might be events- or news-driven. The merchant should also ask what the selling point of its products is from a competitive point of view. Is it the brand name, quality, functionality, or pricing advantage? The merchant needs to determine what niche market it wants to be in. Finally, it needs to make sure it has the agility to react to the dynamics in Chinese market and can deliver goods to consumers in a most efficient way.
- *Choose the right sales channel.* A merchant should carefully weigh the pros and cons of different sales channels. Should it set up its own direct sales website or use e-commerce marketplaces like Tmall.com, JD.com, or Kaola.com? If the latter option is chosen, should one or multiple marketplaces be used? In making

the decision, initial investments required, subsequent costs and cash flows, accessibility of more consumers, logistics, and customers' shopping experience are all factors to consider, along with many others. Most observers would agree that using platforms like Tmall.com or JD.com, which offers more localized shopping experiences, is the most effective way for foreign SMEs to enter into China e-commerce market.

- *Join team marketing efforts.* For small, little-known foreign merchants with constrained marketing budget, one of the biggest challenges is to obtain name recognition by the Chinese consumers. In 2016 alone, for example, 14,500 new foreign brands were introduced in Alibaba's Tmall.com, and the number is only increasing rapidly. How can a merchant make its products sought after by shoppers? A useful strategy could be to team up with other SMEs from the same region. Chinese consumers have some favorable, prototypical perceptions about the products from certain regions such as skincare products from Japan; baby food products from Australia, New Zealand, or the Netherland; wines and fashion products from France or Italy; sporting and cultural products and beers from the USA; maple syrup and winter sporting products from Canada; etc. As another example, when Canadian Prime Minister Justin Trudeau announced the opening of a Canadian pavilion (Canada.tmall.com) on Alibaba's e-commerce platform, there was a great deal of attention drawn to the participating Canadian brands. A small merchant may find it very beneficial to ride on these positive group images and group actions.

- *Utilize social media platforms like WeChat and Weibo.* Compared to American counterparts like Facebook or Twitter, the Chinese social media platforms, WeChat and Weibo, in particular, are much more integrated into e-commerce. A merchant can use the platforms to (1) provide in-app purchase capability, (2) conduct interactive campaigns and offline activities, and (3) provide instant, personalized customer services. The platforms allow for deep customer engagement and therefore are really must-have venues for foreign CBEC merchants.

- *Use third-party service providers strategically.* As discussed before, because of the multitude and complexity of the issues involved along the CBEC process, a merchant inevitably has to enlist the help of third-party service providers. The question is which services should be sourced and to what extent third-party services ought to be employed? The key consideration here is the trade-off between cost savings and quality of services, since most SMEs are budget conscious and keen on profitability. Using premium services hurts short-term profitability, which for some merchants may be hard to accept if they are already operating on thin margin, but may lay a foundation for future growth in the long run due to better customer satisfaction. For example, a DHL study shows that premium shipping could be a differentiator between merchants of certain product categories. Businesses that offer expedited/premium shipping grow 60% faster than peers who only offer standard shipping (DHL Group 2016a).

Conclusion

In this chapter, we discuss the importance of CBEC as a new driver for international trade. We adopt Agarwal and Wu's (2015) i-based N-OLI conceptual framework to understand the recent development of CBEC. Using China's CBEC as a case study, we compare the differences between traditional international trade and CBEC. We introduce a broad picture of China's CBEC. We attribute the success of China's CBEC to the role of e-commerce giants such as Alibaba.com and JD.com in building marketplaces of cross-border e-commerce for Chinese SMEs, the establishment of ten CBEC pilot cities, favorable policies to support CBEC, and big capital inflows into CBEC industry. China's missteps on imposing high duties on CBEC personal products are also discussed.

We think opportunities for future CBEC growth will abound due to governmental pushes for CBEC, the rise of the middle class in emerging countries, technological and infrastructure improvements, and more SMEs to adopt CBEC. Major challenges facing CBEC lie in logistics, payment, and legal and tax regulations. Finally, we outline several strategies for foreign small- and medium-sized merchants that are planning on entering into China's market via CBEC.

We believe that as a new driver of global trade, CBEC has a great prospect in the future, and more and more countries, industries, firms, and individuals will join in and benefit from this new format of e-commerce. We also believe that the success of China's CBEC will offer a shifting paradigm for global marketer. For example, many countries may learn from China to set up CBEC pilot cities or zones. Governments at central and local levels will probably want to provide more, solid support to promote CBEC in their countries. Finally, China's experience has also shown that powerful CBEC platforms, effective global logistics, convenient and safe online payment, and simplified custom clearance are critical to the success of CBEC in a country.

References

Accenture, Plc. 2016. *Cross-border e-commerce report*. White Paper.

Agarwal, J., and T. Wu. 2004. China's entry to WTO: Global marketing issues, impact, and implications. *International Marketing Review* 21 (3): 279–300.

———. 2015. Factors influencing growth potential of e-commerce in emerging economies: An institution-based N-OLI framework. *Thunderbird International Business Review* 57 (3): 197–215.

CECRC (China Electronic Commerce Research Center). 2017. *China e-commerce market data and inspection report in 2016*. White Paper. http://www.100ec.cn/zt/16jcbg/.

CECRC, China Electronic Commerce Research Center. 2016. *The 2015–16 China's cross-border e-commerce development report*. White Paper.

CFTA. 2015. Introduction of Chongqing bonded port area import and export commodities exhibition & trading center.

Chen, N., and J. Yang. 2017. Mechanism of government policies in cross-border e-commerce on firm performance and implications on m-commerce. *International Journal of Mobile Communications* 15 (1): 69–84.

Colliers International. 2015. Crossing borders, changing times – a new model for international e-commerce has strong implications for china's bonded logistics property market. White Paper.

ComScore, Inc. 2015. Reasons for abandoning online shopping carts in Europe in 2015. White Paper.

Deng, Z., and Z. Wang. 2016. Early-mover advantages at cross-border business-to-business e-commerce portals. *Journal of Business Research* 69 (12): 6002–6011.

DHL Group. 2016a. *The 21st century spice trade: a guide to the cross-border e-commerce opportunity*. White Paper.

———. 2016b. *Annual report 2016*. White Paper.

Dunning, J.H. 1995. Reappraising the eclectic paradigm in an age of alliance capitalism. *Journal of International Business Studies* 26: 461–491.

———. 1998. Location and the multinational enterprise: A neglected factor? *Journal of International Business Studies* 29: 45–66.

———. 2000. The eclectic paradigm as an envelope for economic and business theories of MNE activity. *International Business Review* 9: 163–190.

European Commission. 2011. *Bringing e-commerce benefits to consumers*. Commission Staff Working Paper.

———. 2017. *Boosting e-commerce in the EU*. https://ec.europa.eu/digital-single-market/en/boosting-e-commerce-eu.

European Union. 2017. https://ec.europa.eu/taxation_customs/business/vat/.

Forrester. 2014. Seizing the cross-border opportunity: How small and medium-size online businesses can go global, A Forrester Consulting Thought Leadership Paper Commissioned by FedEx.

G20. 2016. *G20 Leaders' communique Hangzhou summit*, 2016.

GAC. 2017. Information on china's importation taxes can be found at the office website of the general administration of customs: http://english.customs.gov.cn/.

Gessner, G.H., and C.R. Snodgrass. 2015. Designing e-commerce cross-border distribution networks for small and medium-size enterprises incorporating Canadian and U.S. trade incentive programs. *Research in Transportation Business & Management* 16: 84–94.

Gomez-Herrera, E., B. Martens, and G. Turlea. 2014. The drivers and impediments for cross-border e-commerce in the EU. *Information Economics and Policy* 28: 83–96.

Lee, M. 2015. *Characteristics of China's cross-border e-commerce, Institute of E-Commerce, China International Electronic Commerce Centre*. White Paper.

Liang, B., Y. Tu, T. Cline, and Z. Ma. 2016. China's e-tailing blossom: A case study, in E-Retailing Challenges and Opportunities in the Global Marketplace (Edited by Shailja Dixit & Amit Kumar Sinha):72–98.

Malhotra, N.K., J. Agarwal, and F.M. Ulgado. 2003. Internationalization and entry modes: A multi-theoretical framework and research propositions. *Journal of International Marketing* 11 (4): 1–31.

Mansfield, C. 2015. *Research on cross border e-commerce & free trade zone*, White Paper.

iMedia Research. 2017. *Survey on perception of CBEC post-sales services among Chinese Internet Users*. White Paper.

Ng, R. 2015. *Cross border e-commerce policy in china – harnessing china' demand for imported products*. Shanghai Lithuania-China Business Forum, Nov. 2015.

Pei, Y., K. Wu, and L. Dai. 2016. An empirical research on the evaluation system of cross-border e-commerce. *WHICEB 2016 Proceedings*. 40. http://aisel.aisnet.org/whiceb2016/40.

Pitney Bowes, Inc. 2014. *Global online shopping survey*. Stamford, CT.

Pitney Bowes. Inc. 2016. *Global online shopping survey*. Stamford, CT.

iResearch. 2014. *The 2014 China cross-border e-commerce report (brief edition)*. www.iresearch-china.com. White Paper.

Singh, N., and S. Kundu. 2002. Explaining the growth of e-commerce corporations: An extension and application of the eclectic paradigm. *Journal of International Business Studies* 33: 679–697.

Sun, D., L. Fang, and J. Li. 2017. Research on the development of cross-border e-commerce in port cities – a case of Manzhouli city. *Proceedings of the Fourth International Forum on Decision Sciences, Uncertainty and Operations Research.* Edited by Li, X., & Xu, X., Springer, Singapore.

Tao, Y., and W. Zhang. 2016. Establishment of cross-border e-commerce credit evaluation system based on big data. *Management & Engineering* 24: 1838–5745.

Terzi, N. 2011. The impact of e-commerce on international trade and employment. *Procedia - Social and Behavioral Sciences* 24: 745–753.

The Brookings Institute. 2017. The unprecedented expansion of the global middle class: An update.

USDC (U.S. Department of Commerce). 2015. Cross-border e-commerce in China.

Xue, W., D. Li, and Y. Pei. 2016. The development and current of cross-border e-commerce. *WHICEB 2016 Proceedings.* 53. http://aisel.aisnet.org/whiceb2016/53.

Yousefi, A. 2015. The impact of cross-border e-commerce on international trade. The *Proceedings of the 16th International Academic Conference*, Amsterdam, Jun 2015: 616–616.

Zhang, M., W. Zuo, and H. Zheng. 2016. Research on the coordination mechanism and improvement strategy of the business model from china's export cross-border e-commerce – based on the theory of coevolution. *WHICEB 2016 Proceedings*, 34. http://aisel.aisnet.org/whiceb2016/34.

Part III
Global Marketing Strategies

Chapter 5
Standardized Global Brand Management Using C-D Maps

Charan K. Bagga and Niraj Dawar

Abstract In this chapter, we describe an application of the centrality-distinctiveness mapping (C-D mapping) methodology in the context of global brand positioning. C-D maps of different countries offer a way to visualize differences in consumer perceptions of brands across markets. Our methodology helps set consistent positioning and performance goals for a global brand across geographical markets. It also helps global brand managers with brand standardization versus localization decisions. Finally, it places actual brand performance in context: it helps explain differences in cross-border performance that are due to different locations on the C-D map for the same brand in different geographies. In sum, we believe that the C-D map methodology provides a means and a vocabulary for strategic conversations about global brand positioning between headquarters and local managers. It also suggests an implementation plan for overcoming brand-positioning challenges in different countries.

The Challenges Faced by Global Brands

Global brands face different consumers, are sold in different market conditions with different regulations, and battle with different competitors in each of their international markets. Yet, their strategy is often centrally determined, and their positioning is expected to be globally uniform.

Indeed, standardization has many benefits. Many successful and global brands such as Apple engage in high levels of standardization (Brand Quarterly 2014) and may consequently achieve greater economies of scale. When successful,

C. K. Bagga (✉)
Haskayne School of Business, University of Calgary, Calgary, AB, Canada
e-mail: charan.bagga@haskayne.ucalgary.ca

N. Dawar
Ivey Business School, Western University, London, ON, Canada

© Springer International Publishing AG, part of Springer Nature 2018
J. Agarwal, T. Wu (eds.), *Emerging Issues in Global Marketing*,
https://doi.org/10.1007/978-3-319-74129-1_5

121

standardization results in significant savings for the global brand. It costs the global brand much less to create a single global advertising campaign, hire one agency, and derive the benefits of being driven by a single strategy (Aaker and Joachimsthaler 1999). However, examples of such a high degree of standardization are few and far between.

Most global brands face brand-positioning challenges as they expand internationally. Examples of brands that faced positioning challenges in international markets abound, Colgate in France, Electrolux in United States, Ford in Brazil, and Ikea in Thailand; the list goes on (Inc.com 2014). The problems with implementing standardized marketing programs are multifold. First, consumers in most countries have trouble relating to generic products and communications that are a function of the corporation's least-common-denominator approach (Holt et al. 2004). Second, a brand's image may not be the same throughout the world. Honda represents quality and reliability in the United States. However, in Japan, where quality is a common factor across competitors, Honda positions itself as youthful and energetic. Consequently, standardized comparison of brands across different positioning dimensions for different countries is not possible (Aaker and Joachimsthaler 1999). Finally, in many cases, country-level managers use their own vocabularies and strategy templates to position the global brand in their respective markets (Aaker and Joachimsthaler 1999). The resulting lack of a common vocabulary and method to make brand management decisions in different countries becomes an impediment to standardized cross-country brand management.

In this chapter, we describe a methodology that examines global brand positioning in international markets at a strategic level. The methodology (C-D maps or centrality-distinctiveness maps) was developed by us and has been featured twice in *Harvard Business Review* in 2015 (Dawar and Bagga 2015a, b). Our method allows brand positioning (across countries) to be analyzed and tracked along the universal cognitive dimensions of centrality and distinctiveness. It also offers global and local brand managers a means and a vocabulary for conversations about positioning. The method we propose does not result in over-standardization that may end up stifling local inventiveness. We subscribe to the view that without some diversity in the organization, marketing standardization will not work (Kashani 1989). Our method permits flexibility by factoring in country-level variables such as country-level competition, country attractiveness, and country-level tactical positioning dimensions among others. From a marketing methodology perspective, our method integrates standardized analysis of positioning across markets with localized implementation recommendations.

The remainder of this chapter is organized as follows. We start with a description of the C-D map methodology. We next discuss why the C-D map methodology is appropriate for global brands and how it compares to other global brand management methodologies. In the subsequent section, we provide detailed guidelines for implementing C-D mapping for global brands in international markets. Finally, we present a comprehensive case study that demonstrates the implementation of the methodology for a company in seven European countries.

What Are C-D Maps?

Brand strategy consists of addressing fundamental business questions including the following: *What is the unique value we offer our customers? How are we positioned against competitors? And why should customers buy our brand?* Answers to these questions help develop a position in the marketplace that customers' value, which competitors have not addressed, and that is profitable. The business value of traditional positioning maps is limited because they fail to link a brands' location on the map to market performance variables such as sales and pricing ability. In the international context, different markets may use different positioning dimensions, making it difficult to compare positioning across markets. In contrast, strategic tools such as the Boston Consulting Group matrix map brands on common business measures such as market share and market growth rate but do not map consumer perceptions of the marketplace.

C-D maps allow companies to connect a brand's location on the positioning map to business outcomes such as sales and pricing (Dawar and Bagga 2015a). The methodology starts with the premise that markets and brands are represented in consumers' minds and that these representations guide consumer behavior, including purchase decisions (Bagga et al. 2016; MacDonald and Sharp 2000). Our methodology maps consumer perceptions of brands on the universal dimensions of centrality (i.e., how representative a brand is of its category) and distinctiveness (i.e., how different a brand is relative to its competitors) and shows how these positions are linked to marketplace outcomes such as sales and the price premium a brand commands. Each positioning choice carries consequences not just for how the brand will be perceived, but for how much will be sold and at what price, and, therefore, ultimately for profitability.

At a high level, C-D mapping involves measuring the centrality and distinctiveness of each brand in a category and plotting the scores on a graph so that each brand is represented by its location on these two dimensions. The graph can then be split into four quadrants consisting of brands that are (a) both central and distinctive, (b) central but not distinctive, (c) distinctive but not central, and (d) neither central nor distinctive. Interpreting the data by examining the nature of brands in each quadrant, we label the four quadrants of the C-D map as follows: the high distinctiveness and low centrality quadrant is labeled, unconventional. For example, in the US passenger car category, this quadrant contains brands such as Smart and Tesla. The quadrant that is low on both centrality and distinctiveness contains peripheral brands such as Kia and Mitsubishi in the US car market. Third, brands that are central but not highly distinctive include brands such as Toyota and Ford in the US passenger car category. We labeled such brands as mainstream brands. Finally, the high distinctiveness and high centrality quadrant is labeled as the aspirational quadrant. Such brands are well differentiated and have wide appeal. See Fig. 5.1 for a C-D map of US passenger car market (Dawar and Bagga 2015a).

We found that each of these positioning choices has consequences in terms of sales, pricing ability, risk, and market influence. More importantly, the C-D map

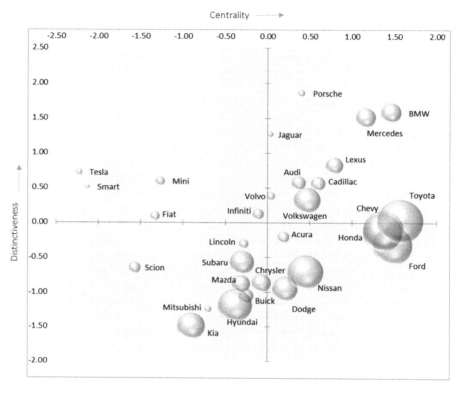

Fig. 5.1 C-D map of US passenger car market (Map reproduced from Dawar and Bagga 2015a)

methodology examined how centrality and distinctiveness impact market performance variables such as sales and pricing. We found that centrality is a significant
positive predictor of sales. In contrast, brand distinctiveness is a significant negative
predictor of sales. Finally, distinctiveness has a significant positive effect on a
brand's price.

The C-D Map Methodology Appropriate for Global Brands

A company that manages a global brand in a standardized manner is often stymied
by differences across markets. The C-D maps of different geographies offer a way
to visualize differences in consumer perceptions of brands across markets. As an
example, Chevrolet and Tide, both highly central brands in the United States, may
be relatively low in centrality and distinctiveness in an emerging market such as
India. Some of these differences may stem from differences in positioning, while
others may be due to market conditions such as consumers' willingness to pay.
Brand location on the C-D map in the different markets is useful at multiple levels.

First, it helps visualize differences in consumer perceptions of brands across markets. Second, it sets consistent performance goals for a global brand that is ranked equivalently on centrality and distinctiveness across a cluster of geographical markets. Third, it helps global brand managers with brand standardization versus localization decisions. Finally, it places actual brand performance in context: it helps explain differences in cross-border performance that are due to different locations on the C-D map for the same brand in different geographies (Dawar and Bagga 2015a). In sum, we believe C-D maps can bridge the gap in the conversation between headquarters and local managers of global brands and can provide a common understanding of the strategy and positioning challenges of global brands in each market.

We also conducted an audit of multiple global brand management methodologies that have been developed by practitioners and academics (Holt et al. 2004; Hsieh 2004; Kish et al. 2001; Ozsomer and Altras 2008; Roth 1992; Steenkamp et al. 2003). We examined the advantages that the C-D mapping methodology provides over prior methods. We noticed many common themes where the existing methodologies fall short. Some of the shortcomings include disjointedness of brand's positioning with its market performance, lack of information on how the brand operates relative to its competition in different countries, and lack of visualization to make managerial interpretation easier. See Table 5.1 for a comparison of the C-D mapping methodology vis-à-vis prior global brand management methodologies.

Implementing C-D Mapping Methodology for Global Brands

In this section, we provide detailed guidelines for implementing C-D mapping for global brands in international markets.

Step 1: Identify the Project Sponsor and Countries

The first step of the process is to identity the project sponsor and the portfolio of countries for which you would like to conduct the analyses. The implementation of the methodology has country-level budgetary implications that may lead to push back from the local level management of certain countries. Therefore, the project sponsor should ideally be a senior C-level executive (e.g., regional CEO) who is in charge of a portfolio of countries under her management. Within a particular portfolio of countries, it is crucial not to limit your analyses only to those countries where your brand is performing poorly. It is imperative to include those countries where the brand is doing well. This will allow additional cross-country analyses of why brand performance varies between countries and what best practices can be shared across borders.

Step 2: Identify the Category Level

The next step of the process is to identity the category level of analyses. The category level should ideally be the basic category level (Loken and Ward 1990)

Table 5.1 Comparison of the C-D mapping method vis-à-vis other global brand management methodologies

Method	Description of method	What shortcomings in the methodology does C-D mapping overcome?
Steenkamp et al. (2003)	Discuss how perceived brand globalness impacts brand purchase likelihood. The authors do a path analysis and analyze three paths through which this relationship operates (direct path, indirect paths though brand quality and brand prestige)	Measure operates in an isolated brand-level context
		It does not provide information on how the brand operates relative to its competition in different countries
		No graphic presentation (of the relative positioning of brands) that makes positioning interpretation easier
		Does not measure the impact of brand's globalness measure with its market performance (sales, profitability) in different countries
Ozsomer and Altras (2008)	Built a model of global brand attitude and purchase likelihood based on the following constructs (brand authenticity, cultural capital, perceived brand globalness, brand credibility, brand quality, social responsibility, prestige, and relative price)	No clear guidelines on how managers can use the model to assess their brand performance in international markets
		Does not measure the impact of brand's global brand attitude on its market performance (sales, profitability) in different countries
Kish et al. (2001)	Measured customer-based brand equity using Equitrak brand equity model. Five measures (awareness, quality, uniqueness, popularity, and favoritism) provide a composite measure of global brand equity	It does not provide information on how the brand operates relative to its competition in different countries
		Does not measure how brand equity is linked with market performance (sales, profitability) in different countries

(continued)

Table 5.1 (continued)

Method	Description of method	What shortcomings in the methodology does C-D mapping overcome?
Holt et al. (2004)	Examined the impact of global brand dimensions (quality signal, global myth, social responsibility) on purchase behavior	Does not measure the impact of brand's globalness on its market performance (sales, profitability) in different countries
		No graphic presentation of the brands positioning to make the interpretation easier
		Some dimensions such as "social responsibility" may carry different meanings in different cultures
Hsieh (2004)	Developed a global brand equity model to assess a brand's value relative to its global competitors	Provides a global measure of brand equity (that has relatively few managerial implications)
Roth (1992)	Examined the impact of brand positioning (depth vs. breadth strategies) on market performance (sales volume, profit margin, and market share) in multiple countries	Based solely on a sample derived from managers in the parent country. Did not include consumer-level perception data
		It does not provide information on how the brand operates relative to its competition in different countries
		No graphic presentation of the brands positioning

and not a subordinate or superordinate category level (Rosch and Lloyd 1978). For instance, cars and beer are basic-level categories. Going one level deeper, we get to the subordinate category levels of sports cars and fruit beers. Zooming one level out, we get to the superordinate category levels of motorized vehicles and alcoholic beverages. Members of basic-level categories are likely to be comparable on more specific sets of attributes than are members of superordinate categories (Mervis and Rosch 1981). It does not make sense to perform C-D analyses at a superordinate level, as the members at the superordinate category level are product types rather than brands that compete against each other. Analysis at a superordinate category level would lead to a proverbial apple and orange comparison with few useful insights. To illustrate, a comparison of Jack Daniels and Budweiser on the same map will provide no actionable insights to either of these brands.

On the other hand, a C-D analysis at a subcategory level would not be very useful as brands offer similar product types within a subcategory, and hence there will be low variance on the distinctiveness dimension at the subcategory level. To illustrate, there is not much distinctiveness between Coca-Cola and Pepsi-Cola at the subcategory level of cola drinks. In contrast, Dr. Pepper is a distinctive basic-level soft drink brand, while Coca-Cola is a central basic-level soft drink brand. In sum, basic-level categories with competing and substitutable brands are most appropriate for conducting a C-D analysis.

Step 3: Identify the Number of Brands

The number of brands should be between 15 and 30. Too few brands will result in lack of statistical power and violate assumptions when conducting regression analyses. Too many brands will result in an unreliable regression model, as small or unknown brands are likely to be outliers in the regression analyses. For example, including specialty car brands such as Rolls-Royce (that has very low sales and very high pricing) in a C-D analysis of the US passenger market will give an inflated impact of distinctiveness on pricing and deflated impact of centrality on sales. Therefore, relevant filters are recommended when identifying the brands to be included in the analyses. An appropriate filter is the market share or level of sales. For instance, in a C-D map analyses we conducted for the consumer banking industry, we used level of deposits and the number of customers as filters. In a C-D map analyses we conducted for the beer industry, the filter we used was the volume of beer sold. Additionally, care should be exercised to include both multinational (common) competitors and active country-specific competitors when finalizing the short list for each country. We also recommend having the same number of brands in each country so that the number of cases for country-specific regression analyses is the same.

Step 4: Identify the Appropriate Dependent Variables for Analyses

The next step is to determine the appropriate dependent variables for analysis. The type of dependent variables depends on what the methodology is used for. For commercial products and services, sales, pricing, and market share are the most appropriate dependent variables. Where data for brand-level market performance variables is not available or where consumer behavior rather than the brand's market performance is of interest, we recommend the use of variables such as consumer consideration and choice. In nontraditional categories, the dependent variables will depend on the nature of the category. In a C-D mapping exercise that we conducted for the US presidential elections (specifically, the Republican Presidential Primary), we used the candidate's share of polling data as the dependent variable. Other variables such as the level of promotional expenditure and number of distribution outlets may also be considered to examine how such variables relate with centrality and distinctiveness.

Step 5: Deciding on Sample Type and Sample Size

The process for determining sample characteristics is similar to any survey-based marketing research studies. The sample should include consumers (or prospects) who have familiarity with the category. This is essential as respondents are asked to rate a battery of brands on whether they are central or distinctive. If respondents have relatively low knowledge of the players in a category, they will be unable to discriminate appropriately on whether the brands vary on centrality and distinctiveness. Therefore, we recommend including awareness and familiarity screener questions.

The sample size is a function of the depth of analyses that is desired. For straightforward analyses, where you are interested in aggregate country-level C-D maps, we have observed stable results with 200–250 respondents. For more advanced analyses, where the manager is interested in understanding how different segments within each market view the category or how centrality and distinctiveness correlate with tactical level positioning dimensions, larger sample sizes of 500+ per market are recommended.

Step 6: Designing the Survey Instrument for Each Country

We recommend that the survey instrument be split into six sections. Sections 1–3 are required. Sections 4, 5, and 6 are optional and are included to gain a deeper understanding of the product category.

Section 1. In the first section, the survey should include appropriate demographic, psychographic, and behavioral questions that will help split the data based on specific segment dimensions that the company uses. Consumers' cognitive representations of the marketplace vary by different segment types. Therefore, to get a richer view of how different segments of consumers view your brand and other brands in the category, collecting such segmentation data is necessary. To illustrate, if the C-D mapping exercise is being done for a product category such as business schools and the sample is prospective business school students, one may want to include questions related to the areas of specialization (e.g., finance, marketing, etc.) and the type of program that students are interested in (e.g., MBA, Executive education). This is relevant as segments of prospective business school students may have very different representations of the business school category.

Section 2. This section should include questions that gauge the awareness of the brands in the C-D mapping exercise. Awareness data can be used to drop low-awareness brands from further analysis. Whether awareness and knowledge about the brand vary across countries will also have managerial implications.

Section 3. This section is the heart of the survey where respondents rate the included brands on a 0–10 point single-item scale for *centrality* or *distinctiveness*. For the centrality measure, the question is accompanied by additional description of what is meant by centrality. Specifically, the question qualifies that centrality implies representativeness and close association with the product category. Additionally, the question should be accompanied by examples of central brands (e.g., McDonalds in fast-food product category). Similarly, the distinctiveness question is accompanied by additional description of what makes a brand distinctive, either by offering something unique (horizontal differentiation) or by offering something superior (vertical differentiation). Just like the centrality question, the distinctiveness question is also accompanied by examples (e.g., Dr. Pepper in soft drinks is different because of its unique flavor, and Starbucks in coffee is distinct because of its perceived premium quality). Participants rate all brands on the centrality and distinctiveness questions. The order in which they respond to either the set of brand centrality questions or the set of brand distinctiveness questions is randomized. Additionally, the order of brands within the set of centrality questions and the set of distinctiveness questions is randomized. Single-item questions are used to avoid respondent fatigue that may arise by asking respondents to rate each brand on multi-item centrality and distinctiveness scales. The centrality scale we recommend has been tested as having high convergent validity with a three-item brand centrality scale used by Loken and Ward (1990). The distinctiveness scale has been tested as having high convergent validity with a three-item brand distinctiveness scale used by Zhou and Nakamoto (2007).

Section 4. Questions on consumer-level dependent variables may be included in this optional section. For instance, we have used this section to collect data on consumer consideration and choice. The consideration question provides respondents with an exhaustive brand list and asks them to check all brands that they may consider (or have considered) in purchase decisions involving the category. A follow-up question on choice presents each respondent with only the short list of brands that the respondent indicated she would consider. It will ask the respondent to choose the most preferred brand from the list of considered brands. As mentioned earlier, if the dependent variables you intend to use are market-based brand-level variables (such as total sales per brand or average selling price for each brand), this section can be skipped.

Section 5. This optional section is a follow-up to Section 4 and should include questions that pertain to finding the reasons why certain brands are more likely to be considered and how they relate to centrality and distinctiveness. This section needs exploratory research to identify the key reasons that drive brand consideration and choice in a particular category. Once an exhaustive list of reasons is created, factor analyses are recommended to obtain a lower number of underlying reasons that are driving brand consideration. For instance, in the beer category, such underlying reasons could include *(a) I find the flavor of the beer delicious, (b) I like what the beer brand stands for, (c) I like the fact that the beer is imported and hence seems exotic,* etc.

Section 6. In the final optional section, the survey can include an implicit measurement exercise that allows managers to examine how tactical positioning dimensions are associated with (a) category brands and (b) the dimensions of centrality and distinctiveness. The first part of the exercise is to draw an exhaustive list of tactical positioning dimensions that are relevant in the category. This will happen prior to the launch of the C-D survey. For example, tactical positioning dimensions in the beer category may include attributes such as ruggedness, sincere, urbane, sophisticated, etc. In the actual C-D survey exercise, each respondent will respond to whether she believes that certain brands are associated with certain positioning dimensions using an implicit attitude measurement method (Perkins and Forehand 2011). Each respondent is asked to associate a randomly chosen subset of brands with a randomly chosen subset of dimensions. This is necessary as asking respondents to associate all brands with all dimensions will lead to severe respondent fatigue. To illustrate, asking a respondent to associate 20 brands with 20 dimensions will require her to provide 400 responses. In contrast, asking the respondent to associate 5 (randomly chosen) brands with 5 (randomly chosen) dimensions requires a less taxing 25 responses from the respondent.

Step 7: Customizing and Implementing Surveys Across Different Countries

Once the master survey is complete, the researcher next needs to localize the survey for each country. The major exercise here is to translate (and reverse or back translate) the survey into the corresponding language for each country and pilot-test it to ensure that participants understand the meaning of questions and that the import of the questions is not lost in translation. Another important point to remember for C-D map surveys across countries is to find country-relevant examples of centrality and distinctiveness questions in each country. Where appropriate, common cross-country examples may be used. For example, Apple is likely a highly central brand in the smartphones category across many countries.

Ideally, the administration of the surveys should be done, either by a single multinational marketing research firm or by a centralized (internal) marketing division within the company, which has access to respondents across the entire portfolio of countries. Additionally, data should be collected across all countries within the same window of time. Consumers' representations of marketplace are dynamic over time. Hence, appropriate cross-country comparison should be conducted within the same period. This will allow the data to be analyzed concurrently and facilitate cross-country comparisons.

Step 8: Analyzing Data

We propose the following analyses to draw the greatest insight from the C-D maps.

Analysis 1 – Country-level mapping. To conduct the C-D mapping, mean-center the centrality and distinctiveness scores for all brands for a particular country. Next, plot all the brands on a 2-D map based on their mean-centered centrality and distinctiveness scores. The X-axis represents centrality and the Y-axis represents distinctiveness. The two axes intersect at the coordinate (0, 0). The magnitude of the dependent variable can be presented as a circle on the C-D map. Label the top right and left quadrants as the aspirational and the unconventional quadrants, respectively. Label the bottom right and left quadrants as the mainstream and the peripheral quadrants, respectively. Repeat this exercise for each country.

Analysis 2 – Impact of centrality and distinctiveness on the dependent variables. Perform multiple linear regression analyses with centrality and distinctiveness scores for each brand as the independent variable and the chosen dependent variable (e.g., sales, price, consideration, etc.) as determined in Step 4. Examine whether and how centrality and distinctiveness affect the chosen dependent variables.

Analysis 3 – Identify your competition. The next analysis is to calculate the Euclidean distances of your brand's position relative to all other brands on the two-dimensional C-D map. The brands that are closest to your brand are your cognitive neighbors. These brands are perceived as being relatively similar in consumers' cognitions. In many categories, cognitive neighbors are also principal competitors. For example, in a C-D map of US passenger cars, Toyota, Honda, Ford, and Chevy are cognitive neighbors. Similarly, Mercedes and BMW are neighbors.

However, cognitive neighbors may not always be competitors. We have observed this in categories where distinctiveness does not vary much between brands. In such categories, an alternate way to find your competitive set is to examine the consideration overlap your brand has with other brands.

Analysis 4 – How far are you from the category leader in different countries? The next recommended analysis is to determine the market leader in each country. The market leader will be determined by your brand's strategy in each market. If the intention is to increase revenue, the leader is the brand with the highest sales. In contrast, if the intention is to increase your profitability, the leader is the brand that has the highest profitability. Once you have identified the leaders across different markets, calculate the Euclidean distance of your brand from the leaders. The country in which your brand has the least distance from the leader is the market where your brand is best positioned to challenge the leader. In contrast, the country in which your brand is the farthest from the leader is the most challenging for your brand.

Analysis 5 – Does your brand differ from the leader along the consumer decision journey? The consumer decision journey begins with awareness of a brand, to considering it and finally choosing it from within her consideration set. Therefore, the next stage of analysis involves examining three key consumer decision metrics, namely, brand awareness, brand consideration, and brand choice. We recommend analyzing these metrics for both your brand and the market leader. It is quite likely that your brand faces very different hurdles across the consumer decision journey and that may explain why your brand is less central or distinctive in certain markets than others. Diagnosing whether you are low on awareness or consideration or choice in different countries will facilitate positioning and promotional decisions in each of the countries under consideration.

Analysis 6 – What are the reasons why your brand is considered, and how do these differ from the reasons why the category leader is considered? This stage of analysis involves a frequency count of the various reasons because of which consumers consider your brand, the market leader's brand, and your competitors' brands. At a minimum, you may want to examine the top three reasons because of which consumers consider the leader and your brand for each country.

Analysis 7 – Market attractiveness. This analysis is based on data that is external to the C-D map survey. Often multinationals operating in multiple markets already have measures or priority rankings of their country markets. These are often based on underlying factors that help determine future market potential and whether the market is currently being served well. This data coupled with the market size provides an indication of the market attractiveness.

Analysis 8 – Which tactical positioning dimensions make more sense? This analysis
  involves two steps. First, examine how centrality and distinctiveness relate to
  different positioning dimensions. Then, short-list those positioning dimensions
  that correlate best with your desired goal (i.e., increasing centrality or distinctiveness or both). Second, analyze the results of the implicit measurement exercise. Examine how the leader associates with the different positioning dimensions
  on the following two measures: (a) frequency count of how many times the
  leader brand is associated with each of the positioning dimensions and (b) the
  time latency (or the speed) of association of different positioning dimensions
  with the leader brand. Identify the positioning dimensions that associate well
  with the leader brand on these measures. Perform these two sets of analyses for
  each country. Next, identify the intersection of the positioning dimensions that
  rated well on these analyses for each country. The intersection presents those
  positioning dimension(s) that are most appropriate to be used across different
  markets.

Analysis 9 – Which intra-country-level differences matter for your brand? The final
  set of analysis is intended to identify how segments within each country view the
  product category. This involves splitting the data based on important segment
  dimensions. Once the data is split, separate segment level C-D maps are created
  for each segment based on the same method presented in Analysis 1 of this section. Once this exercise is completed, a summary matrix is created that guides
  management on how cognitive representations of the category differ between
  segments within each country and whether certain segments need greater attention in that country. In Fig. 5.2, we illustrate the implementation of the C-D
  mapping methodology in international markets.

Step 9: Deriving Strategic Implications

Implication 1: Are you in the appropriate quadrant? The first strategic implication
  that you will draw from different C-D maps is whether you are in the quadrant
  where you expect to be in each country (based on Analysis # 1). Each of the
  quadrants offers a viable positioning that carries different implications for profitability. Your decision regarding whether you intend to target the same quadrant
  across countries or different quadrants in different countries will require different business models. The business model of a brand must be consistent with its
  position on the map.

*Implication 2: What is your competition? How is your competition positioned
  across countries?* The Euclidean distance and consideration overlap analyses
  (Analyses # 3 and # 4) allow you to draw the second set of strategic implications
  regarding your competition. Consumer perceptions of the marketplace and the
  relative positions of each of the competitors are mapped. This analysis also
  informs you how far are your brand is from the market leader and the path it
  needs to take (i.e., whether you need to increase its centrality or distinctiveness)
  in order to get there.

*Implication 3: Should you attempt to increase your centrality and distinctiveness?
  Why?* The regression analyses (Analysis # 2) provide an understanding of the

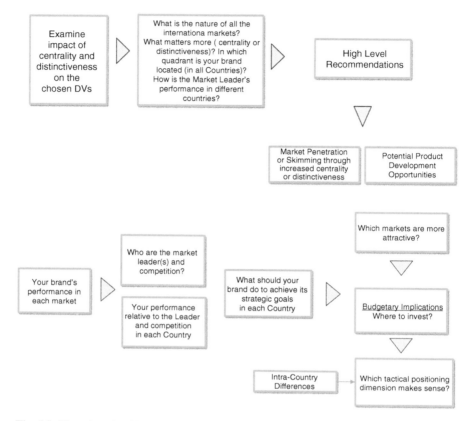

Fig. 5.2 Flow chart detailing C-D mapping implementation in international markets

impact of centrality and distinctiveness on your category. How does an increase in centrality or distinctiveness affect your key dependent variables such as sales, pricing, consideration, choice, etc.? Answering this question guides strategy regarding (a) the relative importance of increasing centrality or distinctiveness in your category, (b) the alignment of increased centrality and distinctiveness with your strategic goals in each country, and (c) the *what-if implications* of increasing centrality and distinctiveness.

Implication 4: What should you do to increase centrality and distinctiveness? The next set of analyses (Analysis # 5, # 6, # 9) provides insight into ways of improving the centrality or distinctiveness of your brand. You learn the points of relative weakness along the consumer decision journey (awareness, consideration, choice) in each country, and this implies where the brand positioning needs improvement.

Additionally, you learn the reasons why consumers are considering your brand, your competition, and the market leader. Depending on the category, such an exercise provides information about the reasons that make some brands more central or distinctive. This provides opportunities for your brand to emulate or outdo the leader's and your competition's strategy in certain countries. Finally, the outcomes of analysis # 9 provide implications regarding whether certain segments need greater attention than others in different countries.

Implication 5: What are the budgetary implications for your brand in each country?
You can derive the budgetary implications for each country based on the outcomes of the market attractiveness analysis and the Euclidean distance analysis (Analysis # 4 and # 7). If the market attractiveness is high and the distance between your brand and the leader is low for a particular country, the firm should allocate an aggressive budget as it presents an opportunity to gain leadership in that country. Conversely, if the attractiveness is low and the distance is far, it makes more sense to have a cautious investment approach in that country.

Implication 6: Which tactical positioning dimension makes more sense? The tactical positioning dimension analysis (Analysis # 8) helps draw implications about dimensions that associate best with centrality and distinctiveness in different countries. If you have an aggressive budget, you may consider customizing the message on different tactical positioning dimensions across countries. Else, you may want to find the tactical positioning dimensions that work best across most countries and create your message on that dimension.

Case Study

We applied the C-D map methodology for a large European company that operates actively in seven European countries. We performed the analyses for the company in the first half of 2017. We disguise the name of the company and the category and have disguised some of the data for proprietary reasons.

The company (fictitious name: *Alpha*) operates in an industry in which the customers use the company's product and services on a subscription-based fee model. Once customers' sign up, they tend to stay with their chosen brand and pay a fee periodically in order to continue to use the company's product. Alpha currently operates actively in the following seven countries: France, Germany, Spain, Poland, Germany, the Netherlands, and Sweden. There are multiple players and brands in the product category. In each country, more than 25 brands compete. Most companies have one flagship brand. Some companies have more than one brand. The industry is around 25 years old. Alpha was launched in the early 2000s. The nature of competition across the seven country markets has a substantive overlap. The competitors fall into four categories:

(a) Common incumbents: These brands operate in all seven countries where Alpha operates. They have been around for 10–15 years longer than Alpha.
(b) Common new entrants: Multiple new brands have entered the product category in the last 5 years. These brands bring relatively unique offerings to the category.

(c) Country-specific regional competition: Most countries have local players that cater to localized geographies within their countries.
(d) Country-specific new entrants: Multiple new brands have entered the product category (that are unique to each market) within the last 5 years. These brands bring relatively unique offerings to the category.

What Alpha Wanted to Understand

At a high level, Alpha wanted to gain an understanding of the following questions:

1. How is it positioned in each of the seven countries? Is it seen as aspirational, mainstream, unconventional, or peripheral in each country?
2. What is the impact of centrality and distinctiveness in each of the seven countries?
3. How is the competition positioned in each of the seven countries?

   (a) Which brand is the market leader?
   (b) Which brands best represents Alpha's competition?
   (c) Are the new entrants (common and country-specific) threatening Alpha's positioning?

4. What should Alpha do to perform better in each of the seven countries?
5. Which markets are attractive? What should Alpha's investment strategy be in each country?
6. Alpha has decided to adopt a new tactical positioning strategy on the dimension of "Authentic." Should it pursue that across the seven countries?

Methodology that Alpha Adopted for Data Collection

We followed the methodology described above in this chapter. The first part of the project (up to data collection) took around 3 months from project inception to the completion of data collection.

Step 1 – Project sponsor. The sponsor of the project was the CEO of Alpha Corporation. All countries rolled up under his management, and he became the project champion of this methodology.
Step 2 – Category level. We performed the analysis at a basic-level category. Consumers clearly understood what the category was and could identify brands in this category.
Step 3 – Short list of brands for the study. Based on the consultation with the CEO, we identified 15 brands in each country. These brands included common incumbents, common new entrants, country-specific regional competition, and

	France	Poland	Spain	Italy	Netherlands	Sweden	Germany
Target Company	Alpha	Alpha	Alpha	Alpha	Alpha	Alpha	Alpha
Common Incumbents	Beta	Beta	Beta	Beta	Beta	Beta	Beta
	Theta	Theta	Theta	Theta	Theta	Theta	Theta
	Delta	Delta	Delta	Delta	Delta	Delta	Delta
	Gamma	Gamma	Gamma	Gamma	Gamma	Gamma	Gamma
Common New-Entrants	Zeta	Zeta	Zeta	Zeta	Zeta	Zeta	Zeta
	Eta	Eta	Eta	Eta	Eta	Eta	Eta
	Kappa	Kappa	Kappa	Kappa	Kappa	Kappa	Kappa
	Phi	Phi	Phi	Phi	Phi	Phi	Phi
Country-specific (Regional) Competition	FRA-L1	POL-L1	SPA-L1	ITA-L1	NET-L1	SWE-L1	GER-L1
	FRA-L2	POL-L2	SPA-L2	ITA-L2	NET-L2	SWE-L2	GER-L2
	FRA-L3	POL-L3	SPA-L3	ITA-L3	NET-L3	SWE-L3	GER-L3
Country-Specific New Entrants	FRA-N1	POL-N1	SPA-N1	ITA-N1	NET-N1	SWE-N1	GER-N1
	FRA-N2	POL-N2	SPA-N2	ITA-N2	NET-N2	SWE-N2	GER-N2
	FRA-N3	POL-N3	SPA-N3	ITA-N3	NET-N3	SWE-N3	GER-N3

Fig. 5.3 Details of alpha and its competition in all seven markets

country-specific new entrants. Figure 5.3 illustrates how the brands across countries were categorized based on the country and the competition type.

Step 4 – Identify the appropriate dependent variables. Market-level variables such as pricing were not readily available for all countries. Therefore, based on our discussions with the CEO, two consumer-level dependent variables, namely, consideration and choice, were identified.

Step 5 – Sample type and size. The sample included both consumers of the category and prospects. Around 500 participants per country responded to the surveys, for a total sample of about 3500.

Step 6/7 – Designing the survey instrument and implementing surveys. The survey instrument was composed of all the six sections that we outline in the methodology section above. A common survey in English was developed. The survey was translated and back translated for seven languages. The survey was conducted on an established panel of respondents over a period of 2 weeks. The data collection was done simultaneously in each of the seven countries.

Analysis and Findings that Alpha Obtained from the Exercise

Finding 1 – Understanding how Alpha is positioned in each of the seven countries. We noticed that Alpha's positioning was different in different countries. In three of the seven countries, the brand was seen as mainstream, and in four countries, the brand was viewed as aspirational. In Fig. 5.4, we present the C-D maps of two of the seven countries, Italy and France. As is visible from the two maps, the nature of category representations for Alpha and other players differs substantively.

Finding 2 – Understanding the impact of centrality and distinctiveness in each of the seven markets. We next conducted regression analyses in which centrality and distinctiveness were the independent variables, and brand consideration (or brand choice) was the dependent variable. We also found that while centrality and distinctiveness were not correlated in two of the seven countries (Germany and France), they had relatively high correlations in the other five countries. In addition, the variance on distinctiveness was consistently lower than the variance on centrality.

Importantly, and consistently, we found (based on the regression analyses) that centrality was a stronger predictor of consideration and choice than distinctiveness. There were multiple takeaways from this analysis. First, the low impact of distinctiveness in this category implies that brands are neither viewed as particularly premium nor particularly unique (there is no brand unique as a Dr. Pepper or as premium as a Starbucks in this market). This implied that the category was relatively undifferentiated. The high impact of centrality means that certain brands were seen as more typical, and consumers made the decision based on a simple heuristic: the more well-known a brand, the better it must be. We also found that the reason centrality and distinctiveness were not correlated in some markets was a function of country-specific local competition who were seen as unconventional in Germany and France. This did not apply to the remaining five countries. Based on these findings, two high-level recommendations emerged:

(a) Market penetration through increased centrality: Given the key role centrality plays in the product category, we recommend that Alpha needs to focus on building cognitive centrality. Centrality is not impacted much by messaging on specific positioning attributes. It is instead a function of the volume of promotions, being readily available through increased distribution, and price competitiveness.

(b) Product development in unconventional quadrants: Given that local incumbents such as FRA-L1, FRA-L2, and FRA-L3 perform well in certain countries (such as France) but not in others such as Italy, we recommended to Alpha to focus on creating new offerings like FRA-L1 in the unconventional quadrant in countries where local incumbents are performing poorly.

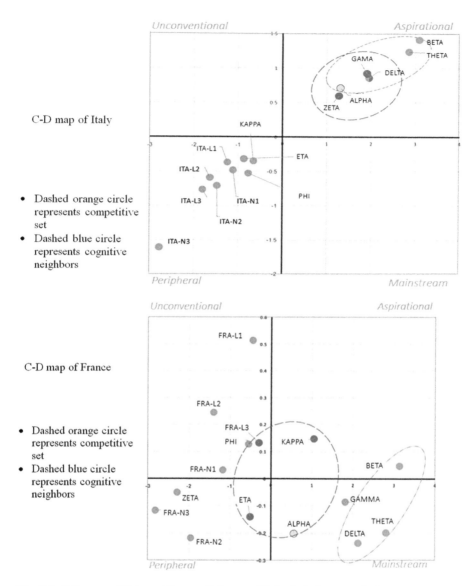

Fig. 5.4 C-D maps of Italy and France. C-D map of Italy, dashed orange circle represents competitive set, dashed blue circle represents cognitive neighbors. C-D map of France, dashed orange circle represents competitive set, dashed blue circle represents cognitive neighbors

Finding 3 – Understanding Alpha's competition and distance from market leader.
The next set of analyses looked at two measures (Euclidean distances and consideration overlap). The first analysis involved calculating distances of Alpha from all other brands (in each of the seven countries). This analysis yielded three

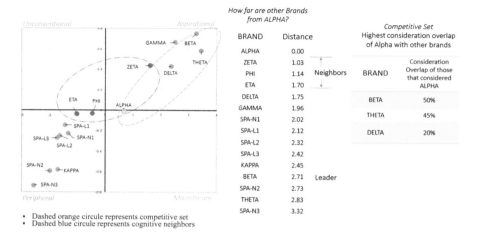

Fig. 5.5 Alpha's cognitive neighbors and competition in Spain. *Dashed orange circle* represents competitive set. Dashed blue circle represents cognitive neighbors

interesting insights. First, we learned who the cognitive neighbors of Alpha were. These brands were closest to Alpha on the C-D map. Second, we learned that the market leader (Beta) was the same across all seven markets. Third, we learned how far Alpha was from Beta in each of the seven markets. The distance from the leader is an interesting standardized cross-country metric as it helps gain an understanding regarding how easy it is for your brand to challenge the market leader. In the second set of analysis, we looked at the consideration overlap between Alpha and other brands in the category. The brands with the highest overlap formed the true competitive set. We found that cognitive neighbors are not always the same as the competitive set. This is especially true in case of product categories where distinctiveness is low. In Fig. 5.5, we present data from Spain that details the C-D map, Alpha's cognitive neighbors and competition. In Fig. 5.6, we present distance of Alpha from Beta in each of the seven countries.

Finding 4 – What should Alpha do differently in different countries? We next examined what Alpha should do differently in each of the seven countries. The first analysis that we conducted was to examine Alpha's performance along the consumer decision journey. We looked at three key metrics, brand awareness, consideration to awareness ratio, and choice to consideration ratio.

These three metrics measured how healthy Alpha was along different points of the consumer decision journey in each of the seven countries (see Fig. 5.7). We noticed that Beta's performance on these metrics was consistent across all the countries. Specifically, the awareness for Beta was largely in the 80(%)s, consideration to awareness ratio was in the 40(%)s, and choice to consideration ratio was in the 70–80(%)s range. In contrast, there was a lot of variance when it came to Alpha's performance across the seven countries. The key implication of this finding was the necessity of conducting an audit of consumer touch-points to understand which controllable touch-points impact awareness, consideration,

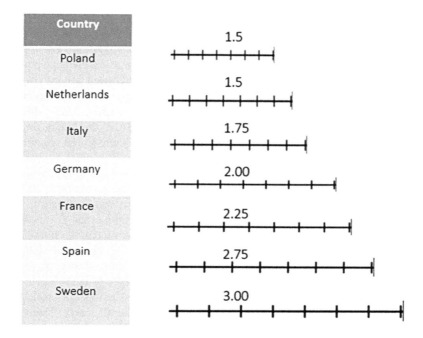

Fig. 5.6 Distance of Alpha from Beta in each of the seven countries

Awareness	Alpha	Beta	Consideration to Awareness Ratio	Alpha	Beta	Choice to Consideration Ratio	Alpha	Beta
Poland	74%	85%	Poland	30%	48%	Poland	45%	75%
Netherlands	70%	90%	Netherlands	10%	50%	Netherlands	25%	75%
Italy	70%	90%	Italy	5%	40%	Italy	55%	85%
Germany	61%	85%	Germany	20%	48%	Germany	25%	75%
France	45%	85%	France	5%	40%	France	40%	85%
Spain	50%	90%	Spain	5%	45%	Spain	35%	75%
Sweden	60%	95%	Sweden	7%	45%	Sweden	35%	75%

Fig. 5.7 Alpha's performance along the consumer's decision-making journey. Dashed red circles represent where Alpha is weak along the customer decision journey

and choice in favor of Alpha. Additionally, this provides an opportunity for Alpha to learn from countries where it is performing better. For instance, Alpha's choice to consideration ratio was quite low in Germany (implying that of the people that considered Alpha in Germany, only one-fourth chose Alpha). This was abysmal compared to Beta in Germany where three-fourths of the people that considered Beta chose it. In this case, Alpha in Germany has a lot to learn from its marketing practices in Italy where its choice to consideration ratio is 55%.

The second analysis we performed was to check the reasons why Beta and Alpha were considered in each of the seven countries. "Reputation" and "attractiveness" were common themes for people that considered Alpha. The top third reason varied across countries. More importantly, we analyzed why respondents were considering Beta over Alpha. Additional analysis showed that the two main reasons for considering Beta across all seven markets were "reputation" and "attractiveness." "User-friendly" was also a popular reason. These three are direct consequences of centrality. The more representative the brand, the more reputed and attractive it is perceived to be. This again underscored why increasing centrality was relevant for Alpha.

Finding 5 – Which markets are more attractive? What should Alpha's investment strategy be? We used secondary country-level data to categorize the seven countries into varying levels of attractiveness. We looked at two measures to determine market attractiveness. First, we looked at market potential. Given that the industry operated on a subscription fee-based business model, we obtained the total number of subscriptions of the product offered by all brands in each of the seven countries. We obtained this data through an international industry research aggregator. We next divided the total number of subscriptions in each country by the population of that country to arrive at an estimate of number of product subscriptions per capita. The second measure was the overall market size (in our case, country's population). The budgetary recommendations were based on two factors, the market attractiveness analysis and the Euclidean distance analysis. Depending on the level of market attractiveness and the distance between Alpha and Beta on the map, we recommended the following course of action for each of the seven countries. See Fig. 5.8. Specifically:

(a) If the market attractiveness is high and the distance between Alpha and Beta (the market leader) is low for a particular country, we recommended that Alpha invest in the country as Alpha has a chance of gaining leadership status in that country. This was true for Poland and Italy.

(b) If the market attractiveness is high and the distance between Alpha and Beta (the market leader) is also high for a particular country, we recommended that Alpha invest (aggressively) in the country as Alpha has a high probability of gaining leadership status in that country. The higher percentage increase in budget (relative to Poland and Italy) was recommended, as it would require greater investments to traverse the longer distance. This was true for Spain.

(c) If the market attractiveness is low and the distance between Alpha and Beta (the market leader) is low for a particular country, we recommended that Alpha maintain its budget in that country. While Alpha is within striking distance of Beta in such a country, the ultimate prize is not lucrative enough, as the market is saturated in such a country (recall that there is little switching once customers subscribe). This situation was true for the Netherlands.

(d) If the market attractiveness is moderate and the distance between Alpha and Beta is in a medium range, we recommend that the budget be increased (slightly). This was recommended, as the size of the markets is large enough

	Distance from Leader	Market Attractiveness	Budget
Poland	1.5	High	Increase
Netherlands	1.5	Low	Maintain
Italy	1.75	High	Increase
Germany	2.0	Moderate	Increase (low)
France	2.25	Moderate	Increase (low)
Spain	2.75	High	Increase (High)
Sweden	3.0	Low	Maintain/Reduce

Fig. 5.8 Budgetary implications for Alpha in each market

that even at moderate levels of growth, the volume of incremental sales is attractive. This was true for France and Germany.

(e) Finally, if the attractiveness is low and the distance is far, it makes sense to have a cautious investment approach and maintain or reduce budget in that country. This situation was true for Sweden.

Finding 6 – Alpha has decided to adopt a new tactical positioning strategy on the dimension of "Authentic." Should it pursue that across the seven countries? Alpha wanted to implement tactical positioning using the "Authentic" dimension. Therefore, in Section 6 of the survey, we included around 20 positioning dimensions (e.g., independent, authentic, reliable, official, international, fun, premium, etc.) that were relevant to the product category. The survey included an implicit measurement exercise that examined how these tactical positioning dimensions corresponded with (a) different category brands and (b) the dimensions of centrality and distinctiveness. Our analyses at this stage involved the following steps.

First, we examined how centrality related to different positioning dimensions. We did not examine the relationship between distinctiveness and positioning dimensions as distinctiveness did not have much impact on consideration and choice. Second, we analyzed how the leader (Beta) associated with the different positioning dimensions on the following two measures: (a) frequency count of how many times Beta is associated with different positioning dimensions and (b) the time latency (or the speed) of association of different positioning dimensions

	# of top tactical positioning dimensions that are statistically equivalent for Beta
Frequency Count Analysis	Cool, Open, Official, Flexible, Premium, Fun, Accessible, Innovative, Authentic
Time Latency Analysis	Steady, Convincing, Premium, Safe, International, Radiant, Engaging Official, Flexible, Premium, Fun, Accessible, Innovative, Authentic

Fig. 5.9 Which positioning dimension makes more sense?

with Beta. We analyzed this data both at the country level and at the aggregate European level.

Based on our analyses, we found that there are no specific attitudinal dimensions (of the 20 examined) that stand out as more *advantageous* than others do. Centrality (that is the key predictor of choice and consideration) correlated very well with all attitudinal dimensions. Additional analyses of Beta at the country level painted a similar picture. Analyses of how Beta correlated with attitudinal frequency count data revealed that no attitudinal dimensions statistically stand out in any of the seven markets. Finally, additional analyses of Beta at the aggregate (European) level yielded similar findings. Multiple attitudinal dimensions intersected (based on frequency count and time latency test analyses). For Beta, we noticed the following eight attitudinal dimensions performed well on both the frequency and the time latency measures – Official, Flexible, Premium, Accessible, Innovative, Authentic and Fun. See Fig. 5.9.

In sum, we concluded that "Authenticity" was a good attitudinal positioning dimension to pursue. However, we inferred that other dimensions such as innovative, official, flexible, premium, fun, and accessible might work just as well. In sum, for Alpha to perform better in this category, it would matter how loud and wide Alpha shouted its message. What message it relayed would not matter much.

Discussion and Conclusion

C-D Methodology and the Shifting Global Marketing Paradigm

Globalization in the previous decades was largely viewed in the context of product and service exchange (Lund et al. 2016). The advent of enabling technologies (the Internet and social media) has *shifted* the traditional globalization *paradigm* to include the phenomenon of digital globalization. Consumers across the world are becoming more similar as they communicate, search, shop, and consume information and entertainment on boundary-less social networks and digital media platforms (Lund et al. 2016). This trend of increased consumer homogeneity across borders is paradoxical. Logically, global brand managers should standardize communication and brand positioning across countries given that consumer perceptions across markets are converging. However, consumer perceptions of a global brand are not created in isolation. Consumers perceive brands within the context of their competitive context, which is very country-specific requiring localized positioning and communication (Wong and Merrilees 2007). These crosscurrents give new urgency to the "standardize versus localize" debate (Levitt 1983).

Levitt (1983) called global companies to ignore country-level idiosyncratic consumer preferences and instead offer globally standardized products. Levitt argued that technology, communication, and travel had led to the convergence of global consumer tastes, which in turn had led to the emergence of global markets for standardized consumer products.

Levitt's argument that standardization is imperative faced counterarguments. First, a plethora of international product failures due to lack of product adaptation suggested that the strategy of extreme standardization was flawed (Kotler 1986). Second, theorists pointed to many impediments against standardization that included country-level differences in consumer tastes and preferences, bureaucratic burdens that make localization necessary, and other management challenges such as insufficient use of formal research and inflexible implementation (Kashani 1989; Kotler 1986). Finally, many local national brands with entrenched local assets and a deep understanding of local consumer tastes continued to defend their home field advantage against global brands that adopted a centralized and standardized approach (Dawar and Frost 1999; Kapferer 2002).

Over the years, the standardization versus localization debate has reached a state of relative equilibrium. Practitioners and researchers recognize that an appropriate balance between standardization and localization is key, and certain elements of the marketing mix are more conducive to standardization than others are (Das 1993; Kapferer 2005; Steenkamp 2017). For instance, there is agreement that global firms should have a standardized core product (with local add-ons) or have a modular product structure to best compete in international markets. In contrast, pricing, sales, and distribution strategy tend to be more country-specific (Steenkamp 2017).

When it comes to brand positioning and advertising, the verdict is similar: strike a careful balance between global and local. Some of the solutions suggested include (a) integrating the global creative strategy with locally conceived execution and (b) developing a series of positioning messages from which local executives can choose the one they like most (Steenkamp 2017).

However, brand positioning in international markets remains tricky. Global brand positioning is unlikely to capture the idiosyncrasies of different markets, but the alternative – locally developed positioning – sacrifices a consistent global message (Matthiesen and Phau 2005; Wind et al. 2013). As discussed earlier, many methodologies developed thus far (Holt et al. 2004; Hsieh 2004; Kish et al. 2001; Ozsomer and Altras 2008; Roth 1992; Steenkamp et al. 2003) to assist international positioning decisions suffer multiple shortcomings. These shortcomings include (a) the omission of country-level competitive environment from the global brand-positioning framework and (b) the disjointedness between country-specific brand positioning and the brands' marketplace performance.

We argue that these methodological challenges that global brand managers face in the context of brand positioning can be overcome by adopting the centrality-distinctiveness methodology. Our methodology solves the global brand-positioning standardization-localization conundrum by integrating standardized analysis of positioning across markets with localized implementation recommendations.

Limitations and Future Research

We note the following limitations of our research methodology. The methodology is unsuitable for product categories that (a) are commoditized, (b) have very few brands, or (c) are monopolistic-led in nature. Here is why. If a product category is viewed as a commodity and consumers make purchase decisions solely on price, brand centrality and distinctiveness are unlikely to matter much in consumer perceptions. Next, brand locations on the C-D map are meaningful in relation to the locations of other brands. The greater the number of brands, the more the constraints on each brand's relative location, and the more reliable are the results. Conversely, few brands will result in less reliable locations. Finally, monopolies that are highly regulated and in which consumers have little choice are unsuitable, as the consumer cognitive space in such categories is largely uncontested.

While our current methodology examines the antecedents of centrality and distinctiveness at a high level, we acknowledge a more nuanced treatment of the topic is merited. Centrality and distinctiveness are complex super-constructs. Research questions in this domain include the following: Do the antecedents (drivers) of centrality and distinctiveness vary by product category? Do the antecedents (drivers) of centrality and distinctiveness vary by culture and country? Which antecedents (drivers) of centrality and distinctiveness are more likely to be shared (be unique) between categories and countries? A related area of future research is to examine whether the relationship between the constructs of centrality and distinctiveness is moderated by consumer-level factors (e.g., need for uniqueness, risk aversion) and category-level factors (e.g., category complexity, category involvement, etc.)

Finally, cultural differences across country markets (Alden et al. 1999; Melewar and Walker 2003; Park and Rabolt 2009; Roth 1995) are likely to affect the reported results. The question is whether the cultural differences are picked up by the methodology and are reflected in the different perceptions of the same brands across markets or whether they affect the methodology itself in some way (e.g., response bias) and distort the positioning maps. Our experience is that the results, and consumer response behaviors, are comparable and that the maps accurately reflect different perceptions across markets. However, this question merits further research.

Conclusion

The C-D mapping methodology detailed in this chapter is mature and tested in the real world. Real corporations in both domestic and international (multi-country) contexts have successfully deployed the C-D mapping methodology. We hope that the C-D map methodology will provide global brand managers a powerful tool to examine brand positioning in international markets at a strategic level. It will also give them a means and a vocabulary for conversations about positioning with country-level managers and provide an implementation plan for overcoming positioning challenges in each market.

References

Aaker, D.A., and E. Joachimsthaler. 1999. The lure of global branding. *Harvard Business Review* 77: 137–146.

Alden, D.L., J.B.E. Steenkamp, and R. Batra. 1999. Brand positioning through advertising in Asia, North America, and Europe: The role of global consumer culture. *The Journal of Marketing* 63: 75–87.

Bagga, C.K., T.J. Noseworthy, and N. Dawar. 2016. Asymmetric consequences of radical innovations on category representations of competing brands. *Journal of Consumer Psychology* 26 (1): 29–39.

Brand Quarterly. 2014. Globalization: Apple's one-size-fits-all approach. http://www.brandquarterly.com/globalization-apples-one-size-fits-approach. Accessed 25 June 2017.

Das, G. 1993. Local memoirs of a global manager, *Harvard Business Review* 71(2): 38–47.

Dawar, N., and C.K. Bagga. 2015a. A better way to map brand strategy. *Harvard Business Review* 93 (6): 90–97.

———. 2015b. A simple graph explains the complex logic of the big beer merger. *Harvard Business Review*. https://hbr.org/2015/10/a-simple-graph-explains-the-complex-logic-of-the-big-beer-merger. Accessed 25 June 2017.

Dawar, N., and T. Frost. 1999. Competing with giants: Survival strategies for local companies in emerging markets. *Harvard Business Review* 77: 119–132.

Holt, D.B., J.A. Quelch, and E.L. Taylor. 2004. How global brands compete. *Harvard Business Review* 82 (9): 68–75.

Hsieh, M.H. 2004. Measuring global brand equity using cross-national survey data. *Journal of International Marketing* 12 (2): 28–57.

Inc.com. 2014. 20 epic fails in global branding. https://www.inc.com/geoffrey-james/the-20-worst-brand-translations-of-all-time.html. Accessed 25 June 2017.

Kapferer, J.N. 2002. Is there really no hope for local brands? *Journal of Brand Management* 9 (3): 163–170.

———. 2005. The post-global brand. *Journal of Brand Management* 12 (5): 319–324.

Kashani, K. 1989. Beware the pitfalls of global marketing. *Harvard Business Review* 67 (5): 91–98.

Kish, P., D.R. Riskey, and R.A. Kerin. 2001. Measurement and tracking of brand equity in the global marketplace-the PepsiCo experience. *International Marketing Review* 18 (1): 91–96.

Kotler, P. 1986. Global standardization—courting danger. *Journal of Consumer Marketing* 3 (2): 13–15.

Levitt, T. 1983. The globalization of markets. *Harvard Business Review* 61: 92–102.

Loken, B., and J. Ward. 1990. Alternative approaches to understanding the determinants of typicality. *Journal of Consumer Research* 17 (2): 111–126.

Lund, S., J. Manyika, and J. Bughin. 2016. Globalization is becoming more about data and less about stuff. *Harvard Business Review*. https://hbr.org/2016/03/globalization-is-becoming-more-about-data-and-less-about-stuff

Macdonald, E.K., and B.M. Sharp. 2000. Brand awareness effects on consumer decision making for a common, repeat purchase product: A replication. *Journal of Business Research* 48 (1): 5–15.

Matthiesen, I., and I. Phau. 2005. The 'HUGO BOSS' connection: Achieving global brand consistency across countries. *The Journal of Brand Management* 12 (5): 325–338.

Melewar, T.C., and C. Walker. 2003. Global corporate brand building: Guidelines and case studies. *The Journal of Brand Management* 11 (2): 157–170.

Mervis, C.B., and E. Rosch. 1981. Categorization of natural objects. *Annual Review of Psychology* 32 (1): 89–115.

Özsomer, A., and S. Altaras. 2008. Global brand purchase likelihood: A critical synthesis and an integrated conceptual framework. *Journal of International Marketing* 16 (4): 1–28.

Park, H.J., and N.J. Rabolt. 2009. Cultural value, consumption value, and global brand image: A cross-national study. *Psychology and Marketing* 26 (8): 714–735.

Perkins, A.W., and M.R. Forehand. 2011. Implicit self-referencing: The effect of nonvolitional self-association on brand and product attitude. *Journal of Consumer Research* 39 (1): 142–156.

Rosch, E., and B.B. Lloyd, eds. 1978. *Cognition and categorization*. Vol. 1, 978. Hillsdale: Lawrence Erlbaum Associates.

Roth, M.S. 1992. Depth versus breadth strategies for global brand image management. *Journal of Advertising* 21 (2): 25–36.

———. 1995. The effects of culture and socioeconomics on the performance of global brand image strategies. *Journal of Marketing Research* 32: 163–175.

Steenkamp, J.B. 2017. *Global brand strategy: World-wise marketing in the age of branding*. London, UK: Springer. https://link.springer.com/book/10.1057/978-1-349-94994-6. ISBN: 978-1-349-94993-9.

Steenkamp, J.B.E., R. Batra, and D.L. Alden. 2003. How perceived brand globalness creates brand value. *Journal of International Business Studies* 34 (1): 53–65.

Wind, J., S. Sthanunathan, and R. Malcolm. 2013. Great advertising is both local and global. *Harvard Business Review*. https://hbr.org/2013/03/great-advertising-is-both-loca

Yin Wong, H., and B. Merrilees. 2007. Multiple roles for branding in international marketing. *International Marketing Review* 24 (4): 384–408.

Zhou, K.Z., and K. Nakamoto. 2007. How do enhanced and unique features affect new product preference? The moderating role of product familiarity. *Journal of the Academy of Marketing Science* 35 (1): 53–62.

Chapter 6
Social Network Brand Visibility (SNBV): Conceptualization and Empirical Evidence

Aijaz A. Shaikh, Richard Glavee-Geo, Adina-Gabriela Tudor, Chen Zheng, and Heikki Karjaluoto

Abstract Social media has become a new way of life that allows for real-time interaction among businesses (B2B) and consumers (P2P/C2C) as well as between business firms and consumers (B2C). Customers are increasingly accessing and using social networking sites (SNS), making it imperative for businesses and organizations to have a presence on these platforms to enhance visibility. The main purpose of this chapter is to provoke an agenda on the study of social network brand visibility (SNBV). We developed and proposed a definition of SNBV and report findings from a preliminary study. We further discuss implications for theory, research, and practice as well as the limitations and options for future research.

Introduction

Recent market trends have suggested that innovative and highly interactive social media platforms are increasingly becoming an integral part of consumer lifestyles. The power of social media resulted in the tremendous success of Pokémon Go in 2016 (Wu 2017). The time that consumers spend on social media is constantly increasing; therefore, the impact of social media on consumers' lifestyles and businesses cannot be underestimated. Capgemini (2014) revealed that the social media user base is expected to increase from 1.47 billion in 2012 to 2.55 billion in 2017. Popular social media platforms include YouTube, Facebook, Twitter, LinkedIn, Snapchat, Instagram, and the recently introduced Musical.ly. Access to these platforms has become more common due to the advent and proliferation of portable devices, including smartphones and tablets. According to Asano (2017), more than

A. A. Shaikh · H. Karjaluoto
Jyväskylä University School of Business and Economics, University of Jyväskylä,
P.O. Box 35, Jyväskylä FI-40014, Finland

R. Glavee-Geo (✉) · A.-G. Tudor · C. Zheng
Department of International Business, NTNU-Norwegian University of Science
and Technology, Postbox 1517, Aalesund, Norway
e-mail: rigl@ntnu.no

© Springer International Publishing AG, part of Springer Nature 2018
J. Agarwal, T. Wu (eds.), *Emerging Issues in Global Marketing*,
https://doi.org/10.1007/978-3-319-74129-1_6

149

60% of consumers' social media time is facilitated by a mobile device. Others (e.g., Agnihotri et al. 2016) have argued that the accessibility of products, services, and information on social media is higher than ever. As a result, both present and prospective customers are becoming better connected to companies, more knowledgeable about products and/or service selections, and more powerful in buyer-seller relationships (Agnihotri et al. 2016).

Confronted with an increasingly competitive global market and the expanding use of social media in everyday life, global technological firms (hi-tech) now seek to enhance their brands through carefully defined content strategy that includes not only producing quality products but also having an active presence on interactive social media. It is widely believed that this content strategy is primarily geared toward creating a unique image for brands online, with the underlying objective being to stimulate product demand from different consumer segments globally. It is now considered imperative for marketing and digital managers to know what is being said about their services, products, and/or brands in general on social media, which constitutes four major domains: collaborative projects, micro-blogs, content communities, and social networking sites (Reyneke et al. 2011; Duane and O'Reilly 2012). These important views, comments, and other information that is posted give brand managers a valuable indication of their brands' "visibility" on social media.

Nonetheless, no previous literature has commented on what social network brand visibility is, its dimensionality, and how it can be measured. Regarding technology-based products, such as smartphones, personal computers, laptops, and tablets, consumers require product knowledge to make informed purchase decisions. Additionally, for brands to achieve high visibility globally, they require an online social media presence/platform (Michaelidou et al. 2011; Kim and Ko 2012; McCarthy et al. 2014), which will provide a medium in terms of SNS for the exchange of information both within and between the brand and the community of users (Callarisa et al. 2012; Gil de Zúñiga et al. 2012; Kaplan 2012; Wang et al. 2012).

Social media marketing should be focused on entertainment, interactions, and electronic word-of-mouth (eWOM) communication (Hoffman and Fodor 2010; Kaplan 2012; Kim and Ko 2012). Thus, increased interactions on SNS provide opportunities for learning about the brand, understanding product features/attributes, and enhancing brand awareness regarding brand recall and recognition (Brown et al. 2007; Chua and Banerjee 2013). The purpose of this chapter is to synthesize the social network marketing literature; define, develop, and show how SNBV is measured; and offer key insights into SNBV, which is a "shifting paradigm" for global branding and marketing. Moreover, this chapter seeks to conceptualize SNBV and to empirically test its effects. To the best of our knowledge, only a few studies have examined the presence of brands on SNS in terms of their visibility. However, even fewer have stressed the importance of advertising in brand awareness (e.g., Buil et al. 2013), the influence of eWOM in consumer product judgment (Lee and Youn 2009), and, quite recently, social media brand building (Cawsey and Rowley 2016).

Visibility is an important aspect of the communication channel strategy, and it is vital to the development and implementation of brand strategy (Chen 2011). Our study departs from that of Reyneke et al. (2011), where visibility was assessed via third-party online data gathering platforms by using an algorithm (e.g., howsociable.com). We sought to measure SNBV from the perspective of either individuals or key informants using a psychometric method. The implications of this study will not only contribute to theory development but also be of practical use to social network marketers, search engine optimizers, and user-generated content providers in assessing the impact of SNS. Our explication and exposition of the mechanisms of SNBV and its effects/outcomes will provide increased understanding and knowledge to digital marketers on how best to overcome the challenges posed by social media and how best to conceive, formulate, and implement global brand building and marketing strategies based on the concepts, findings, and suggestions in this chapter.

Next, we provide a review of the literature on social media, branding, and visibility and develop a working definition for the concept SNBV. This is followed by the hypotheses, methods, results, and discussion. We conclude with limitations and further research.

The Concept and Definition of Online Social Network Brand Visibility

Social media platforms facilitate interactions, collaborations, and the sharing of content, including images, audio, and videos both between and among users. The attribute of interactivity as reciprocal interpersonal communication (Liu and Shrum 2009) is one of the key characteristics of social media because it allows individuals to interact with various people, organizations, and online communities, who share their interests and activities across political, socioeconomic, and geographical barriers (Kim and Kim 2017).

A recent study found that 70% of consumers have visited SNS to get information about a certain product or service, with 49% of these consumers having made a purchase decision based on the information they found on social media and 60% reporting that they were very likely to use SNS to share information as well as make referrals to others. In addition, 45% of those who searched for information through SNS engaged in information sharing by word of mouth (Kim and Ko 2012). In another study, Michaelidou et al. (2011) reported that 93% of social media users believed that companies should have a social media presence, while 85% believed that companies should interact with customers via interactive social media channels. In view of these consumer expectations, most companies have "invaded" SNS and have offered direct links from their corporate websites to Facebook, Twitter, LinkedIn, YouTube, Google+, Pinterest, Tumblr, Flickr, and Instagram. These social websites are now commonly used as promotional tools in support of brand communities (Kaplan and Haenlein 2010). Therefore, it is quite likely that lacking visibility on social media will lead to serious consequences, and companies will not be able to effectively reach out to existing and potential customers as part of their online marketing communication strategy.

As argued by Mangold and Faulds (2009:360), consumers are turning away from traditional advertising methods, such as radio, television, magazines, and newspapers, and demanding more control over their media consumption. Moreover, consumers require on-demand and immediate access to information. In summary, unlike traditional media platforms, social media provides greater user interactivity. Moreover, brand content ("like," "shares," and "comments") is generally transmitted at a quicker rate and to a much larger, more responsive, and more engaged audience than most traditional media; however, the cost is much lower (Qualman 2013). Digital marketers are making use of SNS as an indispensable part of their online brand strategy by raising brand awareness, driving engagement, and increasing conversion rates of brands and products (Phua et al. 2017). Table 6.1 presents a summary of past literature on social network brand visibility.

High visibility is a necessary condition for maximum impact, and it is an important prerequisite for effective communication and the creation of brand awareness. International and global firms are likely to tailor their marketing communication strategies due to the competitive nature of the global market (Wong and Merrilees 2008). Additionally, the global market's changing dynamics dictate an integrated approach to marketing communication; thus, a move to integrated marketing communication represents an adaptation to the changing global market environment (Chen 2011). Integrated marketing communication requires the integration of online, offline, and traditional channels. Here, social media marketing, which is an Internet-based communication channel, is an important source that "closes the gap" between the online, offline, and traditional media/channels. Broadly speaking, we define social network visibility as the degree of exposure a brand, product, service, and/or cause receives on SNS, with the purpose of creating awareness, knowledge, information, and value to build meaningful relationships with existing and potential customers, including communities.

In addition to products, services, brands, and/or causes (in the case of not-for-profit organizations), social network visibility can also be applied to political organizations, figures, and politicians. Thus, a product, a service, an individual, or an organization that is supplanted in a social networking site, either for exposure in the form of review, viral communication, to establish a relationship, to engage, to communicate, to inform, to elicit support, to provide funding for a cause, or to change social behavior, can be gauged by the extent of its visibility. Naturally, online social network visibility can create either a favorable (positive) or an unfavorable (negative) disposition to either the brand, object, individual, product, or service. However, in the present chapter, we have limited this exploratory study to SNBV regarding the brands of a tangible product (laptop), which has service elements that either are or may be intangible, variable, inseparable, and/or perishable.

We conceptualized social network brand visibility to consist of various dimensions. The first conceptualization (see Appendix 6.1) of SNBV consists of six dimensions. Table 6.2 shows both the SNBV dimensions and definitions.

Table 6.1 Summary of past literature on SNBV

Citation	Purpose of study	Major findings
Reyneke et al. (2011)	This study addresses the visibility of luxury wine brands on social media	Some of the brands studied did not have a clearly defined social media strategy. Nonetheless, there are opportunities for luxury wine brand managers to use social media as a tool in their marketing strategies. In addition, some threats may exist should these brands take a laissez-faire approach to social media, particularly when it is becoming at least as influential, if not more so, as conventional media
Botha et al. (2011)	This study describes a tool for collecting brand visibility information by looking at the visibility of various South African university brands and their relative positioning from a social media perspective	The findings indicate that South African university brands are not distinctly positioned in social media, and none of them appears to have a strategy for engaging stakeholders via a particular social media platform. Therefore, there are both opportunities for enthusiastic managers as well as possible threats against those who ignore social media during a time when it is dominating both the Internet and the media
Capitello et al. (2014)	This study analyzes the relationships between the orientation, communication strategies, and Web 2.0 tactics of businesses as well as the social media effect on brand visibility	The results propose a conceptual, three-dimensional approach that integrates a business's strategic orientation with its digital marketing strategy and its social media tactics. This approach also includes specific evaluation criteria to measure the impact on the business's strategic objectives
Yang and Kent (2014)	This study explores the factors that drive organizational social media visibility	The findings reveal that mainstream media coverage significantly affects social media visibility, whereas organizations' social media use patterns have a limited impact on overall organizational visibility
Goswami et al. (2013)	A significant amount of research has been conducted on both social media usability and user engagement. The uniqueness of this research paper is its identification of synergies between the features of social media and user engagement to enhance online brand visibility. In this paper, a conceptual model is explained by developing a social media-user engagement matrix to explain the synergies	The matrix integrates four parameters of user engagement—involvement, interaction, intimacy, and influence—with four social media characteristics, content, relationship, value, and structure, to bring out the essence of interoperability. This paper has identified and listed certain metrics for measuring online brand visibility. The authors believe that the outcome of this paper will make a significant contribution to the existing body of knowledge by uniquely identifying and explaining "social media-user engagement synergy" and listing appropriate metrics for measuring online brand visibility

(continued)

Table 6.1 (continued)

Citation	Purpose of study	Major findings
Davis et al. (2014)	This research explores the consumers' specific motivations for the purpose and structure of the consumption of brands in the social media community. Considering the evolving economic relevance of social consumption, the resulting conceptual model was designed to give a better understanding of the unique branding opportunities and relationships that social media present to brand managers	The findings suggest that consumers expect specific two-way interactions with brands, and social media may be the only way to deliver these demands effectively. This study identifies five core drivers of brand consumption (functional, emotional, self-oriented, social, and relational) in a social media community via the Five Sources Model. These core drivers represent unique opportunities for brands to enhance their relationships with their customers and to increase the likelihood of an active and beneficial online community that is built around their brands

Table 6.2 Six-dimensional social network brand visibility conceptualization

Dimension	Definition/explanation	Citation
Social media presence (SMP)	The importance of either a brand, product, or service on social media, as perceived by individuals, social networkers, communities, and/or businesses	Kim and Ko (2012), McCarthy et al. (2014), Cawsey and Rowley (2016)
Brand awareness	The ability to recognize and recall the brand	Aaker (1991), Kaplan (2012), Kim and Ko (2012)
Value equity	Benefits derived from using the product/service; value derived from interacting with either the brand, other community members, potential users, or customers. Value can be in the form of either the quality of the product/service or in social terms, such as social capital and social values	Callarisa et al. (2012), Gil de Zúñiga et al. (2012), Kim and Ko (2012)
Knowledge	Learning about the product/service and understanding product use, features, etc.	Brown et al. (2007), Chua and Banerjee (2013)
Social media marketing	Online marketing activities in terms of entertainment, interactivity, and eWOM	Hoffman et al. (2010), Kaplan (2012), Kim and Ko (2012)
Information exchange	Social media as a medium for communicating with current and/or potential customers or among peers	Brown et al. (2007), Kaplan (2012), Wang et al. (2012)

We propose that SNBV can have various dimensions in its assessment, depending on the number of these. Previous studies operationalized brand visibility using only one dimension (e.g., Chen 2011; Vianna et al. 2016). In the present study, we empirically test the four-dimensional SNBV, as shown in Fig. 6.1.

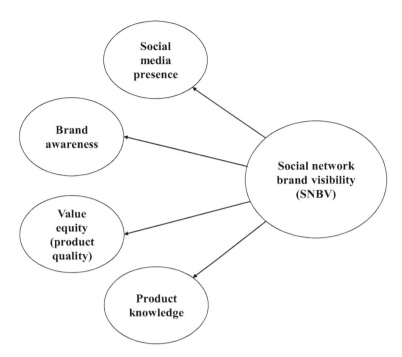

Fig. 6.1 Four-dimensional conceptualization of SNBV

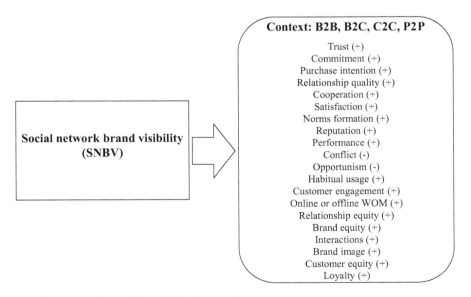

Fig. 6.2 SNBV-relationship variables framework

Additionally, we propose that SNBV can have either a positive or a negative influence on one or more relationship variables. For example, an increase in SNBV can lead to an increase in trust, commitment, purchase intention, cooperation, and brand image among other relationship variables (see Fig. 6.2), while an increase in SNBV can also lead to a reduction in conflict and unethical behaviors between interacting businesses (B2B), a company and its customers (B2C), and among either individual consumers (C2C) or peers (P2P). Figure 6.2 shows the SNBV-relationship variables framework.

Country of Origin Image and Product Evaluation

Country of origin (COO) is considered as the country (or home country) with which a manufacturer's product or brand is associated (Wang and Yang 2008). As a multidimensional construct, COO has been further defined to include country of design, country of assembly, country of brand, country of parts, and country of corporate ownership (Pharr 2005). More than 20 years ago, many products were "made in Taiwan," which conjured positive perceptions of quality similar to the highly-positive perceptions of "made in Japan" in the technology sector. However, 20 years later, the global outlook has radically changed, making it difficult to predict the nature and pace of societal changes (Futurebrand 2014). The widespread growth and usage of the Internet as a medium for both buying and selling products have fundamentally affected many products' availability and distribution as well as their manufacturing, labelling, and promotion processes (Pharr 2005).

COO has been studied extensively as an extrinsic marketing cue since the 1960s, and its effect on consumers' product evaluations has long been established in the literature. However, globalization has made the assessment of COO increasingly complex (Veale and Quester 2009). In today's globalized markets, a product can be designed in one country and have its components sourced from other countries, while manufacturing can be outsourced to either one or more manufacturers in either one or more countries anywhere in the world. For example, the iPad and the MacBook are designed in California (US) but manufactured in China (Minasians 2017). Consumers often use COO stereotypes to evaluate a product's quality. Consumers form opinions of quality through the evaluation of both intrinsic and extrinsic product cues (Bredahl 2003). Therefore, COO has the power to arouse consumers' beliefs about product attributes and hence affect their evaluation of products (Veale and Quester 2009).

Hypotheses

Social Network Brand Visibility (SNBV) and Purchase Intention

Using social media has become a collective social action and a part of daily life for the consumer (Chang and Hsu 2016). A growing body of evidence suggests that the opinions and reviews posted on social media influence consumers' purchase decisions (Shang et al. 2017). Therefore, a growing number of review and opinion sites allow consumers to make informed decisions based on information provided by other consumers who have had experience with either the product, company, brand, or customer care (Karakaya and Barnes 2010). Negative online consumer reviews result in negative consumer product attitudes due to the conformity effect (Lee et al. 2008; Karakaya and Barnes 2010). Thus, SNS are considered to have positive and yet also many negative aspects, such as an unhappy customer posting his/her service failure experiences online as revenge (Zhuang et al. 2013).

However, positive social media communication among potential, current, and former customers about either a product or a firm can enhance brand awareness, while negative communication could negatively affect the brand. A brand name provides memory nodes in consumers' minds; a positive brand attitude over time creates a strong emotional association with that brand. For consumers, awareness of a brand implies learning and formation of an attitude about the brand and hence a strong emotional attachment, which leads to brand loyalty. Consumers must be aware of a brand to prefer it, and social media can provide that awareness. Therefore, visibility on social media should stimulate purchase intention. Vianna et al. (2016) found significant positive associations between brand visibility and purchase intention in the context of viral marketing and online advertising. Hence, we hypothesize the following:

H1 *SNBV is positively associated with purchase intention.*

Conceptual Model A

For validation in the present study, SNBV was conceptualized and operationalized as a higher-order, four-dimensional construct that consists of social media presence, brand awareness, value equity (product quality), and product knowledge. SNBV is subsequently hypothesized to be positively associated with purchase intention. Figure 6.3 shows conceptual model A.

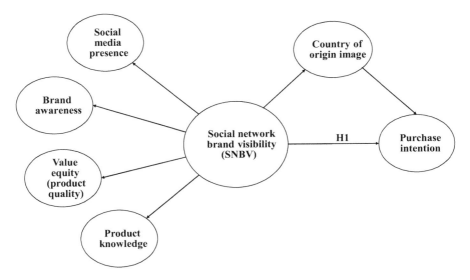

Fig. 6.3 Conceptual model (A)

Social Media Presence (SMP) and Product Knowledge

Global technology companies are now increasingly initiating product support interactions via proactive chat, click-to-talk, short message service (SMS), and web-based social media. Most of these firms have developed and established multichannel means of contacting current and potential customers via online communities and social media. As argued earlier, in view of the dual nature of social media, most technological companies have deployed resources in the form of social media analytics to both guard and moderate their online content using text analytics. These analytic tools flag abusive language, spam, and derogatory content and identify expert users and/or the most qualified customers to provide the most credible information to others (Genpact 2014).

The provision of product support-related services on social media to both current and potential customers is expected to enhance product knowledge. Here, product knowledge refers to both general and product-specific knowledge that customers have about the functional characteristics of the product and/or brand. Product knowledge can also be defined as product-related information that is stored in the memory, such as information about brands, products, attributes, evaluations, decision heuristics, and usage situations (Marks and Olson 1981; Selnes and Grønhaug 1986). Product knowledge involves either customers' familiarity with the product or having the expertise to process product-related information through learning and understanding. Occasionally, consumers are not able to evaluate all the characteristics of a product before purchase, and sometimes they must manage with limited knowledge. The use of tailor-made video content on YouTube can provide product-related information to customers, such as how to either troubleshoot or fix software-related problems for either a smartphone or laptop/PC, to introduce a new product, to explain product features, and how to either operate or use the product. The streaming of videos on Facebook and Twitter, among other SNS, has recently become a popular and common feature. These videos quickly communicate information and knowledge to online social media users and communities.

However, not all the information provided on these SNS originates from the companies; much of it is user generated, while some also stems from third parties. Thus, SNS have the dual role of providing product information and recommendations (Chatterjee 2001), which are important for the consumer decision-making process. Lin and Chen (2006) claim that product knowledge enhances consumer purchase decisions under different product involvement. Therefore, we hypothesize the following:

H2 *SMP is positively associated with product knowledge.*

Brand Awareness, Product Knowledge, and Purchase Intention

Brand awareness is the customer's ability to recognize and recall a brand under different conditions and time pressures (Aaker 1991). Macdonald and Sharp (2000) argued that when a customer chooses a product, there is a strong tendency to choose a well-known brand instead of an unknown brand. Brand is an important antecedent for a consumer's purchase intention (Wang and Yang 2008). Consumers are not able to evaluate all characteristics of a product before they purchase; therefore, they often must judge by their prepurchase evaluation (Rezvani et al. 2012). The term knowledge can best be understood as being created through human interaction with information (Davenport and Prusak 1998). Nonaka and Takeuchi (1995) suggested that knowledge is a dynamic human process of justifying a personal belief toward the truth through the two types of knowledge: *tacit* (personal knowledge) and *explicit* (expressed in words, databases, patents, reports, and documents).

Rezvani et al.'s (2012) study suggested that consumers' attitudes would be more persistent and less affected by country of origin cues over time if they had high product knowledge and the motivation to process product-related information to inform their purchase decisions. The lack of product knowledge decreases the consumer's purchasing intention. If the consumer has never used the product before purchasing the item, there is no "familiarity" in terms of product knowledge. Consumers that have greater knowledge of a product/brand are expected to include that product/brand in their consideration set. Product knowledge is therefore expected to increase consumer purchase intention. In view of the above, we hypothesize the following:

H3 *Brand awareness is positively associated with product knowledge.*

H4 *Product knowledge is positively associated with purchase intention.*

Product Quality, Brand Awareness, and Purchase Intention

A product's ability to fulfill a need relates to its distinctive characteristics and/or attributes, which indicate quality. The expectation that a product can fulfill the stated need is a strong motivation for a consumer to purchase that product. Quality attributes include both the functional and psychological benefits that are provided by the product; they represent what the product is perceived to either do or provide to the consumer (Steenkamp 1990). Expected quality is believed to be one of the most important influencers of consumers' intention to purchase. Based on a study by Papanagiotou et al. (2013), quality expectations relate to intention to buy.

One of the key influencers of the perceived quality of a brand is brand awareness (Aaker 1996; Keller and Lehman 2003) because consumers assign high credibility to prestigious brands due to a lower perceived functional risk. One of the elements that most strongly conditions the perception of a product's quality is the brand name. Many consumers relate recognized brand names to high quality (Rubio et al. 2014). Brand awareness provides a kind of learning advantage for the brand (Keller 2008), and brands that consumers know are more likely to be included in the consumers' consideration set (Schiffman et al. 2012). Therefore, quality products are more likely to create a strong brand image for the product and enhance brand awareness. Such products are more likely to be considered for purchase. Thus, we developed the following hypotheses:

H5 *Product quality is positively associated with brand awareness.*

H6 *Product quality is positively associated with purchase intention.*

Conceptual Model B

We developed a second research model for estimation using the individual sub-constructs of the four-dimensional SNBV based on hypotheses (H2–H6). We hypothesize the following: the SMP of a brand should lead to product knowledge (H2); brand awareness should lead to product knowledge (H3); and product knowledge should be positively related to purchase intention (H4). Value equity, when operationalized as product quality, should lead to brand awareness (H5) and purchase intention (H6). Figure 6.4 shows conceptual model B.

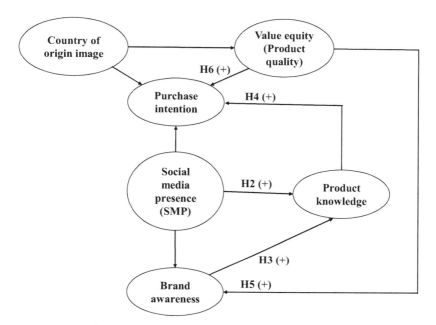

Fig. 6.4 Conceptual model (B)

Methods

Procedure for Developing the Study's Measures

We followed Churchill's (1979) procedure to develop the necessary study measures, with some adaptation. Thus, due to time constraints, we used the "single-phase data collection approach" (see Appendix 6.3). Because the concept of SNBV is new, we reviewed the literature using keywords such as "visibility," "brand visibility," "social media," "online marketing," "branding," "product evaluation," "product knowledge," "purchase intention," and "online interactions." This first step helped in specifying the domain of the construct of SNBV and the development of a working definition. Based on the literature review, we generated a sample of items, some of which were validated scales that were adapted for the study. However, most of the survey items were adapted from previous research, and a few new questions were developed (e.g., social media presence measures). The sources and other information about the survey instrument are summarized in Table 6.3. Country of origin image (COOI) measures were adapted from Martin and Eroglu (1993); purchase intention scales were adapted from Taylor and Baker (1994); value equity-product quality measures were adapted from Lichtenstein et al. (1993); brand awareness measures were developed based on Aaker (1996); and product knowledge measures were developed based on Mark and Olson (1981). All items were anchored in a seven-point Likert scale, from one, "strongly disagree," to seven, "strongly agree."

Table 6.3 Measures and items

Measures and items	Standardized loadings	t-value
Social media presence (SMP)		
The importance of the presence of my favorite personal (laptop) computer brand on social networking sites:		
Facebook	0.818[a]	
Twitter	0.409	4.60
YouTube	0.976	10.20
Google+	0.592	7.02
Country of origin, adapted from Martin and Eroglu (1993)		
The level of economic development of this country is high	0.497[a]	
The level of democratic politics of this country is high	0.535	5.85
The level of industrialization of the country where my laptop originates is high	0.632	5.88
The level of technology of this country is high	0.915	5.76
The product quality of this country is high	0.880	5.70
Personal computers (laptops) from this country are reliable	0.711	5.22
Value equity (product quality), adapted from Lichtenstein et al. (1993)		
This personal (laptop) computer brand is of high technological quality	0.920[a]	
This computer brand manufacturer is very innovative	0.872	12.35
This personal (laptop) computer brand is highly reliable	0.719	11.51
This personal (laptop) computer brand is of high quality	0.821	12.29
Product knowledge developed, based on Mark and Olson (1981)		
The level of my knowledge of this personal computer brand	0.396[a]	
I am willing to know more about this personal (laptop) computer	0.841	4.36
brand After purchase and use of this personal (laptop) computer brand, the accumulated level of what I know about this brand is high	0.597	5.29
I am willing to understand more about this laptop brand	0.944	4.37
Brand awareness, adapted from Aaker (1996)		
I know this brand	0.785[a]	
Regarding laptops, I can immediately recall the brand	0.760	7.14
The name of the manufacturer of my favorite laptop is a well-known computer brand	0.537	5.32
Consumer purchase intention, adapted from Taylor and Baker (1994)		
I would always consider buying this personal computer (laptop) brand	0.602[a]	
It is possible that I will always buy this laptop brand	0.659	7.54
If I was going to buy this laptop/computer, I would buy any model of this brand	0.506	4.85
The possibility that I would consider buying this product is high	0.825	6.98
My willingness to buy this product is high	0.897	7.32
The likelihood of me purchasing this product is high	0.839	7.06

[a]Unstandardized factor loadings fixed

Table 6.4 Demographic characteristics of respondents

Demographic characteristics	Category	Frequency	Percent
Gender	Male	60	49.20
	Female	62	50.80
Age	19–24	62	50.82
	25–30	41	33.61
	31–36	14	11.47
	37–42	3	2.46
	43–48	2	1.64
Monthly income (NOK)	Below 5000	29	23.80
	5000–10,000	58	47.50
	10,000–20,000	22	18.00
	Above 20,000	13	10.70

NOK Norwegian kroner

Data Gathering

The data source consisted of an online survey among former Aalesund University College students who had attended prior to the merger with the Norwegian University of Science and Technology. SNS offer college students the opportunity to connect with friends, family members, and even strangers to engage in social interactions and access information for academic use, such as e-learning. Most users of SNS are young people, with the majority being students of higher education. College students make use of personal computers in their academic work and hence have some basic requirements in terms of products' attributes and functionality.

The proliferation of several PC brands means that college students, as current and potential customers, have many brands from which to choose. However, not all available brands will be included in the consideration set of college students; therefore, this study presents an interesting context for research. In total, 122 responses out of a targeted 3000 students—a response rate of 4%—were obtained. Online surveys usually have low response rates, so 4% is not an uncommon result (Fan and Yan 2010). The sample consisted of 49.1% males and 50.8% females. The majority (84.43%) were between 19 and 30 years of age. Close to 50% of the respondents earned from 5000 to 10,000 Norwegian Kroner (NOK) monthly, with 10.7% earning above 20,000 NOK. The demographic characteristics of the sample are presented in Table 6.4.

Table 6.5 Correlation matrix

	1	2	3	4	5	6
SMP (1)	1	0.043	0.130	−0.040	0.117	0.121
Country of origin (2)		1	0.480**	0.206*	0.202*	0.381**
Value equity-product quality (3)			1	0.485**	0.354**	0.573**
Brand awareness (4)				1	0.482**	0.419**
Product knowledge (5)					1	0.418**
Purchase intention (6)						1
AVE	0.53	0.51	0.70	0.50	0.53	0.54
Cronbach α	0.79	0.86	0.91	0.73	0.91	0.87

SMP Social media presence
*p < 0.05 (2-tailed); **p < 0.01 (2-tailed)

Measure Validation and Data Analysis

As part of the measures purification process (see Appendix 6.3), we first evaluated the psychometric properties of the measures by performing an exploratory factor analysis with varimax rotation. The Kaiser-Meyer-Olkin (KMO) measure of sampling adequacy was 0.796, and Bartlett's test of sphericity was significant at the 0.0001 level, indicating that the data matrix was sufficiently correlated for further analysis. Second, we conducted a confirmatory factor analysis (CFA) using a maximum likelihood estimator in IBM SPSS/AMOS 24 (Arbuckle 2016). This yielded a relatively adequate fit of the model to the data (Chi-square $\chi 2 = 447.53$, df = 303, $p = 0.000$, $\chi 2/df = 1.48$; SRMR = 0.078, RMSEA = 0.063, 90% CI = 0.050, 0.075; CFI = 0.924, TLI = 0.912). The assessment of the measurement model, where all the items were loaded on the designated factor with no cross-loadings, demonstrated both convergent and discriminant validity.

The average variance extracted (AVE) of all the constructs were above the recommended threshold of 0.50 (Fornell and Larker 1981; Hair et al. 2009), which indicated good convergent validity. The AVEs of both COOI and the value equity-product quality were 0.51 and 0.70, respectively. The correlation between these two constructs, as shown in Table 6.5, was 0.48. The square of the correlation between these two constructs was 0.23. The AVE of each construct was greater than the squared correlation between the constructs, which further demonstrated discriminant validity. An examination of the AVEs of other pairs of constructs and their squared multiple correlation demonstrated discriminant validity between the constructs. The Cronbach alpha of all the constructs was above the minimum threshold of 0.70 (Nunnally 1978; Hair et al. 2009). Table 6.5 shows the correlation matrix with a reliability estimate (Cronbach's alpha) and the AVE.

Common Method Variance

Harman's single factor test was used to assess common method variance (CMV), which is present when either a single factor accounts for the factor analysis or one general factor accounts for the majority (Podsakoff et al. 2003.). The exploratory factor analysis, which was conducted with an unrotated factor solution, produced six factors, with the largest factor accounting for 27% of the total variance. An alternative analysis of CMV using CFA (Malhotra et al. 2006), where all observed items were modeled as indicators of a single factor, yielded an unsatisfactory model fit (Chi-square χ^2 = 545.42, df = 282, p = 0.000, SRMR = 0.082, RMSEA = 0.088, 90% CI = 0.077, 0.099; CFI = 0.852, TLI = 0.829), which further supported the claim that CMV is not a potential influencing factor.

Results

Evaluation of Higher-Order Four-Dimensional SNBV and Conceptual Model A

SNBV was both conceptualized and operationalized as a higher-order four-dimensional construct (recall Fig. 6.3) that includes social media presence, brand awareness, value equity (product quality), and product knowledge. The validation of higher-order four-dimensional SNBV was conducted via IBM SPSS/AMOS 24 (Arbuckle 2016). Although the model fit was adequate (Chi-square χ^2 = 104.59, df = 72, p = 0.000, Chi-square χ^2/df = 1.45; RMR = 0.222, RMSEA = 0.062, 90% CI = 0.046, 0.077; CFI = 0.963, TLI = 0.953), the sub-construct social media presence was not as highly related to SNBV (r = 0.02) as expected. The other three sub-constructs were highly related to SNBV [brand awareness (r = 0.95), value equity (r = 0.62), and product knowledge (r = 0.55)]. Appendix 2 shows the results of the evaluation of the four-dimensional SNBV, which was re-specified as a three-dimensional SNBV and estimated. Table 6.6 shows the results of the three-dimensional SNBV with first- and second-order loadings.

Subsequently, conceptual model A with respecification as a three-dimensional SNBV with nomological structural relations with both COOI and purchase intention was estimated to test H1. That estimation yielded a more adequate fit (Chi-square χ^2 = 288.99, df = 197, p = 0.000, Chi-square χ^2/df = 1.47; RMR = 0.178, RMSEA = 0.062, 90% CI = 0.046, 0.077; CFI = 0.942, TLI = 0.933). Figure 6.5 shows the results of the structural model with second-order loadings, while Table 6.7 shows the results of testing H1.

H1, which hypothesizes a positive association between SNBV and purchase intention, is supported (β = 0.86, p < 0.001, t = 3.89) with the R^2 of purchase intention 0.71. Thus, SNBV has a very strong impact on purchase intention. SNBV was also found to have a significant positive effect on COOI (β = 0.50, p < 0.01, t = 3.10).

Table 6.6 Three-dimensional SNBV, with first- and second-order loadings

Measures and items	Loadings#	t-values	(R^2)
Brand awareness (0.96^b)			*0.93*
The name of the manufacturer of my favorite laptop is a well-known computer brand	0.537^a		0.29
Regarding laptops, I can immediately recall the brand	0.746***	5.21	0.56
I know this brand	0.797***	5.29	0.65
Value equity-product quality (0.61^b)			*0.37*
This personal (laptop) computer brand is of high quality	0.804^a		0.65
This personal (laptop) computer brand is highly reliable	0.709***	12.22	0.50
This computer brand manufacturer is very innovative	0.860***	10.95	0.74
This personal (laptop) computer brand is of high technological quality	0.942***	11.80	0.89
Product knowledge (0.55^b)			*0.30*
I am willing to understand more about this laptop brand			
After purchase and use of this personal (laptop) computer brand, the accumulated level of what I know about this brand is high	0.936^a		0.88
I am willing to know more about this personal (laptop) computer brand	0.597***	6.96	0.34
	0.848***	10.28	0.72

Chi-square $\chi^2 = 44.97$, df = 31, $p = 0.000$, RMR = 0.112, RMSEA = 0.061, 90% CI = 0.000, 0.098; CFI = 0.979, TLI = 0.970

[a]Unstandardized factor loadings fixed
[b]Standardized second-order loadings in brackets
R^2 Squared multiple correlations
Standardized first-order loadings
***$p < 0.001$ (two-tailed)

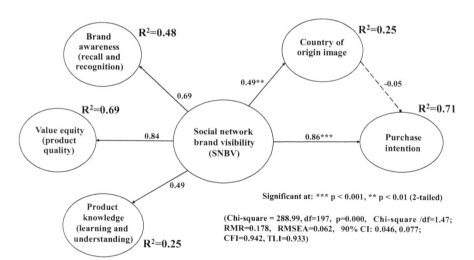

Fig. 6.5 Results of structural model with second-order loadings (model A)

Table 6.7 Results of hypothesis testing (model A)

Hypothesis	Hypothesized effect	Standardized estimate	t-value
H1	SNBV → Purchase intention	0.863***	3.89
	SNBV → Country of origin image	0.497**	3.10
	Country of origin image → Purchase intention	−0.047	0.44

$*p < 0.05$ (2-tailed); $**p < 0.01$ (2-tailed); $***p < 0.001$ (2-tailed)

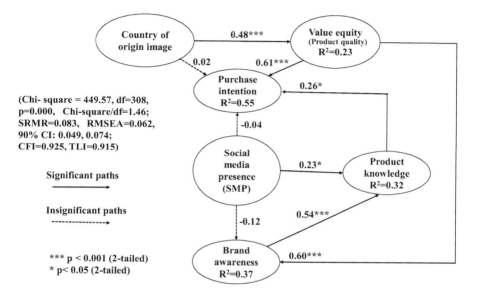

Fig. 6.6 Results of path analysis (structural model B)

No support was found for the effect of country of origin on purchase intention ($\beta = -0.05, p > 0.05$).

Evaluation of Conceptual Model B

To test the hypotheses that are based on conceptual model B (recall Fig. 6.4), we estimated the structural model using a maximum likelihood estimator in IBM SPSS/ AMOS 24 (Arbuckle 2016). Results yielded a relatively adequate fit of the model to the data (Chi-square $\chi 2 = 449.57$, df = 308, $p = 0.000$, $\chi 2/df = 1.46$; SRMR = 0.083, RMSEA = 0.062, 90% CI = 0.049, 0.074; CFI = 0.925, TLI = 0.915). An examination of the fit indices, including the ratio of chi-square to degree of freedom, yielded 1.46; a recommended ratio of chi-square to degree of freedom of less than three is considered acceptable (Schreiber et al. 2006). Standardized root mean square residual (SRMR) and root mean square error of approximation (RMSEA) were 0.083 and 0.062, respectively. Comparative fit index (CFI) and Tucker-Lewis index (TLI)

Table 6.8 Results of hypothesis testing (model B)

Hypothesis	Hypothesized effect	Standardized estimate	t-value
	SMP → Brand awareness	−0.117	1.28
	SMP → Purchase intention	−0.036	0.49
H2	SMP → Product knowledge	0.229*	2.27
H3	Brand awareness → Product knowledge	0.541***	3.41
H4	Product knowledge → Purchase intention	0.255*	2.50
H5	Value equity-product quality → Brand awareness	0.598***	5.56
H6	Value equity-product quality → Purchase intention	0.612***	4.96
	Country of origin → Value equity-product quality	0.484***	3.94
	Country of origin → Purchase intention	0.021	0.25

SMP Social media presence
*$p < 0.05$ (2-tailed); **$p < 0.01$ (2-tailed); ***$p < 0.001$ (2-tailed)

were 0.925 and 0.915, respectively. Values of CFI and TLI that were close to 0.95 or greater were considered indicative of a well-fitting model (Iacobucci 2010; Kline 2016). Figure 6.6 and Table 6.8 show the results of the structural model and the testing of the hypotheses.

The data support H2 and H4 at a 0.05 significance level. Hence, SMP has a significant effect on product knowledge ($\beta = 0.23$, $p < 0.05$, $t = 2.27$), while product knowledge has a significant influence on purchase intention ($\beta = 0.26$, $p < 0.05$, $t = 2.50$). We found support for hypotheses H3, H5, and H6 at a 0.001 significance level. Brand awareness has a significant influence on product knowledge ($\beta = 0.54$, $p < 0.001$, $t = 3.41$), while value equity in terms of product quality has a significant effect on brand awareness ($\beta = 0.60$, $p < 0.001$, $t = 5.56$). The hypothesized relationship between value equity-product quality and purchase intention ($\beta = 0.61$, $p < 0.001$, $t = 4.96$) was also supported by this study.

The squared multiple correlation R^2, which indicates the explanatory power of the model, showed that 55% of the variation in consumer purchase intention was explained by product knowledge, value equity-product quality, social media presence, and COOI. The extent to which COOI serves as an extrinsic cue of value equity-product quality was 23%, while variation in the endogenous variable brand awareness was as much as 37% of value equity-product quality and social media presence.

Discussion

In this chapter, we sought to provoke an agenda on the study of SNBV by reviewing the literature extensively on social media, proposing a definition of SNBV, and reporting findings of a preliminary study. We conceptualized SNBV as related to six key dimensions: social media presence, brand awareness, value equity, knowledge, social media marketing, and information exchange. We operationalized as well as examined a four-dimensional SNBV, and the results showed validity for a three-dimensional SNBV. Through an empirical demonstration, we showed that SNBV can be measured psychometrically, and we found that it is a significant driver of purchase intention. Additionally, we evaluated how the individual dimensions of SNBV can influence each other in a more "rich" nomological structure and found that COOI (an extrinsic cue for product evaluation) predicts value equity (in terms of product quality), which in turn predicts brand awareness.

Brand awareness was found to be a significant predictor of product knowledge, while product knowledge was also shown to be a significant predictor of purchase intention. The presence of a brand on social media is key in knowledge creation. This study was carried out using a hi-tech product (a personal computer); therefore, we propose that for technological firms to stay competitive in today's turbulent PC market, in view of short product lifecycles, increasing changes in preferences of consumers, and the globalization of the PC markets, those firms should engage consumers and potential customers through digital marketing by using social networking. E-commerce has created a paradigm shift in the way business is conducted and has been responsible for blurring national borders through the expansion of businesses into far-flung areas of the globe without the associated costs (Agarwal and Wu 2015).

The authors contend that social media has an important role to play in E-commerce. The E-commerce revolution has occurred not only in developed countries but has spread to emerging economies, such as Brazil, Russia, India, and China, and presents new opportunities to companies to do business on a global scale. Therefore, social networks provide important opportunities for businesses to interact and engage with their customers anywhere in the world. China's entry into the WTO and its impact on trade and global marketing has been the focus of previous studies (e.g., Agarwal and Wu 2004). China, with an Internet user population of approximately 650 million and censorship laws prohibiting its citizens from participating in the dominant SNS (e.g., Facebook), led to the creation of the country's own social platforms and networks (Spencer 2017), such as Tencent Weibo, QZone, Sina Weibo, and Wechat, which each have a user base that exceeds half a billion.

International and global brands have focused large shares of their digital marketing budgets on ads, content, and promotions across the "major" social networks, such as Facebook and Twitter. However, there is still a valuable opportunity to connect with Chinese consumers through Chinese SNS platforms. Internet users in China spend five to six more hours on average online per week than Americans and almost 90 min per day on social networks. It is estimated that 38% of Chinese consumers make product purchase decisions based on recommendations that they read on social networks. Therefore, businesses must engage these users wherever possible (Spencer 2017). Social media tools are critical in generating viral effects, consumer evangelism, and positive WOM advocacy (Järvinen et al. 2012). Thus, social media is an indispensable tool that companies must implement, especially if they want to stay competitive in today's global marketplace.

In line with these predictions, previous research (e.g., Shang et al. 2017) has suggested that Internet-based opinions that are generated and posted on social media channels influence consumers' purchasing decisions. Most authors (e.g., Karakaya and Barnes 2010) are of the view that reviews and opinion sites online lead consumers to make informed decisions based on other consumers' experiences with either the product, company, brand, or a customer service department. Although it is debatable whether the mere presence of brands on social media gives some level of awareness, this chapter has shown the positive role of awareness in enhancing product knowledge. The streaming of videos on YouTube, the use of online chats, and the pursuit of "likes" on Facebook, among other social networking and online activities, create the opportunity for both current and potential customers to learn about a brand as well as interact with it.

Social media provides product information and recommendations that enhance the consumer decision-making process and thus influence consumer purchase intentions. The causal relationship between COOI and product quality has been established by past research (e.g., Zeugner-Roth and Diamantopoulos 2010), while its link with purchase intention has also been studied extensively (Zeugner-Roth and Diamantopoulos 2010). This study provides further support for the role that COOI plays in product evaluation; it is a sign of quality perception that helps consumers make purchase decisions. Consumers' willingness to purchase a product depends not only on how they feel about the product but also on how much they know about it. Thus, quality products enhance brand awareness, which explains the saying "a quality product sells itself." Value, in terms of quality products, creates strong brand recognition and recall; thus, it helps in the processing of product-related information and knowledge.

Conclusion

Implications for Theory, Research, and Practice

One of our key contributions is the agenda for research on social network brand visibility. Specifically, we have developed a working definition for SNBV as well as conceptualized and operationalized the construct, although at an exploratory level. Therefore, this calls for more research on how visibility can be measured psychometrically. We have provided some direction to that effect in this chapter, which is available to scholars. Secondly, consumers' perceptions of the importance of either a product, a brand, or an organization on SNS and how they process information from these sites can influence their attitudes regarding their willingness to purchase. The willingness to purchase a technological product, such as a PC, is strongly influenced by how much consumers know about the product and what they feel are important product quality features and/or attributes from where the product originates.

Hence, businesses must look beyond their borders and develop marketing and promotional programs for global markets. The optimal avenue for that is social media marketing and promotion due to its advantages over traditional offline media. The popularity of Pokémon Go provided an excellent opportunity to marketers (Wu 2017). Indeed some digital content and social media marketing connoisseurs argue that Pokémon Go is a social network in disguise with its origin as the first mobile augmented reality (AR) social media platform. It is a viable channel as a social media platform, which provides additional opportunity for marketers to monetize and drive their businesses through the ever popular (if somewhat ailing) mobile phenomenon (Simpson 2016).

Another important managerial implication of this study is that, although much has been said about the negative impact of the presence of firms on the Internet and social media, there are also numerous opportunities for building brand awareness. The visibility of products and services on SNS by organizations and firms is an effective means of reaching out to current and potential customers on a global scale. As a paradigm shift, firms need to plan, develop, and implement either a proactive social media strategy or digital marketing strategy to fully benefit from such media. Both the tracking of social media to determine how a formulated strategy is working vis-à-vis the competition and monitoring competitor brands are critical to global competitiveness (Reyneke et al. 2011). Regarding branding, social media provides an excellent opportunity to interact with and engage customers, and it provides opportunities for marketers and brand managers to cooperate with consumers to increase brand visibility (Smith et al. 2012).

Thus, in the formulation of marketing strategies for innovative and techno-oriented products, the use of SNS to reach out to market segments and to provide product-related information is key in today's highly competitive global market. Global technological companies involved in the manufacture, sale, and promotion of personal computers (PCs), including laptops, can enhance their brand awareness by focusing on innovative products of high quality. As the old saying goes, "Great products sell themselves." The competitive nature of the PC market means that competitiveness and profitability can only be sustained through value creation and consumer engagement. Social media is an important medium for delivering value, engaging consumers, and providing product/service-related knowledge. Consumers with a significant amount of product knowledge are more likely to make purchase decisions based on this knowledge rather than from where a product originates; hence, a combination of high online social network brand visibility and a favorable COOI of a brand can enhance purchase intentions.

Limitations and Future Research

This study is not without limitations. Firstly, it used data from a cross-sectional survey that was limited to electronic products, such as personal computers. Therefore, the results cannot be generalized, and it is suggested that further research involving multiple products, contexts, and consumer segments should be used. Secondly, this study solicited feedback from college students (mostly millennials) who are not usually representative of the population in terms of demographics, such as age and income; therefore, we advise that further studies use a more representative sample (including generations x and y and baby boomers). Thirdly, longitudinal studies that aim to capture consumers' changing attitudes, perceptions, and buying intentions over a period may provide valuable findings for the industry and scholars and are thus recommended. Fourthly, the scope of our study is limited to only one type of social media: SNS. According to Duane and O'Reilly (2012), social media are divided among four major domains: content communities, collaborative projects, micro-blogs, and SNS. As such, future research should consider other social media domains when investigating social network brand visibility.

Appendix 1

Six-dimensional conceptualization of SNBV

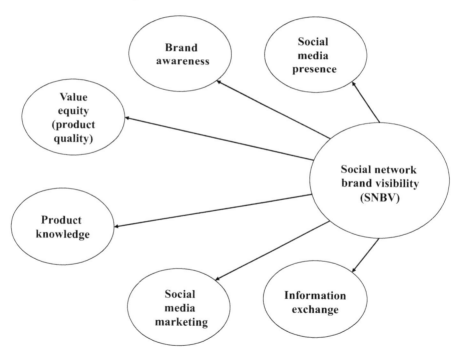

Appendix 2

Standardized parameter estimates (second-order loadings)

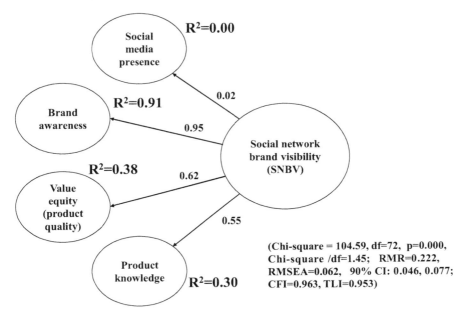

(Chi-square = 104.59, df=72, p=0.000,
Chi-square /df=1.45;   RMR=0.222,
RMSEA=0.062,   90% CI: 0.046, 0.077;
CFI=0.963, TLI=0.953)

Appendix 3

Single-phase data collection procedure for developing measures (Source: Adapted from Churchill 1979:66)

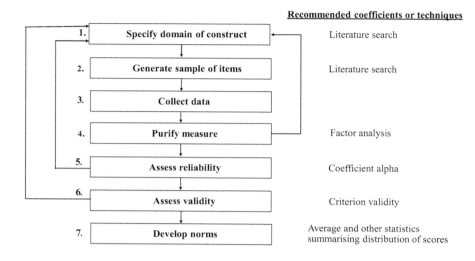

		Recommended coefficients or techniques
1.	Specify domain of construct	Literature search
2.	Generate sample of items	Literature search
3.	Collect data	
4.	Purify measure	Factor analysis
5.	Assess reliability	Coefficient alpha
6.	Assess validity	Criterion validity
7.	Develop norms	Average and other statistics summarising distribution of scores

References

Aaker, D.A. 1991. *Managing brand equity.* New York: The Free Press.
———. 1996. Measuring brand equity across products and markets. *California Management Review* 38 (3): 102–120.
Agarwal, J., and T. Wu. 2004. China's entry to WTO: Global marketing issues, impact, and implications for China. *International Marketing Review* 21 (3): 279–300.
———. 2015. Factors influencing growth potential of E-commerce in emerging economies: An institution-based N-OLI framework. *Thunderbird International Business Review* 57 (3): 197–215.
Agnihotri, R., R. Dingus, M.Y. Hu, and M.T. Krush. 2016. Social media: Influencing customer satisfaction in B2B sales. *Industrial Marketing Management* 53: 172–180.
Arbuckle, J.L. 2016. IBM SPSS AMOS 24.0, Chicago.
Asano, E. 2017. How much time do people spend on social media? http://www.socialmediatoday.com/marketing/how-much-time-do-people-spend-social-media-infographic. Accessed 30 May 2017.
Botha, E., M. Farshid, and L. Pitt. 2011. How sociable? An exploratory study of university brand visibility in social media. *South African Journal of Business Management* 42 (2): 43–51.
Bredahl, L. 2003. Cue utilization and quality perception with regard to branded beef. *Food Quality and Preference* 15: 65–75.
Brown, J., A.J. Broderick, and N. Lee. 2007. Word of mouth communication within online communities: Conceptualizing the online social network. *Journal of Interactive Marketing* 21 (3): 2–20.
Buil, I., L. de Chernatony, and E. Martinez. 2013. Examining the role of advertising and sales promotions in brand equity creation. *Journal of Business Research* 66 (1): 115–122.
Callarisa, L., J.S. García, J. Cardiff, and A. Roshchina. 2012. Harnessing social media platforms to measure customer-based hotel brand equity. *Tourism Management Perspectives* 4: 73–79.

Capgemini, 2014. Social banking: Leveraging social media to enhance customer engagement. https://www.capgemini.com/resource-file-access/resource/pdf/social_banking_leveraging_ social_media_to_enhance_customer_engagement.pdf Accessed 15 May 2017.

Capitello, R., L. Agnoli, D. Begalli, and S. Codurri. 2014. Social media strategies and corporate brand visibility in the wine industry: Lessons from an Italian case study. *EuroMed Journal of Business* 9 (2): 129–148.

Cawsey, T., and J. Rowley. 2016. Social media brand building strategies in B2B companies. *Marketing Intelligence & Planning* 34 (6): 754–776.

Chang, C.M., and M.H. Hsu. 2016. Understanding the determinants of users' subjective well-being in social networking sites: An integration of social capital theory and social presence theory. *Behaviour & Information Technology*: 1–10.

Chatterjee, P. 2001. Online reviews: Do consumers use them? *Advances in Consumer Research* 28: 129–133.

Chen, C.W. 2011. Integrated marketing communications and new product performance in international markets. *Journal of Global Marketing* 24 (5): 397–416.

Chua, A.Y., and S. Banerjee. 2013. Customer knowledge management via social media: The case of Starbucks. *Journal of Knowledge Management* 17 (2): 237–249.

Churchill, G.A., Jr. 1979. A paradigm for developing better measures of marketing constructs. *Journal of Marketing Research* 16: 64–73.

Davenport, T.H., and L. Prusak. 1998. *Working knowledge*. Boston: Harvard Business School Press.

Davis, R., I. Piven, and M. Breazeale. 2014. Conceptualizing the brand in social media community: The five sources model. *Journal of Retailing and Consumer Services* 21 (4): 468–481.

Duane, A.M. O'Reilly, P. 2012. A conceptual stages of growth model for managing an organization's social media business profile (SMBP), Proceedings of the 33rd International Conference on Information Systems, Orlando 2012.

Fan, W., and Z. Yan. 2010. Factors affecting response rates of the web survey: A systematic review. *Computers in Human Behavior* 26 (2): 132–139.

Fornell, C., and D.F. Larcker. 1981. Evaluating structural equation models with unobservable variables and measurement error. *Journal of Marketing Research* 18 (1): 39–50.

Futurebrand. 2014. Made in: the value of origin for future brands. http://www.futurebrand.com/ images/uploads/studies/cbi/MADE_IN_Final_HR.pdf. Accessed 7 Jul 2014.

Genpact. 2014. How Hi-Tech companies can optimize product support to enhance customer satisfaction and increase revenue. White paper, Intelligent enterprise powered by process. http:// www.genpact.com/docs. Accessed 10 July 2014.

Gil de Zúñiga, H., N. Jung, and S. Valenzuela. 2012. Social media use for news and individuals' social capital, civic engagement and political participation. *Journal of Computer-Mediated Communication* 17 (3): 319–336.

Goswami, A., V. Bharathi, R. Raman, A.V. Kulkarni, S. Joseph, and B. Kelkar. 2013. Synergies between social media features and user engagement to enhance online brand visibility-A conceptual model. *International Journal of Engineering and Technology* 5 (3): 2705–2718.

Hair, J.F., W.C. Black, B.J. Babin, and R.E. Anderson. 2009. *Multivariate data analysis*. 7th ed. New Jersey: Prentice-Hall.

Hoffman, D.L., and M. Fodor. 2010. Can you measure the ROI of your social media marketing? *MIT Sloan Management Review* 52 (1): 41.

Iacobucci, D. 2010. Structural equations modeling: Fit indices, sample size and advanced issues. *Journal of Consumer Psychology* 20 (1): 90–98.

Järvinen, J., A. Tollinen, H. Karjaluoto, and C. Jayawardhena. 2012. Digital and social media marketing usage in B2B industrial section. *The Marketing Management Journal* 22 (2): 102–117.

Kaplan, A.M. 2012. If you love something, let it go mobile: Mobile marketing and mobile social media 4 × 4. *Business Horizons* 55 (2): 129–139.

Kaplan, A.M., and M. Haenlein. 2010. Users of the world, unite! The challenges and opportunities of social media. *Business Horizons* 53 (1): 59–68.

Karakaya, F., and N.G. Barnes. 2010. Impact of online reviews of customer care experience on brand or company selection. *Journal of Consumer Marketing* 27 (5): 447–457.

Keller, K.L. 2008. *Strategic branding management: Building, measuring, and managing brand equity.* 3rd ed. Upper Saddle River: Prentice Hall.

Keller, K.L., and D.R. Lehman. 2003. How do brands create value? *Marketing Management* 12 (3): 27–31.

Kim, B., and Y. Kim. 2017. College students' social media use and communication network heterogeneity: Implications for social capital and subjective well-being. *Computers in Human Behavior* 73: 620–628.

Kim, A.J., and E. Ko. 2012. Do social media marketing activities enhance customer equity? An empirical study of luxury fashion brand. *Journal of Business Research* 65 (10): 1480–1486.

Kline, R.B. 2016. *Principles and practice of structural equation modeling.* 4th ed. New York: The Guilford Press.

Lee, M., and S. Youn. 2009. Electronic word of mouth: How eWOM platforms influence consumer product judgment. *International Journal of Advertising* 28 (3): 473–499.

Lee, J., D. Park, and I. Han. 2008. The effect of negative online consumer review on product attitude: An information processing view. *Electronic Commerce Research and Applications* 7: 341–352.

Lichtenstein, D.R., N.M. Ridgway, and R.G. Netemeyer. 1993. Price perceptions and consumer shopping behavior: A field study. *Journal of Marketing Research* 30: 234–245.

Lin, L.-Y., and C.-S. Chen. 2006. The influence of the country-of-origin image, product knowledge and product involvement on consumer purchase decisions: An empirical study of insurance and catering services in Taiwan. *Journal of Consumer Marketing* 23 (5): 248–265.

Liu, Y., and L.J. Shrum. 2009. A dual-process model of interactivity effects. *Journal of Advertising* 38 (2): 53–68.

Macdonald, E.K., and B.M. Sharp. 2000. Brand awareness effects on consumer decision making for a common, repeat purchase product: A replication. *Journal of Business Research* 48 (1): 5–15.

Malhotra, N.K., S.S. Kim, and A. Patil. 2006. Common method variance in IS research: A comparison of alternative approaches and a reanalysis of past research. *Management Science* 52 (12): 1865–1883.

Mangold, W.G., and D.J. Faulds. 2009. Social media: The new hybrid element of the promotion mix. *Business Horizons* 52 (4): 357–365.

Marks, L.J., and Olson, J.C. 1981. Toward a cognitive structure conceptualization of product familiarity. Advances in Consumer Behavior, 145–150.

Martin, I.M., and S. Eroglu. 1993. Measuring a multi-dimensional construct: Country image. *Journal of Business Research* 28 (3): 119–210.

McCarthy, J., J. Rowley, C. Jane Ashworth, and E. Pioch. 2014. Managing brand presence through social media: The case of UK football clubs. *Internet Research* 24 (2): 181–204.

Michaelidou, N., N.T. Siamagka, and G. Christodoulides. 2011. Usage, barriers and measurement of social media marketing: An exploratory investigation of small and medium B2B brands. *Industrial Marketing Management* 40 (7): 1153–1159.

Minasians, C. 2017. Where are Apple products made? How much does the iPhone cost to make? Macworld. http://www.macworld.co.uk/feature/apple/where-are-apple-products-made-how-much-does-iphone-cost-make-india-3633832/. Accessed 28 June 2017.

Nonaka, I., and H. Takeuchi. 1995. *The knowledge creating company: How Japanese companies create the dynamics of innovation.* New York: Oxford University Press.

Nunnally, J.C. 1978. *Psychometric theory.* 2nd ed. New York: McGraw-Hill.

Papanagiotou, P., I. Tzimitra-Kalogianni, and K. Melfou. 2013. Consumers' expected quality and intention to purchase high quality pork meat. *Meat Science* 93: 449–454.

Pharr, J.M. 2005. Synthesizing country-of-origin research from the last decade: Is the concept still salient in an era of global brands? *Journal of Marketing Theory and Practice* 13: 34–45.

Phua, J., S.V. Jin, and J.J. Kim. 2017. Gratifications of using Facebook, Twitter, Instagram, or Snapchat to follow brands: The moderating effect of social comparison, trust, tie strength, and network homophily on brand identification, brand engagement, brand commitment, and membership intention. *Telematics and Informatics* 34 (1): 412–424.

Podsakoff, P.M., S.B. MacKenzie, and N.P. Podsakoff. 2003. Common method biases in behavioral research: A critical review of literature and recommended remedies. *Journal of Applied Psychology* 88 (5): 879–903.

Qualman, E. 2013. *Socialnomics: How social media transforms the way we live and do business*. Hoboken: Wiley.

Reyneke, M., L. Pitt, and P.R. Berthon. 2011. Luxury wine brand visibility in social media: An exploratory study. *International Journal of Wine Business Research* 23 (1): 21–35.

Rezvani, S., G. Shenyari, G.J. Dehkordi, M. Salehi, N. Nahid, and N. Soleimani. 2012. Country of origin: A study over perspective of intrinsic and extrinsic cues on consumers' purchase decision. *Business Management Dynamics* 1 (11): 68–75.

Rubio, N., J. Oubina, and N. Villasenor. 2014. Brand awareness-brand quality inference and consumer's risk perception in store brands of food products. *Food Quality and Preference* 32: 289–298.

Schiffman, L.G., L.L. Kanuk, and H. Hansen. 2012. *Consumer behaviour: A European outlook*. 2nd ed. Upper Saddle River: Prentice Hall.

Schreiber, J.B., A. Nora, F.K. Stage, E.A. Barlow, and J.A. King. 2006. Reporting structural equation modeling and confirmatory factor analysis: A review. *The Journal of Educational Research* 99 (6): 323–338.

Selnes, F., and K. Grønhaug. 1986. Subjective and objective measures of product knowledge contrasted. In *NA – advances in consumer research*, ed. Richard J. Lutz, vol. 13, 67–71. Provo: Association for Consumer Research.

Shang, S.S., Y.L. Wu, and Y.J. Sie. 2017. Generating consumer resonance for purchase intention on social network sites. *Computers in Human Behavior* 69: 18–28.

Simpson, P. 2016. Why Pokémon Go is a social network in disguise. http://www.dmnews.com/social-media/why-pokemon-go-is-a-social-network-in-disguise/article/515003/. Accessed 24 Aug 2017.

Smith, A.N., E. Fischer, and E.C. Yongjian. 2012. How does brand-related user-generated content differ across YouTube, Facebook, and Twitter? *Journal of Interactive Marketing* 26 (2): 102–113.

Spencer, J. 2017. Chinese social media statistics and trends infographic. https://makeawebsitehub.com/chinese-social-media-statistics/. Accessed 28 June 2017.

Steenkamp, J.-B.E.M. 1990. Conceptual model of the quality perception process. *Journal of Business Research* 21: 309–333.

Taylor, S.A., and T.L. Baker. 1994. An assessment of the relationship between service quality and customer satisfaction in the formation of consumers' purchase intentions. *Journal of Retailing* 70 (2): 163–178.

Veale, R., and P. Quester. 2009. Do consumer expectations match experience? Predicting the influence of price and country of origin on perceptions of quality. *International Business Review* 18: 134–144.

Vianna, K.A., J.M.C. de Mesquita, M.R.S. Linhares, and P.C.G. Moreira. 2016. The relationship between viral marketing, purchase intention, and brand visibility: Study with Brazilian customers. In *Rediscovering the essentiality of marketing. Developments in marketing science: Proceedings of the academy of marketing science*, ed. L. Petruzzellis and R. Winer. Cham: Springer.

Wang, X., and Z. Yang. 2008. Does country-of-origin matter in the relationship between brand personality and purchase intention in emerging economies? Evidence from China's auto industry. *International Marketing Review* 25 (4): 458–474.

Wang, X., C. Yu, and Y. Wei. 2012. Social media peer communication and impacts on purchase intentions: A consumer socialization framework. *Journal of Interactive Marketing* 26 (4): 198–208.

Wong, H.Y., and B. Merrilees. 2008. Determinants of SME international marketing communications. *Journal of Global Marketing* 21 (4): 293–305.

Wu, T. 2017. Pokémon Go: Marketing implications for mobile video game. In *Computing in Smart Toys. International Series on Computer Entertainment and Media Technology*, ed. J. Tang and P. Hung, 7–20. Cham: Springer.

Yang, A., and M. Kent. 2014. Social media and organizational visibility: A sample of fortune 500 corporations. *Public Relations Review* 40 (3): 562–564.

Zeugner-Roth, K.P., and A. Diamantopoulos. 2010. Advancing the country image construct: Reply to Samiee's (2009) commentary. *Journal of Business Research* 63 (4): 446–449.

Zhuang, W., M.K. Hsu, K.L. Brewer, and Q. Xiao. 2013. Paradoxes of social networking sites: An empirical analysis. *Management Research Review* 36 (1): 33–49.

Chapter 7
Reconfiguring the Marketing Mix to Counter the Counterfeits in the Global Arena

Karminder Ghuman and Hemant Merchant

Abstract Different strategies have been proposed to counter the global trade in counterfeits, but there is a dearth of the conceptual framework, which coherently organizes the varied anti-counterfeit interventions. In the present article, we employ the construct of marketing mix and extend it further to organize various anti-counterfeiting tactics into a holistic framework. We attempt to answer: how – and to what extent – can the companies reconfigure their marketing mix so that it is tough for the counterfeiters to make and sell the inexpensive replications of their original creations? The present article makes a contribution by reconfiguring the traditional marketing mix for bringing together disparate anti-counterfeiting tactics at the center stage of designing the marketing program.

Introduction

The global trade in counterfeits was estimated at $200 billion in 2005 and USD 250 billion in 2007 (OECD 2009), and it further increased to USD 461 billion in 2013 (OECD/EUIPO 2016). The sheer magnitude and alarming growth have turned it into a wicked problem for corporates as well as the governments around the world. As the majority of efforts by state authorities to curb the trade in counterfeits have not worked as well as expected, the companies cannot afford to remain passive and expect other agencies to resolve the problem for them. In this context, we propose that in addition to the macro-level institutional interventions by governments and international institutions like the World Intellectual Property Organization (WIPO), Interpol, and the World Customs Organization (WCO), the companies need to

K. Ghuman (✉)
LM Thapar School of Management, Thapar University, Patiala, India
e-mail: karminder@thapar.edu

H. Merchant
University of South Florida in St. Petersburg, St. Petersburg, FL, USA

© Springer International Publishing AG, part of Springer Nature 2018
J. Agarwal, T. Wu (eds.), *Emerging Issues in Global Marketing*,
https://doi.org/10.1007/978-3-319-74129-1_7

179

augment further their efforts to lessen the extent of counterfeiting. By employing the framework of marketing mix, we pose a research question, "How and to what extent can the companies reconfigure their marketing-mix, so that it's tough for the counterfeiters to make and sell inexpensive replications of their original creations?"

For the last four decades, several researchers have proposed a multitude of anti-counterfeiting actions; however, very little empirical research has been done to discover what types of tactics companies employ to deter pirates (Chaudhry et al. 2005). Academic literature on counterfeiting is also fragmented, diverse, and often incoherent, calling for synthesizing this extant knowledge (Cesareo 2015). Despite the relative importance, little attention has been paid to the management of counterfeiting; it is a highly under-researched topic, which needs to be tackled within a general, consistent, and synergistic package of measures (Bosworth and Yang 2006). Companies too are investing considerable resources to implement adequate brand and product protection strategies, but their know-how is mostly limited to their own experience and, at best, to some informal exchange among practitioners at brand protection conferences (Staake and Fleisch 2008).

The present study attempts to make a contribution by proposing an extended marketing mix that can be employed to organize various anti-counterfeiting strategies under a single framework. For achieving that, an extensive review of best practices for combating counterfeiting was undertaken, and subsequently they were categorized under the framework of marketing mix. The rationale for employing marketing mix is that it encapsulates all the tactical marketing decisions that the firm employs to pursue its marketing objectives in the target market (Kotler 2000).

Theoretical Background

The pirated goods are products that are exact copies of the original and are typically limited to technology categories (Wilcox et al. 2009). Counterfeits are illegal, low-priced, and often lower-quality replicas of products that typically possess high brand value (Lai and Zaichkowsky 1999). According to the Trade-Related Aspects of Intellectual Property Rights (TRIPS) Agreement, "'counterfeit trademark goods' mean any goods, including packaging, bearing without authorization a trademark that is identical to the trademark validly registered in respect of such goods or that cannot be distinguished in its essential aspects from such a trademark, which thereby infringes the rights of the owner of the trademark in question under the law of the country of importation" (WTO 1994). For this study, counterfeit goods are defined as illegitimately manufactured or adulterated goods, replica or imitation items, pass-offs, look-alikes, and fake products.

Nearly four decades ago, Kaikati and LaGarce (1980) outlined the fundamentals concerning the counterfeit trade by differentiating outright piracy, imitation, and wholesale piracy and international laws protecting the trademarks. Harvey (1987) classified counterfeits as (a) true counterfeit products (closely resemble the original and use the same brand name), (b) look-alikes (duplicates of the original, but bear a different name), (c) reproductions (not exact copies), and unconvincing imitations. From the consumer's awareness perspective, Grossman and Shapiro (1988) further categorized counterfeits into deceptive (consumers unaware that they are buying a counterfeit good) and nondeceptive (consumers aware that the product they are buying is a counterfeit) counterfeits, which are especially prevalent in luxury brand markets (Nia and Zaichkowsky 2000).

The counterfeit producers are not a homogeneous lot. Thorsten et al. (2012) in an empirical study identified five different groups: disaggregators, imitators, fraudsters, desperados, and smugglers. These groups are different from one another in their production capabilities, visual and functional quality, and the accompanying risk (described in detail in Table 7.1).

Table 7.1 Profile of different groups of counterfeit producers

	Disaggregators	Imitators	Fraudster	Desperados	Smugglers
Capabilities	Manufacturing network or manufacturing capability	Substantial engineering skills	A little production capability	Capability to mask forbidden actions	Run a network of criminals
	Agility to promptly comprehend latest trends	Higher-order production capability			Money laundering
					Isolating the stages in distribution chain
Business model	Serve customers with imitated goods reflecting wealth and status	Brand imitation at low prices	Deceiving customers with brand imitations	Misleading customers with brand imitation of dangerous products	Brand imitation and evasion of taxes
Strategic focus	Agility	Competitive advantage	Profit orientation	Profit maximization with no ethical standards	Low production costs
	Products with high demand	Entrepreneurship	Opportunism		Significant power in criminal network
	Exploiting short-term benefits	Learning and growth			Established structures
Typical products	Clothing, accessories, watches, jewelry	Clothing, accessories, FMCGs	Perfume, cosmetics	Pharmaceuticals	Cigarettes

Source: Thorsten et al. (2012)

Consumer Behavior

Consumers' willingness to purchase either genuine or counterfeit brands depends on the attribution of a product (Maldonado and Hume 2005). It was found that a significant proportion of adult consumers would select fake garments over the original labels when there are price advantages (Bloch et al. 1993). Price has often been found to be among the most important factors in the purchase of pirated brands (Cordell et al. 1996), especially counterfeit luxury goods, primarily to optimize resources (Perez et al. 2010).

Customers' desire for counterfeit brands is based on the extent to which such brands fulfill the social goals; by understanding these social goals, it is possible to influence people's counterfeit consumption behaviors (Wilcox et al. 2009). Desires for luxury brands may be driven by social motives such as a desire to portray a particular social class, communicate the desired self-image, or provide self-concept reinforcement, visible proof that the consumer can afford higher prices (Nia and Zaichkowsky 2000).

Consumers tend to attribute counterfeits with greater risk and that such risk may mediate consumers' evaluations and feelings toward fake purchases (Bamossy and Scammon 1985; Chakraborty et al. 1996). Integrity, health, and low-performance risks were found to be the most significant deterrents contributing toward lessening the consumers' buying intentions for counterfeits (Hamelin et al. 2013). Authentic companies strive to upgrade the quality and build company stores after counterfeiters demonstrate the value of disentangling asymmetric information for consumers (Qian 2008).

By stressing upon the inferior quality of fake brands, their demand can be reduced (Chakraborty et al. 1997). The manner in which advertising projects luxury brand's meaning can affect consumers' desire for counterfeit versions of the brand (Wilcox et al. 2009). Even the low-income consumers are likely to switch purchase intention toward original versions of the counterfeit products if their level of awareness is increased through appropriate consumer education and information programs (Maldonado and Hume 2005; Grossman and Shapiro 1988; Nia and Zaichkowsky 2000). More precisely, the degree of consumer consciousness regarding safety (i.e., concerns about risk-security levels related to health, law, and durability) has been found to influence attitudes toward purchasing counterfeit products (Vitell et al. 2001).

To face price rivalry and asymmetric information, authentic producers can use quality differentiation, price, self-enforcement, vertical integration of downstream retail stores, signaling, non-price signals such as holograms, and enforcement devices as strategic instruments to combat counterfeits (Qian 2014). Money-back guarantees also serve as an effective signal for quality (Moorthy and Srinivasan 1995).

Thus, it is evident from the review of literature that a myriad of tactics, such as the product category, brand positioning, and promotional cues, can play a major role in countering the counterfeits (Shavitt et al. 1992). But, at the same time, it has been observed that marketing strategies against counterfeits are still not fully understood (Qian 2014).

Description of the Problem

Geographical Spread

The divide exists between the approaches of developed and developing nations toward intellectual property (IP) rights due to their diverse national interests, which stem from their different levels of economic development (Jackson et al. 2002). Although the WTO's TRIPS Agreement aims to narrow the gap on how IP rights are protected in different countries and to bring them under common international rules, the extent of protection and enforcement of rights significantly varies around the world (WTO).

The problem of counterfeiting is not only confined to the developing and underdeveloped countries, but more than €40 million counterfeit products (original version worth €1 billion) were also detained at the EU external border in 2012 (Basheer and Loizides 2014). Twenty-two thousand eight hundred forty-eight consignments of pirated goods were seized in the USA in the year 2012 (Youill 2016). The Japan Patent Office (JPO) also reported that 21.9% Japanese companies suffered losses due to counterfeiting in the FY 2014. They suffered the highest percentage of damages due to counterfeiting in China followed by the Republic of Korea and the six ASEAN economies and Taiwan. The maximum number of violations was for trademarks (56.4%), next came patents and utility models (34.0%), designs (30.0%), and copyright works (17.4%).

As a result, companies are losing revenue on account of substitution effects by illicit goods and constraints on product pricing (Montoro-Pons and Cuadrado-Garcia 2006). Large numbers of low-cost counterfeits reduce the perceived exclusiveness of luxury goods (Wilke and Zaichkowsky 1999). The unintended IP leakage can affect not only the company's reputation and profitability; but it can also create local or global competitors (Shih and Wang 2013). Preventive measures also lead to considerable enforcement costs, and in cases of counterfeit occurrence, there is a threat of liability claims, customer confusion, and brand dilution (Feinberg and Rousslang 1990; Liebowitz 2005).

Counterfeiting is not just an intellectual property problem; it has also become a criminal issue. Groups like the Maa and Camorra in Europe and the Americas and the Triads and Yakuza in Asia involved in crimes varying from drug and human trafficking to extortion and money laundering have diversified into the illicit trade in counterfeit goods at the same time (OECD 2007; UNICRI 2008). UNODC's research report (2013) has recognized the strategic and operational criminal link between counterfeiting and drug trafficking.

Drivers of Counterfeiting

Wee et al. (1995) identified product variables (image, design, and perceived quality) as the primary drivers influencing consumers' purchase intention toward counterfeit goods. Brand visibility is also an important decisional factor; brands that are globally more visible are concomitantly more susceptible to counterfeiting (Bian and Veloutsou 2007). The various drivers contributing to the trade of counterfeits are:

1. A huge gap in the price of original and the fake product. Consumers hold positive beliefs and expectations that counterfeits are less expensive than the legitimate product (Bamossy and Scammon 1985).
2. Widening income disparities and growing aspirations. It has been observed that younger males of lower income are slightly more likely to be complicit (Stumpf and Chaudhry 2010).
3. Not so strong regulatory and implementation mechanisms in a good number of countries. Imitating proven high-tech know-how from foreign companies, with a limited chance of punishment, is not only the most profitable but also the least risky strategy for many businesses (Schotter and Teagarden 2014).
4. High-technology production, packaging, and printing equipment being easily available to counterfeiters. With luxury brand marketers outsourcing their manufacturing, some factories may add a "ghost shift" to produce counterfeits, which they can sell at higher margins (Phillips 2005).

Although the counterfeits thus produced continue to be typically constructed of inferior materials, they are often made with the same designs, molds, and specifications as the genuine brands (Parloff 2006). Together these factors are creating a big market for the look-alike of the expensive original products. Select reasons for the persistence of this problem are as follows (Fig. 7.1):

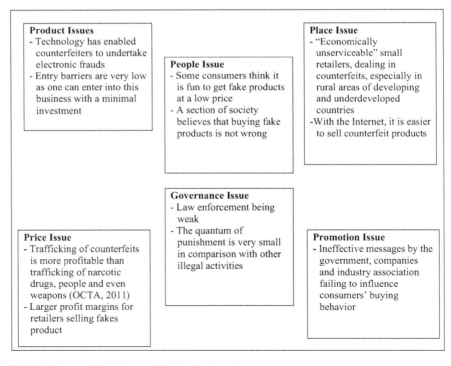

Product Issues
- Technology has enabled counterfeiters to undertake electronic frauds
- Entry barriers are very low as one can enter into this business with a minimal investment

People Issue
- Some consumers think it is fun to get fake products at a low price
- A section of society believes that buying fake products is not wrong

Place Issue
- "Economically unserviceable" small retailers, dealing in counterfeits, especially in rural areas of developing and underdeveloped countries
- With the Internet, it is easier to sell counterfeit products

Governance Issue
- Law enforcement being weak
- The quantum of punishment is very small in comparison with other illegal activities

Price Issue
- Trafficking of counterfeits is more profitable than trafficking of narcotic drugs, people and even weapons (OCTA, 2011)
- Larger profit margins for retailers selling fakes product

Promotion Issue
- Ineffective messages by the government, companies and industry association failing to influence consumers' buying behavior

Fig. 7.1 Counterfeiting issues affecting the brand owners

Consumers too play a vital role in this conundrum either on account of their ignorance or willingness to buy counterfeits. The varied motivations underlying the purchase of counterfeits can be summed up as follows (Chaudhry and Stumpf 2009):

(a) *The consumer thinks that the counterfeit is as good as the legitimate product.*
(b) *The consumer cannot afford a genuine product.*
(c) *The consumers do not believe that it is illegal or immoral to buy counterfeits.*
(d) *The fake product is easy to obtain.*
(e) *The consumers do not like the big organizations that make genuine products.*

In an empirical study of consumer motivation regarding counterfeit goods carried out in seven major countries, the underlying motivations for each counterfeit goods category were found to be different. What was important for Americans was not that important for Russians, Indians, or Brazilians (Chaudhry and Stumpf 2009). In the same study, significant variations were also found across the different product categories; what was perceived as important for bootlegging was not viewed as important for drug peddling. Consumers were found to vary widely even in their beliefs regarding the morality of counterfeit consumption (Hoe et al. 2003; Tom et al. 1998).

E-Commerce and Counterfeiting

E-commerce faces significant deception issues because sellers and buyers have low levels of familiarity with one another, reside in different locations, and normally interact only in a single commercial transaction (Utz et al. 2009). Counterfeiters take full advantage of the online ecosystem to spread their business. Independent websites, online marketplaces, and social media sites are being extensively used by counterfeiters as they offer an easy and cheap method for selling fake goods.

The spatial and temporal separation of online stores enforces information asymmetry as the buyers lack exact information about the product until it is delivered (Pavlou et al. 2007). Product misrepresentation is one of the most common forms of reported online deception (Pavlou Gefen 2005). Product presentation manipulation in the form of exaggerating or overstating product features becomes possible because the majority of retail websites currently convey product information through text and pictures (Lightner and Eastman 2002). The Internet intensifies the risk of counterfeiting because the virtual product presentation does not allow physical inspection of the products (Mavlanova and Benbunan-Fich 2010, 2011). Thus, buyers in the online environments find it difficult to evaluate whether the offered products meet their quality expectations (Ba and Pavlou 2002).

As e-commerce channels present an opportunity to the counterfeiters to anonymously move across the jurisdictions, it has led to the growth of counterfeit sales online. The Japan Patent Office in a survey in 2015 found out that 62.3% of the organizations that suffered from the violation of their intellectual property rights were widely affected by counterfeits sold through the Internet.

WTO and Regulatory Framework

The WTO Agreement on Trade-Related Aspects of Intellectual Property Rights (TRIPS), reached during the Uruguay Round, introduced IP regulations into the multilateral trading system. Membership of WTO requires compliance with agreement on TRIPS and calls for adherence to some minimum standards of sanctions and enforcement with certain flexibilities. It establishes minimum levels of protection that each government has to provide to the IP of the other WTO members. It aims at narrowing down the gaps in the manner in which IP rights are protected in different countries of the world and to bring them under common international rules. Despite controversy regarding the creation of the WTO, many of its provisions are regarded as instrumental to the curtailment of counterfeiting (Shultz II and Saporito 1996). The IPR protection system of the developed countries closely resembled TRIPS Agreement obligations even before its implementation, but the developing countries tightened and strengthened their domestic IPR protection regimes after signing the agreement (Cardwell and Ghazalian 2012).

Shadlen et al. (2005) found external and international pressures to be significant determinants of IPR, but the government's effectiveness was insignificant. As IPRs are often associated with the products of intellectual capital, high rate of education was found to have a positive correlation with patent protection (Ginarte and Park 1997). Cardwell and Ghazalian (2012) observed that domestic factors like education, governance, and R&D intensity play important roles in generating domestic IP and were important determinants of IPR protection and the effects of the TRIPS Agreement vary across regions.

Therefore, the legal system cannot be singularly held responsible for weaker enforcement of IPRs; IPRs can be enforced by changing the whole IP institutional environment over time (Cao 2014). Rightly pointed out by Stan Hart of S. G. Hart & Associates, a brand protection consultancy company: "One has to use multiple protective techniques, and then keep changing them" (Makely 2005). Currently, prevalent protection practices derived from the developed countries are not as effective to protect against the IP violations (Schotter and Teagarden 2014). Even the executives' perceptions of the motives of pirates and purchasers as well as solutions that senior managers deemed most useful differ by country (Chaudhry and Stumpf 2008). There is no one-size-fits-all strategy; executives need to tailor their anticounterfeiting actions to the piracy and consumer demand dynamics of different country markets.

It is evident from the discussion so far that the trade in counterfeit products is affected by multiple constituents that pose different challenges (Fig. 7.2). The decision-makers in organizations must perceive the problem in the context of institutions that their programs are likely to be implemented before initiating an anticounterfeiting program.

Fig. 7.2 Institutional context affecting trade in counterfeits

Reconfiguring Marketing Mix: A Framework for Countering Counterfeiting

Marketing mix is usually configured by an organization at the interface of (1) customer needs, (2) competition scenario, and (3) company competence/strategy (Fig. 7.3), but it does not bring an adequate spotlight on the counterfeiting, which significantly affects the attainment of marketing objectives.

The traditional marketing mix articulates various dimensions of the solution developed by an organization to target/serve a particular market, but it does not specifically address the concern regarding counterfeiting. In this section, extended marketing mix has been developed by incorporating the best practices to counter counterfeiting (Fig. 7.4).

This extension to the marketing mix brings anti-counterfeiting to the center stage of designing of the marketing program for an organization (Fig. 7.5).

Fig. 7.3 Conventional marketing mix

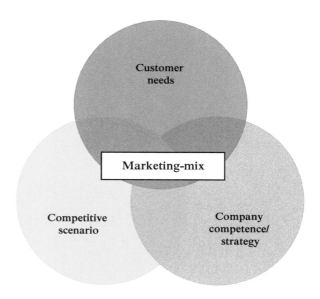

Product Mix

i. *Introducing new variants/products at a faster pace*: The introduction of counterfeits in the market induces incumbent brands to introduce new products (Qian 2012). Innovation can be employed as a response by the authentic firms in response to the counterfeiters. The faster the organization introduces new products, the more difficult it becomes for the counterfeiters to match their corresponding counterfeits with the original brand.

ii. *Proprietary shape of packaging*: By developing a distinctive packaging, which is expensive and difficult to duplicate, organizations selling premium products can create a barrier for counterfeiters. For example, companies can develop impact-extruded shaped cans, which have complex lithographed images and debossed logo, thereby making them distinctive for consumers as well as harder for counterfeiters to imitate.

iii. *Tamper-evident packaging*: Organizations can quickly detect any unauthorized access by using tamper-evident packaging. These packaging technologies include markings, film wrappers, shrinkable seals and bands, breakable caps, bar coding, color-shifting inks, tape seals, blister packs, etc. Organizations can also use holography on the tamper-evident bands, which would make the packaging too costly to imitate. For example, "Bayer CapSeal" innovative packaging technology of Bayer combines visual security features with a QR code, which can be scanned with the help of the company's interactive smartphone app to know about the genuineness of the product.

iv. *Overt and covert packaging technologies*: Simplification of the manufacturing process is making the job of counterfeiters easier (Clark 2000). Therefore, companies are using taggants, tiny identification tags that cannot be identified by the

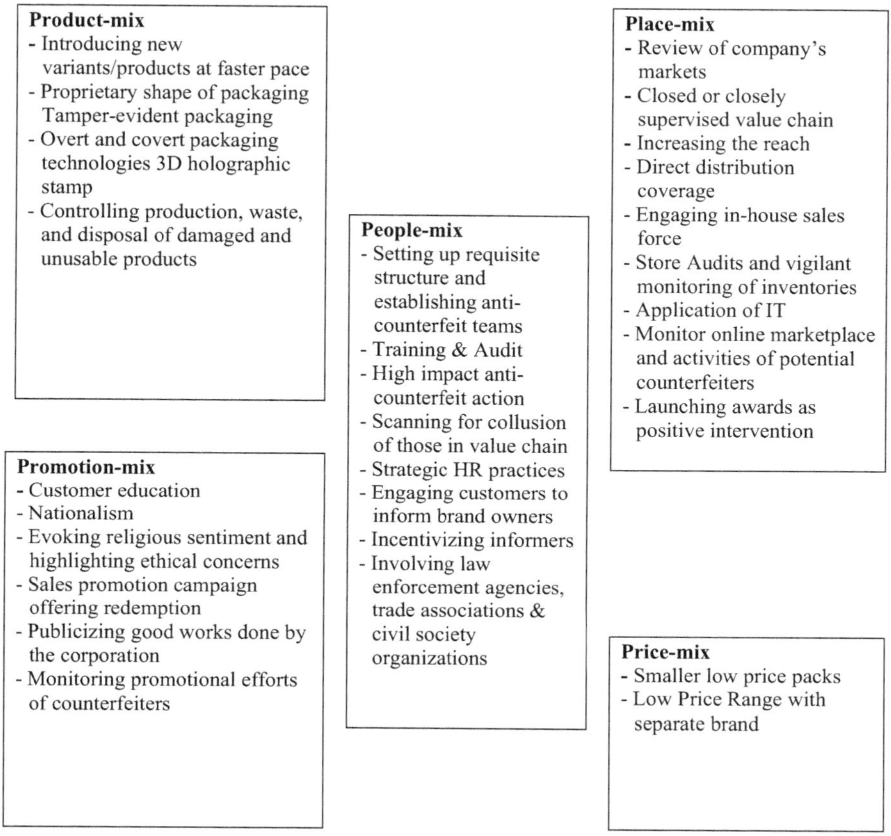

Product-mix
- Introducing new variants/products at faster pace
- Proprietary shape of packaging Tamper-evident packaging
- Overt and covert packaging technologies 3D holographic stamp
- Controlling production, waste, and disposal of damaged and unusable products

People-mix
- Setting up requisite structure and establishing anti-counterfeit teams
- Training & Audit
- High impact anti-counterfeit action
- Scanning for collusion of those in value chain
- Strategic HR practices
- Engaging customers to inform brand owners
- Incentivizing informers
- Involving law enforcement agencies, trade associations & civil society organizations

Place-mix
- Review of company's markets
- Closed or closely supervised value chain
- Increasing the reach
- Direct distribution coverage
- Engaging in-house sales force
- Store Audits and vigilant monitoring of inventories
- Application of IT
- Monitor online marketplace and activities of potential counterfeiters
- Launching awards as positive intervention

Promotion-mix
- Customer education
- Nationalism
- Evoking religious sentiment and highlighting ethical concerns
- Sales promotion campaign offering redemption
- Publicizing good works done by the corporation
- Monitoring promotional efforts of counterfeiters

Price-mix
- Smaller low price packs
- Low Price Range with separate brand

Fig. 7.4 Extended marketing mix constituents to counter the counterfeits

counterfeiters and which can be recognized only through proprietary equipment with brand owners. Covert packaging includes multiple options like using a latent image formation of multi-optical layers to exhibit various kinds of patterns, nano-drip printing, customized holograms, bar codes, digital watermarks, embedded image, and laser coding to mark or engrave an object. Organizations then need to change the designs frequently to identify the original products and distinguish them from counterfeits and fakes.

A 3D holographic stamp wedged between two transparent isotropic polyester layers can be applied on the package to make the product counterfeit-proof and give assurance to buyers that products being purchased by them are genuine. Companies are also using authentication technologies like high-security holograms with 2D and alphanumeric codes, color-changing film, and holographic film on the package to protect their products from being duplicated. Holograms can combine three-layered security features against counterfeiting, with holograms providing evident first-level authentication. The second security layer can

Fig. 7.5 Extended
marketing mix

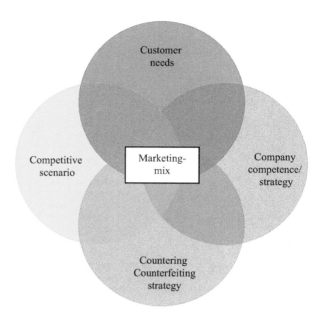

comprise concealed features, like scrambled images, microtext, and copy-proof QR codes, which can be verified with the help of smartphones through the mobile consumer and B2B apps. Companies can give a unique number to each product, which can be checked through its blockchain technology. Microscopic application of UV-sensitive or other specialized inks can also be used for creating second-level authentication, which skilled inspectors can decipher by using the right devices. Serializing of holograms combines authentication with traceability (Pharmaceutical Technology Trends 2008), and binary encrypted holograms, light diffraction hologram, or a combination of a hologram, 2D Datamatrix, and thermal monitoring (Taylor 2011) can provide an effective measure to distinguish originals from fake products. Innovative fluorescent diamonds developed by DiamLite can also be used as overt or invisible permanent markers for putting markings that can't be forged but can be easily deciphered with a portable device for tracking and tracing authenticated products.

TruTag Technologies has created an edible microtag, TruTag®, for identifying, authenticating, and protecting brands and assuring the quality of medicines, food articles, and consumer products. These microtags, which act as covert, heat-resistant, "edible bar codes," have a unique code that can be decoded through the company's proprietary scanners (Thomson 2016).

v. *Controlling production waste and disposal of damaged and unusable products*: Companies must ensure that surplus, damaged, or unusable goods are destroyed or disposed of properly so that their waste does not enter their distribution network (U.S. Chamber of Commerce, & CACP 2006). In some product categories like fashion garments, companies can even sell their slightly defective products at a much lower price without the designer tag to ensure that counterfeiters are not able to benefit from them.

Price Mix

i. *Introducing smaller low-price packs*: In the case of consumer goods, the organizations can make their original products affordable by launching smaller packages. By enabling the customers to try the original product in smaller quantity, the organizations can make the customer understand the finer difference between the original and the fakes. Thus, influencing some of them to adopt genuine products over time. Branded shampoo manufacturers have successfully employed this strategy in India by launching small-quantity sachets to attract customers who wanted to buy original premium branded products but could not afford to pay for them and instead were buying cheaper imitations.

ii. *Introducing low-price range with a separate brand*: The durable companies can launch cheaper variants as distinct lines with different brand names and maybe with different distribution channel so that consumers have an option of buying branded quality products at lower prices instead of buying cheaper imitations.

Place Mix

i. *Review the company's markets*: Before launching a large-scale, organized anti-counterfeiting action, organizations can classify their markets into the following four categories:

  – Major markets that must be defended from fake products.
  – New markets that the organization is planning to enter, which must be defended from counterfeit products.
  – Less important markets: smaller market size, negligible levels of damage to original products/company's brand/image, and costs associated with litigation and enforcement sometimes make "do nothing" or "surveillance only" as the best strategy for this market (Shultz II and Saporito 1996).
  – The markets that have already been lost to counterfeiters.

– This classification can help an organization to direct its efforts to the markets which are significantly important and where these anti-counterfeiting efforts are likely to produce optimum results for the time, effort, and resources invested by it.

ii. *Closed or closely supervised value chains*: Contract manufacturers have been found to produce goods for the ordering right holder as well as for others. Wholesalers and retailers may also buy a cheap version of original products and pass them onto the next level. Therefore, organizations need to closely monitor or close the entire value chain (supply chain) by conducting test purchases and onsite inspections.

Brand owners need to design the contract in such a manner that the concerned factory is deterred from making knock-offs in the "third shift" after making the original products in the scheduled shifts. Organizations also need to put in place such mechanisms that the factories are not in a position to secretly ship the fakes out of their premises. The regular presence of brand right holder at the plant premises and close monitoring of critical technology resources help in preventing IP leakage. Mandatory bag checks for one and all and prohibition of camera phones at factory premises also strengthen the preventive measures.

iii. *Increasing the reach*: Inadequate reach makes the underserved markets vulnerable, especially the economically unserviceable rural markets in large countries like Brazil and India. This want of reach into the widely spread as well as thinly populated markets is not on account of the lack of potential but because of the high costs involved in it. Passive wholesalers serve only those small urban/rural retailers who approach them. As a result, a good number of small retailers in the countryside are neglected as economically unserviceable. This creates an advantageous scenario, which is easily exploited by the manufacturers of fakes, look-alikes, etc. To counter this, the companies can increase their reach by:

   – Appointing exclusive distribution network for the rural market and creating alternative distribution channels to target markets that are unserviceable through traditional channels
   – Subsidizing the cost to serve rural markets by offering reimbursements for extra cost incurred in catering to thinly populated as well as widespread markets

      Hindustan Unilever Limited, the affiliate of Unilever in India, launched the project Shakti Amma to target tiny and economically unserviceable villages, which have a population below 2000. Under this project, the unemployed rural women in villages are employed as distributors for the company products. Subsequently, "Shaktimaans" (usually the husbands or brothers of the Shakti Ammas) were added for selling consumer goods on bicycles in the adjoining villages. With the involvement of more than 70,000 Shakti entrepreneurs, who dispense the company's products in around 162,000 villages, it can now reach out to over four million rural households every month. Consequently, the company has been able to check and counter the fake and pass-off products significantly in the otherwise difficult to target rural market of India.

iv. *Direct distribution coverage*: Some of the organizations are replacing the wholesaler-distributor-retailer model with direct distribution coverage in their key markets. During the transition phase, there might be a short-term drop in sales, but once the direct distribution is established and the beat plans are adequately executed, the organization can build its capacity to counter not only the counterfeits but also a surge in the sales.

v. *Engaging in-house salesforce*: By enlarging the role of the company sales-force to provide leads regarding counterfeiting, the companies can create a surveillance mechanism to identify where the counterfeit goods are being sold. But mechanisms and resources also need to be instituted within the organization to initiate a swift and planned action based on that information so that the salesforce believes their information is being treated seriously.

vi. *Store audits and vigilant monitoring of inventories*: Brand owners can inspect the retail outlets to ascertain and ensure the channel members' trustworthiness. This audit and vigilant monitoring of stocks at various stages in the distribution chain can enable the manufacturers to detect entry sources of diverted, pilfered goods and pass-offs.

vii. *Integrating anti-counterfeit interventions with IT applications*: Increased integration of IT applications can empower the companies to track and trace their supply chain effectively and efficiently. It also creates a mechanism to engage all stakeholders in contributing toward checking the distribution and sale of counterfeit and fake products. Pharmaceutical giant Purdue Pharma employs armored vehicles equipped with GPS and supported by countersurveillance teams to distribute their products across the retail channel to keep them out of the reach of criminal elements.

The integration of big data and Internet of Things (IoT) also strengthens the security harness of products. The following technologies can be employed by companies while distributing their products to the retailers/end consumers:

- *Radio-frequency identification (RFID)*: It assigns an individual identity to the packing used for carrying the goods in transit, which can be traced from a remote location.
- *Electronic pedigree (e-pedigree) system*: The e-pedigree is a tinker-proof report of the movement of medicine through the distribution chain. Every time the drug moves ahead, the organization records the transaction and "signs" the pedigree employing digital certificate. These pedigree records enable the investigators to identify the origin of a problem if any counterfeit medicine somehow enters the distribution network. This can avert the diversion of original medicines or hamper their duplication by enabling the wholesalers and retailers to know the identity and dosage of different drugs (Sukhlecha 2007).
- *Raman spectroscopy*: This novel, low-tech device can be employed as the first line of defense to identify the fake medicine inside their packaging through a handheld refractometer (Sukhlecha 2007). It measures the specific gravity of dissolved drugs, which can be used to figure out the quantity of the ingredients in the medicine.
- *Rapid Alert System (RAS) by WHO*: It is the first Internet-based system for tracking the activities of drug cheats (Sukhlecha 2007).

viii. *Monitoring online marketplace and activities of potential counterfeiters*:
Targeted online data collection and automated web monitoring technologies
can help the organizations to investigate a market swiftly and determine genuine as well as counterfeit trading. By looking for products being sold below
their cost in a particular market, the companies can identify portals/sites selling counterfeits. Online scanning technologies can enable the organizations to
categorize the online distribution network of various sellers and products into
a classified set of legitimate/illegitimate products/organization.

Nearly 80% of all online marketplace traffic occurs at the top ten online
marketplaces. By monitoring these marketplaces through technology, organizations can watch a significant share of online traffic. Organizations can get
the defaulter online marketplace companies relegated to "notorious market
list" if they fail to act on the complaint by the brand owners. Organizations
can also get the counterfeit websites removed from the search results pages of
the search engines on the Internet if they infringe upon their intellectual property. Organizations can send takedown notices directly to Internet service providers; the web-hosting companies can be hugely penalized if they do not
respond to these notices to block the sale of counterfeits on the culprit websites hosted by them. For instance, the National Food and Drugs Monitoring
Association (BPOM) of Indonesia jointly working with the Ministry of
Communications and Information (Kominfo) blocked more than 10,000 websites in the country in 2014 (Santoso 2016). Alibaba Group stated that it
removed 90 million infringing listings in 1 month and spent $160.7 million in
2013 and 2014 on removing counterfeit products and improving online consumers' protection (Shu 2014).

ix. *Launching awards as positive intervention*: Indonesia Anti-Counterfeiting
Society (MIAP) in association with Indonesian Mall Management Association
and the University Award for Copyrights launched the "Clean Mall Award" to
encourage malls to adopt practices that would eliminate counterfeit products
from their premises. Such a certificate assures the consumers that the goods
they are buying from that particular mall are authentic, thus benefiting all the
stakeholders.

Promotion Mix

i. *Customer education*: Sometimes the consumers are unaware of the negative
implications of counterfeited goods. By stressing upon the fact that the counterfeit goods are indirectly funding the criminal or terrorist activities and how
the fake pharmaceuticals are reducing immunity and killing people, companies can create moral pressure on consumers and retailers from buying and
selling spurious products. For instance, four Japanese enterprises that manufacture ED drug in Japan are collaboratively undertaking various actions to

raise the awareness regarding the perils associated with Internet purchase (Shofuda et al. 2014).

The counterfeit antimalarial drug containing a lower dose of the active ingredient creates a situation where the parasite develops a resistance to the genuine medicine. There are around 3000 deaths every year in the G20 countries on account of fake consumer products (BASCAP 2011). As many consumers unknowingly obtain counterfeit drugs, pharmaceutical organizations should highlight how counterfeits hurt patients by giving them ineffective or dangerous treatments (Chaudhry and Stumpf 2009).

Educating consumers by advertising the superiority of original products not only devalues the status of the pirated brand but also has the salutary effect of reinforcing retail distribution alliances (Shultz II and Saporito 1996).

ii. *Nationalism*: Countries and companies can associate their anti-piracy efforts with the feeling of patriotism by demonstrating how the sale of these pirated or counterfeited goods is hurting the nation and society as a whole. By linking counterfeiting to organized crime and showing how the losses resulting from piracy hit the country's economy and industry, China has demonstrated how successful such a strategy for anti-piracy could be.

iii. *Evoking religious sentiment and highlighting ethical concerns*: The Indonesia Ulema Council on the request of Anti-Counterfeiting Society (MIAP) included IP rights in a fatwa, stating that counterfeit goods are *haram*. By appealing to people's conscience regarding what is right and what is wrong, by sensitizing them regarding their civic responsibilities, and by being ethical themselves, the companies can transform the buying behavior of at least some consumers who otherwise buy fake drugs and pirated videos, music, etc. with a clear conscience.

iv. *Sales promotion campaign offering redemption*: Once it is evident that the customer would benefit from the sales promotion campaign only by buying the original product, the retailers would also refrain from selling counterfeit products. In the early 1990s, a new FMCG company with very limited resources, selling Chik Shampoo in rural India where the literacy levels are relatively low and the ability to read and understand the contents printed in English on sachets is very less, launched a campaign to provide one filled shampoo sachet to those consumers who would bring back five empty sachets. Not only the sales increased from 35,000 to 12,00,000 sachets a month in a short time, but the company was also able to prevent counterfeiting as consumers would not get filled sachet for empty sachets of look-alikes.

v. *Publicizing good works undertaken by the organization*: Companies need to highlight the creditable tasks they are performing for the benefit of the consumers and society in general and demonstrate how part of their profits are being channelized for the overall societal benefit through research, CSR, etc. This would provide substantial reasons to the consumers that why the prices of original products are so high, thereby creating an impression that they are not exploiting their customers by charging them exorbitantly. It has been observed that focused corporate social responsibility can build legitimacy that can help insulate companies against IP leakage (Schotter and Teagarden 2014).

vi. *Monitoring promotional efforts of counterfeiters*: Counterfeiters also employ similar effective promotional techniques as used by the genuine organizations, like paid search advertising, posting of information in the social media, black hat SEO tactics, cybersquatting, and spam to direct customer traffic toward their illegitimate products. Monitoring these promotional efforts is necessary to devise responses to counter them.

People Mix

IP leakages often occur through staff transfers or shared practices from foreign multinational corporations to local joint ventures or supply chain partners (Chesbrough et al. 2006). Effective anti-counterfeiting enforcement requires both a determined top management and a perfect coordination between the in-house and external experts. The people dimension is essential for the successful execution of any anti-counterfeiting intervention.

i. *Setting up requisite structure and establishing the anti-counterfeit team*: For taking swift and effective action against the counterfeiters, organizations need to equip themselves with dedicated resources, budgets, training programs, bench strength, as well as networking with other stakeholders. In one such concerted effort against Chinese counterfeiters, eight companies participated in the Electric Dragon project with the Electrical Installation Equipment Manufacturers Association (EIEMA). With the support of the State Bureau of Technical Supervision, 17 factories were raided for 3 days, and over 500,000 counterfeit products were seized and destroyed along with their molds. Seven companies were convicted, and fines ranging from RMB 250,000 to RMB 25,000 were imposed on them (Harris 2001).

For effectively managing various anti-counterfeiting initiatives, an organization needs to create a team comprising in-house counsel, representatives from different corporate functions, external consultants, and legal counsel.

ii. *Training and audit*: Organizations should invest in training, thereby raising awareness among those who could provide information regarding the prevalence of counterfeits in a particular market. Periodic audits can be conducted to assess the knowledge of employees regarding anti-counterfeiting measures and procedures and their consequent implementation. This keeps the employees motivated to learn and implement the best practices to prevent counterfeiting.

iii. *High-impact anti-counterfeit action*: Instead of numerous small-scale surprise checks on the different vendors, it is more efficient to identify where the products are accumulated for assembling, packaging, or dispatching. Once a hit list of offenders is developed, the organization can conduct enforcement action that has a bigger impact.

iv. *Scanning for the collusion of those involved in the value chain*: The first target for the large-scale anti-counterfeiting operations should be to discreetly eliminate the possibility of collusion between the joint venture or commercial partner and the local top management team.

v. *Strategic HR practices*: The most prevalent cause of IP leakage in China was widely seen as staff turnover; strategic human resource practices (understanding of local labor market dynamics and drivers of employee turnover, selecting employees with integrity and compatible ethical values) can help mitigate IP leakage (Schotter and Teagarden 2014). Developing reward systems that resonate with local talent can also assist the organization in reinforcing the desired behaviors among the employees (Bhattacharya et al. 2008).

vi. *Offering incentives to informers*: Provision of incentives to the informers may encourage people to come out and share information about the sale of spurious/counterfeit goods in their vicinity. Coca-Cola has set up a system of around 50 consumer response coordinators in different countries. They along with their teams redress consumer complaints, which also include fake bottling and look-alikes.

vii. *Engaging customers to inform brand owners*: Companies can engage the customers to act as the brands' "eyes and ears" to identify, locate, and share information about the counterfeiting. With customers taking a greater interest in the authenticity of their purchases, providing them with tools to track provenance can become an important part of the marketing mix (New 2010). Through ezTRACK™, a product authentication solution electronic platform, various stakeholders in Hong Kong can track and trace the product information via a mobile application just by scanning the QR code with a smartphone. Brand owners are encouraging such product authentication, through the lure of loyalty programs, price discounts, warranty extensions, and other incentives to connect customers closely with their brands. Similarly, consumers in Delhi in India can use a mobile app (mLiquorSaleCheck) to check the genuineness of the purchased liquor bottle as well as submit their grievances.

Organizations need to identify the factors that drive people in a particular market to buy counterfeits and what can desist them from buying the fakes. Based upon that insight, organization can design a specific message for that particular market.

viii. *Involving law enforcement agencies, trade associations, and civil society organizations*: Brand owners affected by counterfeiting can approach organizations like the International Anti-Counterfeiting Coalition (IACC), Anti-Counterfeiting Group (ACG), and industry-specific organizations, like the American Apparel & Footwear Association (AAFA). These organizations contribute both wherewithals and professional advice on best practices for contesting the counterfeiters. A leadership role has been taken by the World Health Organization (WHO) to curb the prevalence of counterfeit medicines by establishing an extensive network, the International Medical Products Anti-Counterfeiting Taskforce (IMPACT). It includes 193 member countries, global organizations, enforcement agencies, national drug regulatory authorities, customs and police organizations, NGOs, associations of pharmaceutical companies and wholesalers, health professionals, and patient groups for improving coordination among nations to curb the counterfeiting of drugs.

Companies can seek the help of civil society organizations in a particular territory to counter the counterfeiters. Creative Economy Agency (Bekraf), a civil society

Table 7.2 Mapping extended marketing mix to counterfeit issues

Counterfeiting issues	Extended marketing mix element to address that issue
Product issues	Product mix
Technology-enabled electronic frauds	Introducing new variants/products at a faster pace
Low entry barriers	Proprietary shape of packaging
Easy availability of technology to make fakes	Tamper-evident packaging
Collusion of third-party manufacturers	Overt and covert packaging technologies
	Controlling production, waste and disposal of unusable products
Price issues	Price mix
Higher price for original	Smaller low-price packs
Larger profit margins for retailers from fakes	Low price range with separate brand
Place issue	Place mix
"Economically unserviceable" small retailers	Review of company's markets
Online counterfeit sale	Closed or closely supervised value chain
Wholesalers and retailers looking for better margins	Increasing the reach
	Direct distribution coverage
	Engaging in-house salesforce
	Store audits and vigilant monitoring of inventories
	Application of IT
	Monitoring online activities of potential counterfeiters
	Launching awards for distribution entities
Promotion issue	Promotion mix
Ineffective messages by the government	Customer education
Companies and industry association failing to influence consumers' buying behavior	Projecting counterfeiting as anti-national
	Evoking religious sentiments and highlighting ethical concerns
	Sales promotion campaign offering redemption
	Publicizing good works of company
	Monitoring promotion of counterfeiters
People issue	People mix
Some consumers think it is fun to get fakes at a low price	Setting up requisite structure and establishing anti-counterfeit teams
Some think buying fake products is not wrong	Training and audit
Some people think companies are overcharging	Scanning for collusion of those in value chain
Law enforcement being weak in some region/countries	Strategic HR practices
	Incentivizing informers
	Engaging consumers
	Involving law enforcement agencies, trade associations, and civil society organizations

organization in Indonesia, has set a target to increase Indonesia's creative economy, by working for eradicating the IPR violations through a "3Si" dubbed – creation, protection, and commercialization. It created a Music and Film Piracy Task Force in coordination with industry associations, content creators, and the police. It is developing a warning system in collaboration with Telkom Indonesia and the Ministry of Communications and Information (Kominfo) for monitoring music and film content websites and warning the organizations against illegal downloaders.

The various constituents proposed under the extended marketing mix provide countering tactics to the different counterfeiting issues. Table 7.2 maps the various components of the extended marketing mix to specific counterfeiting issues to demonstrate the application of this tool for countering the counterfeiting.

Conclusion

The prevalent marketing mix focusing primarily on customer needs, competition scenario, and company competence/strategy does not provide adequate focus on counterfeiting. The reconfigured marketing mix proposed in this paper brings counterfeiting to the center stage for designing and managing a marketing program to resolve various product, price, place, promotion, and people issues related to counterfeit trade. It adds to the existing marketing literature by bringing together different anti-counterfeiting strategies under a cogent model, which can be operationalized by a practitioner while strategizing against counterfeiting. Counterfeiting is a global phenomenon, and its dynamics varies both across countries and product categories. Organizations need to deeply examine the situation and identify appropriate intervention from the proposed marketing mix to deal with counterfeiting in that particular market.

Challenges and Opportunities

With simplification of manufacturing process, easier availability of technology, and rising aspirations of consumers, the supply and demand side challenges concerning counterfeiting are multifold. The situation calls for a holistic and integrated approach. The proposed extended marketing mix provides a template to bring together different stakeholders: strategic/tactical capacity building of companies, engagement of governments, education, and empowerment of consumers for a concerted action.

Shifting Paradigm of Global Marketing

Significant developments in packaging and printing technology, IT tools for managing distribution chain, changing nature of the marketplace, and increasing adoption of e-commerce warrant that the traditional global marketing frameworks are reexamined and reconfigured to incorporate the effects of these developments. Companies need to strategize for enhancing the engagement of consumers who are empowered with Internet-connected smartphones and applications to play a more active role regarding various facets of marketing. Thus, "people" component, which was primarily related with marketing mix for services, can play a significant role concerning products as well.

Policy Implications

For companies choosing to do business in the emerging economies, the foremost concern is the protection of their IP rights especially when the technology gap is high, and the IP protection regime is weak because local firms may tend to avoid costly R&D and imitate MNEs' technologies (Agarwal and Wu 2015). Therefore, to attract foreign investment, the governments need to strengthen their IP protection mechanisms and support R&D through appropriate policy interventions. This becomes even more important because the country of origin affects consumers' perceptions of product quality, brand image, and purchase decisions (Hong and Wyer 1989). Thus, it is in the long-term interest of governments to be proactive to both safeguard and enhance their national image as a source of original and quality products and not from where the fakes originate.

Given the accelerating growth of counterfeits in the global trade, there is a need to bring together different global marketing interventions under a single academic framework. This paper is an attempt to fill this gap in the literature and to propose a template that can stimulate further research in this important area.

References

Agarwal, J., and T. Wu. 2015. Factors influencing growth potential of e-commerce in emerging economies: An institution-based N-OLI framework and research propositions. *Thunderbird International Business Review* 57 (3): 197–215.

Ba, S., and P. Pavlou. 2002. Evidence of the effect of trust building technology in electronic markets: Price premiums and buyer behavior. *MIS Quarterly* 26 (3): 243–268.

Bamossy, G., and D.L. Scammon. 1985. Product counterfeiting: Consumers and manufacturers beware. In *Advances in consumer research*, ed. Elizabeth C. Hirschman and Morris B. Holbrook, vol. 12, 334–339. Provo: Association for Consumer Research.

BASCAP. 2011. Welcome to BASCAP. http://www.iccwbo.org/advocacy-codes-and-rules/bascap/welcome-to-bascap/.

Basheer, T., and C. Loizides. 2014. Counterfeiting: The challenge to brand owners and manufacturers. http://brandandcommercial.com/articles/show/brand-building/214/counterfeiting-the-challenge-to-brand-owners-and-manufacturers.

Bhattacharya, C.B., S. Sen, and D. Korschun. 2008. Using corporate social responsibility to win the war for talent. *MIT Sloan Management Review* 49 (2. *(winter 2008)*): 37–44.

Bian, X., and C. Veloutsou. 2007. Consumers' attitudes regarding nondeceptive counterfeit brands in the UK and China. *Journal of Brand Management* 14 (3): 211–222.

Bloch, P.H., R.F. Bush, and L. Campbell. 1993. Consumer "accomplices" in product counterfeiting. *Journal of Consumer Marketing* 10 (4): 27–36.

Bosworth, D., and D. Yang. 2006. Conceptual issues of global counterfeiting on products and services. *Journal of Intellectual Property Rights* 11 (January): 15–21.

Cao, Q. 2014. Insight into weak enforcement of intellectual property rights in China. *Technology in Society* 38: 40–47.

Cardwell, R., and P.L. Ghazalian. 2012. The effects of the TRIPS agreement on international protection of intellectual property rights. *The International Trade Journal* 26 (1): 19–36.

Cesareo, L. 2015. Counterfeiting and piracy: A comprehensive literature review. *Spring*: 3–4.

Chakraborty, G., Allred, A.T. and T. Bristol. 1996. Exploring consumers' evaluations of counterfeits: the roles of country of origin and ethnocentrism, in NA – Advances in Consumer Research, eds. Kim P. Corfman and John G. Lynch Jr., Provo, UT: *Association for Consumer Research* 23: 379–384.

Chakraborty, G., A.T. Allred, A.S. Sukhdial, and T. Bristol. 1997. Use of negative cues to reduce demand for counterfeit products. *Advances in Consumer Research* 24: 345–349.

Chaudhry, P., and S.A. Stumpf. 2008. International perspectives on counterfeit trade. *Sloan Management Review* 49 (4): 8–10.

Chaudhry, P.E., and S.A. Stumpf. 2009. Getting Real about fakes. *The Wall Street Journal.* http://www.wsj.com/articles/SB10001424052970204038304574151703747284822.

Chaudhry, P., V. Cordell, and A. Zimmerman. 2005. Modelling anti-counterfeiting strategies in response to protecting intellectual property rights in a global environment. *The Marketing Review* 5 (1): 59–72. 14.

Chesbrough, H., S. Ahern, M. Finn, and S. Guerraz. 2006. Business models for technology in the developing world: The role of non-governmental organizations. *California Management Review* 48 (3): 48–61.

Clark, D. 2000. IP rights protection will improve in China – eventually. *The China Business Review* 27: 22–29.

Cordell, V.V., N. Wongtada, and R.L. Kieschnick Jr. 1996. Counterfeit purchase intentions: Role of lawfulness attitudes and product traits as determinants. *Journal of Business Research* 35: 41–53.

Feinberg, R., and D.J. Rousslang. 1990. The economic effects of intellectual property right infringements. *The Journal of Business* 63 (1): 79–90.

Ginarte, J.C., and W.G. Park. 1997. Determinants of patent rights: A cross-national study. *Research Policy* 26: 283–301.

Grossman, G.M., and C. Shapiro. 1988. Foreign counterfeiting of status goods. *Quarterly Journal of Economics* 103 ((February)): 79–100.

Hamelin, N., S. Nwankwo, and R. Hadouchi. 2013. Faking brands': Consumer responses to counterfeiting. *Journal of Consumer Behaviour* 12: 159–170.

Harris, A. 2001. *Combating counterfeiting: A practical guide for European engineering companies.* Orgalime publication http://www.orgalime.org/sites/default/files/counterfeiting_guide_en.pdf.

Harvey, M. 1987. Industrial product counterfeiting: Problems and proposed solutions. *The Journal of Business and Industrial Marketing* 2 (4. (Fall)): 5–13.

Hoe, L., G. Hogg, and S. Hart. 2003. Fakin' it: Counterfeiting and consumer contradictions. In *European advances in consumer research*, ed. Darach Turley and Stephen Brown, vol. 6, 60–67. Provo: Association for Consumer Research.

Hong, S., and R.S. Wyer Jr. 1989. Effects of country-of-origin and product-attribute information on product evaluation: An information-processing perspective. *Journal of Consumer Research* 16: 175–187.

Jackson, J.H., W.J. Davey, and A.O. Sykes Jr. 2002. *Legal problems of international economic relations: Cases, materials and text.* 4th ed, 962–964. Eagan: West Publishing Company.

Japan Patent Office (JPO). 2015. *Survey report on losses caused by counterfeiting.* http://www.meti.go.jp/english/press/2016/0310_01.html.

Kaikati, J.G., and R. LaGarce. 1980. Beware of international brand piracy. *Harvard Business Review* 58 (2): 52–58.

Kotler, P. 2000. *Marketing Management,* (Millennium Edition), 9. Custom Edition for University of Phoenix, Prentice Hall.

Lai, K.K., and J.L. Zaichkowsky. 1999. Brand imitation: Do the Chinese have different views? *Asia Pacific Journal of Management* 16 (2): 179–192.

Liebowitz, S.J. 2005. Economists' topsy-turvy view of piracy. *Review of Economic Research on Copyright Issues* 2 (1): 5–17.

Lightner, N.J., and C. Eastman. 2002. User preference for product information in remote purchase environments. *Journal of Electronic Commerce Research* 3 (3): 174–186.

Makely, W. 2005. Countering the counterfeits: How brands can protect themselves: You don't have to make it impossible. *Brand Packaging.* July 2005. https://www.brandpackaging.com/articles/83870-countering-the-counterfeiters-how-brands-can-protect-themselves

Maldonado, C., and E.C. Hume. 2005. Attitudes toward counterfeit products: An ethical perspective. *Journal of Legal, Ethical and Regulatory Issues* 8 (2): 105–107.

Mavlanova, T. and Benbunan-Fich, R. 2010. Counterfeit products on the internet: The role of seller-level and product-level information. *International Journal of Electronic Commerce* 15 (2): 79–104.

Mavlanova, T., and R. Benbunan-Fich. 2011. Counterfeit products on the internet: The role of seller-level and product-level information. *International Journal of Electronic Commerce* 15 (2): 79–104.

Montoro-Pons, J.D., and M. Cuadrado-Garcia. 2006. Digital goods and the effects of copying: An empirical study of the music market, paper presented at the 14th International Conference on Cultural Economics, Vienna.

Moorthy, S., and Srinivasan, K. 1995. Signaling quality with a money-back guarantee: *The role of transaction costs. Marketing Science* 14 (4): 442–466.

New, S. 2010. The transparent supply chain. *Harvard Business Review.* October 2010. https://hbr.org/2010/10/the-transparent-supply-chain.

Nia, A., and J.L. Zaichkowsky. 2000. Do counterfeits devalue the ownership of luxury brands? *The Journal of Product and Brand Management* 9 (7): 485–497.

OCTA. 2011. The illicit trafficking of counterfeit goods and transnational organized crime by United Nations office of drugs and crime; Europol, "OCTA 2011: EU Organized Crime Threat Assessment", p. 48, 2011. Available at https://www.europol.europa.eu/sites/default/files/publications/octa2011.pdf.

OECD. 2009. *The magnitude of counterfeiting and piracy of tangible products: An update economic impact of counterfeiting and piracy, part IV,* 19982009. Paris: Organisation for Economic Co-operation and Development.

OECD/EUIPO. 2016. *Trade in counterfeit and pirated goods: Mapping the economic impact.* Paris: OECD Publishing. https://doi.org/10.1787/9789264252653-en.

Organization for Economic Cooperation and Development (OECD). 2007. *The economic impact of counterfeiting and piracy: Executive summary,* 12, Paris: OECD Publishing. Available from https://doi.org/10.1787/9789264037274-en.

Parloff, R. 2006. Not exactly counterfeit. *Fortune* 153 (8): 108–112.

Pavlou, P.A., and D. Gefen. 2005. Psychological contract violation in online marketplaces: Antecedents, consequences, and moderating role. *Information Systems Research* 16 (4): 372–399.

Pavlou, P.A., H. Liang, and Y. Xue. 2007. Understanding and mitigating uncertainty in online exchange relationships: A principal-agent perspective. *MIS Quarterly* 31 (1): 105–136.

Perez, M.E., R. Castaño, and C. Quintanilla. 2010. Constructing identity through the consumption of counterfeit luxury goods. *Qualitative Market Research: An International Journal* 13 (3): 219–235.

Pharmaceutical Technology Trends: Holograms and Anticounterfeiting. 2008. http://pharmtech.findpharma.com/pharmtech/In+the+Field/Trends-Holograms-and-Anticounterfeiting/ArticleStandard/Article/detail/505361.

Phillips, T. 2005. *Knockoff: The deadly trade in counterfeit goods.* Sterling: Kogan Page.

Qian, Y. 2008. Impacts of entry by counterfeiters. *The Quarterly Journal of Economics* 123: 1577–1609.

———. 2012. Brand management and strategies against counterfeits. *The National Bureau of Economic Research.* http://www.nber.org/papers/w17849.

———. 2014. Brand management and strategies against counterfeits. *Journal of Economics & Management Strategy* 23 (2., *summer*): 317–343.

Santoso, R.P. 2016. Countering counterfeiting in Indonesia. https://www.amcham.or.id/manufacturing-industry/5287-countering-counterfeiting-in-indonesia.

Schotter, A., and M. Teagarden. 2014. Protecting intellectual property in China. *MIT Sloan Management Review* summer, 2014: 41–48.

Shadlen, K.C., A. Schrank, and M.J. Kurtz. 2005. The political economy of intellectual property protection: The case of software. *International Studies Quarterly* 49: 45–71.

Shavitt, S., T.M. Lowrey, and S. Han. 1992. Attitude functions in advertising: The interactive role of products and self-monitoring. *Journal of Consumer Psychology* 1 (4): 337–364.

Shih, W., and J.-C. Wang. 2013. Will our partner steal our IP? *Harvard Business Review* 91 (1. *(January–February)*): 137–141.

Shofuda, K., K. Aragane, Y. Igari, K. Matsumoto, and K. Ito. 2014. Anti-counterfeit activities of pharmaceutical companies in Japan: For patient safety. *Yakugaku Zasshi* 134 (2): 203–211.

Shu, C. 2014. Alibaba removed 90m suspicious listing from its sites before IPO. https://techcrunch.com/2014/12/23/alibaba-listings-purge/.

Shultz, C.J., II, and B. Saporito. 1996. Protecting intellectual property: Strategies and recommendations to deter counterfeiting and brand piracy in global markets. *The Columbia Journal of World Business* 31. *Spring*: 18–28.

Staake, T., and E. Fleisch. 2008. *Countering counterfeit trade illicit market insights, best-practice strategies, and management toolbox*, 69–83. Berlin: Springer.

Stumpf, S.A., and P. Chaudhry. 2010. Country matters: Executives weigh in on the causes and counter measures of counterfeit trade. *Business Horizons* 53 (3): 305–314.

Sukhlecha, A. 2007. Counterfeit and substandard drugs: The need for an effective and stringent regulatory control in India and other developing countries. *Indian Journal of Pharmacology* 39: 255.

Taylor, P. 2011. Securing Pharma Label combines holograms, 2D holograms and thermal monitoring. http://www.securingpharma.com/label-combines-holograms-2d-datamatrix-and-thermal-monitoring/s40/a1151/.

Thomson, A. 2016. Top new developers of anti-counterfeit technologies. http://blog.ventureradar.com/2016/02/02/new-developers-of-anti-counterfeit-technologies/.

Thorsten, S., F. Thiesse, and E. Fleisch. 2012. Business strategies in the counterfeit market. *Journal of Business Research* 65: 658–665.

Tom, G., B. Garibaldi, Y. Zeng, and J. Pilcher. 1998. Consumer demand for counterfeit goods. *Psychology & Marketing* 15 (5): 405–421.

U.S. Chamber of Commerce, & Coalition against Counterfeiting and Piracy (CACP). 2006. No trade in fakes supply chain toolkit: Protecting businesses, consumers, and brand integrity. https://sm.asisonline.org/ASIS%20SM%20Documents/counterfeit0507.pdf.

UNICRI. 2008. Illicit trafficking of counterfeit goods, a global spread, a global threat, p. 118. http://www.unicri.it/news/files/2007-12-01_ctf_2k8_final.zip.

UNODC. 2013. Transnational organized crime in East Asia and the Pacific: A threat assessment. p. 127. Available from http://www.unodc.org/toc/en/reports/TOCTA-EA-Pacific.html. 7 Europol, "OCTA 2011: EU Organised Crime.

Utz, S., U. Matzat, and C. Snijders. 2009. On-line reputation systems: The effects of feedback comments and reactions on building and rebuilding trust in on-line auctions. *International Journal of Electronic Commerce* 13 (3): 95–118.

Vitell, S.J., A. Singhapakdi, and J. Thomas. 2001. Consumer ethics: An application and empirical testing of the Hunt-Vitell theory of ethics. *Journal of Consumer Marketing* 18 (2): 153–178.

Wee, C., S. Tan, and K. Cheok. 1995. Non-price determinants of intention to purchase counterfeit goods: An exploratory study. *International Marketing Review* 12 (6): 19–46.

Wilcox, K., H.M. Kim, and S. Sen. 2009. Why do consumers buy counterfeit luxury brands? *Journal of Marketing Research* XLVI ((April)): 247–259.

Wilke, R., and J.L. Zaichkowsky. 1999. Brand imitation and its effects on innovation, competition, and brand equity. *Business Horizons* 42 (6): 9–18.

WTO. 1994. Trade-related aspects of intellectual property rights. Annex 1C of the Marrakesh Agreement Establishing the World Trade Organization. Marrakesh, Morocco: World Trade Organization. 15 April, Annex 1C, Section 4, Article 51 p. 342.

Youill, B. 2016. How to counter the counterfeiters. http://ftijournal.com/article/how-to-counter-the-counterfeiters.

Chapter 8
Bridging Institutional Distance: An Emerging Market Entry Strategy for Multinational Enterprises

Ogechi Adeola, Nathaniel Boso, and James Adeniji

Abstract Despite attractive investment opportunities, multinational enterprises (MNEs) looking to enter emerging markets face multifaceted challenges. While much of the literature tends to infer that emerging markets of all types face similar institutional challenges, this chapter argues that significant differences exist across emerging markets, which may help explain variations in entry mode strategies of MNEs to these markets. Entering an emerging market requires development of a unique market entry strategy that focuses on narrowing the institutional distance (i.e., regulatory, cognitive, and normative) between MNEs' home and targeted host markets. Within the context of the Nigerian market, cognitive and normative institutional distance likely poses a greater challenge to MNE success than regulatory institutional distance. This chapter identifies corporate social responsibility, social media engagement, governmental relations, and informal relational ties as key market entry strategies that enable MNEs to build legitimacy in the Nigerian market, which then helps minimize the costs of the cognitive and normative institutional distances. Thus, this chapter proposes that MNEs can boost emerging market entry success levels when they are able to build and leverage unique market entry strategies to bridge the institutional distance between their home and host country markets.

O. Adeola (✉)
Lagos Business School, Pan-Atlantic University, Lekki, Nigeria
e-mail: oadeola@lbs.edu.ng

N. Boso
KNUST School of Business, Kwame Nkrumah University of Science and Technology, Kumasi, Ghana

J. Adeniji
Leeds University Business School, University of Leeds, Leeds, UK

© Springer International Publishing AG, part of Springer Nature 2018
J. Agarwal, T. Wu (eds.), *Emerging Issues in Global Marketing*,
https://doi.org/10.1007/978-3-319-74129-1_8

205

Introduction

Emerging market literature tends to suggest that emerging markets have similar characteristics. For example, Xu and Meyer (2013) define emerging markets as those that have less institutional support than North American and European markets and have middle-income status as well as rapid GDP growth. However, Hoskisson et al. (2013) improve our understanding of such markets by providing a typology that suggests that emerging markets globally have differing characteristics based on institutional, infrastructural, and factor development, which may help explain the modes of entry for multinational enterprises (MNEs). These different characteristics in institutional development between MNE's home markets and target foreign markets provide an explanation for MNE foreign market entry strategy, otherwise known as institutional distance (Xu and Shenkar 2002). Institutional distance is the degree of similarity or dissimilarity between the cognitive, normative, and regulatory institutions of two countries (Kostova 1996). In the literature, this construct has been linked to two key aspects of MNE operations: (1) the transfer of strategies and practices from parent companies to the foreign subsidiaries (Kostova 1999) and (2) the establishment of legitimacy in the host country (Kostova and Zaheer 1999). Institutional distance is derived from institutional theory – a non-efficiency perspective that sees institutional environment as the key driver of firm behavior (DiMaggio and Powell 1983; Scott 2013; Xu and Shenkar 2002).

It is noteworthy that stakeholder engagement can mitigate the negative effects of institutional distance on MNE entry mode choices. Stakeholder engagement has been defined as "a firm-level set of behavioral practices aimed at exchanging knowledge with the different types of stakeholders so as to incorporate their demands in company's decisions" (Bettinazzi and Zollo 2015). Established, long-term relationships with stakeholders can allow a firm to create more knowledge-creating exchanges than from interactions based on market transactions alone (Harrison et al. 2010). There are many examples of companies who successfully navigated institutional differences with stakeholders as they tried to enter or maintain a competitive advantage in foreign markets, for example, McDonald's in France and Uber in the UK. There are just as many examples of companies that have had to abandon foreign markets because of these same institutional differences, such as Google's short-lived entry into China. Firms must bridge institutional gaps in order to cement successful market entry or at least tailor their entry strategy to mitigate potential negative effects of these gaps (Björkman et al. 2007; Xu and Shenkar 2002). This chapter uses Nigeria as the context of analysis on how stakeholder engagement can overcome the drawbacks of institutional distance on entry mode choices.

Theoretical Framework: Institutional Theory

Institutional theory has emerged as the most popular line of theorizing to explain firm strategies and local contexts (Meyer and Peng 2005; Xu and Meyer 2013). Based on institutional economics in the fashion of North (1990), institutional theory explains how host country institutional environments and the differences between host and home institutions affect MNE location choices (Xu and Shenkar 2002). It emphasizes that organizations must conform to their environment (DiMaggio and Powell 1983; Scott 1995), because institutional isomorphism, both procedural and structural, leads to organizational legitimacy (Dacin 1997).

Kostova and Zaheer turned to institutional theory to suggest that organizational legitimacy is shaped by three sets of factors: "(1) the characteristics of the institutional environment, (2) the organization's characteristics and actions, and (3) the legitimation process by which the environment builds its perceptions of the organization (1999: 67)." Any complexity in these sets of factors (the organization, the institutional environment, and the process of legitimation) makes it more difficult for MNEs to establish and maintain legitimacy.

Institutional theory emphasizes the effects of institutional distance (Kostova 1996), local isomorphism (Robert and Zheying 2012; Rosenzweig and Nohria 1994), and foreignness (Zaheer 1995) on firm survival and success. The deconstruction of institutional distance into the regulatory, normative, and cognitive levels helps in the application of institutional theory to the legitimacy of challenges MNEs encounter in the host country. Legitimacy, the anchor point of institutional theory's explanation of institutional distance, describes the mechanisms by which MNE social embeddedness shapes their behaviors and structures (DiMaggio and Powell 1983). Considering that MNEs operate under multiple institutional demands (D'Aunno et al. 1991), whether local or national in origin (Rosenzweig and Singh 1991), they have to pursue sociopolitical legitimacy and reshaping of institutional environments (Brouthers and Brouthers 2000; Hoskisson et al. 2000) in order to overcome regulatory, normative, and cognitive institutional distance.

Increasingly, institutional theory is being used to explain how various institutional demands (Meyer et al. 1987) drive selection of vital strategic choices in complex environments (Oliver 1991). This is rooted in the understanding that MNEs can gain legitimacy from some sources based on the practices they adopt (D'Aunno et al. 1991). The discretion of MNEs in the formulation of responses to institutional forces is a function of contextual variables such as uncertainty and multiple environmental demands (Goodrick and Salancik 1996; Xu and Shenkar 2002).

Organization theorists find that a particular concern to MNEs under multiple institutional pressures is strategies (e.g., stakeholder engagement) to enhance legitimacy (Kostova et al. 2008). Local partners can help attain legitimacy in the host context (Xu and Meyer 2013). For example, it would be easier for firms to establish legitimacy through stakeholders (e.g., corporate social responsibility officers (CSRs), government representatives, social media, and informal relationships) than through direct reliance on markets because stakeholders are legitimate brand influencers and ambassadors. Stakeholder ties serve as key market entry strategy builders that enable MNEs to build legitimacy in a foreign market, which then helps minimize the cost of institutional distance.

Institutional Distance

The concept of institutional distance relates to international business research seeking to discern degrees of variation in the institutional context of two or more countries where an MNE operates (Salomon and Wu 2012; van Hoorn and Maseland 2016), including ways in which that variation is influenced by formal and informal components (Scott 1995). The concept has been of concern to international business scholars and Western multinational enterprises operating in emerging markets such as Nigeria. According to Ionascu et al., "the more distant a host country is from the organizational centre of a multinational enterprise (MNE), the more it has to bridge differences in culture, in laws and regulation, and in organizational practices and routines. The MNE has to adapt its entry strategies, organizational forms, and internal procedures to manage these differences (2004:3)." Institutional distance can impair internal integration and coordination, particularly when dissimilar national contexts interfere with transfer of knowledge and practices between foreign and local Nigerian affiliates. Ionascu et al. put it thus: "The more different the MNEs origins are from the context that they enter, the greater will be the obstacles to attaining local legitimacy and to practice transfer (2004: 7)."

What this "liability of foreignness" (Zaheer 1995) does is reduce the profits of MNEs compared to their Nigerian counterparts. In a bid to conform to the isomorphic pressures in their home markets and also gain legitimacy in the target foreign market while striving to maintain a cohesive global strategy, MNEs are exposed to institutional dualism (Ionascu et al. 2004). The ease of conformity is thus a function of the MNE's familiarity with the host country's institutional distance (Xu et al. 2004).

Scott (1995, 2001) identified three pillars that drive business strategies in international markets. The three pillars – regulatory, cognitive, and normative – can be seen as a framework for institutional distance (Kostova and Roth 2002). The normative pillar is the beliefs, values, and norms of a culture; the regulatory pillar refers to laws, regulations, and enforcements; and the cognitive pillar is universally shared social knowledge, schemata, and stereotypes (Ionascu et al. 2004).

The Normative Pillar

The normative pillar defines the "what" and "how" of the functional mode of MNEs in the host country. The normative variations that MNEs experience are usually associated with workplace habits and norms that are different from those that are customary in their home countries.

The normative pillar has a direct bearing on the strategic transfer of organizational practices, which is mainly constrained by the normative distance between the home and host countries (Xu and Shenkar 2002). The components of a normative pillar may make the transfer of organizational practices difficult. MNEs with strong, firm-specific, practice-based competitive advantages prefer institutional environments similar to that of the home country. Most MNEs that invest in normatively distant markets lack strong competitive advantages but imitate local practices (Zaheer 1995). Xu and Shenkar found that these latter firms are "not easily constrained by normative distance when making FDI [foreign direct investments] but may purposefully choose to enter normatively distant markets where their freedom to adapt will confer a competitive advantage over MNEs from the same home country that will not adapt (2002: 611)."

The Regulatory Pillar

The regulatory pillar of institutional distance encapsulates the process of stipulating the established rules of the host country, ensuring compliance with those rules, and enforcing the necessary sanctions for failure to meet the rules as they relate to the MNE operational performance. The regulatory pillar, most likely, will not affect MNEs whose organizational practices are not in violation of host country laws. According to Xu and Shenkar, "Differences in the regulatory environment will not have much impact on market choice, because such differences are codified and built into the MNE's routines. The one exception may be where regulatory requirements are perceived to undermine core strategy – for example, where the host country rules require mandatory technology transfer that conflicts with the MNE's proprietary strategy (2002: 612)."

   While it is possible for a government to outlaw a certain practice to keep an MNE out, this is a rare occurrence. In fact as well as practice, regulatory distance is formalized, easily understood by MNEs, and acceptable, according to Ionascu et al. "as a cause for local adaptation (2004: 10)."

The Cognitive Pillar

The cognitive pillar guides the understanding of MNEs on the nature and reality of the cultural context of the host country. This understanding reduces uncertainty about organizational practices within the host country. Cognitive elements are usually associated with beliefs about work and roles. Cultural context guides sustainable organizational changes when the premise of change is internalized and valued by organizational members (Palthe 2014). The cognitive pillar will not affect MNEs that are practice-driven except where the practices challenge the host country identities (Xu and Shenkar 2002). Cognitive distance will have some effect where an MNE's global strategy constitutes a symbolic challenge to local orthodoxy.

   Kostova (1999, cited in Ionascu et al. 2004) states that the higher the level of regulatory, normative, and cognitive institutional distance between an MNE and its host country, the more difficult it is for the MNE to transfer strategic organizational practices. These regulatory, cognitive, and normative pillars of the institutional framework affect the operations and strategies of MNEs, moderating the acceptance of their practices within the host environments, in this case, Nigeria. The three institutional pillars combine to create tensions between the corporate and the Nigerian institutional pressures.

Legitimacy is one of the critical issues faced by MNEs as they invest abroad in multiple host environments. Scott asserts that legitimacy is "not a commodity to be possessed or exchanged but a condition reflecting perceived consonance with relevant rules and laws, normative supports, or alignment with cultural-cognitive frameworks (2008: 59–60)." Suchman calls legitimacy "a generalized perception or assumption that the actions of an entity are desirable, proper, or appropriate within some socially constructed system of norms, values, beliefs, and definitions (1995: 574)." Legitimacy explains the mechanisms by which MNE social embeddedness shapes their behaviors and structures (DiMaggio and Powell 1983); it is institutional theory's anchor point in the explanation of institutional distance.

Where institutional distance is a factor, legitimacy is more imperative for cognitive/normative distance than regulatory distance. Regulatory distance does not create as many obstacles to gaining local legitimacy as cognitive or normative distance. Regulatory institutions are relatively transparent, while norms and cognition demand rigorous cross-cultural communication because they are tacit and not easily understood (Boyacigiller et al. 2004). Regulatory distance is formalized and thus easier to understand by MNEs and more acceptable as a basis for local adaptation. MNEs may find it easier to adapt to local, formalized regulatory pressures without input from local stakeholders, even when regulatory distance is high.

In theory, normative and cognitive differences pose a greater challenge than regulatory differences MNEs who wish to adapt to Nigerian institutional pressures. According to Boyacigiller et al. (2004), while norms and cognition demand rigorous cross-cultural communication that may not be easily understood, and cultural knowledge can be said to be tacit, regulatory institutions are quite clear. High normative and cognitive distance necessitates enhanced levels of interaction with local peers to attain local legitimacy and access the local business networks. The capability to gain legitimacy is inhibited when normative and cognitive distance adversely affects the adoption of parent organization practices by affiliates (Ionascu et al. 2004; Kostova and Zaheer 1999). "A high normative and cognitive distance impedes the adoption of an MNE's practice and restrains the affiliate's capacity to establish legitimacy, while a high regulatory distance is likely to have a negative effect primarily on the adoption of an MNE's practices (Ionascu et al. 2004: 8)." For example, Google effectively had to quit China, whose laws on censorship appear to be politically motivated and are no doubt influenced by normative and cognitive factors.

To obtain legitimacy in a host country, an MNE must understand normative and cognitive distance (Kostova and Zaheer 1999), both of which pose potential constraints on the implementation of an MNE's practice. For example, in Nigeria, workers may be unwilling to adopt or understand and learn a practice if it is not consistent with prevailing local conventions, standards, or cognitive structures.

Therefore, normative and cognitive differences are more challenging than regulatory differences in adaptation to local institutional pressures. However, this may not necessarily be the case in Nigeria since one could argue that elements of the normative and cognitive pillars are instrumental in forming the regulatory pillar and the pillars necessarily influence themselves. For example, in accounting theory and practice, it has been long argued that it would be difficult to have complete comparison between financial statements of corporations belonging to different countries. Even if there were to be a global adoption of IFRS (International Financial Reporting Standards), countries' differing legal frameworks and tax laws, and the effects of culture on auditing practices, could significantly affect the way accounts are presented.

Foreign Direct Investment in Nigeria

As a means of controlling ownership of a business enterprise in a target country, foreign direct investment (FDI) may be made either inorganically (i.e., the acquisition of an existing entity) or organically (i.e., the establishment of a new enterprise). The choice of these modes of entry is crucial in international expansion. Relevant factors influencing the viability of entry include knowledge of local conditions, trade barriers, competition, price localization, and export subsidies. Other factors include brand awareness, sales, and the impact on business stability created by expansion beyond traditional markets into new markets. A high degree of control of capital, technology, and personnel transfer can ensure optimal competitiveness.

Entering the Nigerian market requires development of a market entry strategy which gives due consideration to all relevant factors in choosing the appropriate mode of entry. Nigeria is a major emerging sub-Saharan African market, with expanding financial, communications, entertainment, technology, and hospitality service sectors. Nigeria is ranked as the 21st largest economy in the world in terms of purchasing power parity and the largest in Africa (World Bank Databank 2016). Riches in resources, especially hydrocarbons, have resulted in prosperity, wealth expansion, and the development of a strong middle class (FDIIntelligence.com 2015). Nigeria's 180 million citizens constitute 20% of the sub-Saharan Africa population. The United Nations anticipates that by 2050 there will be 440 million Nigerians, far more than the 400 million population in the USA (The Economist 2014a). According to Goldman Sachs chief economist Jim O'Neill, Nigeria is now one of the Next 11 or N-11 – Bangladesh, the Philippines, Nigeria, Pakistan, Korea, Mexico, Turkey, Vietnam, Egypt, and Indonesia – countries he viewed as having a high potential for economic success in the twenty-first century (Moore 2012) and therefore highly attractive investment destinations. Considering all this, and coupled with the dire need for infrastructure and a slowing European market, Nigeria provides interesting investment opportunities for multinational enterprises looking for new markets for growth.

Nigeria attracted the second highest share of FDI in sub-Saharan Africa (after South Africa) between 2013 and 2014 (Fig. 8.1). Interestingly, Nigeria has the lion's

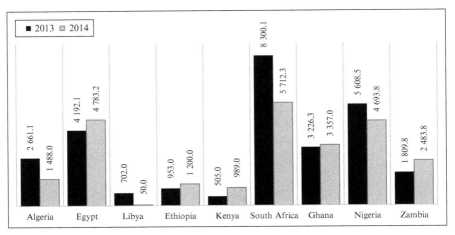

Data Source: UNCTAD: World Investment Report 2015

Fig. 8.1 FDI inflows into Africa ($ Millions) (Data source: UNCTAD: World Investment Report 2015)

share of FDI inflow into West Africa: of the $14,208.4 million inflow into the region in 2013 and $12,763.0 in 2014, Nigeria received 39% and 37%, respectively. On the one hand, the huge FDI inflow to Nigeria may be the result of "abundant natural resources, a low-cost labour pool, and potentially the largest domestic market in Sub-Saharan Africa (KPMG 2012: 17)." On the other hand, the effort to make Nigeria one of the top 20 economies in the world by the year 2020 has impelled the government of Nigeria to enact FDI-magnet economic reforms. The World Economic Forum on Africa has this to say about FDI in Nigeria: "What is equally positive is the increasingly diversified nature of the investment. Although more than 50% of the FDI capital invested into Nigeria since 2007 has been into the capital-intensive resource sectors (primarily oil), nearly 50% of FDI projects are service-orientated. There has been particularly strong growth in investment into telecommunications, with the sector attracting 23.9% of FDI projects between 2007 and 2013. Growth in investment in other service sectors like financial services, consumer products, tourism and business services, further highlights the growing opportunities emerging in these sectors (2014: 2)."

Like most sub-Saharan African markets, Nigeria faces a long list of impediments: poor infrastructure, inadequate power supply, restrictive trade policies, a weak judicial system, inefficient property registration system, the belated passage of legislative reforms, arbitrary policy changes, pervasive corruption, and growing insecurity. Among these often-cited impediments to doing business in Nigeria, the biggest threats are corruption, poor infrastructure, and threats to physical security. Nigeria has one of the lowest per capita national power supply in the world. Reliance on fuel-powered generators adds to the cost of doing business, close to 40% in some sectors (World Economic Forum on Africa 2014). Poorly maintained power sources and infrastructure compel many investors to provide their own power and access roads, adding to costs and undermining competitiveness.

The increases in opportunities on the one hand and the challenges on the other have created a bipolar view of Nigeria. For many investors already doing business in the country "it is an exciting, dynamic, high octane growth market; for some others, often on the outside looking in, it seems chaotic, unstable, and uncertain [...] Nevertheless, the facts support the more positive perspective on Nigeria and its prospects as an investment destination" (World Economic Forum on Africa 2014: 4). Despite the weak institutional environment and high levels of corruption (Holtbrügge and Baron 2013), this large, emerging, sub-Saharan African country has become an attractive investment destination for MNEs seeking growth in foreign markets.

Notably, the most significant FDI flows to Nigeria have been from the home countries of the oil multinationals (Corporate Nigeria 2015). Key FDI partners are Chevron and ExxonMobil from the USA and Shell from the UK. China has become one of Nigeria's important FDI partners via large infrastructure projects. Major motivations of FDI are access to profitable markets, affordable skilled labor, and natural resources, among others (Agwu 2014). Despite the availability of some of these key factors, Nigeria and Africa at large still lag behind in attracting the commensurate benefits of foreign direct investments (UNCTAD 2013).

Market Entry Modes

Though choices of market entry modes remain important to firms in internationalization, the lack of adequate tools to determine effective entry modes remains a challenge (Brouthers 2013). The international business literature suggests that the choice of a market entry mode adopted by an internationalizing firm is determined by the specific characteristics of the firm, the country of operation, and the distinctive features of an industry within which a firm operates (Blomstermo et al. 2006). According to Quer et al., "entry modes abroad can be divided into large groups according to the generic options that are available to an enterprise in order to make the most of its specific advantages beyond the domestic market (2007: 363)." These options include exporting, licensing, global outsourcing, FDI via joint venture or wholly owned subsidiary, among others (Dixon et al. 2015; Quer et al. 2007).

Exporting Exporting, regarded as the dominant mode of internationalization, is considered beneficial for economic growth, particularly in emerging economies (Dixon et al. 2015). This traditional method of internationalization refers to the process of marketing goods produced by one country to other countries, to benefit from economies of scale (Carter 1997; Fernández-Mesa and Alegre 2015). Exporting can be direct (without intermediaries) or indirect (through domestically based export agents). In direct exporting, the organization may use distributors or an overseas subsidiary or act via a government agency that facilitates better control over distribution and capitalizes on economies of scale in production. The advantages of exporting are its low risks and the opportunity to test the foreign markets, while the major disadvantage is the lack of control. Examples of MNEs exporting to Nigeria are Toyota and Samsung. The Toyota brand's entry into the Nigerian market was indirect through domestically based export agents such as Elizade and Mandilas. Currently, Toyota Nigeria Limited has become the sole distributor of Toyota vehicles for Toyota Motor Corporation. Similarly, Samsung's entry into the Nigerian market was indirect through domestically based export agents called authorized dealers.

Joint ventures This is a foreign market entry mode in which two independent organizational partners collaborate within a particular geographical location or product market to create separate organizational entities (Emmanuel and David 2005; Meschi and Wassmer 2013). These entities exist either as an incorporated joint venture contract (where two or more joint venture legal entities are established to carry out a common activity) or as a contractual joint venture that regulates cooperation between parties without the creation of a legal entity (Schneider et al. 2002).

The common goals of joint ventures include technology sharing, risk/reward sharing, market entry, joint product development, government regulation compliance, distribution channel access, and political connections (Foley 1999).

Joint ventures are a common entry mode in emerging markets (Meschi and Wassmer 2013). In Nigeria, most oil exploration activities operate under joint venture contracts between multinationals such as ExxonMobil, Total, Saipem, Shell, BP, and Chevron and the Nigerian National Petroleum Corporation (NNPC), with the NNPC contributing 55–60% of production contracts and budgeted expenditures and claiming the same percentage of total revenues (Table 8.1).

Franchising Franchising can be defined as "a business arrangement wherein a firm (the franchisor) collects up-front and ongoing fees in exchange for allowing other firms (franchisees) to offer products and services under its brand name and using its processes (Combs et al. 2011: 100)." The advantages of franchising are low costs, little political risk, simultaneous expansion, and pooling of financial investment and managerial capabilities; the disadvantages are little control over franchisees and conflicts with franchisees. Franchising in Nigeria has aided entry for some successful international brands such as Avis Car Rental, Kentucky Fried Chicken, Fastrackids, Crestcom, Signarama, Computer Troubleshooters, WSI – Internet Consulting and Education, Precision Tune Auto Care Center, and Hawthorn Suites (Ndumanya and Quadri 2015).

Strategic Alliance A strategic alliance is a purposive mutual association between independent organizational entities, which allows those entities to exchange, share, or co-develop resources, capabilities, processes, and competence with the intent of achieving mutual economic benefits or business objectives while existing as independent entities (Albers et al. 2016; Gulati 1995; Kale and Singh 2009). In sub-Saharan Africa, MNEs in the areas of production, manufacturing, and digital

Table 8.1 Major Nigerian oil production joint ventures (slightly amended to reflect parent name of the companies)

Consortium	Shareholders	Joint venture operator
Shell Petroleum Development Company of Nigeria Ltd.	NNPC (55%), Shell (Dutch/British, 30%) Total (France, 10%), ENI (Italy, 5%)	Shell
Mobil Producing Nigeria Ltd.	NNPC (60%), ExxonMobil (USA, 40%)	ExxonMobil
Chevron Nigeria Limited	NNPC (60%), Chevron (USA, 40%)	Chevron
Nigeria Agip Oil Company	NNPC (60%), ENI (Italy, 20%), Philips (USA, 20%)	ENI
Elf Petroleum Limited	NNPC (60%), Total (France, 40%)	Total
Texaco Overseas (Nigeria) Petroleum Company	NNPC (60%), Texaco (USA, 20%), Chevron (USA, 20%)	Texaco

Source: Nigerian National Petroleum Corporation 2016

technology have been able to leverage strategic alliances to achieve exponentially greater economic strides as they improve levels of market penetration which has helped to transform the nature of competition and strategy in Africa's business economy. An example is the strategic alliance in 2017 between JDR, a technology provider in the global offshore energy industry headquartered in Scotland, UK, and Proserv Instrumentation Nigeria Limited to deliver combined subsea solutions and local content support to West African markets (Africa Oil & Gas report 2017).

It is important to note that regulatory, normative, and cognitive institutional distances complicate entry mode choices. Ionascu et al. point out that regulatory distance may be relevant when considering the desirability of greenfield investments in a context where there are "obstacles to practice adaptation in existing local organizations (2004: 11)," while joint ventures may be preferable option when there are "obstacles to gaining legitimacy (2004: 11)." Normative and cognitive institutional distance is an influence when the entry mode choice is a function of "the relative importance of practice mode adoption and attaining local legitimacy (2004: 11)."

An MNE can, therefore, ease communication through a joint venture when greenfield investors possess less cultural knowledge when communicating with local peers, which impedes the ability to earn legitimacy. High normative and cognitive distance favors joint venture entry because, with an understanding of the Nigerian context, adoption of behaviors and practices as well as gaining legitimacy becomes easy.

Stakeholder Engagement

Generally, emerging markets lack well-developed market-supporting institution, constraining a firm's strategic choices (Ramamurti 2004). In such markets, an MNE's knowledge of the social environment has an uncertainty-reducing effect when entering the market (Hilmersson and Jansson 2012). To mitigate the challenge of institutional gaps in market entry mode choices, particularly in the Nigerian context, effective engagement with relevant stakeholders could be the key to achieving desirable results for the mutual benefit of all parties. Stakeholder engagement and management can be utilized as an informal mechanism to manage challenges of market entry (Freeman 1984; Marquis and Reynard 2015). Also, CSR engagement strategies in a host country can be advantageous when utilized by MNEs to obtain social legitimacy as this connotes an implicit commitment to local stakeholders (Campbell et al. 2012). Therefore, we posit that stakeholder engagement can be utilized to mitigate the drawbacks of institutional distance on entry mode choices.

Donaldson and Preston (1995) defined stakeholders as persons or groups with legitimate interests in procedural and/or substantive aspects of corporate activity. Greenwood (2007) described stakeholder engagement as "practices that the organization undertakes to involve stakeholders in a positive manner in organizational activities (2007: 318)" and thus does not restrict engagement in social responsibility. The need for stakeholder engagement has been proven both in theory and in practice, as businesses are increasingly expected to assume a broad spectrum of social and environmental responsibilities. While observing laws, regulations, and ethics (e.g., regulatory, normative, and cognitive distance), they are, as well, expected to contribute tangibly to the resolution of complex social or environmental issues (Carroll and Buchholtz 2006).

Because potential stakeholders are not a homogenous block for every business, a solid differentiation of pertinent stakeholders is necessary (Post et al. 2002; Hoffmann and Lutz 2013). Stakeholder engagement may take the form of building collaborative relationships with public institutions, participating in CSR activities within communities, or identifying with a particular community to build brand legitimacy. MNEs could use these forms of stakeholder engagement to bridge institutional gaps and thereby cement successful market entry or at least tailor their entry strategy to mitigate potential negative effects of identified deficiencies (Björkman et al. 2007; Xu and Shenkar 2002). Figure 8.2 provides a hypothetical model of how firms could use stakeholder engagement to penetrate foreign markets. The model highlights the complementarities of the ethics and international business domains.

As shown in Fig. 8.2, through stakeholder engagements (e.g., CSR activities, active discussions with government agencies, social media engagement, or informal relationships), MNEs may be able to establish legitimacy with one or multiple groups in a target foreign market. Once established, the stakeholders can then transfer the firm's legitimacy to a wider market where the firm can earn economic benefits such as market share, revenue growth, diversification, and profit. It is important to mention that the number of benefits accrued by a firm may well depend on factors exogenous to the model such as unexpected shocks to the economy that affect consumers' purchasing power. Nevertheless, quantifying the benefits accrued from stakeholder engagement actions helps determine the efficacy of these actions and if the benefits met expectations regarding the return on investment (ROI) in engaging in the foreign market. If ROI is less than expected, a firm may choose to adjust its stakeholder engagement strategy (e.g., perhaps target a different stakeholder group that has better access to market actors) or disengage from the market. For many multinationals, this cost-benefit analysis is a recurring exercise.

Fig. 8.2 Using stakeholder engagement to bridge institutional distance

A stakeholder, as mediator, has the power to influence the success of a firm's foreign market entry in an emerging market such as Nigeria. The stakeholder's position as a mediator is based on the assumption that it is easier for a firm to establish legitimacy through stakeholders rather than primary actors in the market. Stakeholders are legitimate brand influencers, ambassadors, or advocates.

Within the context of the Nigerian market, stakeholder engagements can serve as key market entry strategies that enable MNEs to build legitimacy, which in turn helps minimize the cost of cognitive and normative institutional distances. Thus, MNEs can boost their entry success into the Nigerian market when they build and leverage CSR, social media engagement, governmental relations, and informal relationships.

Corporate Social Responsibility (CSR)

With greater challenges to pursuing a globalization strategy and increased pressure from stakeholders at the local level, firms must seek legitimacy through CSR activities to meet the sustainability expectations of consumers, governments, and shareholders (Crilly 2011; Castelló and Lozano 2011; Hemphill and Lillevik 2011; Campbell et al. 2012; Doh et al. 2017). Community engagement, a subset of stakeholder management strategies, helps companies build legitimacy and gain competitive advantage through continuous dialogue resulting in mutual benefits (Bowen et al. 2010). Similarly, Harting et al. (2006) posit that firms that are able to publicize superior efforts at stakeholder engagements vis-à-vis their competitors are more likely to gain a competitive financial advantage. As a stakeholder engagement strategy, CSR activities have more substance as they truly connect with consumers/ stakeholders who react favorably to sincere and proactive engagement (Fosfuri et al. 2011; Groza et al. 2011).

CSR may be a safe way to connect with new markets. When well-executed, CSR puts in place a strategic direction for sales and human resource requirements. For example, Schneider Electric, Cummins, and CFAO partnered with the Institut Européen de Coopération et de Développement (IECD) and the Institute for Technical Training (ITT) in Nigeria to organize a vocational training program, "Seeds of Hope," to prepare students for careers in electricity. One might speculate that the "Seeds of Hope" project will likely benefit the companies, since the graduates are likely to endorse the sponsors' products in the future employment. The project was of particular importance for Cummins, a relative newcomer to the Nigerian market. While Cummins products have been distributed across Nigeria through its exclusive distributor, Cummins West Africa Limited, the company has only recently attempted to fully enter the Nigerian market in earnest, following infrastructural and policy improvements in the electrical supply industry.

Likewise, Schneider Electric has been involved in several CSR activities in Nigeria including a rural electrification project as part of the Nigerian government's "Light up Nigeria" project. While Cummins and Schneider focused their CSR specifically to their industry and capabilities, Etisalat, a telecoms company, took a wider approach to CSR to include event sponsorship such as the *Etisalat Prize for Literature* and the *Etisalat Prize for Innovation*.

Social Media

While engagement in social responsibility activities helps companies communicate their concern for social development, social media presents itself as a powerful tool for "stakeholder groups to be informed, identify common interests, express and share opinions and demands, organize, and coordinate interventions" (Hoffmann and Lutz 2013: 1). Social media connects and bonds like-minded individuals, supporting political communities, social capital formation, and discursive communication (Boyd and Ellison 2007). Through what Donath and Boyd (2004) call a "foci of interest," organizations can, through social media, "interact directly and within the same paradigms (the same communication tools, the same language and a similar potential for impact) with members of the public (Hoffmann and Lutz 2013: 7)."

The literature has established that social media widens the channels and the forms of customer engagement, increasing richness and interactivity in the exchange relationship (Dabholkar and Sheng 2012; Sashi 2012). Some studies have found that social media participation and interaction smooth "the interaction of producers and consumers and allow for the collaborative creation of value (Hoffmann and Lutz 2013: 1)" under labels that Hoffman and Lutz (2013: 10) refer to as "cocreation," "prosumer," and "open innovation." Social media has therefore birthed professional consumers (prosumers) who "rule social media [and] who consume companies' products and services, but at the same time are information and opinion producers about the very same products and services" (Meisling 2014: 7). As the corporate image becomes a creation of online conversations, an MNE's interaction with prosumers becomes indispensable (Jones et al. 2009). Studies such as that done by Burton and Soboleva (2011) have highlighted legitimacy, trust, and higher favorability as benefits of social media engagement. Fieseler et al. (2010) emphasized the benefit of social media engagement as a means to build strong stakeholder relationships.

Social media engagement proves to informed, twenty-first century stakeholders that an MNE is serious-minded and can listen as well as fulfill their consumer demands. Social media, with its interactive capacities, can enable MNEs to attain and retain legitimacy (Inauen and Schoneborn 2014). For example, MTN – a South African mobile telecommunications company – has built strong social media engagement via Twitter and Facebook. With over 168,000 followers on Twitter and 959,000 likes on Facebook, MTN Nigeria uses social media engagement to interact with customers, offering rewards and prizes, taking questions and suggestions, and posting updates about their services. As well, Jumia, with over 3000 followers on its Twitter account and over 251,000 likes on Facebook, encourages customers to order for goods on both their Twitter and Facebook pages, interacting seamlessly with customers and enabling customers to track their orders on their Twitter account and Facebook pages (Imaralu 2015).

However, MNEs practicing social media engagement in an emerging market such as Nigeria must be cognizant of inequalities in social media access, and the miscellany of groups, and thus be able to discern their relevant demands, antecedents, as well as outcomes. Considering the fluidity of social media, it is important to identify interest groups, evaluate their demands, and design suitable stakeholder engagement. According to Sawhney et al. (2005), open and dialogue-oriented interactions can reduce asymmetries in social media engagement.

Government Relations

Government relations are another important factor in stakeholder engagement. For reasons of policy, host governments intervene in the affairs of MNEs, often establishing rather demanding conditions in order to maintain control over their own national economies. According to Doz and Prahalad (1980), there are two different types of this government intervention: the first sets the fiscal and regulatory frameworks; the second seeks to affect an MNE's internal mechanics. These two constitute a major violation of the MNE's strategic autonomy and represent sensitive issues in the choice of market entry. MNEs operating in the oil sector in Nigeria face these sorts of regulatory distance. Joint venture with the government becomes the desirable option because of "obstacles to gaining legitimacy" (Ionascu et al. 2004: 11). As mentioned earlier, most exploration activities operate under joint venture contracts between MNEs (Table 8.1).

Since stakeholders cut across the spectrum of the Nigerian society, employees and potential employees, nongovernmental organizations, governments and regulators, business partners, investors, local communities, and the media, this spectrum makes the Nigerian market unique and complicated, necessitating the need to speak the language of the Nigerian market. Stakeholder engagement, therefore, underscores real understanding of the Nigerian market and proper positioning of the entry product. It is no good entering a market without all stakeholders taken into consideration and on board. Since studies such as Schoeneborn and Inauen (2014) have established that stakeholder interaction can increase legitimacy, MNEs can, therefore, no longer attain legitimacy by mere public relations; MNEs entering an emerging market such as Nigeria must actively involve all relevant stakeholders.

The Power of Informal Relationships

The strategic marketing literature has highlighted the importance of informal relationships in a firm's entry mode choices (Gabrielsson et al. 2008; Loane and Bell 2006; Ojala 2009; Sharma and Blomstermo 2003; Zain and Ng 2006). Informal relationships are those that are "related to social contacts with friends and family members (Ojala 2009: 4)." *Guanxi* is a classic and often studied form of informal relationships that originated in China. While strategic management and organizational theory literature portray business relationships as impersonal and commercial, *guanxi* demonstrates the power of personal relationships and the reciprocal exchange of favors. Therefore, *guanxi* is a great resource for firms in China to encourage cooperation, manage relationships well, alter the existing network structure, broker structural holes, marshal complementary benefits by arbitraging diverse networks, negotiate between competing networks, and bridge gaps in resource flows between unlinked firms and vital external stakeholders (Park and Luo 2001).

According to Park and Luo, *guanxi* exemplifies "the concept of drawing on a web of connections to secure favors in personal and organizational relations…. It is thus critical for businesses in China, whether foreign or local, to understand and appropriately utilize *guanxi* in order to gain an edge over competitors (2001: 455)." The life force of personal relationships in China (Xin and Pearce 1996) and a crucial variable in firm performance, *guanxi* influences all aspects of Chinese business.

Guanxi has wide-ranging implications for international business practices. It is well known that even in countries described as individualist, many successful business deals have been transacted due to the influence of informal relationships. Lagos, Nigeria's commercial capital, has a reputation for being the country's party capital where millions of dollars are spent every year on life celebrations (e.g., birthdays, weddings, funerals). It is commonplace for business associates to be invited to these life celebrations, which may often blur the boundaries of business and personal relationships. For that reason, MNEs entering into emerging markets such as Nigeria can use the concept of *guanxi* "to manage organizational interdependence and to mitigate institutional disadvantages, structural weaknesses, and other environmental threats (Park and Luo 2001: 456)." Yang states that *"guanxi* operates in concentric circles, with close family members at the core and with distant relatives, classmates, friends, and acquaintances arranged on the periphery according to the distance of the relationship and the degree of trust (1994, as cited in Park and Luo 2001: 456)."

The network model of internationalization sees internationalization as a connection of relationships (Johanson and Vahlne 2003). MNEs develop and maintain their positions in their networks, accessing each other's resources, looking for mutual benefits, and, in the case of internationalization, acting as a bridge to foreign markets (Ojala 2009). Moen et al. (2004) and Zain and Ng (2006) found that firms are often led into new markets by their networks. A firm seeking to enter the Nigerian market can therefore actively build new connections (Loane and Bell 2006), or an importer, customer, intermediary, friends, or family members can open opportunities for the firm (Johanson and Vahlne 2003).

Informal relationships provide MNEs with "a wide range of competitive advantages. When faced with uncertainty in entering new markets, decision makers typically minimize their risks by drawing on their known contacts and connections with others (Zain and Ng 2006: 186)." A classic example is the entry of MTN into the Nigerian market. South African MTN, a young telecoms company in 2001, was led into the Nigerian market by its networks. At the time when the government of Nigeria was selling mobile licenses at an auction, Nigeria, though rich in oil reserves, had just come out of decades of military rule and was dealing with crumbling infrastructure and abject poverty. Confronted with uncertainty about entering the Nigerian market, the firm's boss drew from his web of connections, contacting some friends from his days in pay television and discovering they had ten million customers in Nigeria (The Economist 2014b). The analogy is that if Nigerians could afford pay television, they could also afford a mobile phone. MTN took the gamble, and within 5 years, it had garnered over 32 million customers in Nigeria. Today, although the company is in both Africa and the Middle East, Nigeria remains its largest profit machine.

In summary, for relationship strategies to succeed, an MNE must be well established in one or more relevant networks and be regarded as in insider (Johanson and Vahlne 2009). In Nigeria, SABMiller's Hero lager was successfully marketed as a result of positive interactions with the Igbos (one of the three major ethnic groups in Nigeria) and considerable local consumer insight (Bloomberg Business 2014). "Oh Mpa" (an Igbo phrase that means "Oh Father") is the indigenous name for the SABMiller's Hero beer. "Oh Mpa" was a well-known reference to the late Ojukwu, the hero of the Igbo race who led the failed attempt for an independent Biafra nation; the Hero bottles bear the image of the rising sun found on the Biafran flag. SABMiller used Hero beer to tap into Igbo's nationalist sentiments. SABMiller thus built a local sensation for its beverage via regional traditions, loyalties, and tastes.

The SABMiller example shows that Nigerian market is open to brands that Nigerians trust and could call their own. Nigerians are approachable, welcoming, and open, so MNEs who make an effort to get acquainted with the local populations will find the endeavor worthwhile. From pre-colonization to the present, Nigerian tribes easily adopt strangers into their midst. In fact, in large cities such as Lagos, migrations of people from their cultural homelands have resulted in extensive inter-actions of Nigerians of different tribes with foreigners, particularly Chinese, Indians, Lebanese, and Europeans (Falola 2001).

Connecting via informal relationships can be a great leverage device for MNEs operating in Nigeria. In his discussion of Chinese-African relations, Anedo offered this observation: "Contrary to western countries which have a strong individualism …. China and Africa have a strong collectivism. Individualism-collectivism refers to the relative importance of the interests of the individual versus the interests of the group. In collectivistic societies, the interests of the group take precedence over individual interests ….People see themselves as part of in-groups, and the in-groups look after them in exchange for their loyalty (2012: 93)." Given the strong collectiv-ism in place, groups and institutions are of great significance to Nigerians, empha-sizing loyalty and determining their actions. By connecting with these broad and established networks (i.e., groups and institutions) via network relationships, MNEs can internationalize rapidly in Nigeria (Zain and Ng 2006).

When MNEs internationalize, it is important for them to assimilate knowledge needed to compete and grow in markets where they have little or no experience (Gulko 2014). Therefore, MNEs "must take on completely new knowledge, includ-ing experiential knowledge of specific foreign business practices and institutional norms as well as general experiential knowledge of how to organize for foreign com-petition. Network ties are the means by which this type of knowledge can be obtained, considering that international new ventures lack time and resources to gain experien-tial knowledge themselves (Gulko 2014: 27)." MTN and SABMiller are prime exam-ples of how informal relationships helped access knowledge of the Nigerian market and acquire business information. Informal relationships provide an opportunity for MNEs to build credibility and trust when entering the Nigerian market. Establishing such credibility and trust is "an area that a firm needs to work on in its effort to estab-lish its international presence" [in a developing market, because] "the pace and pat-tern of international market growth and choice of entry mode" [for MNEs is] "influenced by close relationships with customers (Zain and Ng 2006: 187)."

Further Research

From the model shown in Fig. 8.2, we propose the following directions for future research, which together may inform if there are cross-cultural differences in how companies relate to stakeholders to bridge institutional gaps. An interesting out-come of such studies (including samples from multiple sub-Saharan African (SSA) markets) would be data that would show if there are any regional (e.g., West Africa vs East Africa vs Southern Africa; anglophone v francophone countries) differences in institutional distance, which may help explain why some countries receive more FDI than others. SSA, with all its diversity, may require different market entry strat-egies for different country markets. In this direction, researchers might seek to explore the following research question:

Research Question 1: Which aspects of institutional distance – normative, regulatory, or cognitive – affect firms' ability to meet performance targets in foreign markets?

Three pillars of institutional distance – regulatory, cognitive, and normative – have an effect on companies' modes of entry into foreign markets. Over time, the normative pillar informs the cognitive pillar, so that much of a society's shared knowledge stems from normative variables. For example, a society with high power distance (i.e., lower-level staff are submissive to their superiors, particularly when there is an age difference) may have stemmed from traditional values of respect for elders or social hierarchy. The World Bank's *Ease of Doing Business* (2017) rankings provide a useful data set for operationalizing the regulatory pillar of institutional distance. However, due to the qualitative nature of the cognitive and normative pillars, any study would need to be based on perceptions. Thus, a survey method combining the objectivity of the *Ease of Doing Business* rankings with foreign market entrants' perceptions of the host market is considered adequate.

Research Question 2: How do informal relationships bridge institutional distance?

Following economic liberalization in 1979, China was perhaps a fascinating example of a lucrative market with significant barriers due to psychic distance, defined by Johanson and Vahlne as "the sum of factors (cultural and institutional) preventing the sum of information from and to the market (1977, 24)." For foreign firms, joint venture partnerships with Chinese businesses or individuals were helpful in gaining intimate knowledge of the market (Beamish and Wang 1989). However, these firms had to manage important cultural differences to reach their goals.

In a study of 138 Canadian companies doing business in China, Abramson and Ai (1999) found strong and significant links between variables related to local investment, the value of foreign culture experience in a dynamic business environment, and the importance of *guanxi* – an informal relationship system that emphasizes gift giving and favors granting between business partners to ensure mutual financial gain in spite of statutory procedures. *Guanxi* is not unlike compadre in Latin America, *jeito* in Brazil, or *jaan-pehchaan* in India. The advantages of *guanxi* include helping firms to navigate through uncertain economic structures and hedging against universal access to information.

Clearly, informal relationships play a role in the business cultures of many countries, and these relationships are likely difficult to navigate given the possibility of large institutional distances between multinationals and their target foreign market. While many disciplines across management studies have studied and documented the effects of informal relationships, especially *guanxi*, little is known about the sort of informal relationships multinationals entering Nigeria and other African countries may need to cultivate outside of the entry barriers due to institutional distance. An important contribution to the international business literature would be studies that show the effect of informal relationships on business cultures in Nigeria and across Africa, thus informing multinationals about what to expect during business exchanges and how to build and manage relationships with market actors in their target foreign markets.

Conclusion

While businesses can attain more brand awareness, sales, and business stability by expanding beyond their niche market into foreign markets, entering a new market requires developing a market entry strategy which gives due consideration to all stakeholders, including possible competitors and potential customers. Emerging markets around the world have differing characteristics based on institutional and infrastructural development factors, which may explain the importance of MNEs to carefully consider the variety and ultimate value of modes of entry. This consideration is pertinent for MNEs expanding to the Nigerian market. Given the many options available to MNEs in Nigeria, the entry modes used most frequently have been direct and indirect exporting, joint ventures, and franchising.

Emerging markets such as Nigeria lack well-developed market-supporting institutions, thus constraining a firm's strategic choices. The determinants of business strategies in such emerging markets are constituted in the three pillars – regulatory, cognitive, and normative – which can be seen as a framework for institutional distance. The three institutional pillars combine to create tensions between the corporate and the Nigerian institutional pressures. Normative and cognitive differences likely pose higher challenges than regulatory differences in adapting to Nigerian institutional pressures. High normative and cognitive distance necessitates high levels of interaction with local peers in order to attain local legitimacy and to have access to the local business networks. High normative and cognitive distance favors joint venture entry more than greenfield, because with the understanding of the Nigerian context, adoption of behaviors and practices as well as gaining legitimacy is made easier.

Global managers and marketers should therefore recognize this shifting paradigm that suggests that stakeholder engagement is fundamental to success in business. Community engagement, a subset of stakeholder management strategies, helps companies build legitimacy and gain competitive advantage through continuous dialogue resulting in mutual benefits. Apart from engagement in social responsibility, social media is a powerful tool for engaging stakeholders. Since stakeholders of the twenty-first century are better informed through social media engagement, such connections with MNEs demonstrate that the companies are serious-minded and can listen as well as fulfill their demands. Social media, with its interactive capacities, can enable MNEs to attain and retain legitimacy.

Host governments may, for reasons related to policy, intervene in the affairs of MNEs, often establishing rather demanding conditions in order to maintain control over their own national economies. MNEs operating in the oil sector in Nigeria face this sort of regulatory distance. Joint ventures with the government become a desirable option because of "obstacles to gaining legitimacy (Ionascu et al. 2004: 11)." Most exploration activities operate under joint venture contracts between MNEs (i.e., Mobil, Elf, Agip, Shell BP, Chevron, and Texaco) and the Nigerian National Petroleum Corporation (NNPC). Stakeholder engagement, therefore, underscores real understanding of the Nigerian market and good positioning of the entry product in order to bridge the institutional distance.

Furthermore, informal relationships can help facilitate mode of entry into the Nigerian market. Just as *guanxi* in China is noted to have wide-ranging implications for business practices in that country, informal relationships have helped MNEs such as MTN and SABMiller to develop their Nigerian market knowledge and acquire local business information. For that reason, MNEs entering into emerging markets such as Nigeria can actively build new connections into the Nigerian market by utilizing informal relations with key market players to sustain their positions in the market.

References

Abramson, N.R., and J.X. Ai. 1999. Canadian companies doing business in China: Key success factors. *Management International Review* 39 (1): 7–35.

Africa Oil & Gas Report. 2017. JDR to set up umbilicals maintenance base in Nigeria. http://africaoilgasreport.com/2017/03/in-the-news/jdr-to-set-up-umbilicals-maintenance-base-in-nigeria/. Accessed 28 Aug 2017.

Agwu, M.E. 2014. Foreign direct investments: A review from the Nigerian perspective. *Research Journal of Business and Management* 1 (3): 318–337.

Albers, S., F. Wohlgezogen, and E.J. Zajac. 2016. Strategic alliance structures: An organization design perspective. *Journal of Management* 42 (3): 582–614.

Anedo, O. 2012. China-Africa culture differences in business relations. *African Journal of Political Science and International Relations* 6 (4): 92–96.

Beamish, P.W., and H.Y. Wang. 1989. Investing in China via joint ventures. *Management International Review* 29 (1): 57–64.

Bettinazzi, E.L.M., and M. Zollo. 2015. Stakeholder engagement and organizational experiential learning: Evidence from M&A activities. DRUID15 Conference, 15–17 June 2015, Rome.

Björkman, I., G.K. Stahl, and E. Vaara. 2007. Cultural differences and capability transfer in cross-border acquisitions: The mediating roles of capability complementarity, absorptive capacity, and social integration. *Journal of International Business Studies* 38 (4): 658–672. https://doi.org/10.1057/palgrave.jibs.8400287.

Blomstermo, A., D. Sharma, and J. Sallis. 2006. Choice of foreign market entry mode in service firms. *International Marketing Review* 23 (2): 211–229.

Bloomberg Business. 2014. SABMiller's Hero taps into Biafra nostalgia in Nigeria. https://www.bloomberg.com/amp/news/articles/2014-04-09/sabmiller-s-hero-beer-taps-into-nostalgia-for-biafra-in-nigeria. Accessed 29 Aug 2017.

Bowen F, Newenham-Kahindi A and Herremans I (2010) When Suits Meet Roots: The Antecedents and Consequences of Community Engagement Strategy. *Journal of Business Ethics* 95 (2): 297–318

Boyacigiller, N.A., R.A. Goodman, and M.E. Phillips, eds. 2004. *Crossing cultures: Communicating corporate social responsibility*. Bingley: Emerald.

Boyd, D., and N.B. Ellison. 2007. Social network sites: Definition, history, and scholarship. *Journal of Computer-Mediated Communication* 13 (1): 210–230.

Brouthers, K.D. 2013. A retrospective on: Institutional, cultural and transaction cost influences on entry mode choice and performance. *Journal of International Business Studies* 44 (1): 14–22.

Brouthers, K.D., and L.E. Brouthers. 2000. Acquisition or greenfield start-up? Institutional, cultural and transaction cost influences. *Strategic Management Journal* 21 (1): 89–97.

Burton, S., and A. Soboleva. 2011. Interactive or reactive? Marketing with Twitter. *Journal of Consumer Marketing* 28 (7): 491–499.

Campbell, J.T., L. Eden, and S.R. Miller. 2012. Multinationals and corporate social responsibility in host countries: Does distance matter? *Journal of International Business Studies* 43 (1): 84–106.

Carroll, A.B., and A.K. Buchholtz. 2006. *Business and society. Ethics and stakeholder management.* 6th ed. Mason: Thomson.

Carter, S. 1997. *Global agricultural marketing management.* Rome: FAO. http://www.fao.org/docrep/w5973e/w5973e0b.htm. Accessed 26 November, 2015.

Castelló, I., and J.M. Lozano. 2011. Searching for new forms of legitimacy through corporate responsibility rhetoric. *Journal of Business Ethics* 100 (1): 11–29.

Combs, J.G., D.J. Ketchen, C.L. Shook, and J.C. Short. 2011. Antecedents and consequences of franchising: Past accomplishments and future challenges. *Journal of Management* 37 (1): 99–126.

Corporate Nigeria. 2015. Corporate Nigeria – FDI overview. http://www.infomercatiesteri.it/public/images/paesi/23/files/FDI%20CORPORATE%20NIGERIA%20%20012013.pdf. Accessed 29 Aug 2017.

Crilly, D. 2011. Predicting stakeholder orientation in the multinational enterprise: A mid-range theory. *Journal of International Business Studies* 42 (5): 694–717.

D'Aunno, T., R.I. Sutton, and R.H. Price. 1991. Isomorphism and external support in conflicting institutional environments: A study of drug abuse treatment units. *Academy of Management Journal* 34: 636–661.

Dabholkar, P.A., and X. Sheng. 2012. Consumer participation in using online recommendation agents: Effects on satisfaction, trust, and purchase intentions. *Service Industries Journal* 32 (9): 1433–1449.

Dacin, M.T. 1997. Isomorphism in context: The power and prescription of institutional norms. *Academy of Management Journal* 40: 46–81.

DiMaggio, P., and W. Powell. 1983. The iron cage revisited: Institutional isomorphism and collective rationality in organizational fields. *American Sociological Review* 48 (2): 147–160.

Dixon, R., A. Guariglia, and R. Vijayakumaran. 2015. Managerial ownership, corporate governance, and firms' exporting decisions: Evidence from Chinese listed companies.*The European Journal of Finance* 1–39. https://doi.org/10.1080/1351847X.2015.1025990.

Doh, J., S. Rodrigues, A. Saka-Helmhout, and M. Makhija. 2017. International business responses to institutional voids. *Journal of International Business Studies* 48 (3): 293–307.

Donaldson, T., and L.E. Preston. 1995. The stakeholder theory of the corporation: Concepts, evidence, and implications. *Academy of Management Review* 20 (1): 65–91.

Donath, J., and D. Boyd. 2004. Public displays of connection. *BT Technology Journal* 22 (4): 71–82.

Doz, Y.L., and C.K. Prahalad. 1980. How MNCs cope with host-government intervention. *Harvard Business Review, International Business* 58 (2). https://hbr.org/1980/03/how-mncs-cope-with-host-government-intervention. Accessed 29 Aug 2017.

Emmanuel, T., and K. David. 2005. Strategic alliance and models of collaboration. *Journal of Management Decision* 43 (1): 123–148.

Falola, T. (2001). *Culture and customs of Nigeria.* Westport: Greenwood Publishing Group.

FDIIntelligence.com. 2015. Nigerian infrastructure: Building from the base up – locations. http://www.fdiintelligence.com/Locations/Middle-East-Africa/Nigeria/Nigerian-infrastructure-building-from-the-base-up. Accessed 29 Aug 2017.

Fernández-Mesa, A., and J. Alegre. 2015. Entrepreneurial orientation and export intensity: Examining the interplay of organizational learning and innovation. *International Business Review* 24 (1): 148–156.

Fieseler, C., M. Fleck, and M. Meckel. 2010. Corporate social responsibility in the blogosphere. *Journal of Business Ethics* 91: 599–614.

Foley, J. 1999. *The global entrepreneur: Taking your business international.* Chicago: Dearborn Trade. ISBN 1574101242.

Fosfuri, A., M.S. Giarratana, and E. Roca. 2011. Community-focused strategies. *Strategic Organization* 9 (3): 222–239.

Freeman, R.E. 1984. *Strategic management: A stakeholder approach.* Boston: Pitman.

Gabrielsson, M., V.H.M. Kirpalani, P. Dimitratos, C.A. Solberg, and A. Zucchella. 2008. Born globals: Propositions to help advance the theory. *International Business Review* 17 (4): 385–401.

Goodrick, E., and G.R. Salancik. 1996. Organizational discretion in responding to institutional practices: Hospitals and cesarean births. *Administrative Science Quarterly* 41: 1–28.

Greenwood, M. 2007. Stakeholder engagement: Beyond the myth of corporate responsibility. *Journal of Business Ethics* 74 (4): 315–327.

Groza, M.D., M.R. Pronschinske, and M. Walker. 2011. Perceived organizational motives and consumer responses to proactive and reactive CSR. *Journal of Business Ethics* 102 (4): 639–652.

Gulati, R. 1995. Does familiarity breed trust? The implications of repeated ties for contractual choice in alliances. *Academy of Management Journal* 38 (1): 85–112.

Gulko, O. 2014. Importance of networks for International New Ventures entry to Russian and Ukrainian steel industry market. Masters Thesis, University of Oulu, Oulu Business School, Department of Management and International Business.

Harrison, J.S., D.A. Bosse, and R.A. Phillips. 2010. Managing for stakeholders, stakeholder utility functions, and competitive advantage. *Strategic Management Journal* 31 (1): 58–74.

Harting, T.R., S.S. Harmeling, and S. Venkataraman. 2006. Innovative stakeholder relations: When "ethics pays" (and when it doesn't). *Business Ethics Quarterly* 16 (1): 43–68.

Hemphill, T.A., and W. Lillevik. 2011. The global economic ethic manifesto: Implementing a moral values foundation in the multinational enterprise. *Journal of Business Ethics* 101 (2): 213–230.

Hilmersson, M., and H. Jansson. 2012. Reducing uncertainty in the emerging market entry process: On the relationship among international experiential knowledge, institutional distance, and uncertainty. *Journal of International Marketing* 20 (4): 96–110.

Hoffmann C., and C. Lutz. 2013. The impact of social media on stakeholder engagement. 2013 Annual ICA Preconference, Edinburgh. https://www.researchgate.net/publication/259452067_The_Impact_of_Social_Media_on_Stakeholder_Engagement/. Accessed 30 Aug 2017. https://doi.org/10.13140/2.1.2934.9442.

Holtbrügge, D., and A. Baron. 2013. Market entry strategies in emerging markets: An institutional study in the BRIC countries. *Thunderbird International Business Review* 55 (3): 237–252.

van Hoorn, A., and R. Maseland. 2016. How institutions matter for international business: Institutional distance effects vs institutional profile effects. *Journal of International Business Studies* 47 (3): 374–381.

Hoskisson, R.E., L. Eden, C.M. Lau, and M. Wright. 2000. Strategy in emerging economies. *Academy of Management Journal* 43 (3): 249–267.

Hoskisson, R.E., M. Wright, I. Filatotchev, and M.W. Peng. 2013. Emerging multinationals from mid-range economies: The influence of institutions and factor markets. *Journal of Management Studies* 50 (7): 1295–1321.

Imaralu, C. 2015. Top 5 social media savvy companies in Nigeria. http://venturesafrica.com/top-5-companies-with-effective-social-media-presence-in-nigeria/. Accessed 29 Aug 2017.

Inauen, S., & Schoeneborn, D. (2014). Twitter and its usage for dialogic stakeholder communication by MNCs and NGOs. In Communicating Corporate Social Responsibility: Perspectives and Practice (pp. 283-310). Emerald Group Publishing Limited.

Ionascu, D., K.E. Meyer, and S. Estrin. 2004. Institutional distance and international business strategies in emerging economies. https://deepblue.lib.umich.edu/bitstream/handle/2027.42/40114/wp728.pdf. Accessed 28 Aug 2017.

Johanson, J., and J.E. Vahlne. 1977. The internationalization process of the firm: A model of knowledge development and increasing foreign market commitments. *Journal of International Business Studies* 8: 23–32.

Johanson, J., and J.-E. Vahlne. 2003. Business relationship learning and commitment in the internationalization process. *Journal of International Entrepreneurship* 1 (1): 83–101.

———. 2009. The Uppsala internationalization process model revisited: From liability of foreignness to liability of outsidership. *Journal of International Business Studies* 40 (9): 1411–1431.

Jones, B., Temperley, J., & Lima, A. (2009). Corporate reputation in the era of Web 2.0: the case of Primark. *Journal of Marketing Management*, 25 (9–10): 927–939.

Kale, P., and H. Singh. 2009. Managing strategic alliances: What do we know now, and where do we go from here? *Academy of Management Perspectives* 23 (3): 45–62.

Kostova, T. 1996. Success of the transnational transfer of organizational practices within multinational companies. Unpublished doctoral dissertation, Minneapolis: University of Minnesota.

———. 1999. Transnational transfer of strategic organizational practices: A contextual perspective. *Academy of Management Review* 24 (2): 308–324.

Kostova, T., and K. Roth. 2002. Adoption of an organizational practice by subsidiaries of multinational corporations: Institutional and relational effects. *Academy of Management Journal* 45 (1): 215–233.

Kostova, T., and S. Zaheer. 1999. Organizational legitimacy under conditions of complexity: The case of the multinational enterprise. *Academy of Management Review* 24 (1): 64–81.

Kostova, T., Roth, K., and Dacin, M.T. (2008). Institutional theory in the study of multinational corporations: A critique and new directions. *Academy of management review* 33 (4): 994–1006.

Loane, S., and J. Bell. 2006. Rapid internationalisation among entrepreneurial firms in Australia, Canada, Ireland and New Zealand. *International Marketing Review* 23 (5): 467–485.

Marquis, C., and M. Reynard. 2015. Institutional strategies in emerging markets. *Academy of Management Annals* 9 (1): 291–335.

Meisling, C. 2014. Consulting firms' use of Twitter for interactive stakeholder communication. Master Thesis, Frederiksberg: Copenhagen Business School.

Meschi, P.X., and U. Wassmer. 2013. The effect of foreign partner network embeddedness on international joint venture failure: Evidence from European firms' investments in emerging economies. *International Business Review* 22 (4): 713–724.

Meyer, K.E., and M.W. Peng. 2005. Probing theoretically into Central and Eastern Europe: Transactions, resources and institutions. *Journal of International Business Studies* 36: 600–621.

Meyer, J., W.R. Scott, and D. Strang. 1987. Centralization, fragmentation, and school district complexity. *Administrative Science Quarterly* 32 (2): 186–201.

Moen, O., M. Gavlen, and I. Endresen. 2004. Internationalization of small, computer software firms: Entry forms and market selection. *European Journal of Marketing* 38 (9–10): 1236–1251.

Moore, E. 2012. Civets, Brics and the next 11. Financial times. https://www.ft.com/content/c14730ae-aff3-11e1-ad0b-00144feabdc0. Accessed 30 Aug 2017.

Ndumanya, N., and D. Quadri. 2015. Experts tip franchising as an ideal way to tap into Nigeria's huge market. http://www.nigerianfranchise.org/. Accessed 28 Aug 2017.

Nigerian National Petroleum Company. 2016. Joint venture operations. http://nnpcgroup.com/NNPCBusiness/UpstreamVentures.aspx. Accessed 20 Aug 2017.

North, D.C. 1990. *Institutions, institutional change and economic performance*. Cambridge: Cambridge University Press.

Ojala, A. 2009. Internationalization of knowledge-intensive SMEs: The role of network relationships in the entry to a psychically distant market. *International Business Review* 18 (1): 50–59. https://doi.org/10.1016/j.ibusrev.2008.10.002.

Oliver, C. (1991). Strategic responses to institutional processes. *Academy of management review* 16 (1), 145–179.

Palthe, J. 2014. Regulative, normative, and cognitive elements of organizations: Implications for managing change. *Management and Organizational Studies* 1 (2): 59.

Park, S.H., and Y. Luo. 2001. Guanxi and organizational dynamics: Organizational networking in Chinese firms. *Strategic Management Journal* 22 (5): 455–477.

Post, J.E., L.E. Preston, and S. Sachs. 2002. Managing the extended enterprise: The new stakeholder view. *California Management Review* 45 (1): 6–28.

Quer, D., E. Claver, and R. Andreu. 2007. Foreign market entry mode in the hotel industry: The impact of country-and firm-specific factors. *International Business Review* 16 (3): 362–376.

Ramamurti, R. 2004. Developing countries and MNEs: Extending and enriching the research agenda. *Journal of International Business Studies* 35 (4): 277–283.

Robert, S., and W. Zheying. 2012. Institutional distance and local isomorphism strategy. *Journal of International Business Studies* 43 (4): 344–367.

Rosenzweig, P.M., and N. Nohria. 1994. Influences on human resource management practices in multinational corporations. *Journal of International Business Studies* 25 (2): 229–251.

Rosenzweig, P.M., and J.V. Singh. 1991. Organizational environments and the multinational enterprise. *Academy of Management Review* 16 (2): 340–361.

Salomon, R., and Wu, Z. (2012). Institutional distance and local isomorphism strategy. *Journal of International Business Studies* 43 (4): 343–367.

Sashi, C.M. 2012. Customer engagement, buyer-seller relationships, and social media. *Management Decision* 50 (1–2): 253–272.

Sawhney, M., G. Verona, and E. Prandelli. 2005. Collaborating to create: The internet as a platform for customer engagement in product innovation. *Journal of Interactive Marketing* 19 (4): 4–17.

Schneider, M., J. Vulliety, and C. Olsburg. 2002. International joint ventures. International trade forum magazine. http://www.tradeforum.org/International-Joint-Ventures/. Accessed 29 Aug 2017.

Schoeneborn, D., and S. Inauen. 2014. Twitter and its usage for dialogic stakeholder communication by MNCs and NGOs. In *Communicating corporate social responsibility: Perspectives and practice*, ed. R. Tench, W. Sun, and B. Jones, 283–310. Bingley: Emerald Group Publishing Limited.

Scott, W.R. 1995. *Institutions and organizations: Foundations for organizational science*. London: A Sage Publication Series.

———. 2001. *Institutions and organizations*. 2nd ed. Thousand Oaks: Sage Publications.

———. 2008. *Institutions and organizations: Ideas and interests*. 3rd ed. Thousand Oaks: Sage Publications.

———. 2013. *Institutions and organizations: Ideas, interests, and identities*. Thousand Oaks: Sage Publications.

Sharma, D.D., and A. Blomstermo. 2003. The internationalization process of Born Globals: A network view. *International Business Review* 12 (6): 739–753.

Suchman, M.C. 1995. Managing legitimacy: Strategic and institutional approaches. *Academy of Management Review* 20: 571–610.

The Economist. 2014a. Africa's testing ground. https://www.economist.com/news/business/21613341-make-it-big-africa-business-must-succeed-nigeria-continents-largest-market-no. Accessed 28 Aug 2017.

———. 2014b. Nigeria: Africa's new number one. http://www.economist.com/news/leaders/21600685-nigerias-suddenly-supersized-economy-indeed-wonder-so-are-its-still-huge?frsc=dgla. Accessed 28 Aug 2017.

UNCTAD. 2013. World investment report 2013. Global value chains: Investment and trade for development New York and Geneva: United Nations Conference on Trade and Development. http://unctad.org/en/PublicationsLibrary/wir2013_en.pdf. Accessed 29 Aug 2017.

World Bank. 2017. Doing business: Measuring business regulations. http://www.doingbusiness.org/rankings. Accessed 29 Aug 2017.

World Bank Databank. 2016. Gross domestic product 2016, PPP. http://databank.worldbank.org/data/download/GDP_PPP.pdf. Accessed 11 Aug 2017.

World Economic Forum on Africa. 2014. Africa by numbers: A focus on Nigeria. Special Report of World Economic Forum on Africa 2014. http://www.ey.com/Publication/vwLUAssets/EY-Nigeria-Country-Report/$FILE/EY-Nigeria-Country-Report.pdf. Accessed 28 Aug 2017.

World Investment Report. 2015. World investment report 2015: Annex tables. 2015 from http://unctad.org/en/Pages/DIAE/World%20Investment%20Report/Annex-Tables.aspx. Accessed 20 Nov 2015.

Xin, K.R., and J.L. Pearce. 1996. Guanxi: Connections as substitutes for formal institutional support. *Academy of Management Journal* 39: 1641–1658.

Xu, D., and K.E. Meyer. 2013. Linking theory and context: 'Strategy research in emerging economies' after Wright et al. 2005. *Journal of Management Studies* 50 (7): 1322–1346.

Xu, D., and O. Shenkar. 2002. Note: Institutional distance and the multinational enterprise. *Academy of Management Review* 27 (4): 608–618.

Xu, D., Y. Pan, and P.W. Beamish. 2004. The effect of regulative and normative distances on MNE ownership and expatriate strategies. *Management International Review* 44 (3): 285–307.

Yang, M.M. 1994. *Gifts, favors and banquets: The art of social relationships in China*. New York: Cornell University Press.

Zaheer, S. 1995. Overcoming the liability of foreignness. *Academy of Management Journal* 38 (2): 341–363.

Zain, M., and I. Ng. 2006. The impacts of network relationships on SMEs' internationalization process. *Thunderbird International Business Review* 48 (2): 183–205.

Chapter 9
E-Commerce in Emerging Economies: A Multi-theoretical and Multilevel Framework and Global Firm Strategies

James Agarwal and Terry Wu

Abstract Internet usage and e-commerce have taken off like wildfire in developed countries, and emerging economies are rapidly embracing information technology today as well. Using a multi-theoretical and a multilevel framework, this study examines the determinants and deterrents of e-commerce growth potential in emerging economies. Based on the conceptual framework, the study highlights implications for MNEs, both from developed markets and emerging markets, operating in emerging economies.

Introduction

A global revolution, e-commerce has brought about a paradigm shift in the way business is conducted in developed countries as well as emerging economies such as those of Brazil, Russia, India, and China. The growth potential and success of e-commerce vary from country to country and market to market (Gabrielsson and Gabrielsson 2011). Accordingly, a key question worth asking is: What are the determinants and deterrents of e-commerce in emerging economies and how can global marketers better understand the underlying processes from a multi-theoretical perspective so as to better develop and implement growth strategies?

Electronic commerce involves sharing information, maintaining relationships, and conducting transactions in the business world by means of telecommunication networks (Dutta 1997). It spans national borders and expands business opportunities into distant reaches of the planet. Marketing possibilities have burgeoned exponentially. Research on e-commerce development tends to focus on specific areas, such as adoption (Wymer and Regan 2005), strategy (Damanpour and Damanpour

J. Agarwal
Haskayne Research Professor & Full Professor of Marketing at the Haskayne
School of Business, University of Calgary, Calgary, AB, Canada

T. Wu (✉)
Faculty of Business and Information Technology, University of Ontario Institute of Technology,
Oshawa, ON, Canada
e-mail: terry.wu@uoit.ca

© Springer International Publishing AG, part of Springer Nature 2018
J. Agarwal, T. Wu (eds.), *Emerging Issues in Global Marketing*,
https://doi.org/10.1007/978-3-319-74129-1_9

2001), retailing (Zhuang and Lederer 2003), security (Wang et al. 2002), and consumer trust and security (Pavlou 2003; Tan and Thoen 2003). Only a handful of researchers have attempted to develop a framework detailing the drivers and challenges of e-commerce growth (e.g., Dutta 1997; Globerman et al. 2001; Oxley and Yeung 2001; Zwass 1996), and even fewer offer theoretical perspectives (e.g., de la Torre and Moxon 2001; Singh and Kundu 2002). Zwass (1996) puts forth a general framework for e-commerce; his three layers included e-commerce infrastructure, e-commerce services, and e-commerce products and services. Dutta (1997) developed a broader approach identifying technology, social-cultural, commercial, and government/legal infrastructures as essential factors in the growth of e-commerce, in recognition of the importance of human and social factors; however, left unaddressed the underlying motivations and theories of how such factors facilitate e-commerce activity and growth. Oxley and Yeung (2001) argued that physical infrastructure is the most significant factor in determining e-commerce readiness of a country and that factors related to "rule of law" were also significant.

While such frameworks are helpful, the lack of a comprehensive theoretical approach in delineating the factors responsible for e-commerce growth is a major limitation impeding our understanding of the global e-commerce phenomenon. Of note, Dunning's OLI paradigm (Dunning 1995, 1998) was extended by Singh and Kundu (2002), who developed a framework to reflect changes engendered by Internet-based e-commerce companies that made a significant theoretical contribution to our understanding of e-commerce activities. Their revised paradigm, the N-OLI framework (i.e., institution-based network-ownership, location, and internalization), reflects network (N)-based advantages unique to e-commerce, namely, embeddedness, electronic brokerages, and network economics. However, the N-OLI framework fails to clarify the role of institutions in emerging economies that not only have a large institutional distance but are often inflicted with institutional voids. As their share of the world economy increases, emerging nations are expected to become a major part of global economic growth in the coming years (Khanna and Palepu 1997, 2010), a shift that is enabled largely by e-commerce.

The present work advances a multi-theoretical and multilevel framework with implications for global marketers planning e-commerce growth strategies in emerging markets; it aims to explicate the diverse factors arising from multiple levels (i.e., global, national, and transactional levels) that influence the growth potential of e-commerce in emerging economies (Agarwal and Wu 2015). We use multiple lenses of established international business (IB) and international marketing theories that intersect, including transaction cost economics (TCE) theory (Coase 1937; Williamson 1983, 1991), the resource- and knowledge-based view (RBV/KBV) theory (Barney 1991; Wernerfelt 1984), and network theory (Granovetter 1985, 1992; Rowley 1997), along with the overlap of these approaches within the e-commerce framework of the N-OLI paradigm (Dunning 1995, 1998). Institutional theory (DiMaggio and Powell 1983; North 1990) guides our understanding of the institutional effects on firm growth behavior, especially in the context of emerging economies, whereas entrepreneurship theory (Baron 1998; Shane and Venkataraman 2000) emphasizes the enterprising role played by entrepreneurs of opportunity recognition and exploitation amidst institutional voids.

In this chapter, the multi-theoretical framework is based on the premise that no single theory can adequately capture all the factors that promote adoption and expansion of e-commerce firms in the global marketplace. Each theory's set of assumptions possesses unique strengths and weaknesses; collectively, these theories can offer a more complete picture of firms' e-commerce activities (Agarwal and Wu 2015). First, the presumption that knowledge is not equally and universally distributed as in RBV theory (or KBV view theory) in electronic markets has been largely, in principle, debunked. Second, the TCE theory effectively explains vertical integration decisions for e-commerce firms. The theory is limited because firms assess the merits of control not only through reductions in transaction costs but also based on other non-TCE-related features such as capabilities development, value creation, global integration, and market power (Dunning 2000; Madhok 2006). Issues of control and integration as in TCE theory may not be completely relevant (especially in the case of e-commerce firms), because it is possible to simultaneously disinternalize through alliance capitalism and to exercise control due to technological advances and innovation. Finally, the strategic behavior of firms helps explain isomorphism as in institutional theory (DiMaggio and Powell 1983). The advantages of oligopolistic firms—for example, information asymmetry and market imperfections (Hymer 1970)—are minimized for firms engaged in e-commerce activities. Unlike institutions that ultimately tend toward isomorphism, individual and institutional entrepreneurs seek unique opportunities and creative business models (Agarwal and Wu 2015). In general, e-commerce is particularly conducive to business models with low entry barriers and potentially high returns (Amit and Zott 2001). According to the network theory, the speed and extent to which new ventures are established depend on the network density, patterns of relationships, and the alliances formed (Baron 1998; Rowley 1997).

The synergistic combination of multiple theoretical approaches enables us to better understand how e-commerce growth potential results from technological innovation and entrepreneurial activities (Agarwal and Wu 2015). This potential includes minimizing transaction costs and leveraging network and firm-specific resources, along with adapting firm-specific resources and strategies to match differing institutional environments. The next section briefly addresses the institution-based N-OLI framework for e-commerce in emerging economies.

E-Commerce: A Brief Review of the Multiple Theories

Transaction Cost Economics (TCE) Theory

Rooted in the work of Ronald Coase (1937), this theory was notably advanced by Williamson (1983, 1991). It argues that firms exist to provide products and services at lower transaction costs than the market would naturally present. TCE theory identifies conditions specific to firms such as environmental uncertainty, asset specificity, and frequency of transactions—conditions that justify the need for network governance. The level of analysis of TCE is transactions, and the explanatory variables include transaction characteristics of environmental uncertainty, asset specificity, and frequency. Assumptions of TCE are rooted in bounded rationality and opportunism, with the source of competitiveness based on efficient management of transactions, accomplished through minimizing transaction cost. TCE effectively explains vertical integration decisions across firms. However, its weakness lies in its static orientation; furthermore, the theory does not consider non-transaction costs and benefits, and it presents an inherent difficulty in measuring transaction cost.

Resource- and Knowledge-Based View Theory

The growth of e-commerce companies can be explained by RBV and KBV theory of the firm. E-commerce firms tend to be small- or medium-sized entrepreneurial firms with a global competitiveness based on the unique set of resources resident in networks (Singh and Kundu 2002). Today resource-based ownership is increasingly concerned with intangible assets and intellectual property rights as MNEs in OECD economies become asset-light and knowledge-intensive (Mudambi 2004). According to KBV theory, firms are able to take advantage of unique and superior knowledge transfer capabilities based on "higher-order organizing principles" (Kogut and Zander 1993). The level of analysis of RBV/KBV is individual/firm, and the resource characteristics include valuable, rare, inimitable, and nonsubstitutable (VRIN) attributes. The assumptions of RBV/KBV are based on resource exploration and exploitation, while the source of competitiveness depends on efficient management of resources.

Network Theory

With its level of analysis as the organizational field, this theory focuses on explanatory variables that include patterns of relationships between members of the network, the firm's behavior as influenced by the network structure, and its position in the network (Rowley 1997). The networks of social, professional, and economic relations enable the embedded firms to adopt various strategies, products, ideas, and innovations (Granovetter 1985, 1992). Such embeddedness allows adoption and expansion of e-commerce, which is also facilitated by low entry and exit costs as well as low coordination and search costs. The assumptions underlying network theory are rooted in relational orientation, and its source of competitiveness is based on development and exploitation of formal and informal networks.

Ownership-Location-Internalization (OLI) Theory

According to this theory (or paradigm), a firm's international growth and mode of entry depend on advantages of ownership (O), location (L), and internalization (I), which serve as explanatory variables. The level of analysis of OLI theories is the firm. The OLI paradigm stands on bounded rationality and opportunism as assumptions in its effort to explain the growth of e-commerce firms. The sources of competitiveness include O, L, and I advantages for foreign direct investment, at least O advantage for contractual agreement, and O and I advantages for export operation (Agarwal and Wu 2015). In the e-commerce context, the source of O advantage lies in entrepreneurship and innovation, knowledge, and intangible resources; the source of L-advantage is technology-based infrastructure, social capital, and knowledge, interactivity, and IP protection; and the source of I-advantage is vertical or horizontal integration. The OLI paradigm integrates RBV theory, TCE theory, and international trade theory in its multi-theoretical approach, which is a strength.

Institutional Theory

Institutions are built on formal rules (e.g., constitutions, laws, and regulations) and informal constraints (e.g., norms, conventions, and self-imposed codes of conduct) that operate at both national and firm/individual levels (North 1990, 2005). Institutions provide the structure in which firms operate, setting the "rules of the game" and dictating the behavior of individuals and organizations through regulations, collective constructions of social reality, and social obligations. A theory of isomorphism was suggested by DiMaggio and Powell (1983) that explains homogeneity of firms in an organizational field. The level of analysis of institutional theory is macro institutional and the firm's organizational field and the explanatory variables include isomorphism, i.e., coercive, mimetic, and normative isomorphism. The strength of institutional theory is its useful explication of homogeneity across firms; the weakness is its inability to test the effectiveness of individual-level decisions upon collective constructs such as firms in an organizational field.

Entrepreneurship Theory

While institutions devise and enforce rules and regulations, entrepreneurs are the main players in the business world, constantly seeking, identifying, and evaluating fresh opportunities to commercialize new products and services (Shane and Venkataraman 2000). They welcome risk, uncertainty, innovation, and change while also embracing improved methods of allocating resources. Because of entrepreneurs' great need for information search capabilities to assess risk, e-commerce facilitates their pursuit of entrepreneurial opportunities. The adoption of e-commerce also allows entrepreneurs to interact with others in the venture creation process, thus potentially reducing the high knowledge asymmetry that characterizes e-commerce. Furthermore, e-commerce is conducive to business models that feature high competitiveness, low entry barriers, and potentially high returns, all of which are found in entrepreneurial endeavor (Amit and Zott 2001). This theory's level of analysis is the individual or the institution, and the explanatory variables include factors surrounding opportunity recognition, alertness, individual cognitive factors, and opportunity exploitation.

A Multilevel Framework for E-Commerce in Emerging Economies

Which factors at the global, national, and transactional levels help or hinder the growth of e-commerce in emerging economies? Answering this question requires multiple theoretical considerations. Figure 9.1 presents a multilevel framework for e-commerce in emerging economies[1].

Global-Level Factors

Relevant influences on e-commerce at the global level are explored in this section, including multilateral agreements, strategic behavior of firms, and technological innovation.

Multilateral Agreements

The game-changing advent of the Internet grabs the most academic and media attention these days, but it is by no means the only important driver of economic growth in emerging economies. Developments in trade and investment liberalization, regional integration, and the activity of the World Trade Organization (WTO) all play influential roles (Agarwal and Wu 2004, 2015). All WTO member countries have committed to applying WTO rules to international trade in goods and services. The principle of nondiscrimination and national treatment is applied to e-commerce activities. Emerging economies gain from increased access to international markets without trade barriers. Many e-commerce transactions involve technology-related products, and under the framework of the WTO Agreement on Trade-Related

---

[1] Some parts of this paper have been adapted and extended from Agarwal and Wu (2015).

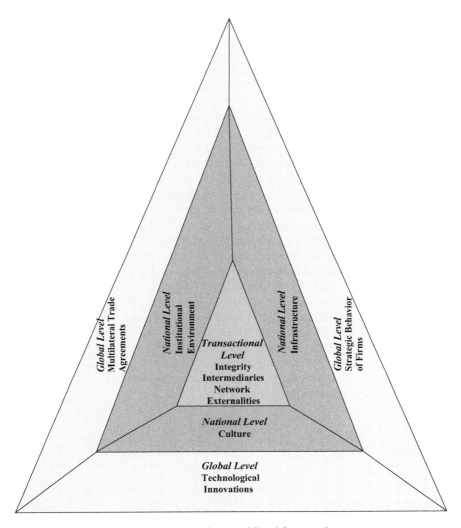

Fig. 9.1 E-commerce in emerging economies: a multilevel framework

Aspects of Intellectual Property Rights (TRIPS), member countries are obligated to protect intellectual property rights.

The opportunities created by multilateral trade agreements under the rubric of the WTO and other trade agreements can be viewed through the lens of institutional theory. The WTO serves as an exogenous global institution with the aim of creating a level playing field for emerging economies traditionally saddled with institutional voids and market imperfections. Its framework ideally reduces market imperfections through collective commitment to the principles of national treatment, transparency, and judicial reviewability. In addition, the WTO attempts to address and overcome information asymmetry in issues related to e-commerce in global markets (Agarwal and Wu 2015).

Trade liberalization achieved through regional trade agreements (RTAs) also triggers and supports growth of e-commerce in emerging economies. Many RTAs include provisions on e-commerce, particularly in the areas of services and investment (Herman 2010).

Institutional changes open doors for entrepreneurial opportunity. Because multilateral agreements reduce most transaction and coordination costs for e-commerce firms to conduct international business transactions, developed-market MNEs have taken advantage of gradual reductions in trade and investment barriers in emerging economies by focusing on their firm-specific and country-specific advantages. Meanwhile, amidst ever-increasing international competition, emerging-market MNEs have followed an alternative model of growth by exploring new resources, capability development and competitive advantage (Dunning 2000; Luo and Tung 2007). Overcoming their late entry into the market through linkages to acquire new technological and financial resources that are leveraged on their path to internationalization (Mathews 2006), emerging-market MNEs tend to expand initially in local markets and then progress to global markets. With phased-in liberalization of the foreign ownership of e-commerce as a result of multilateral trade agreements, the growth trend in e-commerce is likely to continue for both emerging and developed-market MNEs (Agarwal and Wu 2015). While smaller firms from emerging economies may be new in their exploration of e-commerce, spurred by global competition and a desire to catch up with developed-market MNEs (i.e., convergence goals—see next section), these firms tend to rapidly seize e-commerce opportunities in the initial phase of their growth to close the gap.

Strategic Behavior of Firms

Emerging markets are favored foreign direct investment (FDI) destinations, with entrepreneurial entrants into these markets largely depending on e-commerce to conduct their business. This positively impacts the growth of e-commerce in emerging markets, and a mimetic trend multiplies the effect when others follow the industry leaders in their respective field (Zhao and Wang 2009). This form of imitation occurs either because firms perceive other firms to have more information or because they want to converge to maintain competitive parity (Lieberman and Asaba 2006; Wu et al. 2003).

Such a trend can be explained in part by institutional theory (DiMaggio and Powell 1983; North 2005). MNEs that have adopted e-commerce in their home country encourage their global subsidiaries to follow their mandate across geographic borders, thereby fostering isomorphism.

In addition to mimetic isomorphism, a pattern of normative isomorphism is seen among firms influenced by informal institutions that arise externally, such as perceived subjective norms, or internally from social referents within the firm (Agarwal and Wu 2015). For example, in the context of small firms, Iacovou et al. (1995) identified external pressures from partners, rather than perceived benefits or organizational readiness, as an important determinant of IT-related technology adoption. These external pressures ultimately lead to industry standards and best practice models, which help facilitate the adoption and expansion of e-commerce. In general, the convergence of industry standards tends to result in more e-commerce in emerging economies.

Technological Innovations

Technological innovations and knowledge-based experience are key drivers of any firm's strategy and performance (Alon et al. 2013; Gregory et al. 2007; Zhu 2004). Adoption of new technology helps firms gain a competitive advantage, and firms in emerging economies are no exception. Most theories on international knowledge and R&D spillovers focus on transmissions via cross-country trade and FDI, as well as interfirm employee mobility from MNE subsidiaries to local firms. Some studies indicate the positive spillover effects of MNEs on local firms' capacity to innovate (see Buckley et al. 2002; Tian 2007). It should be noted, however, that a high representation of MNE subsidiaries in emerging markets may increase local competition, consequently decreasing the local firms' incentive to innovate (Spencer 2008). It is possible that where the technology gap is high, local firms may try to avoid costly R&D by imitating the technologies of MNEs, especially in economies with a weak IP protection regime. Yet as emerging economies narrow the technology gap over time through technological accumulation, the collective motivation of local firms to innovate will probably increase (Agarwal and Wu 2015).

We noted earlier that entrepreneurial ventures involving opportunity recognition, evaluation, and allocation of resources are driven by individuals and not institutions (Baron 1998). The launching of new ventures is influenced by patterns of relationships and network density.

National-Level Factors

Moving down from the global level of our framework to review some key national-level factors of emerging economies that can help or hinder the growth of e-commerce, this section assesses the influence of government policies and laws, national infrastructures, and local culture.

Institutional Environment: Government Policies and Regulations

Providing significant incentives or disincentives for investment in a particular country, government policies and regulations establish a structure for firms to confidently participate in e-commerce activities or to wisely opt out. The fundamental theoretical basis for government's role can be attributed to institutional theory (DiMaggio and Powell 1983; North 2005). Favorable policies naturally attract business, a phenomenon that Dunning (1995, 1998) attributes to the location or "L pull factor." As firms move in, the location advantage that accrues from government policies can create a critical mass for accelerated growth, as demonstrated by the results of positive e-commerce strategies adopted by several emerging economies (Agarwal and Wu 2015). An open and interrelated set of e-commerce policies and activities further promotes and enables accelerated growth of e-commerce.

However, given complex institutional differences worldwide (i.e., developed versus emerging markets), organizations must adapt their e-commerce practices to fit the institutional environment of the host country—a facet of the neo-institutional theory (Greenwood and Hinings 1996). Ultimately, isomorphic behavior will prevail among organizations in the same environment due to coercive, mimetic, and normative pressures (Agarwal and Wu 2015).

Although governments in emerging economies may enthusiastically promote e-commerce for economic development, some nations remain suspicious of its potential impact on social and political stability, contributing to entrepreneurial uncertainty, problems with asymmetric information and monitoring, and unstable or nonexistent agency relationships within a foreign governmental structure (Agarwal and Wu 2015). Transaction cost economics or TCE theory (introduced early in the chapter and which explains economics-based decisions) is relevant for understanding the cost-benefit situation of political governance and the likely political hazards in emerging markets (Delios and Henisz 2000). When political risk is high, firms may still decide to invest in FDI by considering other arrangements such as forming a regulatory agency or public-private partnership that will mitigate political hazards (Henisz and Zellner 2004). Political alliances constitute firm-specific advantage (based on RBV theory) that developed-market MNEs gain from deep local embeddedness in a given political system, resulting in greater transparency of and access to political information (de la Torre and Moxon 2001). Ample research evidence shows that political connections greatly facilitate economic exchange and firm performance in emerging economies (see Li and Zhang 2007; Li et al. 2008). Such embeddedness and connections give emerging-market MNEs an immediate edge to apply country-specific advantage in order to enhance their firm-specific advantage.

Legal Environment

A political and legal environment offering transparency and protection in online markets is obviously a key driver of e-commerce growth in emerging economies (Oxley and Yeung 2001; Zhou et al. 2008). Not surprisingly, Zhou et al. (2008) conclude that the rule of law has a positive impact on e-commerce diffusion. This effect is more pronounced in emerging economies (Agarwal and Wu 2015); Zhu and Thatcher (2010) note that its importance diminishes as a country reaches a mature stage of e-commerce expansion. Borrowing from institutional theory, Martinez and Williams (2010) found that the quality of national institutions, namely, an open society with a strong rule of law, political stability, regulatory quality, and control of corruption, fosters ICT adoption in both developed and developing countries.

The foremost concern for many firms is protection of intellectual property (IP) rights. When opportunism and uncertainty are high, firms tend to choose hierarchies instead of markets and are likely to initiate internationalization activities in countries with minimal regulatory hazards and a similar legal framework to their own (Coeurderoy and Murray 2008; Hagendoorn et al. 2005). Thus, to attract e-commerce, emerging economies need to develop cyber laws defining a legal framework for Internet transactions. While there is some movement in this direction among emerging economies, other governments are lagging behind (Agarwal and Wu 2015). The main concern is IP protection. Specifically, the quality of the legal environment serves as a key locational determinant (L-advantage) of e-commerce growth (Dunning and Wymbs 2001).

A related issue in terms of legal environment is consumer protection. When governments fail to put sufficient protections and safeguards in place, consumers in emerging economies are reluctant to conduct e-commerce activities. Inadequate consumer rights protection creates an institutional void and barrier to the expansion of e-commerce in emerging economies.

Infrastructural Environment

This section addresses three important forms of infrastructure in any country that affect e-commerce prospects and implementation: physical infrastructure, financial and market infrastructure, and social infrastructure (Agarwal and Wu 2015). All three contribute to what is known as absorptive capacity of a firm, defined as the ability to value, assimilate, and apply new information to commercial ends (Cohen and Leventhal 1990). Zahra and George (2002) distinguished two types of absorptive capacity: "potential" and "realized." The potential absorptive capacity indicates the firm is receptive to acquiring and assimilating external knowledge (Agarwal and Wu 2015).

Taking full advantage of absorptive capacity depends on features of the emerging-nation's economy as well as MNE characteristics. Absorptive capacity differs across firms based on their past experience, knowledge, and organizational learning (Delios and Henisz 2000). Because knowledge accumulation is path-dependent, firms are heterogeneous in their ability to recognize and exploit e-commerce opportunities. While some emerging economies have significantly exploited absorptive capacity in one or more of the infrastructural pillars, others are still exploring and assimilating the future potential of e-commerce. Despite the global reach of the Internet, there remains a gap in the ability MNEs to fully exploit the absorptive capacity of infrastructures in emerging markets.

Physical Infrastructure

Most developed-market MNEs want to invest in countries where resources, capabilities, and physical infrastructure (L-advantage) can enable them to exploit their ownership (O-level) advantage (de la Torre and Moxon 2001). The vital physical components necessary for e-commerce include information technology and telecommunications infrastructure—both hard infrastructure and a telecommunications network—in order to develop and maintain Internet access and hence e-commerce (Dubosson-Torbay et al. 2002; Oxley and Yeung 2001). Poor physical infrastructure results in a stagnant situation where Internet service providers in emerging economies often are unable to justify the cost of investment due to limited activity via e-commerce, even though Internet access is acknowledged as a conduit to economic development.

Financial and Market Infrastructure

One of the chief obstacles to e-commerce activity (including foreign investment) in many emerging economies is the poorly developed nature of financial and market infrastructure. E-commerce requires a network of financial intermediaries to link electronic banking and payment systems including credit and debit card networks with new retail interfaces (Agarwal and Wu 2015). Many nations have to start from the ground up to create an electronic network of banking and investment services, insurance, brokerage, credit rating companies, and other services. Because banks and financial institutions do not support online payment in some countries, citizens are accustomed to paying by bank draft or cash on delivery. While cultural characteristics, history, and politics shape the development of a nation's institutions, both in form and function, it is the government that generally must take the lead in identifying and addressing these institutional voids that impede e-commerce (North 2005).

Social Infrastructure

Social infrastructure refers to the education level of the general population as well as the skilled labor force in a nation (Agarwal and Wu 2015). Relatively recent studies focusing on the human-capital aspects of business recognize the critical contributions of entrepreneurs and other employees (Agarwal and Wu 2015; Graf and Mudambi 2005). While international business models explaining FDI decisions have historically failed to include human capital, the importance of investments in human capital (O-specific advantage) is now more generally acknowledged. For example, in addition to innovation, entrepreneurs often map the institutional context in a foreign country to identify infrastructural voids as entrepreneurial opportunities, thereby promoting the spread of e-commerce. At the firm level, other aspects of human capital make the wheels of business turn. Knowledge is integrated at all levels primarily through human resources, and thus a firm's absorptive capacity largely depends on the absorptive capacity of its employees (Cohen and Levinthal 1990; Kogut and Zander 1993). Many studies suggest that investments in human capital are critical to the expansion of e-commerce in emerging economies (allowing them to "catch up" to more developed economies); studies in this area also note that the rate of economic growth declines as the economies gain more wealth (Contractor and Mudambi 2008; Zhao 2002).

Culture

A nation's infrastructure and formal institutions are largely based upon informal systems of cultural norms and values, and the role of culture is no less important in the adoption and expansion of e-commerce (Agarwal and Wu 2015; Zhu and Thatcher 2010). For example, cultures that hold traditional and survival values as opposed to secular-rational and self-expression values are less ready for e-commerce adoption (Berthon et al. 2008). Furthermore, the distinction between individualistic and collectivistic cultures carries important ramifications for understanding the norms of society as well as the tendencies of individuals in a foreign country. Based on the Hofstede framework (Hofstede 1991), the dimension of individualism-collectivism influences IT adoption in that solitary applications such as online shopping may not be appealing in collectivist cultures, while online community-building sites may prove to generate more interest (Zhou et al. 2007).

Trust is perhaps the most important element of any transaction, and it is certainly a key consideration for an individual to engage in e-commerce. Trust must be present for the adoption of e-commerce because it affects consumers' willingness to participate in online shopping. Since e-commerce is a faceless transaction, trust deficit can slow the growth of e-commerce in emerging economies (Agarwal and Wu 2015). In collectivist societies, people will enter into a transaction only with other people whom they trust. This kind of trust is difficult to develop in a relatively new area like e-commerce, which is not a face-to-face medium. However, network resources often help build a culture of norms and trust, in addition to providing rapid dissemination of information and exchange of complementary assets.

Structured relationships do not serve to bridge disparate groups or subgroups, and therefore change occurs slowly in the society (Granovetter 1983). For this reason, resistance to change (or cultural inertia) is greater in collectivist societies (Agarwal and Wu 2015), and therefore adoption of e-commerce is likely to be slower.

Transactional-Level Factors

Integrity of Transactions

While trust is particularly important in collectivistic cultures or emerging economies where consumers do not have prior trust capital built, integrity of online transactions is critical to the success of e-commerce anywhere (Agarwal and Wu 2015). According to a study by Malhotra et al. (2004), Internet users are concerned with collection of personal data, the control they have over the data, and the awareness of privacy practices. And TCE holds that firms perceiving greater risk in transactions are likely to protect their interests and proprietary knowledge rather than disseminate over the Internet. In short, lack of trust and/or less than full integrity in online transactions will continue to impede the growth of e-commerce in emerging economies (Agarwal and Wu 2015).

Online Intermediaries

Another aspect of e-commerce that emerging economies must supply or create is the network of online intermediaries facilitated by the Internet to enable the efficiencies of e-commerce. This "electronic brokerage" allows firms to engage in partnerships to increase efficiency and avoid redundancies (Agarwal and Wu 2015). Other advantages include quick dispersal of tacit knowledge, lower coordination cost, enhancement of allocative efficiency, and emergence of a network culture of trust (Uzzi 1997). Such a system generally requires reconfiguring industry value chains (Singh and Kundu 2002). Thus, adoption of e-commerce is an important business decision for any MNEs because it calls for significant financial investments and business process changes. Online intermediaries for MNEs based in a foreign country with an emerging economy can help MNEs to overcome cultural and linguistic barriers, acting as a one-stop shop providing comprehensive services. Viewed through the lens of RBV theory, the advantage afforded to firms as a result of their position in networks (cyber and otherwise) is an inimitable resource (Gulati 1999).

Network Externalities and Value Clustering

Network externalities and value clustering are powerful benefits that the network delivers to participating firms. When firms can harness these benefits, e-commerce in emerging economies is enhanced (Agarwal and Wu 2015). The open nature of the Internet and its network externalities is a strong motivation for firms engaging in e-commerce to form alliances in order to explore complementary assets (Agarwal and Wu 2015). In the case of emerging markets where formal institutions are weak, informal institutions such as norms governing interpersonal relationships and networks play a key role in enhancing firm strategies and performance (Peng and Heath 1996; Peng et al. 2008).

Leamer and Storper (2001) suggested that the effect of de-agglomeration and global dispersion of routine and standardized tasks is offset by forces that establish clustering of complex and innovative tasks. Not being embedded in local interactions, historical and cultural nuances, and identity-specific artifacts, differences in norms, values, and beliefs are difficult to detect and manage. Singh and Kundu (2002) argue that the content and type of relationship in the online community are as important as the position and extent (i.e., structural embeddedness) to which firms are interconnected.

Chen and Kamal (2016) examined information and the impact of communication technology (ICT) on a firm's foreign boundary decision to make or buy, and they proposed that ICT adoption reduces both internal and external coordination costs ex post through two effects (a) lowering of communication and search costs and (b) lowering of economic incentive costs in terms of moral hazards and opportunistic behavior.

E-Commerce in Emerging Economies: Firm Strategies

Given similar potentials of e-commerce, firms from developed nations operating internationally and firms within emerging economies exploring their growth possibilities through e-commerce have different advantages, disadvantages, and opportunities. This chapter has explored factors affecting the growth of e-commerce such as cultural differences, institutional voids, different levels of absorptive capacity, and protection of intellectual property rights, among others. Which of these factors can create strategic opportunity, and for which type of firm?

Strategies for Developed-Market Multinationals (DM-MNEs)

1. International agreements, in their effort to standardize business procedures and reduce barriers to trade, serve as a basic framework to dictate and enforce some global rules of the game. Established procedures of the World Trade Organization

(WTO), along with regional trade agreements (RTAs), help reduce market imperfections and information asymmetries. These umbrella organizations and treaties create opportunities for DM-MNEs to exploit their firm-specific assets and for emerging-market MNEs (EM-MNEs) to explore firm-specific assets.

The gradual inclusion of more and more individual markets in the global business sphere, and particularly the e-commerce realm, continues to widen the windows of opportunity. Brazil and India were among the first to join the WTO, then China and later Russia's memberships continued to level the playing field for multilateral trade and investment (Agarwal and Wu 2015). The Chinese government actively promotes domestic firms' technological innovation processes by establishing supportive policies (e.g., national innovation system or NIS), making institutional arrangements, and even engaging in direct intervention. Through incremental organizational learning, Chinese firms are gradually shifting from production capability to technological innovation capability to compete with DM-MNEs.

2. DM-MNEs must adapt their approach to e-commerce in each new country due to large variations in culture and institutional structure. While many governments in emerging economies have adopted an open-door policy for foreign firms and encourage privatization and decentralization (Child and Tse 2001), national security concerns remain a major consideration in public policy and can impede both growth of e-commerce and investment. In China, for example, the government censors and monitors through its four-tier system all kinds of subject matter in its society, including news, publications, radio broadcasts, TV programs, as well as the Internet (Yao 2006). Global managers from DM-MNEs need to be aware of the political hazards in their transaction cost assessment, as well as the benefits of political knowledge and alliances with the government. Even powerful DM-MNEs (e.g., Google in China) are not exempt from political hazards (Agarwal and Wu 2015). In this regard, DM-MNEs can invest in internal and external networking.

3. Continuing with the issue of intellectual property rights (IPR), this is a serious problem when laws protecting these rights are not enforced, which tends to be the case in emerging economies more than developed nations. Properly addressing these valid concerns will open up many opportunities for firms of all types. For developed-market MNEs operating in emerging economies, neither formal methods of protection nor complementary methods are effective safeguards against IPR violation (Agarwal and Wu 2015). In addition, it is clear that developed-market MNEs are unlikely to win lawsuits because institutions in emerging economies are plagued by nepotism and corruption, and the court system lacks judicial independence and transparency. However, DM-MNEs from multiple countries can jointly lobby with global institutions such as the WIPO (World Intellectual Property Organization) to attempt to work out treaties with different nations to agree on common guidelines. Consumer rights constitute another arena where strict enforcement is lacking (Agarwal and Wu 2015). Laws protecting consumers exist in both countries, but they are not strictly enforced so consumers do not receive much protection.

4. Because local culture dominates consumer attitudes toward online shopping in emerging economies, DM-MNEs often fare better by using online local intermediaries to overcome the complexities of cultural and other social barriers. Firms practicing marketing orientation to generate and disseminate intelligence regarding customers and competition need to adopt high-touch intelligence generation activities instead of large-scale marketing studies that may not work in some countries due to large institutional distance and institutional void (Agarwal and Wu 2015). Establishing trust between companies and customers is a key problem in many countries, due to both cultural constraints and lack of consumer protections.

Strategies for Emerging-Market Multinationals (EM-MNEs)

1. Emerging-market MNEs must actively work to close institutional voids in order to catch up with developed economies. Hence, EM-MNEs are forced to be innovative and gain "adversity advantage" and "latecomer advantage" by circumventing institutional voids, thus acquiring greater levels of firm-specific advantage (Khanna and Palepu 2006; Mathews 2006). Further, emerging-market MNEs rely heavily on DM-MNEs that have entered their country to set examples and take initial risks. The presence of DM-MNEs facilitates isomorphic behavior among domestic firms, leading to convergence in industry standards and reduction in technology gaps through technological accumulation.
2. Domestic firms in emerging markets can creatively utilize structural and cultural factors in their home country to gain advantage where foreign entrants cannot. For the latter, these factors are hindrances. For instance, relative to DM-MNEs, EM-MNEs are better placed to circumvent their home country's institutional voids. Emerging-market entrepreneurs have an advantage over foreign multinationals in dealing with local institutional voids due to their cultural familiarity. Both the adoption of new technology and the advantages of the Internet itself facilitate emerging-market domestic firms to innovate and to diffuse their innovations rapidly. E-commerce enables entrepreneurs in emerging economies in their information search capabilities, risk assessment, and interaction with other actors in the venture creation process. E-commerce provides a number of opportunities for local entrepreneurs to create "cultural capital" as a source of competitive advantage (e.g., Buscape in Brazil, Flipkart in India, and Taobao in China) that will position these economies advantageously in their path to economic development (Agarwal and Wu 2015).
3. EM-MNEs can capitalize on the fact that DM-MNEs tend to be reluctant to adapt their brands, business models, and organizational culture in foreign markets, and as a result they seldom reach beyond the "global" segment in the host-country markets. This creates an opportunity for EM-MNEs. In the e-commerce industry, the codification of knowledge is further allowing EM-MNEs to fill information gaps and to tap into the global knowledge base, making it easier

for them to move up the value chain and compete against foreign MNEs. New technologies keep operating costs low for EM-MNEs and enable companies to deliver high-quality products and services.

4. Exploiting absorptive capacity in one or more of the infrastructural dimensions could also be an effective business strategy for EM-MNEs. As noted earlier, emerging economies are at different levels of absorptive capacity along the dimensions of physical infrastructure, financial and market infrastructure, and social infrastructure (Agarwal and Wu 2015). Financial and market infrastructure seems to be the most immediately pressing barrier for DM-MNEs. The development of intermediaries and marketing institutions that provide credibility and transparency is vital to the development of e-commerce in emerging economies (Ramamurti and Singh 2009). For e-commerce transactions, credit cards are considered to be the most acceptable means of payment, yet this is a major problem in most emerging economies. To address the deficiencies in payment systems (a financial infrastructure issue), many EM-MNEs allow cash on delivery for larger items and both payment and pick-up at the local postal office (Martinsons 2008).

5. Calming consumer concerns around trust is a cultural issue that can often be accomplished more successfully by a domestic firm compared to a DM-MNE, and this can serve as another source of advantage and opportunity for firms in emerging markets. As mentioned earlier, many consumers are reluctant to shop online in emerging economies given security and privacy concerns over online transactions. Contrary to conventional wisdom, this may create an opportunity for EM-MNEs, as demonstrated by eBay and Alibaba in China (Agarwal and Wu 2015).

Conclusion

This chapter presents a multi-theoretical foundation to explore multiple factors influencing e-commerce in emerging economies. With this multilayered approach to understanding the growth potential of e-commerce, the salience of each factor depends largely on the specific circumstances of each emerging economy. This chapter has several managerial implications. First, the e-commerce development in emerging economies can be explained by multiple theories in IB, marketing, management, and economics. Second, the growth potential of e-commerce is not influenced by a single factor. Rather, it is influenced by diverse factors, including global, national, and transactional ones. Third, firm strategies for DM-MNEs and EM-MNEs are quite different with respect to e-commerce. Specifically, EM-MNEs have a distinct advantage over DM-MNEs in dealing with institutional voids due to their knowledge over local conditions.

In sum, DM-MNEs who wish to succeed in the Internet space would best stick to areas that focus on job creation and economic gain that do not overlap with broader social and political challenges. While the research presented here is anchored in a multi-theoretical template, it is exploratory in nature, and the entrepreneurial efforts of firms around the world are vital to advancing knowledge about how e-commerce can and will be conducted in the future.

References

Agarwal, J., and T. Wu. 2004. China's entry to WTO: Global marketing issues, impact, and implications for China. *International Marketing Review* 21 (3): 279–300.

———. 2015. Factors influencing growth potential of e-commerce in emerging economies: An institution-based N-OLI framework. *Thunderbird International Business Review* 57 (3): 197–215.

Alon, I., O. Yeheskel, M. Lerner, and W. Zhang. 2013. Internationalization of Chinese entrepreneurial firms. *Thunderbird International Business Review* 55 (5): 495–512.

Amit, R., and C. Zott. 2001. Value creation in e-business. *Strategic Management Journal* 22 (6–7): 493–520.

Baker, W.E., and J.M. Sinkula. 2007. Does market orientation facilitate balanced innovation programs? An organizational learning perspective. *Journal of Product Innovation Management* 24: 316–334.

Barney, J.B. 1991. Firm resources and sustained competitive advantage. *Journal of Management* 17 (1): 99–120.

Baron, R.A. 1998. Cognitive mechanisms in entrepreneurship: Why and when entrepreneurs think differently than other people. *Journal of Business Venturing* 13 (4): 275–294.

Berthon, P., L. Pitt, D. Cyr, and C. Campbell. 2008. E-readiness and trust: Macro and micro dualities for e-commerce in a global environment. *International Marketing Review* 25 (6): 700–714.

Buckley, P., J. Clegg, and C. Wang. 2002. The impact of inward FDI on the performance of Chinese manufacturing firms. *Journal of International Business Studies* 33 (4): 637–655.

Cantwell, J.A. 2009. Location and the multinational enterprise. *Journal of International Business Studies* 40 (1): 35–41.

Cantwell, J.A., J.H. Dunning, and S.M. Lundan. 2010. An evolutionary approach to understanding international business activity: The co-evolution of MNEs and the institutional environment. *Journal of International Business Studies* 41 (4): 567–586.

Chen, W., and F. Kamal. 2016. The impact of information and communication technology adoption on multinational firm boundary decisions. *Journal of International Business Studies* 47: 563–576.

Child, J., and D.K. Tse. 2001. China's transition and its implications for international business. *Journal of International Business Studies* 32 (1): 5–21.

Coase, R. 1937. The nature of the firm. *Economica* 4 (16): 386–405.

Coeurderoy, R., and G. Murray. 2008. Regulatory environments and the location decision: Evidence from the early foreign market entries of new technology-based firms. *Journal of International Business Studies* 39 (4): 670–687.

Cohen, W.M., and D.A. Levinthal. 1990. Absorptive capacity: A new perspective on learning and innovation. *Administrative Science Quarterly* 35 (1): 128–152.

Contractor, F.J., and S.M. Mudambi. 2008. The influence of human capital investment on the exports of services and goods: An analysis of the top 25 services outsourcing countries. *Management International Review* 48 (4): 433–445.

Damanpour, F., and J.A. Damanpour. 2001. E-business e-commerce evolution: Perspective and strategy. *Managerial Finance* 27 (7): 16–33.

De la Torre, J., and R.W. Moxon. 2001. E-commerce and global business: The impact of the information and communication technology revolution on the conduct of international business. *Journal of International Business Studies* 32 (4): 617–639.

Delios, A., and W.J. Henisz. 2000. Japanese firms' investment strategies in emerging economies. *Academy of Management Journal* 43 (3): 305–323.

DiMaggio, P., and D. Powell. 1983. The iron cage revisited: Institutional isomorphism and collective rationality in organizational fields. *American Sociological Review* 48 (2): 147–160.

Dubosson-Torbay, M., A. Osterwalder, and Y. Pigneur. 2002. E-business model design, classification, and measurements. *Thunderbird International Business Review* 44 (1): 5–23.

Dunning, J.H. 1995. Reappraising the eclectic paradigm in an age of alliance capitalism. *Journal of International Business Studies* 26 (3): 461–491.

———. 1998. Location and the multinational enterprise: A neglected factor? *Journal of International Business Studies* 29 (1): 45–66.

———. 2000. The eclectic paradigm as an envelope for economic and business theories of MNE activity. *International Business Review* 9 (1): 163–190.

———. 2009. Location and the multinational enterprise: A neglected factor? *Journal of International Business Studies* 40 (1): 5–19.

Dunning, J.H., and C. Wymbs. 2001. The challenge of electronic markets for international business theory. *International Journal of the Economics of Business* 8 (2): 273–302.

Dutta, A. 1997. The physical infrastructure for electronic commerce in developing nations: Historical trends and the impact of privatization. *International Journal of Electronic Commerce* 2 (1): 61–83.

Gabrielsson, M., and P. Gabrielsson. 2011. Internet-based sales channel strategies of born global firms. *International Business Review* 20 (1): 88–89.

Ghoshal, S., and P. Moran. 1996. Bad for practice: A critique of the transaction cost theory. *Academy of Management Review* 21 (1): 13–47.

Globerman, S., T.W. Roehl, and S. Standifird. 2001. Globalization and electronic commerce: Inferences from retail brokering. *Journal of International Business Studies* 32 (4): 749–768.

Graf, M., and S. Mudambi. 2005. The outsourcing of IT-enabled business processes: A conceptual model of the location decision. *Journal of International Management* 11 (2): 253–268.

Granovetter, M. 1983. The strength of weak ties: A network theory revisited. In *Sociological theory*, ed. R. Collins. Hoboken: Wiley.

———. 1985. Economic action and social structure: The problem of embeddedness. *American Journal of Sociology* 91 (3): 481–510.

———. 1992. Problems of explanation in economic sociology. In *Networks and organizations: Structure, form and action*, ed. N. Nohria and R. Eccles. Boston: Harvard Business School Press.

Greenwood, R., and C.R. Hinings. 1996. Understanding radical organizational change: Bringing together the old and the new institutionalism. *Academy of Management Review* 21 (4): 1022–1054.

Gregory, G., M. Karavdic, and S. Zou. 2007. The effects of e-commerce drivers on export marketing strategy. *Journal of International Marketing* 15 (2): 30–57.

Gulati, R. 1999. Network location and learning: The influence of network resources and firm capabilities on alliance formation. *Strategic Management Journal* 20 (5): 397–420.

Hagendoorn, J., D. Cloodt, and H.V. Kranenburg. 2005. Intellectual property rights and the governance of international R&D partnerships. *Journal of International Business Studies* 36 (2): 175–186.

Henisz, W.J., and B.A. Zellner. 2004. Explicating political hazards and safeguards: A transaction cost politics approach. *Industrial and Corporate Change* 13 (6): 901–915.

Herman, L. 2010. Multilateralising regionalism: The case of E-commerce. OECD Trade Policy Working Papers, No. 99, OECD Publishing.

Hofstede, G.H. 1991. *Cultures and organizations: Software of the mind*. London: McGraw-Hill.

Hymer, S.H. 1970. The efficiency (contradictions) of multinational corporations. *American Economic Review* 60 (2): 441–448.

Iacovou, C.L., I. Benbasat, and A.S. Dexter. 1995. Electronic data interchange and small organizations: Adoption and impact of technology. *MIS Quarterly* 19 (4): 465–484.

Khanna, T., and K. Palepu. 1997. Why focused strategies may be wrong for emerging markets. *Harvard Business Review* 75 (4): 41–51.

———. 2006. Emerging giants: Building world-class companies in developing economies. *Harvard Business Review* 84 (10): 60–70.

———. 2010. *Winning emerging markets: A road map to strategy and execution*. Boston: Harvard Business Press.

Kogut, B., and U. Zander. 1993. Knowledge of the firm and the evolutionary theory of the multinational corporation. *Journal of International Business Studies* 24 (4): 625–645.

Kostova, T., and S. Zaheer. 1999. Organizational legitimacy under conditions of complexity: The case of the multinational enterprise. *Academy of Management Review* 24 (1): 64–81.

Leamer, E.E., and M. Storper. 2001. The economic geography of the internet age. *Journal of International Business Studies* 32 (4): 641–665.

Li, H., and Y. Zhang. 2007. The role of managers' political networking and functional experience in new venture performance: Evidence from China's transition economy. *Strategic Management Journal* 28 (8): 791–804.

Li, J., J. Poppo, and K.Z. Zhou. 2008. Do managerial ties in China always produce value? Competition, uncertainty, and domestic versus foreign firms. *Strategic Management Journal* 29 (4): 383–400.

Lieberman, M., and S. Asaba. 2006. Why do firms imitate each other? *Academy of Management Review* 31 (2): 366–385.

Lim, K.H., K. Leung, C.L. Sia, and M.K.O. Lee. 2004. Is e-commerce boundary-less?: Effects of individualism-collectivism and uncertainty avoidance on internet hopping. *Journal of International Business Studies* 35 (6): 545–559.

Luo, Y.R., and R.L. Tung. 2007. International expansion of emerging market enterprises: A springboard perspective. *Journal of International Business Studies* 38 (4): 481–498.

Madhok, A. 2006. Opportunism, trust and knowledge: The management of firm value and the value of firm management. In *Handbook on trust*, ed. R. Bachmann and A. Zaheer. Cheltenham: Edward Elgar.

Malhotra, N.K., S.S. Kim, and J. Agarwal. 2004. Internet users' information privacy concerns (IUIPC): The construct, the scale, and a causal model. *Information Systems Research* 15 (4): 336–355.

Martinez, C.A., and C. Williams. 2010. National institutions, entrepreneurship and global ICT adoption: A cross-country test of competing theories. *Journal of Electronic Commerce* 11 (1): 73–91.

Martinsons, M.G. 2008. Relationship-based e-commerce: Theory and evidence from China. *Information Systems Journal* 18 (4): 331–356.

Mathews, J.A. 2006. Dragon multinationals: New players in 21st century globalization. *Asia Pacific Journal of Management* 23: 5–27.

Molla, A., and P.S. Licker. 2005. Perceived e-readiness factors in e-commerce adoption: An empirical investigation in a developing country. *International Journal of Electronic Commerce* 10 (1): 83–110.

Mudambi, R. 2004. International business and the eclectic paradigm: Developing the OLI framework. *Journal of International Business Studies* 35 (5): 456–458.

North, D. 1990. *Institutions, institutional change and economic performance*. Cambridge: Cambridge University Press.

———. 2005. *Understanding the process of economic change*. New Jersey: Princeton University Press.

Oxley, J.E., and B. Yeung. 2001. E-commerce readiness: Institutional environment and international competitiveness. *Journal of International Business Studies* 32 (4): 705–723.

Ozgen, E., and R.A. Baron. 2007. Social sources of information in opportunity recognition: Effects of mentors, industry networks, and professional forums. *Journal of Business Venturing* 22 (2): 174–192.

Pavlou, P. 2003. Consumer acceptance of electronic commerce: Integrating trust and risk with the technology acceptance model. *International Journal of Electronic Commerce* 7 (3): 101–135.

Peng, M.W., and P. Heath. 1996. The growth of the firm in planned economies in transition: Institutions, organizations, and strategic choices. *Academy of Management Review* 21 (2): 492–528.

Peng, M.W., D.Y.L. Wang, and Y. Jiang. 2008. An institution-based view of international business strategy: A focus on emerging economies. *Journal of International Business Studies* 39 (5): 920–936.

Ramamurti, R., and J.V. Singh. 2009. *Emerging multinationals in emerging markets*. Cambridge: Cambridge University Press.

Rowley, T.J. 1997. Moving beyond dyadic ties: A network theory of stakeholder influences. *The Journal of the Academy of Management* 22 (4): 887–910.

Shama, A. 2005. An empirical study of the international marketing strategies of e-commerce companies. *Thunderbird International Business Review* 47 (6): 695–709.

Shane, S., and S. Venkataraman. 2000. The promise of entrepreneurship as a field of research. *Academy of Management Review* 25 (1): 217–226.

Shareef, M., U. Kumar, and V. Kumar. 2008. Role of different electronic commerce quality factors on purchase decision: A developing country perspective. *Journal of Electronic Commerce* 9 (2): 92–113.

Singh, N., and S. Kundu. 2002. Explaining the growth of e-commerce corporations: An extension and application of the eclectic paradigm. *Journal of International Business Studies* 33 (4): 679–697.

Slater, S.F., and J.C. Narver. 1995. Market orientation and the learning organization. *Journal of Marketing* 59 (3): 63–74.

Spencer, J.W. 2008. The impact of multinational strategy on indigenous enterprises: Horizontal spillovers and crowding out in developing countries. *Academy of Management Review* 33 (2): 341–361.

Straub, D., M. Keil, and W. Brenner. 1997. Testing the technology acceptance model across cultures: A three country study. *Information Management* 33 (1): 1–11.

Tan, Y.H., and W. Thoen. 2003. Electronic contract drafting based on risk and trust assessment. *International Journal of Electronic Commerce* 7 (4): 55–71.

Tian, X. 2007. Accounting for sources of FDI technology spillovers: Evidence from China. *Journal of International Business Studies* 38 (1): 147–159.

Uzzi, B. 1997. Social structure and competition in interfirm networks: The paradox of embeddedness. *Administrative Science Quarterly* 42 (1): 35–67.

Verbeke, A., and N. Greidanus. 2009. The end of the opportunism versus trust debate: Bounded reliability as a new envelope concept in research on MNE governance. *Journal of International Business Studies* 40 (9): 1471–1495.

Wang, W., Z. Hidvegi, and A. Whinston. 2002. Designing mechanisms for e-commerce security: An example from sealed-bid auctions. *International Journal of Electronic Commerce* 6 (2): 139–156.

Wernerfelt, B. 1984. A resource-based view of the firm. *Strategic Management Journal* 5 (2): 171–180.

Williamson, O.E. 1983. Credible commitments: Using hostages to support exchange. *American Economic Review* 73 (4): 519–538.

———. 1991. Comparative economic organization: The analysis of discrete structural alternatives. *Administrative Science Quarterly* 36 (2): 269–296.

Wu, F., V. Mahajan, and S. Balasubramanian. 2003. An analysis of e-business adoption and its impact on business performance. *Journal of the Academy of Marketing Science* 31 (4): 425–447.

Wymer, S.A., and E.A. Regan. 2005. Factors influencing e-commerce adoption and use by small and medium businesses. *Electronic Markets* 15 (4): 438–453.

Yao, W. 2006. Factors affecting e-commerce diffusion in China in the 21st century. *International Journal of Electronic Business* 4 (2): 162–176.

Zaheer, S., and S. Manrakhan. 2001. Concentration and dispersion in global industries: Remote electronic access and the location of economic activities. *Journal of International Business Studies* 32 (4): 667–686.

Zahra, S.A., and G. George. 2002. Absorptive capacity: A review, reconceptualization, and extension. *Academy of Management Review* 27 (2): 185–203.

Zhao, H. 2002. Rapid internet development in China: A discussion of opportunities and constraints on future growth. *Thunderbird International Business Review* 44 (1): 119–138.

Zhao, L., and Y. Wang. 2009. China's pattern of trade and growth after WTO accession: Lessons for other developing countries. *Journal of Chinese Economic and Foreign Trade Studies* 2 (3): 178–210.

Zhou, L., L. Dai, and D. Zhang. 2007. Online shopping acceptance model – a critical survey of consumer factors in online shopping. *Journal of Electronic Commerce Research* 8 (1): 41–62.

Zhou, H., S. Kim, T. Suh, and J. Du. 2008. Social institutional explanations of global internet diffusion: A cross-country analysis. In *Selected readings on global formation technology*, ed. H. Rahman. Hershey: Information Science Reference.

Zhu, K. 2004. The complementarity of information technology infrastructure and e-commerce capability: A resource-based assessment of their business value. *Journal of Management Information Systems* 21 (1): 167–202.

Zhu, L., and S.M.B. Thatcher. 2010. National information ecology: A new institutional economics perspective on global e-commerce adoption. *Journal of Electronic Commerce Research* 11 (1): 53–72.

Zhuang, Y., and A. Lederer. 2003. An instrument for measuring the business benefits of e-commerce retailing. *International Journal of Electronic Commerce* 7 (3): 65–99.

Zwass, V. 1996. Electronic commerce: Structure and issues. *International Journal of Electronic Commerce* 1 (1): 3–2.

Part IV
Global CSR, Sustainability, and Macromarketing Issues

Chapter 10
CSR-Driven Entrepreneurial Internationalization: Evidence of Firm-Specific Advantages in International Performance of SMEs

Maria Uzhegova, Lasse Torkkeli, Hanna Salojärvi, and Sami Saarenketo

Abstract This study examines an emerging yet somewhat neglected theme in international and global marketing literature, namely, the role of corporate social responsibility (CSR) and market-sensing capability in international enterprises. Specifically, we illustrate how CSR and market-sensing capability impact international performance in the context of small- and medium-sized enterprises (SMEs). The results from a sample of 85 internationalized Finnish SMEs indicate that social responsibility serves as a mediator of market-sensing capability on international performance. Moreover, market-sensing capability along with social responsibility also has a positive direct effect on an SME's international performance. Thus, the study links global marketing, strategic management, and sustainability literatures to explain the emerging paradigm of sustainable international entrepreneurship.

Introduction

A major emerging issue in global marketing is the role of corporate social responsibility (CSR) in international entrepreneurial firm growth and expansion. Today, companies are increasingly expected to exhibit CSR, i.e., the "duty of every corporate body to protect the interest of the society at large" (Holme and Watts 1999). However, as we have seen from the public scandals of companies that in some cases have previously been on top of CSR rankings (e.g., Volkswagen), societal and customer expectations related to CSR can have a complex impact on the behavior of corporations globally. Moreover, the extant research on CSR in the context of global marketing has prevalently aimed to explain the phenomenon in the context of large multinational companies (MNCs; e.g., Jamali et al. 2009; Kolk and Van Tulder

M. Uzhegova (✉) · L. Torkkeli · H. Salojärvi · S. Saarenketo
School of Business and Management, Lappeenranta University of Technology,
Lappeenranta, Finland
e-mail: maria.uzhegova@lut.fi

© Springer International Publishing AG, part of Springer Nature 2018   257
J. Agarwal, T. Wu (eds.), *Emerging Issues in Global Marketing*,
https://doi.org/10.1007/978-3-319-74129-1_10

2010), leaving several topics mostly unexplored. However, the majority of the companies in the world, particularly in the EU, are small- and medium-sized companies, with SMEs being responsible for 99.8% of all business in the nonfinancial sector in the EU. Being important employers, with 66.8% of jobs and accounting for more than half of the gross value added generated, they are critical for the growth and social integration of the region (European Commission 2015/2016).

With CSR having emerged previously as an issue for MNCs, nowadays SMEs witness that CSR has grown to be a global concern that they need to address, especially if they are involved in international operations. Hence, the first of these unexplored gaps is the impact of CSR on international entrepreneurial growth and internationalization. Studies of international entrepreneurship (IE) have not included CSR as part of the research ontology (see Jones et al. 2011). The IE as a research field is defined by McDougall and Oviatt (2000: 903) as "…a combination of innovative, proactive and risk-seeking behaviour that crosses national borders and is intended to create value in organizations," with the topics of firm behavior and value creation being the primary focus of the field. Yet, in SMEs, CSR is manifested differently from MNCs (Perrini et al. 2007), and despite a growing body of literature on socially responsible practices of large firms engaged in business globally, the role of SMEs remains under-researched (Hoogendoorn et al. 2014). For instance, while large companies are known for extensive marketing of their CSR practices, leading to an increased corporate reputation and differentiation from competitors (Gallego-Álvarez et al. 2010), SMEs do not tend to articulate their CSR commitment widely (Nielsen and Thomsen 2009). Moreover, even though CSR is more often attributed to the large firm, the research field of international business (IB), which primarily has a large multinational company as a research unit, is still lacking a holistic approach to CSR issues (Pisani et al. 2017).

Second, with most of the studies focused on investigating the antecedents of CSR in large corporations (i.e., Yang and Rivers 2009; Crilly et al. 2008), in the context of SMEs and IE, this topic is currently under-researched. The extant literature in the emerging IE research field does not explain the role of CSR, which is playing an increasingly important role in business today in the internationalization of SMEs. Economic, political, and social factors are shaping CSR activities around the world (Baughn et al. 2007) as consumers have become more interested in CSR in the past two decades (Carrigan and Attalla 2001; Maignan 2001). Not only are SMEs the important business players in home markets, they are also increasingly involved in international operations and sustainability efforts, thereby presenting a rich context for studying CSR.

Third, international entrepreneurial growth and expansion strategy may come to depend on both CSR and other firm-specific advantages, such as the extent of their organizational characteristics and capabilities (Torugsa et al. 2012). SMEs may be engaged in CSR because of family tradition, the entrepreneur's personal values, community embeddedness, or feeling the need to contribute to the wider society (Ellerup Nielsen and Thomsen 2009; Looser and Wehrmeyer 2015). However, until now there has been scant evidence of either in the international context; hence, there is still a limited understanding of whether and how CSR affects international performance of SMEs.

On top of all that, a recent literature review of Eteokleous et al. (2016) pointed out that the research field of international marketing still lacks evidence of performance outcomes of CSR activities. In addition, the integrative models incorporating mediators and moderators are called upon to identify the conditions under which CSR leads to specific outcomes. On a firm level, a competitive intensity may serve as an enabling condition for CSR being a moderator in the marketing capability–performance relationship (Kemper et al. 2013).

We seek to respond to these omissions by illustrating how CSR drives entrepreneurial internationalization among SMEs and how firm-specific advantages in the form of market-sensing capability and the orientation toward responsible practices are intertwined with these dynamics. This study presents a view into the shifting paradigms in international and global marketing. This is done by illustrating global marketing in a transition stage from being primarily a concern of large corporations, which have already learned how to operate under the grown concern for business responsibility, to SMEs. At the same time, the traditional approach of SMEs to internationalization is nowadays challenged toward the need to communicate their commitment to the stakeholders globally in the host countries. This study reveals that responsible business behavior opens the new opportunities if combined with the responsiveness toward the global market needs and thus presents a shifting paradigm with SMEs in global marketing. In doing so, we apply regression modeling on a data of 85 internationally operating SMEs originating from Finland and adapt Turker's (2009) CSR measure while conducting mediation analysis.

This study continues as follows: First, we outline the literature suggesting the role of CSR and market-sensing capability in the context of SMEs, with particular focus on internationalizing SMEs. We then follow that with the quantitative study, where we examine the dynamics of market-sensing capability and CSR on SME internationalization in detail. We conclude by discussing the results and their implications on the theory and practice of SME internationalization and growth.

Literature Review

CSR

The definitions of the concept of CSR are many. In the research papers and in the practitioners' reports, it is ambiguous and sometimes referred to as a "complex jungle of CSR definitions" (Crane et al. 2013: 9). One of the early definitions is "the conduct of a business so that it is economically profitable, law-abiding, ethical and socially supportive in order to fulfill economic, legal, ethical and philanthropic responsibilities" (Carroll 1983: 608). Another definition, also used in the international marketing field according to the review of Eteokleous et al. (2016), captures the issue of CSR activities being something more than what is already required by law: "actions that appear to further some social good, beyond the interests of the firm and that which is required by law" (McWilliams and Siegel 2001a, b: 117). Often, research papers adopt the definition of the European Commission, "a concept whereby companies integrate social and environmental concerns in their business operations and in their interaction with their stakeholders on a voluntary basis" (Commission of the European Communities 2001: 8), which emphasizes the voluntary nature of these actions. The voluntary aspect is also seen in this definition used in the Marcel van Marrewijk (2003: 102) review: "company activities – voluntary by definition – demonstrating the inclusion of social and environmental concerns in business operations and in interactions with stakeholders." In the study of SMEs' CSR communications, Parker et al. (2015: 364) define CSR as "voluntary values, technologies and practices which directly or indirectly result in a positive (or reduce negative) impact on the environment, employees or external stakeholders."

Key concepts from the above definitions of CSR are economic, interaction with stakeholders, social and environmental concerns, and voluntariness. Indeed, in the attempt of systematization, Dahlsrud (2006) has analyzed 37 definitions and outlined five dimensions of the CSR concept, with those dimensions used most often being *stakeholder* and *social*, followed by *economic* and *voluntariness*, with *environmental* being the least used.

Moore and Spence (2006) argue that CSR, as a term, does not capture the approach required for SMEs. Studies of CSR in the SME context adopt the various definitions of CSR: some of the definitions are not that specific about the size of the company as Wood (1991) explains – "company's configuration of social responsibility, social responsiveness, policies, programs, and observable outcomes as they are related to the company's relationship with society." Others emphasize the importance of entrepreneurs' personal values as Maclagan (1998) does: "a process in which business owner-managers take responsibility for identifying and accommodating stakeholder interests."

The differences in the CSR definitions used in the studies of large companies and SMEs are embedded in the organizational characteristics of different-sized firms. A number of characteristics in regard to CSR are listed in Table 10.1.

The updated definition from the European Commission does not refer to voluntary nature or "going beyond the regulation" features, nor does it address the issue of size, stating that CSR is "the responsibility of enterprises for their impacts on society" (European Commission 2011:6). In line with Cavusgil and Cavusgil's study (2012) which claims that "stakeholders are more vocal and actively seek solutions to a wide array of environmental and social issues," we propose that SMEs are able to answer this call, though not through the implementation of standardized and formalized CSR practices but rather through responsible business behavior (RBB). Used in Avram and Kühne's (2008) study of Austrian SMEs, RBB is "an instrument to develop a sustained competitive advantage by relating social and environmental issues to the value chain of the company." Adopted in this study in place of CSR, RBB, being universal, isn't constrained by size, sector, or geographical scope and can therefore be applied to SMEs operating in an international context. In its core,

Table 10.1 Differences in CSR between MNCs and SME

	MNC	SME
Conceptual definition of CSR	Often includes one or several of following dimensions: *stakeholder*, *social*, *economic*, *voluntariness*, and *environmental*	Often includes one or several of the same five dimensions, but also the *individual dimension* such as responsibility of firm's owner–manager, leader, or entrepreneur is emphasized
CSR integration into the company	Explicit leadership support by the CEO and the board, the existence of CSR coordination unit (person or a department) which is responsible for dealing with CSR	The owner–manager, often highly involved into SME's operations, has an influence on the values and culture of the company and thus may expose CSR throughout the company
	Incentive systems and trainings to promote CSR awareness among employees, as well as for performance evaluation and reporting	Low hierarchy in management and more open and fluid communication within the company facilitate the involvement of all employees in CSR through the informal measures
CSR's integration with marketing strategy	Integrated approach – the brand and CSR operate in synchrony (firm tells one compelling story)	Use involvement and communication-oriented activities such as cause-related marketing and corporate advertising
	Selective approach – CSR manifests itself in very specific, targeted ways, i.e., in the form of sub-brands	Having high adaptability, SMEs are able to quickly respond to the market needs with the products or services with the environmental/social benefits in their value
	Invisible approach – CSR is present only in strategic level guiding the company but hidden in external communications and initiatives	
Public expectations in terms of CSR	Proactive participation and "activity level" by which they contribute to collaborative CSR initiatives (i.e., UN global compact)	Collective involvement with other SMEs or suppliers to mutually address CSR issues, i.e., in the form of CSR-related networks, such as industry associations
	Maintaining the relationships with the external stakeholders such as NGOs	

(continued)

Table 10.1 (continued)

	MNC	SME
Communications and positioning strategy of CSR	Develop solutions for issues of global public concern on human rights or climate change, such as codes of conduct or corporate policies	SMEs run by informal management approaches lack proper communication tools for reporting
	Make extensive public commitments to CSR and regularly publish CSR reports	Transparency of activities toward third parties is disclosed only on demand
		Account on indirect word-of-mouth communication with internal and local stakeholders
Form of implementation	Support initiatives which involve "material" support such as giving and sponsorships	Small firms implement responsible behaviors toward specific categories of stakeholders through owner's personalized relations between firm and the society
		Medium-sized firms commit to their community through volunteering

Adapted from Baumann-Pauly et al. (2013), Blomkqvist and Posner (2004), Jenkins (2009), Nielsen and Thomsen (2009), and Russo and Tencati (2009)

responsible business behavior constitutes the consciousness about the environment and society. With it, the firm's competitive advantage can either be facilitated or constrained by the strategic and operational decisions taken.

Global Marketing and CSR

Marketing and CSR are intertwined topics, especially in the area of global marketing and multinational corporations. In their reflection about the future of international marketing in the era of transformations and a truly global marketplace, Cavusgil and Cavusgil (2012: 210) note that CSR "will rise as a marketing theme and will drive strategies." Indeed, the study of Hadjikhani et al. (2016) illustrates how CSR is used as an MNC's marketing strategy, which aided the firm's entry through investments into the social and environmental issues in the target country. Such tracking of the customers' social concerns and further application of them into the marketing strategy for the good of the company are referred to as a social marketing concept (Crane and Desmond 2002). CSR, in the form of the triple bottom line (social, environmental, and economic), does not include the customers as the stakeholders. However, firms that have market-focused sustainability, by integrating the customers among other stakeholders into their marketing strategy, have an opportunity to create a marketing strategy that is valuable, rare, inimitable, and difficult to substitute (Barney 1991; Wernerfelt 1984). Customers' trust, loyalty, and perceptions of corporate reputation are influenced by the perceived CSR (Stanaland et al. 2011). CSR can serve as a tool for the positive perception of the company. Company's products or services are positively perceived especially by those consumers seeking identification with the firm (Bhattacharya and Sen 2004), with this kind of customer loyalty leading to wider customer support (Luo and Bhattacharya 2006).

Besides being attentive to customers, companies also need to be able to adapt their CSR practices on a global scale. The importance of maintaining an image of social responsibility can vary between both emerging and developed markets (Li et al. 2010) and within different developed economies (Maignan and Ralston 2002).

CSR also brings added challenges to global marketing. This is due to the cultural disposition of customers, which can determine how they view CSR activities of foreign firms compared to domestic ones. This can cause the effectiveness of cause-related marketing to vary at the global level (Choi et al. 2016). At the same time, having a global brand can still have a positive impact on consumer perceptions, assuming that the foreign company is sufficiently agile to account for local culture and taste (Becker-Olsen et al. 2011).

An emerging paradigm in this discussion is the role of CSR in international entrepreneurship, which seeks to explain how entrepreneurial internationalization drives companies to international and global markets. The context of SMEs is particularly in need of further clarification, as the ways in which small companies address the issues related to CSR are different from the large corporations (Perrini 2006), which means that extant research conducted with large multinationals is not generalizable for SMEs. For instance, the CSR communication, as a part of marketing activities, is addressed by MNCs in a more systematic way compared to small firms: through the wide variety of channels such as corporate web sites, annual reports, and other publicly available documents (Baumann-Pauly et al. 2013). Thus, from the global marketing standpoint, SMEs present a phenomenon that is both emerging and distinct from most of the extant research on international and global marketing. Having business activities which are less visible to the wider public and media, SMEs are less likely to see a significant benefit in a publicity-driven approach to CSR communication and reporting (Baumann-Pauly et al. 2013), preferring instead to have an informal reporting in the form of face-to-face interaction with stakeholders (Spence 2004). Moreover, firms in manufacturing industries tend to communicate more CSR, being exposed to a wider variety of environmental, labor, and social issues compared to service firms (Lattemann et al. 2009). In sum, for all of the reasons mentioned above, clarifying the role of CSR in internationalization outcomes of SMEs provides a novel contribution to both literature on global marketing and to that of international entrepreneurship.

Hypothesis Development

Through the empirical part of this study, we aim to posit three factors that drive international SMEs to achieve higher international performance: market-sensing capability, social responsibility, and environmental responsibility. These linkages suggested in our conceptual model are elaborated in the following sections, thereby deriving the testable hypothesis.

According to the resource-based view (RBV), every organization has unique resources (Barney 1991) and capabilities (Song et al. 2007). Capabilities are defined by Day (1994) as "complex bundles of skills and collective learning, exercised through organizational processes that ensure superior coordination of functional activities." Such organizational capabilities are an integral part of how MNCs operate at the international and global level (Augier and Teece 2007; Teece 2014).

Particularly, market-sensing capability is critical among other capabilities for successful business development (Day 1994). According to capability classification by Hooley et al. (1999), a market-sensing capability is one of the strategic marketing capabilities – a group of capabilities which is defined as the ability of senior management to examine the surroundings. The concept of market-sensing capability refers to a firm's ability to learn about its market environment, be aware of change in it, and to use this knowledge in a way to guide its marketing actions (Day 1994). These abilities to sense the markets have been found particularly important when entering international markets (Armario et al. 2008a, b).

According to Day (1994), market-sensing capability precedes market orientation which has been regarded as the foundation and thus a central concept in the marketing discipline (Drucker 1954; Gebhardt et al. 2006; Kotler 2000). Market orientation concept includes two major subdimensions: customer orientation and competitor orientation (Hagen et al. 2012). In the literature, there are two mutually complementing perspectives of market orientation (Armario et al. 2008). A cultural perspective conceptualizes market orientation as a part of organizational culture that includes creation and delivery of value to the customers (Narver and Slater 1990), whereas a behavioral one considers market orientation in terms of specific behaviors of the organization (Kohli and Jaworski 1990).

In line with that, Lindblom et al. (2008) stresses that market-sensing capability is an essential element of market-oriented behavior since it includes organizational learning regarding, e.g., customers' explicit and latent needs. Market orientation, in turn, according to the previous literature has a positive impact on business performance, including the financial performance (Han et al. 1998; Kirca et al. 2005; Kohli and Jaworski 1990; Narver and Slater 1990; Slater and Narver 1994) and customer-centric performance (O'Cass et al. 2012). Although market orientation research in the international context remains relatively sparse and recent, support for the positive relationship between market orientation and international performance has also been found, for example, by Kwon and Hu (2000), Cadogan et al. (2003), and Armario et al. (2008).

However, despite the positive performance outcomes, the ability of market orientation to explain market performance has also been criticized as such positive outcomes are often directly explained by constructs that either mediate or moderate the relationships, rather than by the status of market orientation (Olavarrieta and Friedmann 2008). As a result, it has been suggested that more attention should be paid to market-sensing capability as a key antecedent of firm performance, as ultimately it is market-sensing capability that captures well the main elements of the market orientation construct as defined by Kohli and Jaworski (1990). At the same time, however, it is likely to provide a more direct path to explaining why some firms perform better than others (see Olavarrieta and Friedmann 2008).

In general, marketing capabilities, such as the capabilities for brand management (e.g., Angulo-Ruiz et al. 2014; Merrilees et al. 2011; Möller and Anttila 1987), innovation (e.g., Ngo and O'Cass 2009), customer linking (O'Cass et al. 2012; Fahy et al. 2000), channel bonding (e.g., Prasad et al. 2001; Ripolles and Blesa 2012), networking (e.g., Perez-Cabanero et al. 2012), external and internal marketing capabilities (Morgan et al. 2012), and specialized marketing capability (Elango and Pattnaik 2007), all are found to relate positively to the firm's performance. In addition, dynamic marketing capabilities such as global marketing capabilities (Chang 1996; Kotabe et al. 2002) and market-sensing capability (Day 1994, 2002) have been found to have performance implications in the global context (Prange and Verdier 2011).

According to Lindblom et al. (2008), high level of market-sensing capability of entrepreneurs can lead to higher growth in firms. Market-sensing capability has also a positive effect on the speed to market (Ardyan 2016) and product innovativeness (Zhang and Wu 2013). Firms with sensing capabilities are known for their ability to constantly detect the emerging trends and thus behave proactively rather than responding only to the clear signals (Day 2011). Following this, it can be assumed that market-sensing capability may also influence the international performance of the company.

An emerging theme is the role of dynamic capabilities in internationalization of SMEs (see Knight and Cavusgil 2004; Autio et al. 2011; Torkkeli et al. 2012), where marketing strategy in general (Knight 2000) and marketing-related capabilities in particular (Lee and Hsieh 2010; Weerawardena et al. 2007) influence the ways in which the enterprises conduct marketing and operations abroad. Based on Day (2002) and Vorhies and Morgan (2005), it is assumed that firms with developed market-sensing activities gain competitive advantage and superior business performance.

International performance is one of the main outcomes that research on entrepreneurial internationalization has sought to explain (e.g., Knight 2001; Kuivalainen et al. 2004; Leonidou et al. 2002; Zou and Stan 1998). It can be explained either through the degree of internationalization (cf. Sullivan 1994) or through subjective assessments of how well a given enterprise has succeeded in their operations abroad and to what extent they have reached their goals for internationalization. International performance measures in the literature are mainly of the latter type

(Leonidou et al. 2002) and should be favored when aiming to operationalize international performance in this type of research (Zou and Stan 1998). Thus, in this study we also refer to international performance as the extent of success internationally as assessed by the managers of the enterprises and aim to operationalize it through a Likert scale measure.

As market-sensing capability can be linked to increased overall performance, we propose that it is also linked to increased *international* performance: other types of organizational capabilities have been linked to international performance in extant literature (e.g., Jantunen et al. 2005; Lu et al. 2010; Torkkeli et al. 2012). There is also some evidence of the relationship between market orientation and international performance (Armario et al. 2008). Moreover, marketing capabilities in general can foster international commitment and, subsequently, performance (Blesa and Ripolles 2008). While the extant studies have neither assessed market-sensing capability directly nor examined the role of CSR as part of their study setting, they provide a basis to hypothesize the following:

H1 *Market-sensing capability will increase firm's international performance.*

Since the CSR practices as applied in large corporations are hardly applicable to the small firms as such, there was an attempt to reposition the CSR concept to better fit SMEs by Ryan et al. (2010). They reconsider CSR to the concept of responsible business practice in order to apply it for the small firms. The difference between these two concepts is that the former is understood by the authors as an organizational response of large corporations to prominent calls for businesses to not only avoid doing harm but to also have a positive impact on the society. Consequently, in a large firm, CSR involves a wide variety of practices, which SMEs are hard put to replicate and implement due to the resource constraints. On contrary, an SME's owner/manager, on account of their central role in the SME, can make personal decisions about the issues related to the engagement of the firm to the elements of responsible business practices (RBPs), such as environmental and/or social responsibility. The concept of RBP is also in line with the responsible business behavior (RBB) concept we picked up for this study. RBP topology in a form of matrix is presented in Table 10.2.

In this topology, small firms are differentiated according to the RBPs they adopt, which in turn are dictated by the firms' unique features. Environmentally responsible firms, sometimes also referred as to ecopreneurs, are involved in environmentally sustainable practices due to various reasons which can be categorized into five

Table 10.2 A typology of responsible business practice orientation

| | | Environmental mission | |
		High	Low
Social mission	High	Sustainable enterprises	Socially responsible enterprises
	Low	Environmentally responsible enterprises	Market-driven responsible enterprises

Adapted from Ryan et al. (2010)

groups: resistant, reactive, anticipatory, innovation-based, and sustainability-driven behavior (Klewitz and Hansen 2014). Out of these, the reactive behavior of SMEs is rooted in the answer to the external pressure to engage in responsible practices. Such stimuli may be environmental regulations (Bianchi and Noci 1998) or actors in public–private partnerships that SMEs are involved in (Hansen and Klewitz 2012). Post and Altman (1994) divide the environmentalism according to its drivers, one of which is market-driven environmentalism, i.e., adhering to market incentives in the firm's actions.

The same logic may be applied to socially responsible enterprises which, in the context of SMEs, are referred to as social entrepreneurship. Compared to entrepreneurship, social entrepreneurship is different in terms, i.e., measuring the performance through social impact rather than financial indicators (Spear 2006). However, even if they are not engaged in social entrepreneurship, SMEs are known to have strong relationships between the firm, its employees, and the local community (European Commission 2003).

Different SMEs are attributed to different types of RBP, and they can change their type depending on the time and situation. For instance, RBP may be initiated for market reasons; thus, the enterprise will be called market-driven responsible enterprise, meaning a firm that has made significant changes to the processes or products in order to be considered responsible. While shifting from such a short-term competitive response to more strategic adaptations, such firms may change to another type of RBB throughout the company's operations. However, market-driven RBB is a first step in this process. In other words, these firms are responsive to external, market-driven influence and therefore need to possess a market-sensing capability which may drive their responsible behavior further toward sustainable enterprise. Based on these notions, we hypothesize that:

H2a *Market-sensing capability will increase the social responsibility of an international SME.*

H2b *Market-sensing capability will increase the environmental responsibility of an international SME.*

Derwall et al. (2005) claim there are a number of benefits associated with environmental initiatives, such as business risk reduction, reputation increase, and new markets development. Focusing on large US firms, several quantitative studies have demonstrated the positive linkage between environmental performance of large firms and their financial performance (Russo and Fouts 1997; Karagozoglu and Lindell 2000; Clarkson et al. 2011).

The scarce amount of recent studies shows mixed results in this regard in the international and global context. CSR can either facilitate or hinder innovation and internationalization efforts depending on their type (Costa et al. 2015), while the impact of environmentally friendly export strategies on competitive advantage in foreign markets is complex (Leonidou et al. 2015). For instance, since the firm's responsibility increases consumer and employee trust in the organization, it can be assumed that this will positively affect the firm's activities also in the foreign markets. Indeed, a support for it was demonstrated in the study of MNC in Hadjikhani et al. (2016), with a reason for this being that CSR "creates a reputation that a firm is reliable and honest" (McWilliams and Siegel 2001: 120).

Overall, there is a lack of empirical evidence when it comes to the environmental performance of smaller firms (Qian and Xing 2016). Molina-Azorín et al. (2009), in their review of the impact of green management on financial performance, found that most of the studies show a positive impact. However, all these studies that were reviewed have a large listed company as a unit of analysis, whereas there is as yet no research proving that the same positive trend is prevalent in privately owned firms. In the same vein, there is a lack of research that investigates the link between a company's responsibility and international performance, with the rare evidence indicating that CSR can have a positive impact on performance (Ben Brik et al. 2010). Thus, we hypothesize that:

H3a *Social responsibility will increase SMEs' international performance.*

H3b *Environmental responsibility will increase SMEs' international performance.*

Research Framework

Based on the literature review and the subsequent hypotheses developed, this study argues that market-sensing capability and responsible business practices are important in the internationalization processes of SMEs, contributing to their international performance. In this research framework, a firm's responsibility for the environment and for the society is considered to be two parts of business responsibility.

The framework proposes a direct relationship between market-sensing capability and the responsibility to the society and the environment, as well as the mediating role of business responsibility between the market-sensing capability and an SME's international performance. Overall, the research framework implies that a firm's market-sensing capability improves the responsibilities to society and the natural environment, which then improve international performance. The research framework is presented in Fig. 10.1, showing the interrelations and five hypotheses discussed above.

Research Design

Data Collection

First, in order to test the hypotheses, we collected data through an online survey. The sample data for this study was collected in May–September 2014 via a web-based survey instrument. The initial sample of SMEs with the employee head

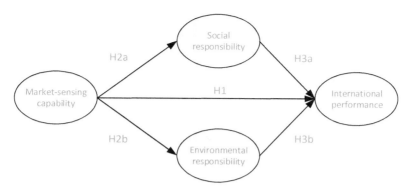

Fig.10.1 A research framework

count within the limits of 10–250 employees was drawn from the Amadeus online database of Finnish small- and medium-sized companies. The yielded sample of 1130 companies was a cross-industrial one including firms from several industries: forest industry, chemical industry, metal industry, other manufacturing activities and mining and quarrying, energy supply, water supply, waste management, and construction.

As a result, we identified a total of 1130 firms to be contacted by phone. A total of 78 of them were judged non-eligible, with the eligibility determined by the requirement that the respondents needed to have independence in terms of strategic decision-making. Because of this, subbranches and Finnish subsidiaries of foreign firms, for example, were excluded from the study. The respondents were typically CEOs or other higher-level managers. Three hundred eleven firms declined to participate in the study, with the most common reason being the lack of time. Three hundred six firms were not reached despite several efforts. At the end, final responses were received from 148 firms, thus resulting in a 14% response rate (148/1052). After clearing the data from duplicates, allowing only one filled-in survey per company, 141 companies constituted a sample. Out of this sample, 85 SMEs with international operations constituted the final sample used in this study. The distribution of the final sample by industry is presented in Fig. 10.2.

Concerning international operations, companies had on average 20.3 years of international operations in an average of 8.5 countries. The countries of the first international entry were Sweden for 31% of companies, Germany for 12%, Russia for 11%, Estonia for 9%, and the Soviet Union for 4% of companies. On average, the international operations constituted 26.9% of turnover at the moment of data collection. As shown in Fig. 10.3, own exports (58%) were the most used primary international entry mode, followed by exports with a retailer/distributor (24%).

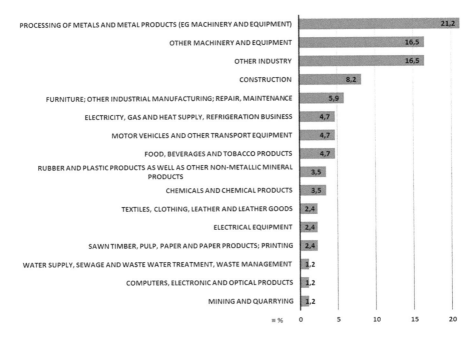

Fig. 10.2 Distribution of sample by industry, % from total sample

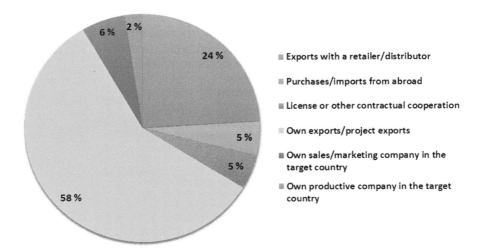

Fig. 10.3 A primary international entry mode

Measurement of Key Variables

International performance was evaluated based on the decision-maker's perception of the firm's performance in foreign markets. The six-item scale was borrowed from Nummela et al. (2004) study, and one item was added and measured on a seven-point Likert scale (1 = strongly disagree to 7 = strongly agree).

This and other scales in this study were measured on a seven-point Likert scale (1 = strongly disagree to 7 = strongly agree). The international performance scale items converged on a single factor that explained 66.8% of the total variance. Kaiser–Meyer–Olkin (KMO) measure of sampling adequacy value was 0.81, and Bartlett's test of sphericity was statistically significant (sig. <0.01).Communality values ranged between 0.53 and 0.75, while the individual factor loadings ranged between 0.72 and 0.91 (see Appendix 1 for the detailed listing). The Cronbach's alpha value of this resulting scale was 0.92, indicating a reliable measure. We further ensured reliability and convergent validity through calculating composite reliability (CR) and average variance extracted (AVE) values for each scale. CR values should in general be above 0.60 (Bagozzi and Yi 1988), while AVE values of 0.50 or higher indicate sufficient convergent validity (Hair et al. 2009). For the international performance scale, the CR value was 0.93 and AVE 0.66, indicating sufficient convergent validity. The resulting scale items were the following:

1. *Generally speaking, we are satisfied with our success in the international markets.*
2. *We have achieved the turnover objectives we set for internationalization.*
3. *We have achieved the market share objectives we set for internationalization.*
4. *Internationalization has had a positive effect on our company's profitability.*
5. *Internationalization has had a positive effect on our company's image.*
6. *Internationalization has had a positive effect on the development of our company's expertise.*
7. *The investments we have made in internationalization have paid themselves back well.*

Five items measuring social responsibility were adapted from Turker's (2009) study. CSR to society was regarded as a responsibility to social and nonsocial stakeholders. The items for CSR converged in a single factor explaining 71% of the total variation. Communalities ranged from 0.59 to 0.79 and individual factor loadings between 0.77 and 0.89. KMO value was 0.74, and Bartlett's test is again significant. Cronbach's alpha value for the resulting measure was 0.90, AVE value was 0.71, and CR was 0.92, altogether suggesting a sufficiently reliable and valid scale, with the following items:

1. *Our company participates to the activities which aim to protect and improve the quality of the natural environment.*
2. *Our company makes investment to create a better life for the future generations.*
3. *Our company implements special programs to minimize its negative impact on the natural environment.*

4. *Our company targets a sustainable growth which considers to the future generations.*
5. *Our company contributes to the campaigns and projects that promote the well-being of the society.*

Environmental responsibility has been measured by eight self-developed items based on reviewing available literature on sustainability (e.g., Menguc and Ozanne 2005). For the environmental responsibility scale, again, the factor analysis converged on a single scale explaining 52% of the total variation, with a KMO value of 0.82 and a significant ($p < 0.01$) Bartlett's test of sphericity. Communality values of the individual items ranged between 0.39 and 0.65, with factor loadings ranging between 0.62 and 0.81. The corresponding AVE value was 0.55 and CR 0.89. Cronbach's alpha value was 0.85, indicating sufficient reliability of the scale with the following items:

1. *We pay much attention to the environmental hazards resulting from the manufacture of our products.*
2. *We apply the lifecycle analysis when we assess the environmental friendliness of our products.*
3. *We set waste reduction goals for our suppliers.*
4. *We actively advance the recycling and reuse of our products.*
5. *Our products are part of the process reducing environmental hazards and/or climate change.*
6. *Our company utilizes clean technology (incl. products, services, processes, technologies), which prevents or reduces negative environmental effects of business activities.*
7. *Preventing damage to nature is a central goal of our business activities.*
8. *Production that saves natural resources is a central goal of our business activities.*

Items measuring market sensing were conceptualized on the basis of Day's (1994, 2002) work. The items of the market-sensing capability similarly converged in a single factor, explaining 54.7% of the total variation. KMO value was 0.74 and Bartlett's test again significant at the 0.01 risk level. Communalities ranged between 0.38 and 0.76, while individual factor loadings ranged between 0.62 and 0.87 (see Appendix 1). Cronbach's alpha value for the resulting scale was 0.77, AVE value was 0.54, and CR was value 0.85. The resulting measure included the following five items:

1. *We have systematic processes, with which we interpret prevailing trends in the market environment.*
2. *We actively follow our competitors' procedures.*
3. *Our company's employees regularly discuss the effect of market trends and new products on our activities.*
4. *We quickly analyze and interpret changes taking place in market demand.*
5. *We regularly envision what our industry will look like after the next 20 years.*

In addition, two control variables – firm age and firm size – were included. A firm's size was measured by the number of its employees, and the firm's age was operationalized by the number of years passed since the firm's establishment; thus, the effects on dependent variables (social responsibility, environmental responsibility, and international performance) are controlled. The choice for the control variables in this case was clear, as firm size and firm age are the control variables that are used most often in marketing studies (Kamboj and Rahman 2015). The firm size difference, even within the SME category, was noticed in the study of Preuss and Perschke (2009), where medium-sized firms differed from small and micro firms in their approach to CSR, while the study of Hoogendoorn et al. (2014) demonstrated that an SME's age is not related to the environmental practices of the firm. Firm age may relate to the level of experience and managerial competences of the firm; hence, it may affect the firm's performance (Zhan and Luo 2008).

Finally, we accounted for several potential biases and ensured further validity of the survey setting through several means: In order to minimize potential common method variance (CMV) and increase data reliability, we took both ex-ante and post-hoc measures, seeking to adhere to the guidelines set forth by Podsakoff et al. (2003). Namely, we guaranteed confidentiality and anonymity to respondents, and, as the survey was part of a larger project covering a variety of issues relevant to SMEs, it is unlikely that the responses would have been consciously aligning themselves with the expected theoretical linkages. Some questionnaire items were negatively worded in order to avoid the halo effect, and the scales used in this study were also inquired upon in different parts of the questionnaire. Moreover, we conducted Harman's single-factor test as a post-hoc test against CMV. In the test, the first factor accounted for 33.4% of the variance, indicating that CMV should not have been a concern in the analysis. In addition to testing for CMV, we tested for convergent validity of the scales through the examination of AVE and CR values as mentioned above. For discriminant analysis, we compared AVE values of constructs to the squared correlations between them, with the former being higher than the latter in all cases, thus indicating discriminant validity.

Results

Hypotheses Testing

Table 10.3 reports the descriptive statistics and zero-order correlations associated with study variables. The mean age of the firms in our sample is 34 years, and their size in terms of employees is relatively small with a mean of 60 employees. The correlation coefficients and variance inflation factors (VIF; not tabulated, but all below 10; Hill and Adkins 2001) do not raise a concern for multicollinearity.

Models 1 and 3 (Table 10.4) included only control variables – firm size and firm age. Neither firm age nor firm size was significantly related to social or environmental responsibility. In Model 2, with the inclusion of control variables, social responsibility

Table 10.3 Descriptive statistics and correlations of key variables

	Mean	Std. dev.	1	2	3	4	5	6
1. Market-sensing capability	4.22	0.98	1					
2. Environmental responsibility	4.05	1.29	0.34**	1				
3. Social responsibility	4.22	1.35	0.42**	0.74**	1			
4. International performance	4.26	1.37	0.24*	0.18	0.36**	1		
5. Firm age	34.18	25.78	0.06	0.02	0.08	0.19	1	
6. Firm size	59.078	53.09	0.05	0.17	0.20	0.27*	0.25*	1

$*p < 0.05$, $**p < 0.01$

Table 10.4 Results of hypotheses test

Independent variables	Model 1 social responsibility		Model 2 social responsibility		Model 3 environmental responsibility		Model 4 environmental responsibility		Model 5 international performance	
	β	t-value	β	t-value	β	t-value	β	t-value	β	t-value
Market-sensing capability	–	–	0.42	4.25***	–	–	0.34	3.23**	0.23	2.12*
Environmental responsibility	–	–	–	–	–	–	–	–	−0.19	−1.31
Social responsibility	–	–	–	–	–	–	–	–	0.32	2.11*
Control variables										
Firm age	0.03	0.33	0.03	0.33	−0.01	−0.13	−0.01	−0.17	0.19	1.95
Firm size	0.20	1.75	0.19	1.84	0.17	1.52	0.16	1.54	0.24	2.30*
Model estimation										
R^2	0.04		0.22		0.03		0.14		0.29	
adj. R^2	0.02		0.19		0.00		0.11		0.24	
F	1.80		7.51***		1.18		4.36**		5.91***	

$*p < 0.05$, $**p < 0.01$, $***p < 0.001$

regressed on market-sensing capability. In Model 4, with the inclusion of control variables, environmental responsibility regressed on market-sensing capability. In Models 2 and 4, market-sensing capability positively affected the social responsibility ($\beta = 1.80$, $t = 4.59$, $p < 0.001$) and environmental responsibility ($\beta = 0.38$, $t = 3.66$, $p < 0.001$) of the firm. Thus, H2a and H2b were supported.

Model 5 considered a firm's environmental responsibility, social responsibility, and market-sensing capability as sources for international performance. The result showed that both market-sensing capability ($\beta = 0.23$, $t = 2.12$, $p < 0.05$) and social responsibility ($\beta = 0.32$, $t = 2.11$, $p < 0.05$) positively affected perceived international performance, whereas environmental responsibility ($\beta = -0.19$, $t = -1.31$, $p > 0.05$) did not. Thus, H3a and H1 were supported, but H3b was not. It was found that firm size was positively associated with international performance. The SMEs with more employees may possess a variety of resources including human resources and capital to maintain international operations and, consequently, be more satisfied with the international business goal execution.

Mediation

Since the links between social responsibility–market-sensing capability and social responsibility–international performance were positive, this study further analyzed the mediating role of social responsibility in the relationship between market-sensing capability and international performance. For these purposes, multiple regression analyses were run to asses each component of the proposed mediation model (Fig. 10.4).

It was found that all paths in Fig. 10.2 were significant: path a (market-sensing capability–social responsibility) ($\beta = 0.50$, $t = 3.95$, $p < 0.001$), path b (social responsibility–international performance) ($\beta = 0.28$, $t = 2.41$, $p < 0.05$), and path c (market-sensing capability–international performance) ($\beta = 0.38$, $t = 2.89$, $p < 0.01$). Next, mediation analyses were tested using the bootstrapping method with bias-corrected confidence estimates (MacKinnon et al. 2004; Preacher and Hayes 2004). In this study, the 95% confidence interval of the indirect effects was obtained with 5000 bootstrap samples (Preacher and Hayes 2008). Figure 10.5 displays the results.

As a result, it was found that the mean indirect effect from the bootstrap analysis is positive and significant ($a \times b = 0.141$), with a 95% confidence interval excluding zero (0.0389–0.3115). In the indirect path, a unit increase in market-sensing capability increases social responsibility by $a = 0.5012$ units. Since $b = 0.2813$, with market-sensing capability staying constant, a unit increase in social responsibility increases international performance by 0.2813 units on a 0–1 scale. The direct effect c' (0.2461) became nonsignificant ($p = 0.0872$), meaning there is no direct effect of market-sensing capability on international performance in this case. The results of the mediation analysis confirmed the mediation role of social responsibility in the

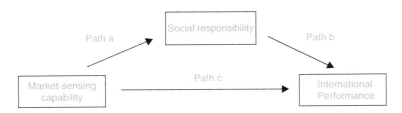

Fig. 10.4 A mediating model

Fig. 10.5 Indirect effect of market-sensing capability through social responsibility on international performance (Note: *$p < 0.05$, **$p < 0.01$, ***$p < 0.001$)

Fig. 10.6 Indirect effect of environmental responsibility through social responsibility on international performance (Note: *$p < 0.05$, **$p < 0.01$, ***$p < 0.001$)

relation between market-sensing capability and international performance, and since a × b is significant and c' is nonsignificant, it is an indirect-only mediation (Zhao et al. 2010) or "full mediation."

Even though the environmental responsibility was nonsignificant in regression model 5, we conducted an additional mediation analysis using the aforementioned bootstrapping method with bias-corrected confidence estimates, a 95% confidence interval, and 5000 bootstrap samples. This mediation analysis tests if there is an indirect effect of environmental responsibility through the social responsibility on international performance. For this mediation analysis, the model is the following: path *a* is environmental responsibility–social responsibility ($\beta = 0.76$, $t = 9.44$, $p < 0.001$), path *b* is social responsibility–international performance ($\beta = 0.49$, $t = 3.13$, $p < 0.01$), and path *c* is environmental responsibility–international performance ($\beta = 0.19$, $t = 1.62$, $p > 0.05$). Figure 10.6 displays the results.

The results of the analysis indicated that mean indirect effect is positive and significant (a × b = 0.3779), with a 95% confidence interval excluding zero (0.1208–0.6707). The direct effect c'(−0.1854) remained nonsignificant ($p = 0.2635$), and since a × b is significant with c' being nonsignificant, an indirect-only mediation was found, meaning environmental responsibility increases international performance through the mediation of social responsibility in this case.

Discussion and Implications

Theoretical Implications

The results of this study highlight how the combination of firm-specific advantages in the form of organizational characteristics and capabilities is intertwined with responsible business practices, which together enhance international entrepreneurial growth. The results suggest that responsible business behavior results from sensing the market; however, responsible behavior does not necessarily facilitate SMEs' international performance. The findings demonstrated that market-sensing capability led to both higher social responsibility and environmental responsibility. While market-sensing capability, socially responsible behavior, and firm size together directly enhance international performance (H3a), environmentally responsible behavior does so through social responsibility only. In addition, social responsibility was confirmed to be a mediator between market-sensing capability and international performance. Thus, the empirical part of this study provided evidence that market-sensing capability serves as a source for international performance (H1) as well as for both social responsibility (H2a) and environmental responsibility (H2b).

The direct positive relationship found between market-sensing capability and international performance is contrary to the studies that considered the market-sensing capabilities among the SMEs. These studies have not found strong evidence for market-sensing capability directly influencing firm performance, as in the study of Lindblom et al. (2008) where positive effect on profitability was not confirmed. However, that study did not assess the international dimension, and thus our results extend those findings to also account for performance and growth of internationalizing SMEs.

Market-sensing capability had a positive relationship on both types of responsibilities in the sample firms as hypothesized. This result suggests that it is easier for a company to notice and incorporate the responsible practices into its operations when it is responsive to customers and competitors. Contrary to evidence in extant literature supporting the positive role of environmental responsibility on a firm's performance, this study found no direct relationship between environmental responsibility and international performance (H3b). This insignificant finding implies that environmental responsibility by itself has no direct effect on the international performance of the SME. Contrary to environmental responsibility, higher levels of social responsibility were found to predict better international performance (H3a). The explanation for that might be is that social responsibility involves less resource-consuming actions, as it may occur along with the embeddedness of the SME to the local community and may be maintained through the interaction with it. Environmental responsibility, on the other hand, may require major operational changes, i.e., during the process of obtaining the environmental certifications or standards. Hence, these differences may become crucial for an SME with relatively scarce resources at its disposal and thus indirectly impact the international performance. As noted by Gelbmann (2010), SMEs often find sustainable practices challenging, as adhering to such practices may require significant additional time and investment for communicating them to stakeholders, leaving less resources for the company for use in its internationalization process, most notably its marketing abroad.

Moreover, we found a mediating role of social responsibility between market-sensing capability and international performance in the analysis, as well as between environmental responsibility and international performance. In the first case, this means that market-sensing capability should help SMEs achieve social responsibility in order to achieve a better international performance. The role of market-sensing capability indirectly impacting the performance of an SME is visible in the study of Ardyan (2015), who found that market-sensing capability has a positive effect on the success of product innovativeness, which then serves as a mediator between market-sensing capability and the performance of an SME. In the second case, this means that environmentally friendly practices executed by the company contribute to the well-being of the local society and enhanced international performance.

The higher international performance in this study resulted partially from firm size, meaning SMEs with more employees may be more successful in managing activities in multiple international locations. This result is in line with Manolova et al. (2010), where firm size in terms of employees was positively associated with an SME's export intensity. Increased human resources allow for the broadening of the firm's consumer base, hence decreasing the coordination costs and potentially achieving a higher sales volume, which results in economies of scale and scope (Aulakh et al. 2000; Gomes and Ramaswamy 1999). This is also contrary to findings that indicate that small firms perform better than medium-sized firms (Wolff and Pett 2000).

This study therefore has implications on the emerging issues in global marketing in several ways: First, it clarifies the role of CSR in a form of responsible behavior toward society and toward the environment in the context of international entrepreneurial growth. Then, it also posits the necessity of strategic management through social responsibility and market-sensing capability. This provides an opportunity for internationalizing SMEs to align with the global market dynamics and perform better when internationalizing.

The greatest impact of responsible business behavior in the internationalization of SMEs would be on product development decisions. By sensing the demand of host markets, the same product could be sold simultaneously in several countries to groups with similar levels of demand for social and environmental issues. Moreover, products in line with a certain level of standards for responsibility being in demand in one country can be targeted in the future to countries that now have lower responsibility requirements. Such a lower level of responsibility requirements in some countries, combined with the current product alternatives being unaffordable for consumers, may launch a product redesign or adaptation processes, in order to consider entry into this market as a step of international entrepreneurial growth.

In terms of promotion, SMEs often tend to have a lack of disclosure of their responsible practices. The market sensing brings the knowledge of a consumer type on the host market and thus allows the adjustment of communication of responsibility-related issues while internationalizing. Depending on the needed communication type, SMEs may maintain their image and facilitate the acceptance of their products in host countries if matched right.

Then, dictated by the international entry mode, the distribution should also be adjusted to the market conditions and to the partners' strategies concerning the responsible business practices if resellers are involved. Consequently, pricing policy for different markets might be built taking into account, in addition to the market knowledge, such factors as different pricing for products marketed as "responsible" or "sustainable" (as a differentiation strategy) or requirements from a distribution channel.

As a result, the SME's marketing strategy, including product, promotion, distribution, and pricing, should be carefully planned in accordance with the knowledge received from target markets. The responsible business practices used should match the varying levels of demand in various countries while considering new market entry.

Academically, this study extends previous approaches to the organizational capability–international performance relationship in a few aspects. First, this study confirms that market-sensing capability has a critical role in the SME's international performance, providing empirical evidence for it being an antecedent of organizational change in behavior.

Second, while integrating the IE and CSR perspectives, this study enhances our understanding of the market-sensing capability–international performance relationship by employing social responsibility as a mediator, since it appears partially in response to the market situation and contributes to the performance in international markets. Given the limited research on both market-sensing capability and responsible business practices in the internationalization of SMEs, this finding is unique in the literature since the mediating roles of responsible business behavior have not been examined when explaining the market-sensing capability–international performance relationship.

Third, it links the SMEs' internal firm-specific advantages in social responsibility as major determinants of their responsible business behavior. In doing so, it extends the studies in global marketing on CSR (Becker-Olsen et al. 2011; Choi et al. 2016) and marketing-related capabilities (e.g., Prasad et al. 2001) to the SME context, thus bringing forth additional contribution to complement those from the large MNC context (Jamali et al. 2009; Kolk and Van Tulder 2010). CSR and the increasing prevalence of software start-ups and other SMEs in the markets globally bring forth emerging themes also for research on international marketing. As the results of this study show, both are relevant and linked to marketing through specific marketing-related dynamic capabilities.

In sum, we found that the impact of market-sensing capability on international performance is mediated by the extent of social responsibility exhibited by the SME. Thus, social responsibility has a central role in entrepreneurial internationalization, and this impact is both fostered and tempered by organizational capabilities and operational characteristics of the enterprise. The results help clarify the mixed evidence in previous literature concerning the effect that CSR activities can have on company performance (Ben Brik et al. 2010; Husted and Allen 2007; Margolis and Walsh 2003; McWilliams and Siegel 2000; Orlitzky and Benjamin 2001; Orlitzky et al. 2003), specifically by outlining how the two elements of CSR, namely, social responsibility and environmental responsibility, affect the international performance of SME. Clarifying the role of market-sensing capability brings up another novel finding: Even though extant literature has investigated the mediating role of innovation capabilities and competitive advantages in the market orientation–performance relationship (Han et al. 1998; Zhou et al. 2005, 2008), there is still limited knowledge about the processes which are influenced by market-sensing capability and implications for the international performance of firms. This study contributes to adding to that knowledge and linking it to CSR and performance specifically.

Managerial Implications

The findings of this study can help SMEs develop effective management strategies. Our findings – that market-sensing capability improves responsible business behavior which then contributes to international performance of SMEs – may improve the understanding of SME managers regarding the importance of the development of a firm's capabilities. This study posits that market-sensing capability is not only a key for better international performance, but, combined with social responsibility, it brings more results for the company. As this study demonstrated, the market sensing may serve as a source for improvement of responsible practices in the firm; thus, SMEs need to find ways to develop and maintain the market sensing both at home and in host countries, from diverse perspectives. Consequently, paired with the well-developed market-sensing capability, the international operations of the SMEs may become better. To achieve this, market sensing should be strategized and maintained so that the acquisition of the needed market knowledge can be achieved.

Social responsibility is often operationalized in small companies through their strong embeddedness with the local community and employment of the locals affecting the well-being of the local community. Entrepreneurs and owner–managers in charge of decision-making in small businesses should consider the advantages of responsible business behavior for international performance. For SMEs, both internationalization and responsible business practices are activities which require a contribution of often limited resources and prioritizing; hence, managers are assessing in what way RBB and "doing good" will influence their company as they conduct internationalization strategy. Our finding that social responsibility contributes positively to international performance suggests that managers can obtain competitive advantages and benefit by contributing resources into issues related to social responsibility while already having international operations. For instance, they can improve their international operations by explicitly emphasizing the socially important issues for the host market's local community.

Our findings also suggest that firms are not always able to benefit from responsible business behavior. Environmentally responsible behavior will pay off and improve international performance only through social responsibility and thus shouldn't be totally ignored despite not showing a direct effect. Rather, it should be combined with social responsibility. Indeed, internationalized SMEs should realize that contribution to responsibility can represent a beneficial strategy, particularly in recent times, when the stakeholders are expressing their social and ecological concerns. To managers, this means that improving the business' responsible practices is an important intermediate step in converting organizational capabilities into performance gains.

It is an emerging issue that SMEs involved in responsible business practices neither have them prominently positioned within the company's strategy nor in the external communication. Though SMEs are not advised be pushed by policies to disclose this information as opposed to large companies, government officials and policymakers should take a step further in order to lead the SMEs toward more open communication about their commitments. Starting from the home countries, the bodies and state agents that provide consultation about exports and internationalization for SMEs should include advice on what would be the most beneficial tactic for a particular SME when going abroad, especially regarding the responsibility issues in the host market with the use of international marketing instruments.

Limitations and Future Research

The results and their interpretation must be considered in the context of this study's limitations. One of the limitations is that this study is a one-country study with Finland having its own specific features, making the results less generalizable for all countries. Thus, future studies might consider the differences of the host markets for the internationalization strategies of SMEs and, consequently, different socially responsible behavior in regard toward what the customers' values and expectations are in this market. Also, the research which compares developed and emerging economies as both home and host countries may reveal interesting insights.

Several methodological limitations may restrict the generalizability of our findings, including using a relatively small sample size and applying Likert scale items across the variables. Hence, expanding the scale of the sample and incorporating objective measures for international performance are beneficial for future studies. Moreover, since the dynamics of the effect of responsible practices over international performance may differ along with the internationalization process, the longitudinal study that examines the effects of internationalization over several years may reveal certain differences. For a further investigation, it is advised to measure a firm size as a composite measure combining number of employees with i.e., few-year average yearly revenues.

Conclusion

The aim of this study was to highlight an emerging area linking global marketing and international entrepreneurship research, the impact of CSR, and dynamic capabilities related to marketing in an international and global context. Specifically, the empirical part of the study examined how market-sensing capability and CSR are interlinked in explaining the international performance of SMEs. In doing so, the present study has contributed, by linking together global marketing, strategic management, and CSR-themed research, to explaining how SMEs operating internationally and globally can benefit from developing marketing-related capabilities while maintaining socially responsible business practices in the process.

Appendix 10.1

International performance, market-sensing capability, social responsibility, and environmental responsibility

International performance		
AVE = 0.66, CR = 0.93		
	Communalities	Factor loadings
IP1	,740	,860
IP2	,559	,748
IP3	,633	,796
IP4	,750	,866
IP5	,610	,781
IP6	,528	,727
IP7	,833	,913
Market-sensing capability		
AVE = 0.54, CR = 0.85		
	Communalities	Factor loadings
MS1	,437	,661
MS2	,562	,750
MS3	,764	,874
MS4	,590	,768
MS5	,385	,620
Environmental responsibility		
AVE = 0.55, CR = 0.89		
	Communalities	Factor loadings
ER 1	,654	,809
ER 2	,590	,768
ER 3	,410	,640
ER 4	,412	,642
ER 5	,529	,727
ER 6	,387	,622
ER 7	,583	,764
ER 8	,662	,814
Social responsibility		
AVE = 0.71, CR = 0.92		
	Communalities	Factor loadings
SR 1	,792	,890
SR 2	,737	,859
SR 3	,639	,800
SR 4	,784	,885
SR 5	,587	,766

References

Angulo-Ruiz, F., N. Donthu, D. Prior, and J. Rialp. 2014. The financial contribution of customer-oriented marketing capability. *Journal of the Academy of Marketing Science* 42 (4): 380–399.

Ardyan, E. 2015. Market sensing capability, entrepreneurial orientation, product innovativeness success, speed to market and SMEs performance. *International Journal of Business Intelligence Research* 6 (2): 18–32.

———. 2016. Market sensing capability and SMEs performance: The mediating role of product innovativeness success. *DLSU Business & Economics Review.* 25 (2): 79–97.

Armario, J.M., D.M. Ruiz, and E.M. Armario. 2008a. Market orientation and internationalization in small and medium-sized enterprises. *Journal of Small Business Management* 46 (4): 485–511.

Armario, J., D. Ruiz, and E. Armario. 2008b. Market orientation and internationalization in small and medium-sized enterprises. *Journal of Small Business Management* 46 (4): 485–511.

Augier, M., and D.J. Teece. 2007. Dynamic capabilities and multinational enterprise: Penrosean insights and omissions. *Management International Review* 47 (2): 175–192.

Aulakh, P., M. Kotabe, and H. Teegen. 2000. Export strategies and performance of firms from emerging economies: Evidence from Brazil, Chile, and Mexico. *Academy of Management Journal* 43 (3): 342–361.

Autio, E., G. George, and O. Alexy. 2011. International entrepreneurship and capability development – qualitative evidence and future research directions. *Entrepreneurship Theory and Practice* 35 (1): 11–37.

Avram, D., and S. Kühne. 2008. Implementing responsible business behavior from a strategic management perspective: Developing a framework for Austrian SMEs. *Journal of Business Ethics* 82 (2): 463–475.

Bagozzi, R.P., and Y. Yi. 1988. On the evaluation of structural equation models. *Journal of the Academy of Marketing Science* 16 (1): 74–94.

Barney, J.B. 1991. Firm resources and sustained competitive advantage. *Journal of Management* 17 (1): 99–120.

Baughn, C., N.L. Bodie, and J.C. McIntosh. 2007. Corporate social and environmental responsibility in Asian countries and other geographical regions. *Corporate Social Responsibility and Environmental Management* 14: 189–205.

Baumann-Pauly, D., C. Wickert, L. Spence, and A. Scherer. 2013. Organizing corporate social responsibility in small and large firms: Size matters. *Journal of Business Ethics* 115 (4): 693–705.

Becker-Olsen, K.L., C.R. Taylor, R.P. Hill, and G. Yalcinkaya. 2011. A cross-cultural examination of corporate social responsibility marketing communications in Mexico and the United States: Strategies for global brands. *Journal of International Marketing* 19 (2): 30–44.

Ben Brik, A., B. Rettab, and K. Mellahi. 2010. Market orientation, corporate social responsibility, and business performance. *Journal of Business Ethics* 99 (3): 307–324.

Bhattacharya, C.B., and S. Sen. 2004. Doing better at doing good: When, why, and how consumers respond to corporate social initiatives. *California Management Review* 47 (1): 9–24.

Bianchi, R., and G. Noci. 1998. "Greening" SMEs' competitiveness. *Small Business Economics* 11 (3): 269–281.

Blesa, A., and M. Ripolles. 2008. The influence of marketing capabilities on economic international performance. *International Marketing Review* 25 (6): 651–673.

Blomqvist, K.H., and S. Posner. 2004. Three strategies for integrating CSR with brand marketing. *Market Leader*, (summer): pp.33–6.

Cadogan, J.W., C.C. Cui, and E.K.Y. Li. 2003. Export market-oriented behavior and export performance: The moderating roles of competitive intensity and technological turbulence. *International Marketing Review* 20 (5): 493–513.

Carrigan, M., and A. Attalla. 2001. The myth of the ethical consumer – do ethics matter in purchase behaviour? *Journal of Consumer Marketing* 18 (7): 560–577.

Carroll, A.B. 1983. Corporate social responsibility: Will industry respond to cut-backs in social program funding? *Vital Speeches of the Day* 49: 604–608.

Cavusgil, S.T., and E. Cavusgil. 2012. Reflections on international marketing: Destructive regeneration and multinational firms. *Journal of the Academy of Marketing Science* 40 (2): 202–217.

Chang, T.L. 1996. Cultivating global experience curve advantage on technology and marketing capabilities. *International Marketing Review* 13 (6): 22–42.

Choi, J., Y.K. Chang, Y.J. Li, and M.G. Jang. 2016. Doing good in another neighborhood: Attributions of CSR motives depend on corporate nationality and cultural orientation. *Journal of International Marketing* 24 (4): 82–102.

Clarkson, P.M., Y. Li, G.D. Richardson, and F.P. Vasvari. 2011. Does it really pay to be green? Determinants and consequences of proactive environmental strategies. *Journal of Accounting and Public Policy* 30 (2): 122–144.

Commission of the European Communities. 2001. Promoting a European Framework for Corporate Social Responsibilities. COM (2001) 366 final, Brussels.

Costa, C., L.F. Lages, and P. Hortinha. 2015. The bright and dark side of CSR in export markets: Its impact on innovation and performance. *International Business Review* 24 (5): 749–757.

Crane, A., and J. Desmond. 2002. Societal marketing and morality. *European Journal of Marketing* 36 (5): 548–569.

Crane, A., D. Matten, and L.J. Spence. 2013. *Corporate social responsibility: Readings and cases in a global context*. 2nd ed, 3–26. Abingdon: Routledge.

Crilly, D., S. Schneider, and M. Zollo. 2008. Psychological antecedents to socially responsible behavior. *European Management Review* 5 (3): 175–190.

Dahlsrud, A. 2006. How corporate social responsibility is defined: An analysis of 37 definitions. *Corporate Social Responsibility and Environmental Management* 15 (1): 132–146.

Day, G.S. 1994. The capabilities of market-driven organizations. *Journal of Marketing* 58 (4): 37–52.

———. 2002. Managing the market learning process. *Journal of Business & Industrial Marketing* 17 (4): 240–252.

———. 2011. Closing the marketing capabilities gap. *Journal of Marketing* 75 (4): 183–195.

Derwall, J., N. Guenster, R. Bauer, and K. Koedijk. 2005. The eco-efficiency premium puzzle. *Financial Analysts Journal* 61 (2): 51–63.

Drucker, P.F. 1954. *The practice of management*. New York: Harper and Row. Escriba-Esteve.

Elango, B., and C. Pattnaik. 2007. Building capabilities for international operations through networks: A study of Indian firms. *Journal of International Business Studies* 38 (4): 541–555.

Ellerup Nielsen, A., and C. Thomsen. 2009. CSR communication in small and medium-sized enterprises. *Corporate Communications: An International Journal* 14 (2): 176–189.

Eteokleous, P., L. Leonidou, and C. Katsikeas. 2016. Corporate social responsibility in international marketing: Review, assessment, and future research. *International Marketing Review* 33 (4): 580–624.

European Commission. 2003. *Responsible entrepreneurship: A collection of good practice cases among small and medium-sized enterprises across Europe*, 1–53. Brussels: Enterprise Publications, European Commission.

———. 2011. *A renewed EU Strategy 2011–2014 for corporate social responsibility, Public Law 681*. Communication from the Commission to the European Parliament, the Council, the European Economic and Social Committee and the Committee of the Regions, Com.

———. 2016. *A partial and fragile recovery. Annual Report on European SMEs 2015/2016*. November 2016. Available online at https://ec.europa.eu/growth/smes/business-friendly-environment/performance-review-2016.

Fahy, J., G. Hooley, T. Cox, J. Bercas, K. Fonfara, and B. Snoj. 2000. The development and impact of marketing capabilities in central Europe. *Journal of International Business Studies* 31 (1): 63–81.

Gallego-Álvarez, I., J.-M. Prado-Lorenzo, L. Rodríguez-Domínguez, and I.-M. García-Sánchez. 2010. Are social and environmental practices a marketing tool? Empirical evidence for the biggest European companies. *Management Decision* 48 (10): 1440–1455.

Gebhardt, G.F., G.S. Carpenter, and J.F. Sherry Jr. 2006. Creating a market orientation: A longitudinal, multiform, grounded analysis of cultural transformation. *Journal of Marketing* 70: 37–55.

Gelbmann, U. 2010. Establishing strategic CSR in SMEs: An Austrian CSR quality seal to substantiate the strategic CSR performance. *Sustainable Development* 18 (2): 90–98.

Gomes, L., and R. Ramaswamy. 1999. An empirical examination of the form of the relationship between internationalization and performance. *Journal of International Business Studies* 30: 173–188.

Hadjikhani, A., J. Lee, and S. Park. 2016. Corporate social responsibility as a marketing strategy in foreign markets. *International Marketing Review* 33 (4): 530–554.

Hagen, B., A. Zucchella, P. Cerchiello, and N. De Giovanni. 2012. International strategy and performance – clustering strategic types of SMEs. *International Business Review* 21 (3): 369–382.

Hair, J.F., W.C. Black, B.J. Babin, and R.E. Anderson. 2009. *Multivariate data analysis*. 7th ed. Upper Saddle River: Prentice Hall.

Han, J., N. Kim, and R.K. Srivastava. 1998. Market orientation and business performance: Is innovation a missing link? *Journal of Marketing* 62 (4): 30–45.

Hansen, E.G., and J. Klewitz. 2012. The role of an SME's green strategy in public-private eco-innovation initiatives: The case of Ecoprofit. *Journal of Small Business Entrepreneurship* 25 (4): 451–477.

Hill, R.C., and L.C. Adkins. 2001. Collinearity. In *A companion to theoretical econometrics*, ed. B. Baltagi, 256–278. UK: Blackwell Publishing.

Holme, R., and P. Watts. 1999. *Corporate social responsibility*. Geneva: World Business Council for Sustainable Development.

Hoogendoorn, B., D. Guerra, and P. van der Zwan. 2014. What drives environmental practices of SMEs? *Small Business Economics* 44 (4): 759–781.

Hooley, G., J. Fahy, T. Cox, J. Beracs, K. Fonfara, and B. Snoj. 1999. Marketing capabilities and firm performance: A hierarchical model. *Journal of Market-Focused Management* 4 (3): 259–278.

Husted, B., and D. Allen. 2007. Strategic corporate social responsibility and value creation among large firms lessons from the Spanish experience. *Long Range Planning* 40 (6): 594–610.

Jamali, D., M. Zanhour, and T. Keshishian. 2009. Peculiar strengths and relational attributes of SMEs in the context of CSR. *Journal of Business Ethics* 87 (3): 355–377.

Jantunen, A., K. Puumalainen, S. Saarenketo, and K. Kyläheiko. 2005. Entrepreneurial orientation, dynamic capabilities and international performance. *Journal of International Entrepreneurship* 3 (3): 223–243.

Jenkins, H. 2009. A 'business opportunity' model of corporate social responsibility for small- and medium-sized enterprises. *Business Ethics: A European Review* 18 (1): 21–36.

Jones, M.V., N. Coviello, and Y.K. Tang. 2011. International entrepreneurship research (1989–2009): A domain ontology and thematic analysis. *Journal of Business Venturing* 26 (6): 632–659.

Kamboj, S., and Z. Rahman. 2015. Marketing capabilities and firm performance: Literature review and future research agenda. *International Journal of Productivity and Performance Management* 64 (8): 1041–1067.

Karagozoglu, N., and M. Lindell. 2000. Environmental management: Testing the win-win model. *Journal of Environmental Planning and Management* 43 (6): 817–829.

Kemper, J., O. Schilke, M. Reimann, X. Wang, and M. Bretter. 2013. Competition-motivated corporate social responsibility marketing capabilities-CSR-firms performance. *Journal of Business Research* 66 (10): 1954–1963.

Kirca, A., S. Jayachandran, and W.O. Bearden. 2005. Market orientation: A meta-analytic review and assessment of its antecedents and impact on performance. *Journal of Marketing* 69 (2): 24–41.

Klewitz, J., and E. Hansen. 2014. Sustainability-oriented innovation of SMEs: A systematic review. *Journal of Cleaner Production* 65: 57–75.

Knight, G. 2000. Entrepreneurship and marketing strategy: The SME under globalization. *Journal of International Marketing* 8 (2): 12–32.

Knight, G.A. 2001. Entrepreneurship and strategy in the international SME. *Journal of International Management* 7 (3): 155–171.

Knight, G.A., and S.T. Cavusgil. 2004. Innovation, organizational capabilities, and the born-global firm. *Journal of International Business Studies* 35 (2): 124–141.

Kohli, A., and B. Jaworski. 1990. Market orientation: The construct, research propositions and managerial implications. *Journal of Marketing* 54 (1): 1–18.

Kolk, A., and R. Van Tulder. 2010. International business, corporate social responsibility and sustainable development. *International Business Review* 19 (2): 119–125.

Kotabe, M., S.S. Srinivasan, and P.S. Aulakh. 2002. Multinationality and firm performance: The moderating role of R&D and marketing capabilities. *Journal of International Business Studies* 33 (1): 79–97.

Kotler, P. 2000. *Marketing management.* Millennium Ed. Upper Saddle River: Prentice Hall.

Kuivalainen, O., S. Sundqvist, K. Puumalainen, and J.W. Cadogan. 2004. The effect of environmental turbulence and leader characteristics on international performance: Are knowledge based firms different? *Canadian Journal of Administrative Science* 21 (1): 35–50.

Kwon, Y.C., and M.Y. Hu. 2000. Market orientation among small Korean exporters. *International Business Review* 9 (1): 61–75.

Lattemann, C., M. Fetscherin, I. Alon, S. Li, and A. Schneider. 2009. CSR communication intensity in Chinese and Indian multinational companies. *Corporate Governance: An International Review* 17 (4): 426–442.

Lee, J.S., and C.J. Hsieh. 2010. A research in relating entrepreneurship, marketing capability, innovative capability and sustained competitive advantage. *Journal of Business & Economics Research* 8 (9): 109.

Leonidou, L.C., T.A. Fotiadis, P. Christodoulides, S. Spyropoulou, and C.S. Katsikeas. 2015. Environmentally friendly export business strategy: Its determinants and effects on competitive advantage and performance. *International Business Review* 24 (5): 798–811.

Leonidou, L.C., C.S. Katsikeas, and S. Samiee. 2002. Marketing strategy determinants of export performance: a meta-analysis. *Journal of Business Research* 55 (1): 51–67.

Li, S., M. Fetscherin, I. Alon, C. Lattemann, and K. Yeh. 2010. Corporate social responsibility in emerging markets. *Management International Review* 50 (5): 635–654.

Lindblom, A., R. Olkkonen, L. Mitronen, and S. Kajalo. 2008. Market-sensing capability and business performance of retail entrepreneurs. *Contemporary Management Research* 4 (3).

Looser, S., and W. Wehrmeyer. 2015. An emerging template of CSR in Switzerland. *Corporate Ownership and Control* 12 (3): 541–560.

Lu, Y., L. Zhou, G. Bruton, and W. Li. 2010. Capabilities as a mediator linking resources and the international performance of entrepreneurial firms in an emerging economy. *Journal of International Business Studies* 41 (3): 419–436.

Luo, X., and C.B. Bhattacharya. 2006. Corporate social responsibility, customer satisfaction, and market value. *Journal of Marketing* 70 (4): 1–18.

MacKinnon, D., C. Lockwood, and J. Williams. 2004. Confidence limits for the indirect effect: Distribution of the product and resampling methods. *Multivariate Behavioral Research* 39 (1): 99–128.

Maclagan, P.W. 1998. *Management and morality.* London: Sage.

Maignan, I. 2001. Consumers' perceptions of corporate social responsibilities: A cross-cultural comparison. *Journal of Business Ethics* 30 (1): 57–72.

Maignan, I., and D.A. Ralston. 2002. Corporate social responsibility in Europe and the US: Insights from businesses' self-presentations. *Journal of International Business Studies* 33 (3): 497–514.

Manolova, T.S., I.M. Manev, and B.S. Gyoshev. 2010. In good company: The role of personal and inter-firm networks for new-venture internationalization in a transition economy. *Journal of World Business* 45 (3): 257–265.

Margolis, J., and J. Walsh. 2003. Misery loves companies: Rethinking social initiatives by business. *Administrative Science Quarterly* 48: 268–305.

McDougall, P.P., and B.M. Oviatt. 2000. International entrepreneurship: The intersection of two research paths. *Academy of Management Journal* 43 (5): 902–906.

McWilliams, A., and D. Siegel. 2000. Corporate social responsibility and financial performance: Correlation or misspecification? *Strategic Management Journal* 21 (5): 603–609.

McWilliams, A., and D. Siegel. 2001a. Corporate social responsibility: A theory of the firm perspective. *Academy of Management Review* 26 (1): 117–127.

———. 2001b. Corporate social responsibility: A theory of the firm perspective. *The Academy of Management Review* 26 (1): 117–127.

Menguc, B., and L.K. Ozanne. 2005. Challenges of the "green imperative": A natural resource-based approach to the environmental orientation–business performance relationship. *Journal of Business Research* 58 (4): 430–438.

Merrilees, B., S. Rundle-Thiele, and A. Lye. 2011. Marketing capabilities: Antecedents and implications for B2B SME performance. *Industrial Marketing Management* 40 (3): 368–375.

Molina-Azorín, J.F., E. Claver-Cortés, M.D. López-Gamero, and J.J. Tarí. 2009. Green management and financial performance: a literature review. *Management Decision* 47 (7): 1080–1100.

Möller, K., and M. Anttila. 1987. Marketing capability – a key success factor in small business? *Journal of Marketing Management* 3 (2): 185–203.

Moore, G., and L. Spence. 2006. Responsibility and small business. *Journal of Business Ethics* 67 (3): 219–226.

Morgan, N.A., C.S. Katsikeas, and D.W. Vorhies. 2012. Export marketing strategy implementation, export marketing capabilities, and export venture performance. *Journal of the Academy of Marketing Science* 40 (2): 271–289.

Narver, J., and S. Slater. 1990. The effect of a market orientation on business profitability. *Journal of Marketing* 54: 20–35.

Ngo, L.V., and A. O'Cass. 2009. Creating value offerings via operant resource-based capabilities. *Industrial Marketing Management* 38 (1): 45–59.

Nielsen, A.E., and C. Thomsen. 2009. CSR communication in small and medium-sized enterprises: A study of the attitudes and beliefs of middle managers. *Corporate Communications: An International Journal* 14 (2): 176–189.

Nummela, N., S. Saarenketo, and K. Puumalainen. 2004. A global mindset – A prerequisite for successful internationalization? *Canadian Journal of Administrative Sciences.* 21 (1): 51–64.

O'Cass, A., L. Ngo, and V. Siahtiri. 2012. Examining the marketing planning–marketing capability interface and customer-centric performance in SMEs. *Journal of Strategic Marketing* 20 (6): 463–481.

Olavarrieta, S., and R. Friedmann. 2008. Market orientation, knowledge-related resources and firm performance. *Journal of Business Research* 61 (6): 623–630.

Orlitzky, M., and J.D. Benjamin. 2001. Corporate social performance and firm risk: A meta-analytic review. *Business & Society* 40 (4): 369–396.

Orlitzky, M., F. Schmidt, and L.S. Rynes. 2003. Corporate social and financial performance: A meta-analysis. *Organization Studies* 24 (3): 403–441.

Parker, C., E. Bellucci, A. Zutshi, L. Torlina, and B. Fraunholz. 2015. SME stakeholder relationship descriptions in website CSR communications. *Social Responsibility Journal* 11 (2): 364–386.

Perez-Cabanero, C., T. Gonzalez-Cruz, and S. Cruz-Ros. 2012. Do family SME managers value marketing capabilities contribution to firm performance? *Marketing Intelligence & Planning* 30 (2): 116–142.

Perrini, F. 2006. SMEs and CSR theory: Evidence and implications from and Italian perspective. *Journal of Business Ethics* 67 (3): 305–316.

Perrini, F., A. Russo, and A. Tencati. 2007. CSR strategies of SMEs and large firms. Evidence from Italy. *Journal of Business Ethics* 74 (3): 285–300.

Pisani, N., Kourula, A., Kolk, A., and R. Meijer. 2017. How global is international CSR research? Insights and recommendations from a systematic review. *Journal of World Business* 52 (5): 591–614.

Podsakoff, P.M., S.B. MacKenzie, J.Y. Lee, and N.P. Podsakoff. 2003. Common method biases in behavioral research: A critical review of the literature and recommended remedies. *Journal of Applied Psychology* 88 (5): 879.

Post, J., and B. Altman. 1994. Managing the environmental change process: Barriers and opportunities. *Journal of Organisational Change Management* 7 (4): 64–81.

Prange, C., and S. Verdier. 2011. Dynamic capabilities, internationalization processes and performance. *Journal of World Business* 46 (1): 126–133.

Prasad, V.K., K. Ramamurthy, and G.M. Naidu. 2001. The influence of internet-marketing integration on marketing competencies and export performance. *Journal of International Marketing* 9 (4): 82–110.

Preacher, K.J., and A.F. Hayes. 2004. SPSS and SAS procedures for estimating indirect effects in simple mediation models. *Behavior Research Methods, Instruments, & Computers* 36 (4): 717–731.

———. 2008. Asymptotic and resampling strategies for assessing and comparing indirect effects in multiple mediator models. *Behavior Research Methods* 40 (3): 879–891.

Preuss, L., and J. Perschke. 2009. Slipstreaming the larger boats: Social responsibility in medium-sized businesses. *Journal of Business Ethics* 92 (4): 531–551.

Qian, W., and K. Xing. 2016. Linking environmental and financial performance for privately owned firms: Some evidence from Australia. *Journal of Small Business Management*. http://onlinelibrary.wiley.com/doi/10.1111/jsbm.12261/epdf

Ripolles, M., and R. Blesa. 2012. International new ventures as 'small multinationals': The importance of marketing capabilities. *Journal of World Business* 47 (2): 277–287.

Russo, M., and P. Fouts. 1997. A resource-based perspective on corporate environmental performance and profitability. *Academy of Management Review* 40 (3): 534–559.

Russo, A., and A. Tencati. 2009. Formal vs. informal CSR strategies: Evidence from Italian micro, small, medium-sized, and large firms. *Journal of Business Ethics* 85 (S2): 339–353.

Ryan, A., L. O'Malley, and M. O'Dwyer. 2010. Responsible business practice: Re-framing CSR for effective SME engagement. *European Journal of International Management* 4 (3): 290.

Slater, S.F., and J.C. Narver. 1994. Does competitive environment moderate the market orientation–performance relationship? *Journal of Marketing* 58: 46–55.

Song, M., C.A. Di-Benedetto, and R.W. Nason. 2007. Capabilities and financial performance, the moderating role of strategic type. *Journal of the Academy of Marketing Science* 35 (1): 18–34.

Spear, R. 2006. Social entrepreneurship: a different model? *International Journal of Social Economics* 33 (5–6): 399–410.

Spence, L. 2004. Small firm accountability and integrity. In *Corporate integrity and accountability*, ed. G. Brenkert. London: Sage.

Stanaland, A., M. Lwin, and P. Murphy. 2011. Consumer perceptions of the antecedents and consequences of corporate social responsibility. *Journal of Business Ethics* 102 (1): 47–55.

Sullivan, D. 1994. Measuring the degree of internationalization of a firm. *Journal of International Business Studies* 25 (2): 325–342.

Teece, D.J. 2014. A dynamic capabilities-based entrepreneurial theory of the multinational enterprise. *Journal of International Business Studies* 45 (1): 8–37.

Torkkeli, L., K. Puumalainen, S. Saarenketo, and O. Kuivalainen. 2012. The effect of network competence and environmental hostility on the internationalization of SMEs. *Journal of International Entrepreneurship* 10 (1): 25–49.

Torugsa, N.A., W. O'Donohue, and R. Hecker. 2012. Capabilities, proactive CSR and financial performance in SMEs: Empirical evidence from an Australian manufacturing industry sector. *Journal of Business Ethics* 10 (4): 483–500.

Turker, D. 2009. Measuring corporate social responsibility: A scale development study. *Journal of Business Ethics* 85 (4): 411–427.

van Marrewijk, M. 2003. Concepts and definitions of CSR and corporate sustainability: Between agency and communion. *Journal of Business Ethics* 44 (2): 95–105.

Vorhies, D.W., and N.A. Morgan. 2005. Benchmarking marketing capabilities for sustainable competitive advantage. *Journal of Marketing* 69 (1): 80–94.

Weerawardena, J., G.S. Mort, P.W. Liesch, and G. Knight. 2007. Conceptualizing accelerated internationalization in the born global firm: A dynamic capabilities perspective. *Journal of World Business* 42 (3): 294–306.

Wernerfelt, B. 1984. A resource-based view of the firm. *Strategic Management Journal* 5 (2): 171–180.

Wolff, J., and T.L. Pett. 2000. Internationalization of small firms: An examination of export competitive patterns, firm size, and export performance. *Journal of Small Business Management* 38 (2): 34–47.

Wood, D. 1991. Corporate social performance revisited. *Academy of Management Review* 16: 691–718.

Yang, X., and C. Rivers. 2009. Antecedents of CSR practices in MNCs' subsidiaries: A stakeholder and institutional perspective. *Journal of Business Ethics* 86 (2): 155–169.

Zhan, W., and Y. Luo. 2008. Performance implications of capability exploitation and upgrading in international joint ventures. *Management International Review* 48 (2): 227–253.

Zhang, J., and W.-p. Wu. 2013. Social capital and new product development outcomes: The mediating role of sensing capability in Chinese high-tech firms. *Journal of World Business* 48 (4): 539–548.

Zhao, X., J.G. Lynch Jr, and Q. Chen. 2010. Reconsidering Baron and Kenny: Myths and truths about mediation analysis. *Journal of Consumer Research* 37 (2): 197–206.

Zhou, K.Z., J.J. Li, N. Zhou, and C. Su. 2008. Market orientation, job satisfaction, product quality, and firm performance: Evidence from China. *Strategic Management Journal* 29: 985–1000.

Zhou, K.Z., C.K. Yim, and D.K. Tse. 2005. The effects of strategic orientations on technology-and market-based breakthrough innovations. *Journal of Marketing* 69 (2): 42–60.

Zou, S., and S. Stan. 1998. The determinants of export performance: A review of the empirical literature between 1987 and 1997. *International Marketing Review* 15 (5): 333–356.

Chapter 11
Case Study of Corporate Social Responsibility in Japanese Pharmaceutical Companies: A Comparison with Western Firms

Terry Wu and Yuko Kimura

Abstract In recent years, the awareness of corporate social responsibility (CSR) and its role have been on the rise in the business world. Japanese pharmaceutical companies got a late start on CSR activities compared to their Western counterparts. This study focuses on CSR in the pharmaceutical industry utilizing a comparison of Japanese and Western firms. We examine a sample of eight pharmaceutical companies: four Japanese-based firms and four Western-based firms. Our objective is to assess whether there is any difference between Japanese and Western firms in terms of the level of CSR.

Introduction

In recent years, there has been a growing awareness of corporate social responsibility (CSR) in the business world. In the past, profit-focused businesses paid little, if any, attention to the environment, education, health, poverty, or sustainable development. There was a perception that these social issues did not affect business firms, directly or indirectly, nor did these firms bear responsibility for a common good. Nevertheless, the topic of business ethics has received increasing attention in the news media, and today, companies are under tremendous pressure to practice CSR given the extensive media coverage of ethics as well as the environment, child labor, and other pressing issues of sustainability in developing nations and worldwide. In most countries, CSR is gaining growing acceptance in the corporate sector. Many companies have adopted CSR as an integral part of their business strategy and public value offering.

T. Wu (✉)
Faculty of Business and Information Technology, University of Ontario Institute of Technology, Oshawa, ON, Canada
e-mail: terry.wu@uoit.ca

Y. Kimura
School of Business, University of Leicester, Leicester, UK

© Springer International Publishing AG, part of Springer Nature 2018
J. Agarwal, T. Wu (eds.), *Emerging Issues in Global Marketing*,
https://doi.org/10.1007/978-3-319-74129-1_11

CSR is not a new concept in business. Levitt (1958) introduced the concept of social responsibility in business more than 60 years ago. Extending Levitt's notion that "government's job is not in business" (Levitt 1958), Friedman applied the agency theory to explain the role of CSR in business (Friedman 1970), arguing that a firm's primary objective is to increase profits, thus implying that there is no need for CSR, which is a waste of corporate resources. Using the stakeholder theory, Freeman (1984) argued that a firm is not just responsible to the shareholders or owners of the firm. Rather, a firm is required to include all stakeholders such as customers, employees, suppliers, and the public. Kotler and Lee (2004) defined CSR as "a commitment to improve community well-being through discretionary business practices and contributions of corporate resources."

Building on the stakeholder theory, Donaldson and Preston (1995) asserted that it is good business to be socially responsible in conducting business. Jones (1995) combined the stakeholder theory and classical economic theory to postulate that trust and ethical behavior result in high returns due to repeated business. The institutional theory was used to stress the role of institutions in establishing "ecologically sustainable organizations" (Jennings and Zandbergen 1995).

In a pioneering study on resource-based view (RBV) of the firm, Barney (1991) argued that a firm is able to possess "sustained competitive advantage derived from resources and capabilities it controls," providing a useful framework analyzing competitive advantage and performance. The RBV framework can be applied to the study of CSR because it offers insights into how a firm's resources are being used to influence performance (Barney 1991, 2001). Using RBV, Hart (1995) analyzed a firm's performance from an environmental perspective. Similarly, Russo and Fouts (1997) applied the CSR from a RBV perspective and argued that a firm's competitive advantage is reflected by its corporate environmental performance. McWilliams and Siegel (2001) modified the theory of the firm by adding the "social" component to business as a competitive advantage.

Being socially responsible is not only important for business firms, but it is also advantageous for them to enhance values for stakeholders. In particular, marketers can use CSR to strengthen relationships with customers, improve ties with suppliers, and increase brand equity. There is a consensus that CSR and marketing are closely linked. One relevant group of stakeholders is consumers, who may influence firms to conduct CSR activities (Lii and Lee 2012; Sen et al. 2006). Companies need to create a positive corporate image when consumers expect and demand ethical behavior and philanthropic activities of business entities. CSR is a key factor in enhancing a company's image and public value, while also ensuring corporate success both at home and abroad.

The marketing literature ties CSR-related activities to marketing strategy. Marketing studies have focused on several streams of research: corporate marketing (Balmer and Greyser 2006), brand extension (Kitchin and Schultz 2002), marketing communication (Jahdi and Acikdilli 2009), consumer reactions (Sen and Bhattacharya 2001), and purchase intentions (David et al. 2005). Of particular interest is that most studies focus on the impact of CSR on domestic marketing (Lai et al. 2010; Luo and Bhattacharya 2006). While CSR is crucial to enhancing corporate image in international markets, there are only a few studies on international marketing with respect to CSR (Muller 2006; Polonsky and Jevons 2009). Some studies suggest that CSR may enhance global brand image in emerging markets (Torres et al. 2012). However, when entering foreign markets, global companies may not achieve cause-related marketing results by spending on CSR due to cultural differences in attitudes toward CSR (Choi et al. 2016).

One of the issues that has generated considerable interest related to CSR is its impact on a firm's performance. A business case can be made by linking CSR activities to corporate performance outcomes. Since the 1990s, there has been a great deal of research on CSR. Some studies suggest a link between corporate success and CSR activities (Orlitzky et al. 2003; Waddock and Graves 1997). This perspective is based on an underlying assumption that CSR activities may improve a company's image, thereby enhancing consumer trust in its products and services (Turker 2009). Some scholars explore the effects of CSR activity on numerous stakeholders (Sen and Bhattacharya 2001; Smith 2003; Waddock and Smith 2000). Building on the idea of CSR as a competitive advantage, Greening and Turban (2000) found a positive relationship between CSR activity and job-seeking intention. This is consistent with the reputation literature, in which corporate reputation is the organization outcome of CSR (Agarwal et al. 2014; Walker 2010). Some management scholars have argued that CSR has a positive impact on decisions of professional investors (Sen and Bhattacharya 2001).

Despite numerous studies on the relationship between social responsibility and financial performance, the empirical results are somewhat inconclusive and inconsistent (McWilliams and Siegel 2000; Orlitzky et al. 2003; Ullman 1985; Waddock and Graves 1997). Although some studies indicate a positive relationship (Margolis and Walsh 2003; Orlitzky et al. 2003), other studies suggest a negative relationship (Aupperle et al. 1985; Friedman 1970). Several studies conclude that the relationship is insignificant (Aupperle et al. 1985; Surroca et al. 2010). Other scholars have found the relationship in asymmetric form (Jayachandran et al. 2013), U-shaped form (Barnett and Salomon 2012), and even inverted U-shaped form (Lankoski 2008).

Given CSR is used as a business strategy, research is still needed due to these inconclusive and contradictory results (Orlitzky et al. 2003). Some scholars even suggest that previous research work was futile since it did not provide conclusive and clear answers (Ullmann 1985; Margolis and Walsh 2001). Moreover, a review of the literature reveals that most studies are based on industrial and financial firms (Surroca et al. 2010). Yet none of the studies examines the relationship between CSR and firm performance in the pharmaceutical industry especially in the Japanese context. This research void is not surprising for three reasons. First, in general, little academic research is conducted on the business approach of Japanese pharmaceutical industry due to secrecy surrounding the confidential nature of new drugs and product developments. Second, CSR data are not readily available in the Japanese pharmaceutical industry due to less rigorous reporting requirements in Japan. Third, the time frame for CSR involvement in Japanese pharmaceutical industry is much shorter. To fill the research gap, this study explores the nature of the relationship between CSR and firm performance for Japanese pharmaceutical companies in comparison with their Western counterparts. The pharmaceutical market is a typical case of global marketing because prescription drugs are sold on a worldwide basis. The reason for choosing Western firms for comparison is that they currently dominate the global pharmaceutical market.

This study examines CSR in the pharmaceutical industry, using a case study to explore the reach and importance of CSR in Japanese pharmaceutical firms in comparison with Western firms, as well as the impact of CSR on the financial performance of Japanese versus Western firms. The study is organized as follows. The next section discusses research on CSR in the pharmaceutical industry. Using a sample of four Japanese and four Western pharmaceutical firms, we offer some preliminary results from our investigation of the CSR activities of these firms. Concluding remarks are presented in the last section.

CSR in the Pharmaceutical Industry

The pharmaceutical industry is a key industrial sector that is vital to most developed economies such as the United States, U.K., Germany, Japan and even emerging economies such as China and India. This industry develops new drugs and biopharmaceutical products, as well as a variety of generic drugs. The industry is multifaceted, with numerous stakeholders ranging from patients, doctors, pharmacists, scientists, employees, shareholders, health professionals, drug stores, hospitals, and government to the general public. Unlike most other consumer products, people are willing to pay a higher price for pharmaceutical products to maintain good health and long life. This sector generates substantial profits for pharmaceutical companies while also providing significant foreign exchange earnings for high-producing countries in the industry. More importantly, this sector is critical to innovation and scientific discovery in developed and emerging economies.

However, the pharmaceutical industry is facing negative publicity all the time. There are questions about the reliability of clinical trial data for new drugs and their safety. There is also a perception of questionable marketing behavior by pharmaceutical companies in terms of financial relationships involving manufacturers, physicians, and teaching hospitals. While the pharmaceutical industry is highly profitable, many people believe that the industry is inclined to restrict access to its products. Of particular note is the observation that pharmaceutical companies are reluctant to offer inexpensive drugs and medical supplies to developing countries; it is widely perceived that big pharmaceutical and biopharmaceutical companies are partly responsible for the lack of access to basic medicine in those countries. According to the Ipsos Global Reputation Centre, the pharmaceutical industry is viewed negatively in many key markets such as the USA, Canada, China, and Germany (Ipsos Public Affairs 2012). One study concluded that pharmaceutical companies are often regarded with considerable suspicion by the general public in the Western world, which has a tendency to think that the industry overcharges for its products and that it carries out irresponsible animal testing (Esteban 2008). It is widely believed that the pharmaceutical industry is highly profitable because it controls the supply of medicine worldwide (Kreiner 1995).

Members of the general public often do not recognize that the pharmaceutical industry invests heavily in R&D and takes significant risks in developing drugs, many of which never reach the market. For pharmaceutical companies, finding the right balance between provision of healthcare and the generation of profits is a challenging one. Most companies are under pressure to reduce costs and improve access to their products. While CSR has been recognized as a central issue in business, there is no consistent approach to CSR in the pharmaceutical industry. In the USA, CSR is related to the environment or "sustainable development." In Japan, the focus of CSR is on social contributions. In most European countries, the emphasis is on socially responsible activities.

The pharmaceutical industry has maintained that it is required to operate a profitable business with an objective to improve people's health. However, beginning with the global HIV/AIDS pandemic, large drug companies have received negative publicity due to a perception that they are not being socially responsible (Leisinger 2005; Smith 2008). In 2000, in terms of global access to basic medical supplies, the United Nations and 189 nations made a commitment to free people from extreme poverty and multiple deprivations. This pledge was later converted into the eight Millennium Development Goals (MDGs) for the year 2015. These goals were intended to (i) eradicate extreme poverty and hunger; (ii) achieve universal primary education; (iii) promote gender equality and empower women; (iv) reduce child mortality; (v) improve maternal health; (vi) combat HIV/AIDS, malaria, and other diseases; (vii) ensure environmental sustainability; and (viii) develop a global partnership with companies for development (United Nations 2015). Many of these initiatives are health-related and thus require pharmaceutical companies to support the goals.

In response to these MDGs, large pharmaceutical companies have started to develop strategies for implementation. Moreover, Kofi Annan, the Secretary-General of the United Nations, announced the UN Principles for Responsible Investment in 2006 (Principles of Responsible Investment 2006), emphasizing the need for corporations to consider a more long-term perspective for their investment decisions and the implications for investors. Against this backdrop, there is a higher expectation for companies to incorporate transparency, environment, governance, and social responsibility in their business operations.

In light of these initiatives and activities, several Western pharmaceutical companies have begun to formulate CSR strategy as an integral part of their business operations. It was recognized that it is relatively risky to allocate extensive resources to CSR activities in "big pharma" due to the existing burden of R&D expense in the already high cost structure (Smith 2008). While it is not mandatory to report CSR, many large pharmaceutical companies have chosen to publish CSR reports.

In 2012, the London Declaration was launched to represent a new, coordinated push to accelerate progress toward eliminating or controlling ten neglected tropical diseases (NTDs) by the end of the present decade (World Health Organization 2012). Partners pledged to work together to improve the lives of the 1.4 billion people affected worldwide, most of them among the world's poorest. Original endorsers include more than ten global pharmaceutical companies as well as the Bill & Melinda Gates Foundation, the World Bank, UK Aid, US Aid, Drug for Neglected Disease Initiative (DNDi), and other important endorsers (World Health Organization 2012). The Japan-based pharmaceutical company Eisai endorsed this declaration. Other major pharmaceutical companies such as GlaxoSmithKline, Johnson & Johnson, and Merck also supported this initiative by carrying out more strategic and comprehensive thinking in CSR arenas such as R&D, intellectual property, affordable pricing, corporate governance, and social contribution activities and to act globally.

The Japanese Pharmaceutical Industry

Japan is not a global leader in the pharmaceutical industry, though it is one of the few countries in the world that discovers new prescription drugs (Umemura 2014). Prior to the 1990s, the Japanese pharmaceutical industry focused primarily on its domestic market. However, during the last two decades, this sector has started to globalize and to explore international markets. Due to the removal of trade barriers, the Japanese pharmaceutical industry has experienced a large number of mergers and restructuring initiatives (Nivoix and Nguyen 2012).

In contrast to their Western counterparts, Japanese pharmaceutical companies have formulated CSR strategy later, due to differences compared to Western companies in market outreach and historical and geographic distances to emerging markets. The Japan Business Federation (Nippon Keidanren) defined CSR as the effort "to understand economic, environmental and social aspects comprehensively to make them sources of competitiveness and improve corporate values" (Japanese Business Federation 2004). This definition was received as a reactive declaration compared to the attitude of other countries. In this context, the UN Global Compact (2000) pledged to promote activities by companies with a strategic policy initiative for businesses committed to aligning their operations and strategies with ten universally accepted principles in the areas of human rights, labor, environment, and anti-corruption (United Nations 2000). In 2010, the International Organization for Standardization (ISO) released a document entitled *ISO26000 Guidance on Social Responsibility*, providing guidance on how businesses and organizations can operate in a socially responsible way, although this compliance cannot be certified, unlike some other well-known ISO standards (International Organization for Standardization 2010). In response, Japanese corporations have started to participate in the UN Global Compact and declare they will follow ISO26000 in their future business plans.

The Japan Association of Corporate Executives (Keizai Doyukai) is a private, nonprofit, nonpartisan organization that was formed in 1946 by 83 farsighted business leaders united by a common desire to contribute to the reconstruction of the Japanese economy. In consideration of the emerging global CSR activities and market paradigm shift, the Japanese Association of Corporate Executives proposed very active declarations in both 2011 and 2012 on how to evolve companies toward a corporation for co-creating social value aimed at sustainable, synergetic development of society and businesses (Japan Association of Corporate Executives 2011, 2012). With the influence of these declarations and the impacts of the severe financial recession and rapid business paradigm shift within emerging countries, CSR-based business strategy began to penetrate Japanese companies in a convincing way. Therefore, it is starting to be recognized in Japan that CSR can and should be expanded beyond social contribution or regulatory compliance to become a strategic investment and set of embedded activities situated at the core of any business proposition. CSR is integral to public reputation, public value, and future competitiveness. Furthermore, Japanese companies have long practiced a traditional philosophy of business ethics known as *sanpou-yoshi* (trilateral good), guaranteeing a "three-way satisfaction" among key stakeholders: buyers, sellers, and society (Oshika and Saka 2017). In recent years, many Japanese executives have done some soul-searching and self-reflection about corporate social responsibility, especially in the aftermath of the Tohoku earthquake in 2011. There is some evidence that Japanese companies have become more active in their philanthropic activities in an attempt to contribute positively to society and promote a more responsible corporate image with a broader and longer-term orientation.

While there are no regulatory or statutory requirements for pharmaceutical companies to adopt CSR in Japan, there is a growing recognition that CSR is actually good for business. In 1981, the Japan Pharmaceutical Manufacturers Association (JPMA) introduced an industry-wide Code of Practice in line with the ethical criteria for industry developed by the World Health Organization (JPMA 2013). Specifically, since 2013 JPMA has published regularly updated transparency guidelines for the relation between corporate activities and medical institutions and the disclosure of such relations. The trend towards increased transparency has been accelerated by two factors: (1) big pharmaceutical companies' unethical activities for sales and marketing in the USA and (2) US government requirements for payment disclosure. Ethical behaviors should be the baseline of any business implementation; however, this is now part of the discussion related to the CSR perspective.

Although JPMA does not specify the components of CSR, it recognizes its importance for the industry as a whole in its Code of Practice:

> It is also important for the pharmaceutical industry to perceive Corporate Social Responsibility (CSR), which has recently been requested by society as an important mission. (JPMA 2013)

In order to remain globally competitive, Japanese pharmaceutical companies started to focus on R&D and internationalization after the 2008 global financial crisis (Douai and Wu 2014). In the decade of the 2000s, the Japanese pharmaceutical industry experienced substantial transformation including rapid mergers and acquisitions, patent cliffs in 2010, and a paradigm shift to sell drugs to emerging markets. Of the 20 largest pharmaceutical companies in the world, 4 of them are Japanese firms with headquarters in Japan. These four Japan-based multinational pharmaceutical companies are not only leaders in the Japanese pharmaceutical market; they are active players in the global market.

1. Takeda

With more than 29,000 employees worldwide, the Osaka-based Takeda Pharmaceutical Company Ltd. (*Takeda Yakuhin Kōgyō Kabushiki Kaisha*) is the largest pharmaceutical company in Japan in terms of global sales (Takeda 2016). Takeda is a public company that was originally founded in 1781 and incorporated in 1925. It has offices around the world with R&D centers in many countries.

2. Astellas Pharma Inc.

Astellas Pharma Inc. (*Asuterasu Seiyaku Kabushiki Kaisha*) is the second largest pharmaceutical company in Japan, headquartered in Tokyo (Astellas Pharma 2016). The public company was established in 2005 after a merger of Fujisawa Pharmaceutical Company and Yamanouchi Pharmaceutical Company. It used to specialize in a variety of post-transplant and antifungal pharmaceutical products such as Prograf and Mycamine in the past. The company has 17,000 employees worldwide, with research and development offices in Japan, Europe, and the USA.

3. Daiichi Sankyo

Daiichi Sankyo Company (*Daiichi Sankyō Kabushiki Kaisha*) is a leading Japanese pharmaceutical company based in Tokyo with more than 14,670 employees (Daiichi Sankyo 2016). Formed in 2005 after a merger of Daiichi Pharmaceutical Company and the century-old Sankyo Company Limited, the combined Daiichi Sankyo is actively involved in global operations. Daiichi Sankyo produces and markets a large variety of pharmaceutical products and drugs globally. The company has research centers mainly in Japan.

4. Eisai Co., Ltd.

Eisai Co., Ltd. (*Eisai Kabushiki Kaisha*) was originally established as Nihon Eisai in 1941 (Eisai 2016). A few years later in 1944, the company chose to merge with Sakuragaoka Research Laboratory. Eisai is currently a public company with its headquarters in Tokyo. There are nearly 10,000 employees.

Research Propositions

Dunning's institution-based ownership-location-internalization (OLI) theory provides a solid framework for describing the situation of international firms entering foreign markets (Dunning 1998, 2003). Most pharmaceutical companies are exploiting their location, along with any internalization advantages in foreign markets as they sell pharmaceutical products on a global basis. In the pharmaceutical industry, the source of competitiveness also includes ownership (O-level) advantage, which is critical because most pharmaceutical companies are R&D intensive. Reputation and public perceptions would be an important factor when entering a foreign market. Since the pharmaceutical industry has been the target of constant criticisms for unethical behavior, it has recognized that adoption of CSR may mitigate or even reverse a negative corporate image.

A company's investment in CSR can be beneficial because of positive impact on the image of a company (Sen and Bhattacharya 2001; Waddock and Smith 2000). Hence, consumers are more willing to purchase the company's products and services. This suggests that CSR activities generate returns to the company (Luo and Bhattacharya 2006; Luo and Homburg 2008). Acknowledging that CSR can be used as a competitive advantage, the world's top 20 pharmaceutical companies have positioned the CSR approach as their overall business strategy. Dow Jones Sustainability Index and FTSE4GOOD would be recognized as among the most important indexes to measure and identify companies that meet globally approved corporate responsibility standards (Dow Jones Sustainability Index 2012; FTSE4GOOD 2012).

The concept of CSR is rooted in the philosophy and ideology of Anglo-American and European principles of liberal democratic rights, justice, and societal structures (Fukukawa and Teramoto 2009). An obvious question is whether it is appropriate to apply the Anglo-American corporate values to Confucian-oriented societies (Miles 2006). While Japanese companies appear to endorse CSR, they are also uneasy about its uncritical adoption (Fukukawa and Teramoto 2009). Nakano (2007) argues that the uniqueness of Japanese business could be at odds with Western values due to differences in Japanese social customs, employee motivations, as well as organizational values.

As discussed before, most studies on the relationship between CSR and firm performance are contradictory and inconclusive over the last three decades (Orlitzky et al. 2003). A number of studies have attempted to provide theoretical explanations for this causal pattern without success (Aupperle et al. 1985; McWilliams and Siegel 2001; Ullmann 1985). Most research focus on industrial and financial firms (Surroca et al. 2010). Although the subject of CSR has gained an increasing attention in Japan, there is scant research in this area. A review of the literature reveals that there are only a few studies on CSR with respect to Japanese firms (Fukukawa and Moon 2004; Fukukawa and Teramoto 2009; Nakano 2007). However, none of the research is on Japanese pharmaceutical industry. As Japanese pharmaceutical companies become more international-oriented and increasingly globalized, they have gradually adopted and adapted CSR in the context of Japanese social customs and organization values. It is unclear whether adoption of Anglo-American theoretical framework of CSR for Japanese pharmaceutical companies will yield better financial performance. Thus, we posit:

Proposition 1 *With increasing globalization and overseas operations, Japanese pharmaceutical companies are inclined to adopt the Anglo-American CSR practices in global markets. Thus, an increase in CSR activities will lead to better financial performance for Japanese pharmaceutical companies.*

In 2000, the Japanese pharmaceutical industry experienced a major transformation due to rapid mergers and acquisitions, accompanied by increased innovation through patents. To achieve a stronger international market presence, Japanese firms established R&D centers and marketing divisions in major markets (Mahlich 2007). Currently, four Japanese-based multinational pharmaceutical companies such as

Takeda, Astellas, Daiichi Sankyo, and Eisai lead the market in Japan and expand internationally to global markets. On the one hand, globalization has brought new overseas markets for Japanese pharmaceutical products. On the other hand, they must compete with more established Western firms. In Japan, a company is closely tied to the formation of a local community, forming the basis of a society to which an individual employee belongs (Fukukawa and Moon 2004). Unlike the Anglo-American model of community, both individuals and companies are responsible to society as members in this society (Tange 2001). Fukukawa and Teramoto (2009) argue that Japanese CSR is different from the Anglo-American styles of CSR. Specifically, the current Japanese CSR management by Japanese multinational companies is balanced in terms of the three dimensions of the triple bottom line: economic, environmental, and social dimensions (Fukukawa and Teramoto 2009). The pharmaceutical industry presents a unique case study to analyze whether there are any differences between sample Japanese companies and Western firms. It is expected that there are significant differences in financial performance between Japanese firms and Western firms. Thus, we posit:

Proposition 2 *In light of the differences between Japanese CSR and Anglo-American CSR practices, Japanese pharmaceutical firms are expected to have a weaker financial performance than Western firms.*

Case Study

There are three underlying problems in collecting data for this study. First, most Japanese pharmaceutical companies do not provide details of their philanthropic contributions. In the absence of reliable information, it is difficult to compare them with Western pharmaceutical companies. Second, there is no commonly accepted standard in CSR activities across countries. What is accepted as CSR in Japan may not be acceptable in the USA and in Europe. Third, the financial disclosure rules for listed companies in Japan differ significantly from those of the USA and Europe. Hence, the financial performance indicators are not consistent for comparison purposes.

Since Japanese pharmaceutical companies have undertaken their CSR activities only in the last few years, there are not enough data for any statistical analysis. However, we can use some preliminary data for an exploratory study. We have used available data in the Access to Medicine Index, a widely accepted index for analyzing access to medicine in developing countries. Specifically, the Access to Medicine Index provides rankings for the world's 20 largest pharmaceutical companies on seven performance indicators: access to medicine, market compliance, research and development (R&D), pricing, patents, capacity building, and donations (Access to Medicine Index Foundation 2016).

Of the 20 largest pharmaceutical companies in the world, four of them are Japan-based multinational firms: Takeda, Astellas, Daiichi Sankyo, and Eisai. Takeda has undertaken a holistic approach to CSR activities, introducing the "Takeda Initiative" healthcare support program as part of the global fund to fight AIDS, tuberculosis, and malaria in Africa (Takeda 2016). Astellas has focused on new drugs and offered support to a local healthcare system in Indonesia (Astellas 2016). Daiichi Sankyo started to provide mobile healthcare vans to deliver medical care in India, Cameroon, and Tanzania in 2011 in collaboration with international NGOs (Daiichi Sankyo 2016). Eisai offered a comprehensive access to medicine with free supply of diethylcarbamazine citrate (DEC) tablets to eliminate lymphatic filariasis. The first shipment was sent to India in November 2013 (Eisai 2016).

Using the definition by Kotler and Lee (2004), we consider all corporate resources that are used to improve social well-being as CSR. The measurement of CSR activities can utilize corporate spending or third-party ratings (Graves and Waddock 1994). In order to compare the level of CSR activities between Japanese and Western pharmaceutical companies on a consistency basis, we decided to use company ranking index and donation data reported in the Access to Medicine Index (Access to Medicine Foundation 2016). We selected eight companies for analysis: four Japanese firms and four Western firms. In addition to the Access to Medicine Index, we have used annual reports of various companies for the financial performance. When measuring financial performance, other studies suggest a number of indicators such as sales revenue, return on investment (ROI), market share, and profits (Pentina et al. 2009; VanderWerf and Mahon 1997). We decided not to use profits and return on investment as indicators of financial performance given the unique nature of the pharmaceutical industry with its high costs of R&D. Due to availability of data in our sample, we selected sales revenue as the financial performance indicator for consistency purposes.

Discussions

Drawing on the data collected from company annual reports and the Access to Medicine Index, we examine a sample of eight pharmaceutical companies: four Japanese-based firms and four Western-based firms. The four Japanese firms are Eisai, Takeda, Astellas, and Daiichi Sankyo. For comparison, we chose four non-Japanese leading Western firms: GlaxoSmithKline (GSK), Johnson & Johnson (J & J), Novartis, and Merck. Our objective is to assess whether there are any differences between Japanese and Western firms in terms of the level of philanthropic activities.

The Access to Medicine Index ranks companies on their efforts to provide access to medicine, vaccines, and diagnostic tests to people living in 88 countries (Access to Medicine Foundation 2016). Table 11.1 shows the company rankings and ratings in access to medicine of four Japanese pharmaceutical firms as well as four Western firms. All four Japanese companies are in the last ten positions, ranging from 11th for Eisai to 20th for Astellas. Of the 20 largest pharmaceutical companies, GlaxoSmithKline (GSK) and Johnson & Johnson (J & J) are ranked first and second, respectively.

Pharmaceutical companies are increasingly aware of their public image. To meet their CSR commitments, they have engaged in drug donation programs and other health-related infrastructure activities. Table 11.2 shows the product donations and philanthropic activities of Japanese and Western firms. With the exception of Eisai in the 4th position, the other three Japanese firms are low in ranking, with Takeda 16th, Daiichi Sankyo 18th, and Astellas 20th. In contrast, GlaxoSmithKline, Merck, and Johnson & Johnson are ranked as the top three, followed by Novartis at fifth. It is evident that Japanese pharmaceutical companies are not able to reach the level of Western firms in terms of donations and philanthropic activities, as reflected by the level of CSR.

We have used company annual reports to compile some financial data for comparison. Table 11.3 provides financial information for these eight companies for the fiscal year 2016. It is interesting to note that GlaxoSmithKline, Johnson & Johnson, and Novartis are leaders in terms of sales. Johnson & Johnson, for example, sold more products than the four Japanese companies combined. It is noteworthy that the profit after taxation is very low for all the Japanese firms in comparison with Western firms.

Over the last three decades, many scholars have examined the relationship between CSR and firm performance (Aupperle et al. 1985; McWilliams and Siegel 2001; Waddock and Graves 1997). Their results are contradictory and inconclusive (Grewatsch and Kleindienst 2017; Orlitzky et al. 2003), though many studies suggest a small but positive relationship between CSR and firm performance (Margolis and Walsh 2003; Orlitzky et al. 2003). Siegel and Vitaliano (2007) argue that CSR is influenced by the type of products and market profits trends. By all accounts, Japan is a step behind the global trends in CSR practices. Given the Japanese traditional focus on customers and employee relationships, there are some doubts about the universality of CSR causal relationship that is based on an Anglo-American conceptual frame-

Table 11.1 Overall ranking and rating (2016)

Japanese firms	Company ranking	Index	Non-Japanese firms	Company ranking	Index
Eisai	11	2.34	GlaxoSmithKline	1	3.43
Takeda	15	1.77	Johnson & Johnson	2	2.93
Daiichi Sankyo	18	1.61	Novartis	3	2.87
Astellas	20	1.32	Merck	4	2.83

Source: Access to Medicine Foundation (2016)

Table 11.2 Product donations and philanthropic activities index (2016)

Japanese firms	Company ranking	Index	Non-Japanese firms	Company ranking	Index
Eisai	4	3.5	GlaxoSmithKline	1	4.0
Takeda	16	1.7	Merck	2	3.8
Daiichi Sankyo	18	1.1	Johnson & Johnson	3	3.8
Astellas	19	1.1	Novartis	5	3.5

Source: Access to Medicine Foundation (2016)

Table 11.3 Company financial information for fiscal year 2016

Firms	Eisai	Takeda	Astellas	Daiichi Sankyo	GSK	J&J	Novartis	Merck
Net sales	539	1,732	1,312	955	37,929	71,890	48,518	39,807
	(bil. yen)	(bil. yen)	(bil. yen)	(bil. yen)	(US$mil.)	(US$mil.)	(US$mil.)	(US$mil.)
(US$ bil.)	4.6	14.8	11.2	8.2	37.9	71.9	48.52	39.81
Cost of products sold or cost of sales	36%	32.3%	24%	36.6%	33.3%	30.2%	36.1%	34.9%
Cost of selling, general, and administration[a]	33%	35.7%	36%	31.7%	33.6%	27.7%	29.3%	24.5%
R&D expense	21%	18.0%	15.9%	22.4%	13.0%	12.7%	18.6%	18.1%
Profit for the year	39.4	115	219	47.5	1,240	16,540	6,698	5,691
	(bil. yen)	(bil. yen)	(bil. yen)	(bil. yen)	(US$mil.)	(US$mil.)	(US$mil.)	(US$mil.)
Diluted earnings per share	137.41 yen	146.26 yen	103.55 yen	79.44 yen	US$0.253	US$6.76	US$2.80	US$2.04
Stock price (year-end)	6,638 yen	4,835 yen	1,624 yen	2,392 yen	US$38.51	US$115	74.1 CHF	US$58.87
No of employees	9,877	29,900	17,202	14,670	99,333	126,400	123,000	69,000
Ranking in ATM 2016	11th	15th	20th	18th	1st	2nd	3rd	5th
Product donation index	3.5	1.7	1.1	1.1	4.0	3.8	3.5	3.5

Sources: Access to Medicine Foundation (2016), 2016 Annual Financial Reports of Each Company

[a]For Japanese company: selling, general, and administration cost-R&D expense

work. Thus, there is a need to verify the validity of this causal pattern in the context of Japanese pharmaceutical companies vis-à-vis their Western counterparts. Due to lack of sufficient data for an empirical analysis, this study is exploratory in nature.

The relationship between philanthropic activities and corporate performance is illustrated in the donation-performance matrix in Fig. 11.1. The four Western pharmaceutical firms (GSK, Merck, Johnson & Johnson, and Novartis) are rated highly in CSR with an index of more than 3.5 in each case. In fact, GSK and Johnson & Johnson obtained huge revenues with US$37.9 billion and US$71.9 billion, respectively. In contrast, the Japanese firms are located in the first and third quadrants with lower revenues. With the exception of Eisai, the other three Japanese firms recorded low scores in donations and philanthropic activities. While CSR is no guarantee for positive financial results, the data suggests a possible relationship between CSR and financial performance.

Among the eight pharmaceutical companies, the Western companies ranked in the top four in the Access to Medicine Index. Novartis ranked fifth in the product donations and philanthropic activities index. GSK remained at the top of the league according to the Access to Medicine Index but by a narrower margin due to newcomers' efforts such as Johnson & Johnson and Sanofi. Japan-based pharmaceutical companies' efforts gradually came to the evaluation in the Access to Medicine Index. There are still significant differences between Japanese and Western pharmaceutical companies. This trend relates to the companies' financial performance. Looking at

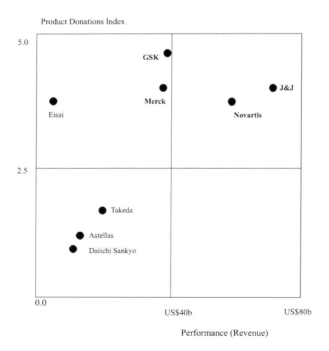

Fig. 11.1 Product donations-performance matrix

the number of employees, we see that recently Takeda increased its size to be comparable with the level of their Western counterparts, by acquiring global pharmaceutical company of Nycomed. Japanese pharmaceutical companies will be pressured to be increasingly more CSR-conscious in their business strategies and operations in order to meet their responsibility in the global society.

Managerial Implications

Using a case study, this study explores the impact of CSR on firm performance in the Japanese pharmaceutical industry. This is a case study based on a small sampling of Japanese and Western pharmaceutical companies which appeared to have achieved positive performance resulting from CSR. One conclusion drawn from this study is that CSR can affect business performance in the pharmaceutical industry worldwide. It is evident that CSR can be an element of the marketing strategy that can yield positive firm performance (Maignan and Ferrell 2004).

It would be beneficial for Japanese pharmaceutical firms to refer to the Anglo-American mode of CSR and adapt it to Japanese business practices. While Japanese business ethics can be quite different from the Western norms, Japanese senior management can modify their management behavior by adapting CSR in their firms. This is particularly true for those Japanese pharmaceutical companies that are expanding globally.

The Japanese pharmaceutical industry is experiencing tremendous changes in the global market. The combination of economic stagnation and declining population has forced Japanese firms to expand internationally in search for overseas markets and increased customer base. The industry has shifted from pursuing a closed, small domestic market to an open, large global system. For Japanese firms, the traditional approach to CSR with a focus on "sanpou-yoshi" (trilateral good) may not be sufficient to address the complexities of the global economy. Japanese companies need to consider a new approach to CSR in light of global competition and market opportunities. Due to increasing globalization, there is evidence that Japanese firms are willing to incorporate the Western concept of CSR. Facing a paradigm shift in global marketing, Japanese pharmaceutical companies are likely to adopt marketing strategies from a domestic-based system to a global-based orientation.

Conclusion

The pharmaceutical industry has long been criticized for ever-escalating drug prices and excessive profits at the expense of consumers. However, prescription drugs are not ordinary goods on the market. Consumers are vulnerable to these products that can potentially save lives and preserve health. Thus, many pharmaceutical companies face a host of economic, moral, and legal issues in relation to their activities for the production and distribution of drugs.

A review of the literature reveals that there is currently no study on CSR relating to Japanese pharmaceutical companies. Understanding the complex issues of CSR in the Japanese pharmaceutical industry is not an easy task due to availability of limited data. This study is a first attempt to analyze the CSR for Japanese pharmaceutical firms in comparison with Western firms. In this study, we have used some preliminary data to compare Japanese pharmaceutical firms and Western pharmaceutical firms.

The findings in this study are exploratory in nature. As with any research, this study has several limitations. First, due to lack of data for empirical work, we have adopted a simple framework to analyze the complexities of CSR. However, the relationship on CSR and firm performance is a very complex one, involving an array of multiple factors. Hence, our analysis has oversimplified the CSR situation. Second, our current sample size is relatively small, with four Japanese pharmaceutical firms and four Western firms. These eight firms may not be representative of the pharmaceutical industry in both Japan and the West. Hence, caution must be taken in interpreting these results on the relationship between CSR and firm performance. Third, we have chosen several large Western firms for our sample. There could be some sampling biases when we use them to compare with Japanese firms. A more meaningful comparison would be Western firms that are of similar size to those Japanese firms. Lastly, given the Japanese tradition of social norms and organizational values, this study is unable to capture the impact of these variables on CSR. Despite the difficulties in obtaining company data, future studies should focus on empirical analysis in order to understand the impact of CSR on firm performance in the Japanese pharmaceutical industry. It is hoped that this study will lead to further research in this area.

References

Access to Medicine Foundation. 2016. The access to medicine index. https://accesstomedicineindex.org/media/atmi/Access-to-Medicine-Index-2016.pdf.

Agarwal, J., O. Osiyevskyy, and P.M. Feldman. 2014. Corporate reputation measurement: Alternative factor structures, nomological validity, and organizational outcomes. *Journal of Business Ethics* 130 (2): 485–506.

Astellas. 2016. Annual report 2016. https://www.astellas.com/en/ir/library/pdf/160905_2016AR_en.pdf. Accessed 30 May 2017.

Aupperle, K.E., A.B. Carroll, and J.D. Hatfield. 1985. An empirical examination of the relationship between corporate social responsibility and profitability. *Academy of Management Journal* 28 (2): 446–463.

Balmer, J.M.T., and S.A. Greyser. 2006. Corporate marketing: Integrating corporate identity, corporate branding, corporate communications, corporate image and corporate reputation. *European Journal of Marketing* 40 (7/8): 730–741.

Barnett, M.L., and R.M. Salomon. 2012. Does it pay to be really good? Addressing the shape of the relationship between social and financial performance. *Strategic Management Journal* 33 (11): 1304–1320.

Barney, J.B. 1991. Firm resources and sustained competitive advantage. *Journal of Management* 17 (1): 99–120.

————. 2001. Resource-based *theories* of competitive advantage: A ten-year retrospective on the resource-based view. *Journal of Management* 27 (6): 643–650.

Choi, J., Y.K. Chang, Y.J. Li, and M.G. Jang. 2016. Doing good in another neighborhood: Attributions of CSR motives depend on corporate nationality and cultural orientation. *Journal of International Marketing* 24 (4): 82–102.

Daiichi Sankyo. 2016. Corporate social responsibility report 2016. http://www.daiichisankyo.com/about_us/responsibility/philanthropy/medicalaccess/b2c2.html.

David, P., S. Kline, and Y. Dai. 2005. Corporate social responsibility practices, corporate identity, and purchase intention: A dual-process model. *Journal of Public Relations Research* 17 (3): 291–313.

Donaldson, T., and L. Preston. 1995. The stakeholder theory of the corporation: Concepts, evidence, and implications. *Academy of Management Review* 20: 65–91.

Douai, A. and Wu, T. 2014. News as business: the global financial crisis and Occupy movement in the Wall Street Journal. *Journal of International Communication* 20 (2): 148–167.

Dow Jones Sustainability Indexes. 2012. Annual review 2012. http://www.sustainability-indexes.com/review/annual-review-2012.jsp. Accessed 12 Jan 2013.

Dunning, J.H. 1998. Location and the multinational enterprises: A neglected factor. *Journal of International Business Studies* 29: 45–66.

————. 2003. Some antecedents and international theory. *Journal of International Business Studies* 34: 108–115.

————. 2016. Company. http://www.eisai.com/company/atm/index.html.

Esteban, D. 2008. Strengthening corporate social responsibility in the pharmaceutical industry. *Journal of Medical Marketing* 8 (1): 77–79.

Freeman, R.E. 1984. *Strategic management: A stakeholder approach.* Boston: Pitman Publishing Inc.

Friedman, M. 1970. The social responsibility of business is to increase its profits. *New York Times Magazine*, September 13.

FTSE4GOOD. 2012. Index website. http://www.ftse.com/ftse4good.

Fukukawa, K., and J. Moon. 2004. A Japanese model of corporate social responsibility? *Journal of Corporate Citizenship* 16: 45–59.

Fukukawa, K., and Y. Teramoto. 2009. Understanding Japanese CSR: The reflections of managers in the field of global operations. *Journal of Business Ethics* 85 (1): 133–146.

Graves, S.B., and S.A. Waddock. 1994. Institutional owners and corporate social performance. *Academy of Management Journal* 37 (4): 1034–1046.

Greening, D.W., and D.B. Turban. 2000. Corporate social performance as a competitive advantage in attracting a quality workforce. *Business and Society* 39 (3): 254–280.

Grewatsch, S., and I. Kleindienst. 2017. When does it pay to be good? Moderators and mediators in the corporate sustainability-corporate financial performance relationship: A critical review. *Journal of Business Ethics* 145 (2): 383–416.

Hart, S. 1995. A natural resource-based view of the firm. *Academy of Management Review* 20: 986–1014.

International Organization for Standardization. 2010. ISO 26000 guidance on social responsibility. https://www.iso.org/standard/42546.html.

Ipsos Public Affairs. 2012. Global consumers to the pharmaceutical industry: Focus on innovation, safety and affordability. https://www.ipsos.com/en-us/global-consumers-pharmaceutical-industry-focus-innovation-safety-and-affordability.

Jahdi, K.S., and G. Acikdilli. 2009. Marketing communications and corporate social responsibility: Marriage of convenience or shotgun wedding? *Journal of Business Ethics* 88 (1): 103–113.

Japan Association of Corporate Executives (Keizai Doyukai). 2011. CSR in the global era: Meet the expectations of an ever-changing society and enhance competitiveness. http://www.doyukai.or.jp/en/policyproposals/2011/110404.html.

————. 2012. Policy proposal: Evolution toward a corporation for co-creating social value aiming for sustainable, synergetic development of society and companies. http://www.doyukai.or.jp/en/policyproposals/2012/120613a.html.

Japan Business Federation (Nippon Keidanren). 2004. Basic views on CSR promotion (in Japanese).

Japan Pharmaceutical Manufacturers Association (JPMA). 2013. JPMA code of practice. http://www.jpma.or.jp/english/policies_guidelines/pdf/code_practice03.pdf.

Jayachandran, S., K. Kalaignanam, and M. Eilert. 2013. Product and environmental social performance: Varying effect on firm performance. *Strategic Management Journal* 34 (10): 1255–1264.

Jennings, P., and P. Zandbergen. 1995. Ecological sustainable organizations: An institutional approach. *Academy of Management Review* 20: 1015–1052.

Jones, T. 1995. Instrumental stakeholder theory: A synthesis of ethics and economics. *Academy of Management Review* 20: 404–437.

Kitchin, P. J. and Schultz, D.E. 2002. Managing reputation: global issues and problems", paper presented at the 7th Annual Conference on Corporate and Marketing Communications, 29-30 April.

Kotler, P., and N. Lee. 2004. *Corporate social responsibility: Doing the most good for your company and your cause*. Hoboken: Wiley & Sons, Inc.

Kreiner, A. 1995. The ethics of the pharmaceutical industry and the need for a dual market system. *Journal of Medical Humanities* 16 (1): 55–68.

Lai, C.S., C.J. Chiu, C.F. Yang, and D.C. Pai. 2010. The effects of corporate social responsibility on brand performance: The mediating effect of industrial brand equity and corporate reputation. *Journal of Business Ethics* 95 (3): 457–469.

Lankoski, L. 2008. Corporate responsibility activities and economic performance: A theory of why and how they are connected. *Business Strategy and the Environment* 17 (8): 536–547.

Leisinger, K.M. 2005. The corporate social responsibility of the pharmaceutical industry: Idealism without illusion and realism without resignation. *Business Ethics Quarterly* 15 (4): 577–594.

Levitt, T. 1958. The dangers of social responsibility. *Harvard Business Review* 36 (5): 41–50.

Lii, Y.S., and M. Lee. 2012. Doing right leads to doing well: When the type of CSR and reputation interact to affect consumer evaluations of the firm. *Journal of Business Ethics* 105 (1): 69–81.

Luo, X., and C.B. Bhattacharya. 2006. Corporate social responsibility: Customer satisfaction and market value. *Journal of Marketing Research* 70: 1–18.

Luo, X., and C. Homburg. 2008. Satisfaction, complaint, and the stock value gap. *Journal of Marketing* 72: 29–43.

Mahlich, J. 2007. The Japanese pharmaceutical industry in transition: Has higher research orientation resulted in higher market values? *Asian Business and Management* 6: 75–94.

Maignan, I., and O.C. Ferrell. 2004. Corporate social responsibility and marketing: An integrative framework. *Journal of the Academy of Marketing Science* 32 (1): 3–19.

Margolis, J. D. and Walsh, J. P. 2001. People and Profits? The Search for a Link between a Company's Social and Financial Performance. Mahwah, NJ: Lawrence Erlbaum and Associates.

Margolis, J.D., and J.P. Walsh. 2003. Misery loves companies: Rethinking social initiatives by business. *Administrative Science Quarterly* 48: 268–305.

McWilliams, A., and D. Siegel. 2000. Corporate social responsibility and financial performance: Correlation or misspecification. *Strategic Management Journal* 21 (5): 603–609.

———. 2001. Corporate social responsibility: A theory of the firm perspective. *Academy of Management Review* 26 (1): 117–127.

Miles, L. 2006. The application of Anglo-American corporate practices in societies influenced by Confucian values. *Business and Society Review* 111 (3): 305–321.

Muller, A. 2006. Global versus local CSR strategies. *European Journal of Management* 24 (2–3): 189–198.

Nakano, C. 2007. The significance and limitations of corporate governance from the perspective of business ethics: Towards the creation of an ethical organizational culture. *Asian Business & Management* 6: 163–178.

Nivoix, S., and P. Nguyen. 2012. Characteristics of R&D expenditures in Japan's pharmaceutical industry. *Asia Pacific Business Review* 18 (2): 225–240.

Orlitzky, M., F. Schmidt, and S. Rynes. 2003. Corporate social and financial performance: A meta-analysis. *Organization Studies* 24: 403–441.

Oshika, T., and C. Saka. 2017. Sustainability KPIs for integrated reporting. *Social Responsibility Journal* 13 (3): 625–642.

Pentina, I., L.E. Pelton, and R.W. Hasty. 2009. Performance implications of online entry timing by store-based retailers: A longitudinal investigation. *Journal of Retailing* 85 (2): 177–193.

Polonsky, M., and C. Jevons. 2009. Global branding and strategic CSR: An overview of three types of complexity. *International Marketing Review* 26 (3): 327–347.

Principles of Responsible Investment. 2006. The UN principles for responsible investment. http://www.unpri.org/. Accessed 12 Jan 2013.

Russo, M., and P. Fouts. 1997. A resource-based perspective on corporate environmental performance and profitability. *Academy of Management Journal* 40 (3): 534–559.

Sen, S., and C.B. Bhattacharya. 2001. Does doing good always lead to doing better? Consumer reactions to corporate social responsibility. *Journal of Marketing Research* 38: 225–243.

Sen, S., Bhattacharya, C. B. and Korschun, D. 2006. The role of corporate social responsibility in strengthening multiple stakeholder relationships: A field experiment. *Journal of the Academy of Marketing Science* 34: 158–166.

Siegel, D.S., and D.F. Vitaliano. 2007. An empirical analysis of the strategic use of corporate social responsibility. *Journal of Economics and Management Strategy* 16 (3): 773–792.

Smith, N.C. 2003. Corporate social responsibility: Whether or how? *California Management Review* 45 (4): 52–76.

Smith, A.D. 2008. Corporate social responsibility practices in the pharmaceutical industry. *Business Strategy Series* 9 (6): 306–315.

Surroca, J., J.A. Tribo, and S. Waddock. 2010. Corporate responsibility and financial performance: The role of intangible resources. *Strategic Management Journal* 31 (5): 463–490.

Takeda. 2016. Annual report 2016. http://www.takeda.com/investor-information/annual/pdf/index/ar2012_en.pdf.

———. 2016. CSR http://www.takeda.com/csr/community/.

Tange, H. 2001. *A study of the social nature of corporate management (Kigyo Keiei no Syakaisei Kenkyu).* Tokyo: Chuo Keizaisha.

Torres, A., T.H.A. Bijmolt, J.A. Tribo, and P. Verhoef. 2012. Generating global brand equity through corporate social responsibility to key stakeholders. *International Journal of Research in Marketing* 29: 13–24.

Turker, D. 2009. How corporate social responsibility influences organizational commitment. *Journal of Business Ethics* 89: 189–204.

Ullman, A.E. 1985. Data in search of a theory: A critical examination of the relationships among social performance, social disclosure and economic performance of U.S. firms. *Academy of Management Review* 10 (3): 540–557.

Umemura, M. 2014. Crisis and change in the system of innovation: The Japanese pharmaceutical industry during the lost decades, 1990–2010. *Business History* 56 (5): 816–844.

United Nations. 2000. UN Global Compact 2000. https://www.unglobalcompact.org/what-is-gc/mission/principles.

———. 2015. The Millennium Development Goals Report 2015. http://www.un.org/millennium-goals/2015_MDG_Report/pdf/MDG%202015%20rev%20(July%201).pdf.

VanderWerf, P.A., and J.F. Mahon. 1997. Meta-analysis of the impact of research methods on findings of first-mover advantage. *Management Science* 43 (11): 1510–1519.

Waddock, S.A., and S.B. Graves. 1997. The corporate social performance–financial performance link. *Strategic Management Journal* 18 (4): 303–320.

Waddock, S., and N. Smith. 2000. Relationships: The real challenge of corporate global citizenship. *Business and Society Review* 105 (1): 47–62.

Walker, K. 2010. A system review of the corporate reputation literature: Definitions, measurement, and theory. *Corporate Reputation Review* 12 (4): 357–387.

World Health Organization. 2012. London declaration on neglected tropical disease. http://www.who.int/neglected_diseases/London_Declaration_NTDs.pdf.

Chapter 12
How Do Western Luxury Consumers Relate with Virtual Rarity and Sustainable Consumption?

Anne-Flore Maman Larraufie and Lucy Sze-Hang Lui

Abstract Despite the fact that different industries have been putting efforts into promoting sustainability in their businesses, little effort was initially shown in the luxury industry. Even though some companies have included responsibility and sustainability as a source of competitive advantage, thus becoming central to their strategic vision, the sector has been regularly criticized for its lack of sustainable development imperatives. It has led to an extensive discussion in the academic field on whether luxury and sustainable development are by nature compatible or not. It is the objective of the present chapter to challenge this hypothesis, confronting it with the market perspective. Studying the views of Western regular luxury consumers toward the two concepts should ultimately help luxury managers design more efficient, and hopefully effective, strategies to promote sustainability in their companies.

Introduction

Ever since sustainable development was brought up in the United Nations in 1987, sustainability has been one of the top priorities in the policy-making process of different governments as well as different companies. Despite the fact that different industries have been putting efforts into promoting sustainability in their businesses, little effort was initially shown in the luxury industry. Even though some companies have included responsibility and sustainability as a source of competitive advantage, thus becoming central to their strategic vision (Pavione et al. 2016), the sector has been regularly criticized for its lack of sustainable development imperatives. It has led to an extensive discussion in the academic field on whether luxury and sustainable development are by nature compatible or not. Some scholars suggest

A. -F. Maman Larraufie (✉)
SémioConsult® & ESSEC Business School, Paris, France
e-mail: maman@essec.edu

L. S. -H. Lui
Fendi, Paris, France

© Springer International Publishing AG, part of Springer Nature 2018
J. Agarwal, T. Wu (eds.), *Emerging Issues in Global Marketing*,
https://doi.org/10.1007/978-3-319-74129-1_12

the two concepts can indeed coexist as they share many similarities. They suggest that virtual rarity is the key to increase the motivation of luxury consumers for sustainable luxury purchase. However, no further studies have concerned the relation between virtual rarity and sustainable luxury. It is the objective of the present chapter to challenge this hypothesis, confronting it with the market perspective. Studying the views of Western regular luxury consumers toward the two concepts should ultimately help luxury managers design more efficient, and hopefully effective, strategies to promote sustainability in their companies. This chapter does not refer to any luxury company or brand in particular. We rather explore the concept of luxury facing sustainability and drive implications about how to take advantage of that for a luxury company.

To achieve this objective, the chapter is organized into the following parts. First, a thorough literature review helping define the concepts of virtual rarity and of sustainable luxury, and ultimately merging both. Then, the qualitative methodology used to conduct the study is explained, along with a detailed description of the methods used for data collection and data analysis. The chapter then focuses on the most important theoretical and managerial findings, still acknowledging further research developments due to research limitations.

Background

The Concept of Luxury

The concept of luxury is quite hard to define and has been explained via different approaches. Mortelmans (2005) has made a detailed summary of the discussion around this debate and suggests that four elements contribute to luxury: scarcity, extra value, high quality, and price. He states that luxury must be limited in production and highly exclusive, having a unique design that provides aesthetic value and displaying a high-quality control as well as a detailed craftsmanship on the products that end up being expensive (Mortelmans 2005). People tend to purchase luxury products to make a social statement (Wattanasuwan 2003), from group-fitting to distinguishing from other groups lower on the status scale. Purchasing luxury goods can also help achieve an "ego ideal" that commands the respect of others and inspires self-love. Furthermore, luxury is also a primary source of excitement as a unique experience and enjoyment. These are the reasons that led philosophers such as Plato and Aristotle to condemn luxury that they considered by nature negative and immoral (Mortelmans 2005) and thus unnecessary and superficial. Needs are limited to the three basic necessities of survival (Plato 1945), i.e., food, shelter, and clothing, and the demand for luxury would break the harmony of the polis[1]. It would erode their society's strength and lead to some unending struggle for wealth and

---

[1] City in ancient Greek

material possessions. No matter which approach one adopts, it seems that luxury is more of a desire serving different purposes than a basic necessity one needs to rely on to survive (Mortelmans 2005).

Luxury branding is composed of five different dimensions: conspicuousness, uniqueness, perceived extended self, hedonism, and quality (Fionda and Moore 2009; Patrick and Hagtvedt 2015; Vigneron and Johnson 2004). Conspicuous consumption suggests that the consumption of luxury products is very important to individuals in search of social representation and position, while the sense of uniqueness is a way to enhance self-image (Vigneron and Johnson 2004). The extended self refers to the fact that consumers tend to purchase luxury products to distinguish themselves from others with social referencing and the construction of one's self, thus being decisive to luxury consumption (Vigneron and Johnson 1999). Hedonism means that the purchase of luxury products allows consumers to have personal reward and fulfillment: they focus on their subjective satisfaction rather than on the functional values of the luxury products they purchase (Patrick and Hagtvedt 2015). Lastly, quality is also a key component in luxury branding: it is expected from luxury companies to offer superior product quality and performance (Mortelmans 2005).

Luxury Facing Sustainability

While luxury focuses on excessive desires, sustainability relates more to fundamental human needs (Maslow 1943). Sustainability is the result of some growing awareness upon environmental problems and socioeconomic issues that deal with the future welfare of humanity (Hopwood et al. 2005). It is commonly associated with values of altruism, sobriety, and moderation, in contrast to those of personal pleasure and superficiality for luxury. Even when related to luxury, sustainable development is approached as a way to promote the conservation of biodiversity and natural resources and to strengthen social equity (Kapferer 2010). Hence, luxury companies include CSR through the design of materials used for manufacturing or through saving consumption of natural resources during the conduct of their operations (Doval et al. 2013).

Some scholars suggest that the two concepts are conflicting and are thus incompatible. The lifestyle of excess, indulgence, and waste that luxury embraces would hinder sustainable development, for it encourages every human being to live a life disconnected from needs and environmental-focus, which lessens the influence of sustainability and ethics in the decision-making process for luxury consumers (Davies et al. 2012). Besides, the demand for secondary desires of showing-off and of unique experiences exceeds the limits of being focused only on core basic needs. As these two concepts are suggesting two different kinds of lifestyle, it would be impossible to produce sustainable luxury (DeWeese-Boyd and DeWeese-Boyd 2007).

Other scholars advocate a positive correlation between luxury and sustainability. Kapferer (2012) suggests that even if luxury highlights social inequality, it does not create it. In fact, there are similarities between the two concepts as they both focus on durability. Despite the fact that luxury is associated with wastefulness, there are luxury products that are inherited through generations. Many luxury products focus on the durability and everlasting timepieces that can be passed from generation to generation (Kapferer 2012). This exact same idea is embraced by sustainable development: the environment should be preserved to guarantee sufficient resources for future generations (Hasna 2006).

Apart from durability, the concept of rarity is also shared by luxury and sustainability (Kapferer 2012). Mortelmans (2005) suggests that luxury value is based on the objective rarity of materials. He states that scarcity is one of the most important elements in defining luxury: limited production preserves the notion of exclusivity. This is mainly achieved by transforming rare materials, e.g., exotic skins, into high-quality products. Thus, luxury production relies upon rare natural resources. This should encourage luxury companies to focus on the sustainability of their resources instead of simply exploiting them (Kapferer 2010). Ensuring sufficient supply of the materials is the underlying factor of the organic growth of luxury companies, so luxury itself requires sustainability. This makes the two concepts compatible.

Some other scholars also suggest that consumers' change of concerns and sources of satisfaction also fosters luxury to be tied in with sustainability (Moscardo and Benckendorff 2010). Luxury products standing in one's extended self, one's values should affect one's decision to buy luxury (Hennings et al. 2013; Parker 2009). Luxury consumers would then be the major force fostering luxury companies to adopt sustainability within their corporate strategies. Actually, buying sustainable luxury products is triggered by three values: social cultural, ego-centered and eco-centered values (Cervellon and Shammas 2013). As it is a way for consumers to show their concern for the environment and eco-friendly practices, it communicates positively about their personality (Griskevicius et al. 2010).

However, bad management of "sustainable actions" done by luxury companies might backfire. For instance, using CSR components has a negative impact on the quality perception of luxury goods when communication is made about social-oriented CSR and not about environmental-oriented CSR (no impact in that case) (Alharbi et al. 2017). Besides, the owner of non-sustainable luxury goods would be endowed with more status, social power and prestige (Beckham and Voyer 2014), so for luxury brands associated with the self-enhancement concept CSR activities might have negative consequences (Torelli et al. 2011). Therefore, it is important for luxury companies to understand up to which point they can communicate with their consumers on their CSR actions, and which "aspects" they should stress out.

Luxury and Rarity

Rarity plays some active role in luxury consumers' decision-making process (Joy et al. 2012). This is to be linked with the natural desire that people have to be unique and distinctive (Snyder and Fromkin 1980). The possession of scarce goods (due to low supply) helps a lot in this vein. Low supply might be real or virtual, with virtual rarity being introduced to keep the dream and desirability for luxury products alive (Kapferer and Bastien 2012). Virtual rarity builds some perception of scarcity instead of strengthening real scarcity. It is naturally correlated with the perception of desirability, value, and purchase intention (Brock 1968; Sevilla and Redden 2014), as long as the rare products are priced more (Lynn 1989).

Managing rarity is thus a strategic issue for luxury companies, which articulate it through limited editions, individualized approaches, special events, and one-to-one and two-step marketing actions (Catry 2007). Some subjective rarity is built as well, thanks to price, distribution, and advertising choices.

Rarity is naturally associated with scarcity, esp. in link with limited quantity as far as luxury goods are concerned. Scarcity messages interact with the brand concept and will positively affect the purchase intention for a symbolic brand (i.e., all luxury ones) without cheapening its image (Aggarwal et al. 2011). Besides, perceived uniqueness has also a strong impact on purchase intention for scarce products (Wu et al. 2012); and scarcity appeals that enhance value perception increase purchase intention through a self-serving motivation related to an enhanced perceived influence on the self vs. others (Eisend 2008; Gunther and Mundy 1993).

We therefore argue that luxury companies could package sustainable luxury through promoting rarity in the production process and at the retail and communication levels.

Research Question

The objective of this study is to investigate the importance of virtual rarity in promoting sustainable luxury in luxury companies by studying how consumers relate and merge the concepts of virtual rarity and sustainable luxury. By studying the relations of these two concepts, it is expected that luxury companies can set their marketing strategies in successfully promoting sustainable luxury in the market, which directly increase the sustainability in the luxury industry.

Methodology

In order to investigate Western luxury regular consumers' standpoints toward virtual rarity and sustainable luxury, an interpretive qualitative interview research methodology was adopted, as it is considered to be the most appropriate approach for exploratory research (Legard et al. 2003). With no previous works dealing with the topic, this study aimed at gathering rich and descriptive data, exploring the views, experiences, beliefs, and/or motivations of individuals on specific matters. Besides, qualitative methods, such as interviews, are believed to provide a deeper understanding of social phenomena than would be obtained from purely quantitative methods (Silverman 2010).

Table 12.1 List of participants

Name	Sex	Age	Country	Occupation	Education	Income (per month)
Pierre-Yves	M	38	France	Acoustic technician	University	2300
Karla	F	30	Mexico	Shop owner	Master	1500
Vincent	M	31	Belgium	Computer consultant	University	3200
Sarah	F	27	Brazil	Boutique director	University	4500
Simone	M	39	Italy	Interior designer	College	2000
Alex	M	40	USA	Property manager	University	4600
Magalie	F	32	France	Consultant	College	2000
Sophia	F	25	UK	Flight attendant	College	2500
Raymond	F	31	Spain	Store manager	Master	4500
Andrea	F	34	Peru	Hotel receptionist	College	1200
Yan	F	28	USA	Sales assistant	Master	2200
Laura	F	29	Belgium	Bank customer service	University	1800
Carla	F	36	Brazil	Psychiatrist	University	1900
Helen	F	25	USA	Freelancer	University	1800
Cindy	F	36	UK	Secretary	University	1600
Nael	F	28	USA	Brain researcher	University	3500
Mario	M	30	Mexico	Chocolatier	College	1500
Pier	M	38	Denmark	Doctor	University	4400
Francesco	M	33	Italy	Chef	College	3400
Sarah	F	25	USA	Music teacher	Master	2800

Twenty males and females from 25 years old to 40 years old were interviewed on their views toward virtual rarity and sustainability in luxury (see Table 12.1). They were all regular luxury consumers. Their understanding of the luxury concept as well as the driving motivation for purchasing luxury products served as an indicator to understand the relations between virtual rarity and sustainable luxury. They were all Western consumers, as sustainability is still a topic more studied in Western countries. Respondents were European (10), North American (5), and Latin American (5). Data has been collected until no new information emerged from the respondents' verbatims, following the saturation principle.

The interview was structured in three main parts. At the beginning of the interview, participants were asked about their basic information including their names, nationalities, age, and occupation. The interview continued with asking participants about their purchasing habits in luxury products including the frequency of their luxury purchases and eventually brands. This part is to make sure the participants fit with the sampling stated above. The third part was the core part of the interview and was divided into three sections. The first section aimed at understanding the views of the participants toward the concept of luxury as well as the importance of rarity in luxury products. Questions such as photo comparisons of luxury and premium bags, word associations with rarity, and their purchase motivations were asked to understand how they see rarity in the luxury industry. The second section aimed at understanding their knowledge of sustainable luxury and how they look at the concept. The final section was set to understand how participants correlate the concepts of rarity and of sustainable luxury. Questions such as the importance of rarity in sustainable luxury and sustainable luxury launching strategy were asked.

All interviews were conducted in a private setting and transcribed. Content analysis was used to analyze the data (Cole 1988). Some inductive approach was used (Elo and Kyngäs 2008) following the three standard steps of open coding, conceptualization, and then theorization. During the open coding process, data is organized and examined. Important points and pieces of information are identified as different codes and phrases for different sections. These codes and phrases normally summarize participants' views and opinions toward the concept of virtual rarity, the concept of sustainable luxury as well as the relation between the two concepts. By doing this, we can understand how participants share the same views or diverge. During the data-sorting process, the codes and phrases taken down are identified into different themes and concepts. Through identifying different themes and concepts, data from different participants was connected and related. By doing this, we can summarize all the similar data that appeared in the 20 interviews and get a better understanding of participants' positive or negative opinions. Abstraction is the last step in content analysis. During this process themes and concepts, as generated in the previous categorization process, are interpreted to make explanatory accounts and meanings on how participants view the two concepts and how they relate the two concepts together.

Results and Findings

The purpose of this study is to understand Western regular luxury consumers' perspective upon virtual rarity and sustainable luxury as well as to identify how they merge the two concepts together. The findings are broken down into three parts that relate to the research question: (1) the view of virtual rarity, (2) the view of sustainable luxury, and (3) the view toward merging the two concepts.

View of Virtual Rarity

Western regular luxury consumers hold four different views toward the concept of virtual rarity in luxury: (1) it serves as a symbolic effect, (2) it is a driving factor for conspicuous consumption, (3) rarity as a marketing tool, and (4) quality and design as the driving forces of luxury purchase.

Rarity as a Symbolic Effect

As shown by the literature review, rarity is a very important element naturally intertwined with the luxury concept: it suggests some exclusivity. Such exclusivity makes luxury a luxury. To the participants, apart from the exclusivity that it generates, rarity is shown as a symbolic component, also highly essential in luxury (Mortelmans 2005).

> Well, I think rarity is the first thing you think about luxury. For a brand it is very important, it makes you buy a brand. You don't need to hard sell luxury, but for a brand you need to have rarity. (Yan, USA)

Some participants also think that rarity is the core of a brand as it makes customers dream for the brand so that they are motivated to buy premium products from the company.

> You must have luxury, then you have that image and this image attracts customers to buy the products at the bottom of the pyramid. You know those perfumes and make up and stuff. People may not necessarily buy products that are rare, but this is a must to keep the image and you buy the cheap products in the brand. They are products that can really earn money. (Helen, USA)

In terms of virtual rarity, participants also suggested that it serves as an attraction to introduce a new brand to the consumers and the market.

> There are so many brands in the world and how do I know they are good or not if I have never heard of the name? I would just look at some magazines and see if any brand is special. If I know oh that brand has one of the most limited productions or they have some skills that other brands don't have, of course I will pay more attention to that. (Francesco, Italy)

Based on the above statements, we can conclude that to Western regular luxury consumers, rarity is an important brand component that can be leveraged to introduce some brand to the market or to maintain the desire of consumers to purchase the products of the brand.

Rarity Contributing to Conspicuous Consumption

In the interviews conducted, many participants suggested that rarity is a driving factor for conspicuous consumption.

> If I have one Kelly bag I am like in a different world you know. Looking at the others which are still asking for the bag every time they go to the store, but look I already have one. (Karla, Mexico)

Some participants also stated that purchasing rare products is a way to distinguish themselves from others.

> When I think about luxury, that is what I think. I don't want everybody to have it... It's like... it is difficult to get, to me at least. And that is what I call luxury so I don't want everybody to have it. (Karla, Mexico)

From the above analysis, we can see that rarity plays a role in conspicuous consumption. As rarity often implies high price and exclusivity, consumers would associate the purchase of the rare luxury products to a way of showing the others that they have high economic power and that they are different from others.

Rarity as Marketing Tool

Rarity is not a driving factor that encourages luxury purchase for the respondents. Most of them suggest that it serves as an attraction, some marketing tool to attract consumers' attention. In other words, it is a very useful tool to communicate with the consumers and raise their interest for the brand.

> I will be interested in knowing the products if you tell me they are rare. Like I would do some research on them and see how rare they are. (Helen, US)

> If a product is rare, I will focus more on that and I would want to know more about that. (Magalie, France)

Therefore, rarity in this case is not a motivation to buy a luxury product, but more of a given feature of any luxury retail or product characteristics.

Quality and Design as the Driving Forces of Luxury Purchase

When asked whether rarity is the main driving force that encourages luxury purchase, many participants suggested that it is not a driving force but a good marketing tool for a company to catch people's attention. So, the interviewer elaborated upon this statement, trying to understand the participants' driving force(s) behind luxury consumption.

> I think the design is very important. If the design is not good, even it is rare, I don't care I won't buy it. (Vincent, Belgium)

Apart from the design, some participants also emphasized the importance of quality in luxury products. They suggested that durability as well as good craftsmanship would be the main criteria for good quality luxury products.

> Of course, the quality has to be good, if I have to pay so much money, I would expect to buy something I can use for a long time, with the good quality. I don't just buy the crocodile skin or any other material, I buy when it is really with good quality, when the production process is good, the sewing and finishing is good. (Pierre-Yves, France)

View on Sustainable Luxury

In the second part of the interview, participants were asked about their views toward sustainable luxury. Three opinions emerged: (1) sustainable luxury is doubtful; (2) encouraging sustainability in different forms should be done, instead of making sustainable products; and (3) quality and design as the driving forces behind luxury purchase (again).

Sustainable Luxury Is Doubtful

Although the literature review suggests that consumers are well-aware of the sustainability concept, they do not think it could be applied in the luxury business. Many consumers still see the luxury business as one of the exceptional industries that should not emphasize on sustainability.

> What do you mean by sustainability? I don't think it can be done. Because luxury is about precious leather, it is about waste, excess. You cannot emphasize on sustainability if a lot of your products are about excessive materials and production. I think sustainability is just a slogan. (Yan, USA)

> I don't even pay attention to sustainability. I don't think it has anything to do with luxury. I don't find luxury products with this sustainability concept very attractive. Maybe to some people it is very important, just like people who eat organic food. But for me, I simply don't care. (Sophie, UK)

Therefore, even if the sustainable concept has been encouraged in the luxury industry, the acceptance of this concept (as far as it deals with the product itself) by its consumers is not as high as scholars were predicting.

Sustainability in Different Form

Many participants suggested that adding the sustainability concept to luxury products would not increase their motivation to buy the products.

> I don't really care about whether the products are sustainable or not. I mean, if I like it, I will buy. It is not because the product is sustainable. It is because I like it. (Yan, US)

> I won't think about that really. I just respond to my impulse. If I have a desire to buy a leather product, I will do so. I won't ask myself not to buy because it is not good for the environment. (Simone, Italy)

However, some participants suggested that there are different ways to support sustainability instead of buying sustainable luxury goods, such as donating money to environmental associations.

> I don't want to buy sustainable luxury goods. I can pay more money and the brand can donate some of the money to preserve sustainability. I think this is more practical. (Laura, Belgium)

> I think donating money to some organizations to me is a more attractive way to preserve the environment. Like I want to take care of the environment. But if I have to sacrifice my want of buying luxury products, I cannot. (Karla, Mexico)

Hence, it sounds that regular consumers are reluctant to change their ways of purchasing to match the sustainability concept, at least when it deals with luxury. But that does not mean that they do not care. Rather than purchasing sustainable luxury products, they would prefer to use other ways to support this concept.

Quality and Design as the Driving Forces of Sustainable Luxury Purchase

When asked about what would mostly encourage them to purchase a sustainable luxury product, participants mentioned quality and design once again as the most important driving forces in their decision-making process. For regular customers, quality is the key element that attracts them to buy certain luxury products, including sustainable ones.

> I am more interested in classical products, but if it is presented properly, why not? But the quality has to be good. (Pierre-Yves, France)

> I think luxury products, sustainable or not, quality is always the most important thing. Because this is why we call it luxury. (Karla, Mexico)

Apart from quality, the design is also a driving factor that makes consumers buy certain luxury products.

> Having sustainable design is good, but not enough. I will look at the design, the design and sustainable, I will buy only when the two things are present in the products. (Helen, US)

> Of course the design should be good, otherwise why should I choose you? There are so many brands in this industry and I don't need to stick with this brand. (Francesco, Italy)

Therefore, it appears that regular luxury consumers still hold quality and design as the driving forces that make them buy luxury products, even if sustainable.

Virtual Rarity vs. Sustainable Luxury

At the end of the interview, participants were asked about the importance of virtual rarity in sustainable luxury as well as about their opinions toward launching a sustainable luxury product. The findings were twofold: (1) rarity serves as a marketing strategy and (2) sustainability serves as an added value in sustainable luxury.

Rarity as Marketing Strategy

Same as previously found regarding the role of rarity in the concept of luxury, rarity is essential, but not the most important factor in encouraging sustainable luxury purchase.

> I really don't think I will buy sustainable luxury products just because you tell me the production is limited and the materials are so rare that you don't find it in anywhere else. I mean I won't respond to that even when I buy normal luxury products. So why would it be exceptional for sustainable luxury products? (Yan, USA)

Even though rarity is not the driving factor of sustainable luxury purchase, according to many participants, rarity is a very good tool to increase people's attention to a certain campaign or certain product, which is useful to promote the product.

I will put this rarity concept into the promotional campaign because even they don't want to buy, at least they know this thing exists. You know you have so many new products launching every year, if you want to stand out from the crowd, you have to speak louder than the others. I think rarity is a microphone. (Vincent, Belgium)

After all, I think the quality and the design are the most important, whether it is a normal luxury product or it is the sustainable luxury product. But I think you can still add this element. Because you don't know if anyone would be interested in rare products. It is a good communication tool, especially to the new luxury consumer. (Helen, USA)

In terms of communication tools, participants also suggested that rarity can be backed up by a history. They stated that it is a very good way to create a good image to the consumers and this packaging tool would increase the consumer's desire to know more about the company as well as the products.

History. Really beautiful history. And how good it is. Show me that it worth buying. I will say something about the sustainable luxury crap but I will put more my effort in creating the desire. (Karla, Mexico)

You have to have a very good packaging when it comes to sustainable luxury. Rarity does not have to be about very rare materials or very rare production process. You can simply say that having this sustainable concept is already unique. This idea of buying sustainable products is rare. I think rarity can be presented like this in sustainable luxury. (Vincent, Belgium)

Therefore, rarity serves as a very important marketing tool from the consumers' perspective, and it appears essential to promote sustainable luxury.

Sustainability as Added Value in Sustainable Luxury

In the interview, participants suggested that sustainability is not an important factor in the sustainable luxury concept. There is no doubt that the sustainability part is essential as it is the only factor that distinguishes sustainable luxury goods from other ordinary luxury goods. However, sustainability is not a motivating attraction for consumers to purchase the products as it is only one of the essences in sustainable luxury.

I think sustainability is important because this is the main focus of sustainability. However, I don't think you can sell people just like this. I think it is one part of sustainable luxury. After all, you are still in the luxury business. Sustainability is only an added value. I don't think you can motivate people to buy just because it is sustainable. (Pierre-Yves, France)

Some participants also mentioned that paying attention at the audience's perspective is fundamental to understand how much added value is the sustainable nature of the luxury product.

I am skeptical. If I am to launch a sustainable luxury product, I focus on how the product is desired by individuals. We are not selling the product to the environment. If I am selling this to the environment I will say how this product is good for itself. But we are not. We are selling that to individuals. Of course you say the product is good for them! You have to pay attention to the audience after all, in any business! (Yan, USA)

> I will launch the product like how I launch other normal luxury products. Maybe I will mention a bit about the sustainability of course. But I think that's it. I won't spend my money showing how the product is good to the environment. I show them how consumers should have the product because it changes their lives. (Helen, US)

Based on the above arguments of sustainability being just an essence in sustainable luxury, some participants stated that luxury should be put with more emphasis than sustainability. They suggested that the luxury part of the products should override the sustainability part and should be more communicated upon.

> Even you are sustainable, you are still a luxury product. If you are a luxury product, you have a specific way to make consumers buy. You emphasize on the quality, the design, the rarity, maybe or even the high price. Because these are the things that make you a luxury. These are the things that differentiate you from other cheap products. (Laura, Belgium)

Some participants even suggested that sustainability can be neglected in the communication process.

> You can say that. But there is nothing wrong even you don't say that. It is after all just a credit. You need to build up a name first. And then when people start having the buying desire and they keep buying the products, you can say this additional value to reinforce their desire. (Carla, Brazil)

The literature review has explained that there is some active debate in the academic field on whether sustainable luxury is feasible. Many scholars have proven that the two concepts have a lot of factors and dimensions in common. Sustainable luxury would therefore be some feasible solution for luxury companies to increase their social responsibility to the environment. However, despite all the arguments suggested by the scholars in terms of promoting sustainable luxury, luxury consumers are still feeling uncomfortable with the idea. In fact, in the present study a lot of participants express doubt as to the feasibility of sustainable luxury. Most of them suggest that the luxury business is mostly about unusual materials, such as exotic leathers and furs, and that these raw materials are the fundamental ingredients for luxury products. They also suggest that the preciousness of raw materials is the major distinction between luxury products and ordinary products and that it stands as a strong driving force for luxury purchase. Such a view toward sustainable luxury shows that there is a gap between theory and practice, when having a consumer-centric approach.

Besides, despite some of the regular luxury consumers declaring they pay little or no attention to sustainable luxury, some participants in the interview suggest that they do realize the importance of sustainability for the environment. This echoes with the literature suggesting luxury consumers are aware of sustainability. The literature also suggests that with such awareness, luxury consumers would be willing to purchase sustainable luxury goods as part of the luxury's essence. This is not supported by the findings from the present study which shows that while luxury consumers agree that the level of sustainability should be increased in the luxury business, they are reluctant to purchase sustainable luxury goods. Instead, they would prefer to donate to some environmental organizations to do something for the environment as they are not willing to give up their choices around some luxury goods.

Importance of Brand Name

In the process of understanding how luxury consumers view the concepts of virtual rarity and sustainable luxury, the importance of brand name to luxury consumers is discussed. In the interview, participants have been asked about what would encourage them to purchase a sustainable luxury product. Surprisingly, when the importance of brand name in luxury industry was evoked, all the 20 participants suggested that brand name is not a determining factor for them to purchase a luxury product. They suggested that they pay little or even no attention to brand names as it does not mean anything to them. They explained that they have a long and solid experience in purchasing luxury goods and they understand how the industry works. They also suggested that they do not need to purchase a luxury product with big brand names because they do not need to distinguish themselves from others by a brand name. Therefore, they would not spend money just to buy a product with a famous brand name. Rather, they would focus on the products themselves in the purchasing process. They focus more on the quality and design of the products than the brand name. This is consistent with the literature (Mortelmans 2005) that posits scarcity, extra value, high quality, and price as the four elements contributing to the luxury-building.

Rarity as Marketing Tool

Scholars suggest that virtual rarity is the key for developing sustainable luxury in the near future (Gault et al. 2008): enacting rarity through the production process or artificially inducing it through limited editions and communication, luxury consumers' dream and desirability for the products should increase. The findings from the present study sound contradictory. In fact, the respondents are aware of the communication strategy of luxury companies. Including rarity in it does not necessarily increase the motivation for purchasing. Many of the participants suggested that if a specific luxury product is portrayed as rare, due to its limited production or rare materials, it will only increase their motivation to look for the product and find out more details about that specific product. In other words, the concept of virtual rarity only serves as an effective marketing tool to communicate with the consumers but not as a driving force to increase the motivation of purchasing that product. More refined research should be conducted with experimental design to double-check such finding.

Quality and Design as Driving Forces for Luxury Purchase

As mentioned previously the present study shows that instead of virtual rarity, other factors affect consumers' decisions about purchasing a sustainable luxury good. As Mortelmans (2005) has suggested, one of the most important elements of luxury is the quality of the product. And this is exactly what respondents (regular luxury consumers) are looking for. Nearly all participants mentioned that when they try to purchase a luxury good, they will look at the quality of the product. If they do not find quality, whatever the price of the product, the brand name, and the sustainable aspect of it, they are reluctant to buy it. In their eyes, quality is the only thing that can differentiate luxury products from ordinary ones. And this element of quality serves as a strong driving force for them to buy luxury products.

Apart from quality, the design of the products is a driving force. This finding is consistent with past literature (Joy et al. 2012). The prerequisite for buying thus appears as being quality, while design would be more of an emotional driver.

Implication: Shifting Paradigm in Luxury

Figure 12.1 summarizes the findings of our study, pointing on the conceptual framework that may disrupt how luxury business conduct might be shifting based on the evolving definition of the concept of luxury as shown previously, when confronted to the notion of sustainability.

Luxury consumers do not appear so much convinced about sustainable luxury if it is not carefully managed by luxury companies. The "dream" has to be kept true whatever the circumstances for purchase or usage of the products. Virtual rarity shares the conspicuity nature of luxury goods in the eyes of the consumers and brings some added value to their sustainable nature.

Still, quality and design appear as two fundamental components when approaching sustainable luxury if companies want to trigger purchase intention.

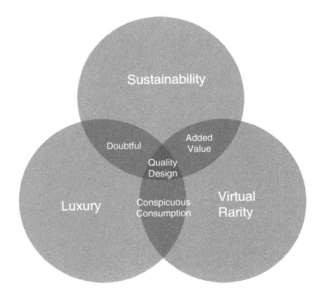

Fig. 12.1 Conceptual framework

This is some shift in the luxury concept management for luxury companies. Traditionally, managers have taken these two brand characteristics as a given, something they could not compromise upon, but have very little used them in their strategic processes toward consumers. They have been focusing upon exploiting the brand imagery and meaning. It would appear that if luxury companies want to speak about sustainability, they have to go back to basics and reassure consumers on their brand characteristics. We provide practical managerial recommendations hereafter in this direction.

Managerial Implications

The objective of this study was to investigate the importance of virtual rarity in promoting sustainable luxury in luxury companies by studying how consumers relate and merge the concepts of virtual rarity and sustainable luxury. Through studying the relationships between these two concepts, there are a few implications that can help luxury companies to set their marketing strategies to successfully promote sustainable luxury in the market.

Marketing Implications

In terms of marketing actions, there are two points that luxury companies could take from this study: (1) launch sustainable luxury products as any ordinary luxury products and (2) do not overestimate the effect of brand names.

1. In this study, luxury regular consumers sound little aware of sustainable luxury or tend to discount this information. A luxury company trying to launch sustainable luxury products should always keep in mind that sustainable luxury is sold in the luxury industry, and not like in any other industry. Given that the target audience is "ordinary" luxury consumers, they should be addressed as luxury consumers rather than environment activists. In other words, luxury companies should not put too much emphasis on the sustainability part of the sustainable luxury product. Rather, luxury companies should focus on creating the dream and desire of the product to increase purchase motivation. When the consumers have the desire of owning those sustainable luxury products, sustainable luxury will be ready to be pushed in the industry. This is already being done in one sector of activity: luxury hospitality. It has been empirically found by managers that it was more productive to discount the existence of "sustainable" actions in the hotel when selling it. However, lots of public relations and press releases are issued on a continuous pace by luxury resorts/lodges/hotels to still show their stakeholders (including their clients) that they care about the CSR-related topics.

However, in the rest of the industry, esp. in fashion/accessories/shoes, etc., all exemplars of luxury companies designing and selling a sustainable product have done it in some "activist" way. The success of these products remains mitigated (e.g., the "synthetic fur coat" by Stella McCartney).

2. Apart from creating the dream and the desire for sustainable luxury products, luxury companies should avoid focusing and emphasizing the brand name. This is valid not only for sustainable luxury products but also for the other ordinary luxury products. It is important not to focus on the brand name, especially when the target audience is regular luxury consumers as they pay little attention to it. It is more essential for companies to focus on the products themselves instead of taking advantage of the brand name and expect consumers to purchase the new sustainable luxury products because of a famous brand name. While for traditional goods a brand name is a signal of quality (Rao and Monroe 1989), for luxury goods it conveys more imaginations and values that are not associated with quality (quality being a prerequisite for belonging to the luxury category, like a filter), especially for Western consumers or third generation of luxury consumers in Asia (Ozcan et al. 2012). Therefore, caution should be put on associating the brand name with the "sustainable" nature of a given product as the brand identity and values might be non-compatible with sustainability. For instance, Chanel's values are around the aesthetics of disruption (Floch 1990) and of control, two values that cannot be so easily reconciled with sustainability which is ontologically longitudinal (vs. disrupting) and linked to some adaptability/fit with the environment (vs. controlling it). This does not mean that Chanel cannot issue a luxury sustainable product, but just that the brand name should not be too much associated with the product. In some way that might be one of the reason that refrain luxury companies to expand their brand in sustainability.

Communication Implications

In the present study, rarity is found a useful communication tool to promote sustainable luxury. Regular luxury consumers respond to the virtual rarity principle and generate interest in luxury products if portrayed as rare. It might not necessarily be the driving force of luxury purchase, but it serves as an attraction to consumers who would then try to look for more details about the specific products. Therefore, rarity is a very important communication tool to increase attention as well as to create some word-of-mouth in the luxury market. Luxury companies could emphasize production processes, quality-focused, savoir faire, and craftsmanship. Such communication could be exclusive to create a sense of rarity and exclusiveness to the regular luxury consumers, recreating some sense of rarity around sustainable products. Some companies have already engaged in the process (e.g., LVMH with the "Journées particulières" event once in a year that allows clients to visit the factories), but rarely in link with their sustainable actions, these being touched upon briefly during the visits, for instance (e.g., visiting the Guerlain factory, visitors learn about the orchid plantation management in Asia, made to preserve the natural ecosystem of the area). No examples of sustainable-dedicated communication using rarity could be found, even in other studies related to luxury hospitality that is quite in advance compared to the other sectors in the luxury industry (Maman Larraufie 2017).

Besides, sustainability can be communicated upon by creating the perception that owning a sustainable luxury product is a rare and exclusive concept that not many consumers have access to. In that sense, the concept of sustainability is packaged-based on the concept of rarity under the main goal of luxury – to create a dream or desire to purchase certain luxury products. This is a possible method to relate sustainability and virtual rarity. However, it is noted that no matter how luxury companies communicate with their consumers, they should keep in mind the target audience and communicate in the way they communicate in luxury in general. Thus, they should still aim at creating desire and dream, otherwise any attempts of promoting or communicating about sustainable luxury would be vain. Again, to our knowledge, this communication strategy has not been already used by luxury companies. It has rather been used by premium ones or in fast fashion (e.g., H&M).

Opportunities and Costs for Managers

The marketing and communication solutions we propose in this chapter should help luxury managers to better tackle their love and hate relationship with sustainability, focusing on their clients' perceptions that are also shifting and becoming more and more prominent in the luxury consumption landscape (Cervellon and Shammas 2013). We believe that if done properly such actions would not damage luxury brands' images and respective identities but rather propose their clients with new ways to strengthen their relationship with the brand thanks to some enhanced perception of exclusiveness (rarity communication) and enhanced product experience (with some unexperienced disconnection between the product and the brand name). Besides, designing sustainable products without stressing their sustainable nature is a good way to address the cognitive dissonance that exists in clients' minds when consuming luxury goods, downsizing the guilt feeling (Cervellon 2013). And even if this might not be the primary objective, acting in such ways should reconcile the environment activists that criticized the luxury industry with these, why not engaging them to consume sustainable luxury products as well.

Such actions are not cost-free, but these costs are no more than the usual costs associated with product-development and communication-design plans. We believe the most important cost will be a human one as all this requires some change of mindsets, since few luxury companies do inscribe in their very operational DNA (including HR processes, i.e., choice of employees) features of sustainability and CSR, with Kering being an exception (Maman Larraufie 2016).

Limitations of the Study

The current study has some limitations, mainly due to its explorative nature. First, the sample was only composed of Western consumers, which limits the results to such set, even though research has shown that wealthy Asian consumers share the same concerns of sustainability than Western ones (Chadha and Husband 2010), but they might express it in a different way than through virtual rarity. The small size of the sample is also quite problematic if one wants to get results that could be statistically representative. However, since the focus of the research was not to generalize findings but to go deep in the understanding of one phenomenon thanks to theoretical sampling and stop of data collection thanks to the saturation principle, we believe the results are still valid in the validity definition of qualitative research (Mucchielli 1991).

Then, there is a natural bias that may happen when interviewing people on sensitive and socially related topics (social desirability bias). That may have limited the set and nature of the replies and unstated thoughts could remain unexplored. Projective techniques could help in that direction. Finally, our sample was mainly composed of Generation X and older consumers. Therefore the results do not reflect what Millennials and Generation Z might have said and cannot be generalized to these sets of consumers.

Conclusion

Since the luxury industry has often been criticized for its lack of motivation to promote sustainability, this study aimed at finding ways to encourage luxury companies to increase their social responsibility. The literature review suggested that the concept of virtual rarity would serve as a driving force for more luxury purchases of sustainable luxury. We then tried to study the relationship between the concepts of luxury and sustainability, from regular luxury consumers' standpoints. Several conclusions have been reached, each of them being eligible as a source of inspiration for managerial implications.

First of all, even if sustainability sounds trendy nowadays, in hypermodern times of consumption (Lipovetsky 2004), Western regular luxury consumers are still reluctant to accept the concept of sustainable luxury in the luxury industry. This is probably the reason why luxury companies are not as responsive as other industries in terms of promoting sustainability. Secondly, this study shows that, unlike what past academic research suggested, virtual rarity is not the main driving force for luxury purchase to regular luxury consumers. Rather, it serves as a communication tool that arouses the attention of regular luxury consumers to know more about the sustainable luxury product. Thirdly, regular luxury consumers are extremely attentive to the quality as well as to the design of luxury products. These are the underlying motivations for them to purchase certain luxury good, including sustainable ones.

Therefore, luxury companies that would like to promote sustainable luxury need to pay attention to their target audience and keep in mind that sustainable luxury is still in the sphere of luxury and should be communicated upon in certain ways, such as aiming at creating the dream and the desire for that product instead of emphasizing on the sustainability aspect of the products. Besides, virtual rarity would be a good tool to increase the attention or even cause a stir in the market. Finally, the results have shown that quality and design are the most important qualities in luxury products and that every luxury company should make sure their products are of good quality and good design to maintain its market share in the industry.

Of course, this study is a first step in understanding a little explored area. Therefore, further studies should be conducted to have a deeper knowledge about consumer behavior facing sustainable luxury. This research proves that quality and design are the underlying factors of luxury purchase to regular luxury consumers. However, further investigation should be conducted to understand how quality and design play a role in the consumer decision-making process as well as what exactly consumers are looking for in quality and design when it comes to sustainable luxury.

This study chose to focus on Western and regular luxury consumers and studied their views toward the concepts of virtual rarity and sustainable luxury. Based on their opinions, recommendations are made to luxury companies. However, apart from Western consumers and regular luxury consumers, Asian consumers as well as non-regular consumers should also be considered in setting luxury marketing strategies to promote sustainable luxury. The conduct of further studies examining the views of these two groups of consumers is suggested to get a holistic picture of the target audience in the luxury industry. The studying of the consumer behavior of all the types of consumers is the only way to truly promote sustainable luxury, and in the long run, to increase the sustainability of the whole luxury business.

References

Aggarwal, P., S.Y. Jun, and J.H. Huh. 2011. Scarcity messages. *Journal of Advertising* 40 (3): 19–30.

Alharbi, F., S. Dekhili, and M. A. Achabou. 2017. Developpement durable et luxe: Partagent-ils la notion de qualite exceptionnelle? Une etude experimentale aupres de consommateurs saoudiens. *33ème édition du congrès international de l'AFM* Tours (France).

Beckham, D., and B.G. Voyer. 2014. *Can sustainability be luxurious? A mixed-method investigation of implicit and explicit attitudes towards sustainable luxury consumption*. Duluth: ACR North American Advances.

Brock, T.C. 1968. Implications of commodity theory for value change. *Psychological Foundations of Attitudes* 1: 243–275.

Catry, B. 2007. Le luxe peut être cher, mais est-il toujours rare? *Revue Française de Gestion* 2: 49–63.

Cervellon, M.-C. 2013. Conspicuous conservation – using semiotics to understand sustainable luxury. *International Journal of Market Research* 55 (5): 695–717.

Cervellon, M.-C., and L. Shammas. 2013. The value of sustainable luxury in mature markets: A customer-based approach. *The Journal of Corporate Citizenship* 52: 90–101.

Chadha, R., and P. Husband. 2010. *Cult of the luxury brand: Inside Asia's love affair with luxury.* London: Nicholas Brealey Publishing.

Cole, F.L. 1988. Content analysis: Process and application. *Clinical Nurse Specialist* 2 (1): 53–57.

Davies, I.A., Z. Lee, and I. Ahonkhai. 2012. Do consumers care about ethical-luxury? *Journal of Business Ethics* 106 (1): 37–51.

DeWeese-Boyd, I., and M. DeWeese-Boyd. 2007. The healthy city versus the luxurious city in Plato's republic: Lessons about consumption and sustainability for a globalizing economy. *Contemporary Justice Review* 10 (1): 115–130.

Doval, J., E.P. Singh, and D.G.S. Batra. 2013. Green buzz in luxury brands. *Review of Management* 3 (3–4): 5–14.

Eisend, M. 2008. Explaining the impact of scarcity appeals in advertising: The mediating role of perceptions of susceptibility. *Journal of Advertising* 37 (3): 33–40.

Elo, S., and H. Kyngäs. 2008. The qualitative content analysis process. *Journal of Advanced Nursing* 62 (1): 107–115.

Fionda, A.M., and C.M. Moore. 2009. The anatomy of the luxury fashion brand. *Journal of Brand Management* 16 (5): 347–363.

Floch, J.-M. 1990. *Sémiotique, Marketing et Communication: Sous les Signes, les Stratégies.* Paris: PUF.

Gault, A., Y. Meinard, and F. Courchamp. 2008. Less is more: Rarity trumps quality in luxury markets. *Nature Precedings.*

Griskevicius, V., J.M. Tybur, and B. Van den Bergh. 2010. Going green to be seen: Status, reputation, and conspicuous conservation. *Journal of Personality and Social Psychology* 98 (3): 392–404.

Gunther, A.C., and P. Mundy. 1993. Biased optimism and the third-person effect. *Journalism Quarterly* 70 (1): 58–67.

Hasna, A.M. 2006. Dimensions of sustainability. *Journal of Engineering for Sustainable Community Development* 1 (2): 47–57.

Hennings, N., K.-P. Wiedmann, C. Klarmann, and S. Behrens. 2013. Sustainability as part of the luxury essence. *Sustainable Luxury: A special theme issue of The Journal of Corporate Citizenship* 52 (11): 25–35.

Hopwood, B., M. Mellor, and G. O'Brien. 2005. Sustainable development: Mapping different approaches. *Sustainable Development* 13 (1): 38–52.

Joy, A., J.F. Sherry Jr., A. Venkatesh, J. Wang, and R. Chan. 2012. Fast fashion, sustainability, and the ethical appeal of luxury brands. *Fashion Theory* 16 (3): 273–295.

Kapferer, J.-N. 2010. All that glitters is not green: The challenge of sustainable luxury. *European Business Review*: 40–45.

———. 2012. Abundant rarity: The key to luxury growth. *Business Horizons* 55 (5): 453–462.

Kapferer, J.-N., and V. Bastien. 2012. *The luxury strategy: Break the rules of marketing to build luxury brands.* 2nd ed. London: Kogan Page Ltd..

Legard, R., J. Keegan, and K. Ward. 2003. In-depth interviews. In *Qualitative research practice: A guide for social science students and researchers*, ed. Jane Ritchie and Jane Lewis. London: Sage Piblications.

Lipovetsky, G. 2004. *Les temps hypermodernes.* Paris: Ed. Grasset.

Lynn, M. 1989. Scarcity effects on desirability: Mediated by assumed expensiveness? *Journal of Economic Psychology* 10 (2): 257–274.

Maman Larraufie, A.-F. 2016. Multicultural Human capital in luxury companies. In *Luxusmarkenmanagement*, ed. Wermer Thiene. Germany: Springer.

———. 2017. Strategic image management of CSR for luxury brands – the case of Luxury Hotels. *7th Advances in Hospitality and Tourism Marketing and Management Conference (AHTMM).* Famagusta (North Cyprus).

Maslow, A.H. 1943. A theory of human motivation. *Psychological Review* 50 (4): 370.

Mortelmans, D. 2005. Sign values in processes of distinction: The concept of luxury. *Semiotica* 2005 (157): 497–520.

Moscardo, G., and P. Benckendorff. 2010. *Sustainable luxury: Oxymoron or comfortable bedfellows?* Mbombela: International Tourism Conference on Global Sustainable Tourism.

Mucchielli, A. 1991. *Les méthodes qualitatives*. Paris: Presses Universitaires de France.

Ozcan, T., A.-F. Maman Larraufie, and Z. Turk. 2012. Consumer attitudes toward counterfeit products: Three-country analysis. *Journal of Euromarketing* 21 (2–3): 91–109.

Parker, B.T. 2009. A comparison of brand personality and brand user-imagery congruence. *Journal of Consumer Marketing* 26 (3): 175–184.

Patrick, V.M., and H. Hagtvedt. 2015. Luxury brands. In *Next practices in marketing*, ed. Rajendra Srivastava and Greg Thomas. Atlanta: Emery Marketing Institute.

Pavione, E., R. Pezzetti, and M. Dall'ava. 2016. Emerging competitive strategies in the global luxury industry in the perspective of sustainable development: The case of Kering group. *Management Dynamics in the Knowledge Economy* 4 (2): 241–261.

Plato. 1945. *The republic of Plato*. New York: Oxford University Press.

Rao, A.R., and K.B. Monroe. 1989. The effect of price, brand name, and store name on buyers' perceptions of product quality: An integrative review. *Journal of Marketing Research* 26: 351–357.

Sevilla, J., and J.P. Redden. 2014. Limited availability reduces the rate of satiation. *Journal of Marketing Research* 51 (2): 205–217.

Silverman, D. 2010. *Qualitative research*. London: Sage.

Snyder, C.R., and H.L. Fromkin. 1980. *Uniqueness: The human pursuit of difference*. New York: Plenum Press.

Torelli, C.J., A.B. Monga, and A.M. Kaikati. 2011. Doing poorly by doing good: Corporate social responsibility and brand concepts. *Journal of Consumer Research* 38 (5): 948–963.

Vigneron, F., and L.W. Johnson. 1999. A review and a conceptual framework of prestige-seeking consumer behavior. *Academy of Marketing Science Review* 1: 1–15.

———. 2004. Measuring perceptions of brand luxury. *Journal of Brand Management* 11 (6): 484–506.

Wattanasuwan, K. 2003. The young nouveau riche and luxury-brand consumption. *Journal of Commerce and Accountancy* 97: 61–86.

Wu, W., et al. 2012. The effects of product scarcity and consumers' need for uniqueness on purchase intention. *International Journal of Consumer Studies* 36 (3): 263–274.

Chapter 13
Putting African Country Development into Macromarketing Perspective

Mark Peterson and Saman Zehra

Abstract Macromarketing takes a holistic approach to marketing activity in order to understand the interactions among markets, marketing, and society. Using the Sustainable Society Index, this study performs an analysis of country and regional development for Africa. Accordingly, the human, environmental, and economic well-being for societies across Africa will be compared with (1) the rest of the world, (2) other developing countries, and (3) regions of the world. In terms of the sustainability dimensions of people, planet, and profit, Africa does well on the planet (environmental) dimension but lags in the people and profit dimensions (human and economic development).

African Mystery

Africa remains a mystery to many in global marketing. Mahajan (2009) has led an "Africa Rising" narrative (ARN) by reminding business persons about the market potential of African countries based on the millions of consumers on the African continent who are gradually moving out of poverty and into roles of purchasers of goods and services year after year. Other authors such as Berman (2013), Rotberg (2013), as well as Bright and Hruby (2015) have reinforced the ARN.

While all authors acknowledge that challenges and obstacles to genuine development in Africa remain, Chitonge (2015) questions whether the recent cheering about the prospects for development in Africa will be another false start for Africa. Likewise, Onyeiwu (2015) asks whether the proposed African Renaissance is merely a mirage. Sheth (2017) sees promise in an African awakening but asks "When will the giant wake up?" This book chapter will address these questions of Chitonge, Onyeiwu, and Sheth. The chapter will put country development in Africa

M. Peterson (✉) · S. Zehra
College of Business, University of Wyoming, Laramie, WY, USA
e-mail: markpete@uwyo.edu

© Springer International Publishing AG, part of Springer Nature 2018
J. Agarwal, T. Wu (eds.), *Emerging Issues in Global Marketing*,
https://doi.org/10.1007/978-3-319-74129-1_13

into macromarketing perspective by analyzing the triple bottom line for sustainable development of human well-being, environmental well-being, and economic well-being (Peterson 2013).

A special focus on this study will be on assessing the sustainability achievements in African societies. One notable achievement is South Africa's mandate for publicly traded firms to produce annual nonfinancial reporting on topics, such as the impact on the natural environment, as well as the impact on employees and other stakeholders (Eccles and Kruz 2015). This is a remarkable move by South Africa. In December 2016, the European Commission issued a directive requiring nonfinancial reporting similar to South Africa (Oxford Business Law Blog 2017). This series of events suggests how Africa can jump to the lead in certain aspects of sustainability.

The core of the study's assessment of African societies' sustainability achievements (or lack of achievements) will use the Sustainable Society Foundation's Sustainable Society Index (SSI) (Van de Kerk and Manuel 2013). Large-scale global indexes such as the Sustainable Society Index (SSI), which has been published biannually since 2006, offer valuable insights into important issues related to macromarketing and sustainability. Simkins and Peterson (2016) assessed the value of the SSI for macromarketing research. These researchers found that the SSI compared favorably to three other society-level indexes, such as (1) the Legatum Prosperity Index, (2) Transparency International's Corruption Perceptions Index, and (3) the Euromoney Country Risk Index. In this way, Simkins and Peterson recommend the SSI to researchers interested in analyzing countries on the sustainability dimensions of the SSI.

Focus of the Study

The Sustainable Society Index and Four Research Questions

The core of the study's assessment of Africa's sustainable development will use the Sustainable Society Foundation's Sustainable Society Index (SSI) (Van de Kerk and Manuel 2013). The SSI has been published biannually since 2006 and offers valuable insights into important issues related to macromarketing and sustainability. As part of a shifting paradigm today, firms are increasingly adopting sustainable business practices because of consumers' concern for the natural environment and firm leaders' awareness that business can be a positive influence in addressing problems for societies and local communities (Peterson 2013).

The SSI is an index including 154 countries of the world, and it is particularly well-suited to measure and study sustainability on a global scale. The SSI is one of the very few indexes that includes all three well-being dimensions: (1) human, (2) environmental, and (3) economic. All three dimensions of well-being complement each other in examining issues of sustainability. Quality of life or well-being studies have served as important dimensions of macromarketing scholarship since the inception of macromarketing (Fisk 1981).

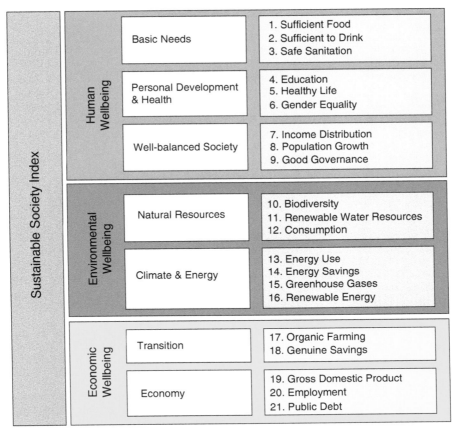

Fig. 13.1 The SSI's 3 dimensions, 7 categories, and 21 dimensions (Source: Sustainable Society Foundation http://www.ssfindex.com/ssi/framework/)

The SSI includes 21 dimensions for rating sustainability across seven categories and three dimensions of well-being. Figure 13.1 depicts the framework of the SSI. Table 13.1 presents the measures and sources of the measures representing the dimensions of the SSI.

Table 13.2 presents the SSI dimensions and the corresponding Sustainable Development Goals (SDGs) of the United Nations (2017). As can be seen, 16 of the 21 SSI dimensions have a corresponding SDG. There are no corresponding SDGs for (1) population growth, (2) renewable water resources, (3) organic farming, (4) genuine savings, and (5) public debt. Similarly, there are no SSI dimensions for the SDGs of (1) industry, innovation, and infrastructure, (2) sustainable cities and communities, (3) life below water, and (4) partnerships for the goals. In sum, an analysis of Table 13.2 suggests that the SSI and the UN's SDGs overlap significantly. This suggests the relevance of the SSI to issues of country development.

Table 13.1 SSI dimensions, measures, and source of measures

Name	Measure	Source
Sufficient food	Number of undernourished people in percent of total population	Food & Agr. Org. of UN
Sufficient to drink	Number of people in percent of total population, with sustainable access to an improved water source	Food & Agr. Org. of UN
Safe sanitation	Number of people in percent of total population, with sustainable access to improved sanitation	Food & Agr. Org. of UN
Education	Gross enrollment ratio for primary, secondary, and tertiary education (combined)	UNESCO
Healthy life	Life expectancy at birth in number of healthy life years	WHO HALE
Gender equality	Gender Gap Index	WEF
Income distribution	Ratio of income of the richest 10 percent to the poorest 10% people in a country	World Bank
Population growth	5-year change in total population size (percent of total population)	World Bank
Good governance	Sum of the six worldwide governance indicators	World Bank
Biodiversity part a—forest area	10-year change in forest area	Protected Planet
Biodiversity part a—protected area	Size of protected land area (in percent total land area)	Protected Planet
Renewable water resources	Annual water withdrawals (m3 per capita) as percent of renewable water resources	FAO Aquastat
Consumption	Ecological footprint minus carbon footprint	GFN
Energy use	Energy use (tons of oil equivalent per capita)	IEA
Energy savings	Change in energy use over 4 years (percent)	IEA
Greenhouse gases	CO2 emissions per person per year	IEA
Renewable energy	Consumption of renewable energy as percent of total energy consumption	IEA
Organic farming	Area for organic farming in percent of total agricultural area of a country	FiBL
Genuine savings	Genuine savings (adjusted net savings) as percent of gross national income (GNI)	World Bank
GDP	Gross domestic product per capita, PPP, current international $	IMF
Employment	Number of unemployed people in percent of total labor force	World Bank
Public debt	The level of public debt of a country in percent of GDP	IMF

Four research questions shape the analysis in this study focused on SSI ratings for 2016. First, how does Africa compare to the rest of the world on SSI ratings? Second, how does Africa compare to other developing countries of the world on SSI ratings? Third, how do the five regions as defined by the United Nations compare against each other in terms of changes in the SSI ratings from 2006 to 2016. Fourth, how do the regions of Africa compare against the regions of the world as defined by

Table 13.2 The dimensions of the SSI and corresponding dimensions of the UN's sustainable development goals

SSI dimensions	UN's sustainable development goals
Sufficient food	2. Zero hunger
Sufficient to drink	6. Clean water and sanitation
Safe sanitation	6. Clean water and sanitation
Education	4. Quality education
Healthy life	3. Good health and well-being
Gender equality	5. Gender equality
Income distribution	10. Reduced inequalities
Population growth	
Good governance	16. Peace, justice, and strong institutions
Biodiversity part a—forest area	15. Life on land
Biodiversity part a—protected area	15. Life on land
Renewable water resources	
Consumption	12. Responsible consumption and production
Energy use	7. Affordable and clean energy
Energy savings	7. Affordable and clean energy
Greenhouse gases	13. Climate action
Renewable energy	7. Affordable and clean energy
Organic farming	
Genuine savings	
GDP	1. No poverty
Employment	8. Decent work and economic growth
Public debt	
	9. Industry, innovation, and infrastructure
	11. Sustainable cities and communities
	14. Life below water
	17. Partnerships for the goals

the United Nations? By answering these research questions, one can better understand how global marketing strategies for firms might need to change because of new realizations about sustainable development in Africa.

Africa Compared to the Rest of the World and to Other Developing Countries

Figure 13.2 depicts the SSI ratings for Africa (solid line) and the rest of the world (dotted line). These ratings represent the average for 40 African countries and the average of the 110 non-African countries. A scale of 0–10 is used with higher values representing increasingly favorable ratings for sustainability. Reviewing Fig. 13.2 by beginning at the top of the radar chart and moving in a clockwise direction, one

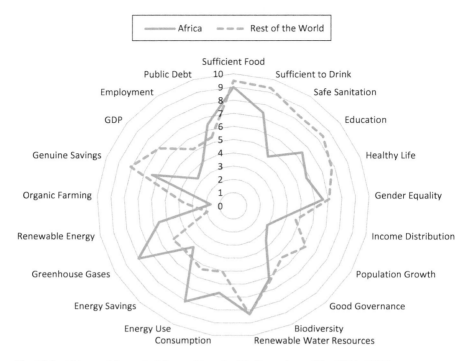

Fig. 13.2 Africa and the rest of the world on the 21 dimensions of the SSI in 2016

can see how close Africa comes to the rest of the world regarding sufficient food. However, Africa markedly lags the rest of the world on the dimensions of (1) sufficient drinking water, (2) safe sanitation, (3) education, and (4) a healthy life. Another noticeable gap for Africa comes in terms of having a less favorable score on population growth (which represents a burgeoning population for Africa). Africa also lags on good governance but has parity with the rest of the world on biodiversity and renewable water resources.

Continuing moving in a clockwise direction, Africa begins posting better scores than the rest of the world on (1) consumption, (2) energy use, (3) greenhouse gases, and (4) renewable energy. Africa's slightly lower score on energy savings represents Africa's slightly less favorable increase in energy consumption in the last 4 years than the rest of the world. Finally, the economic dimensions show the rest of the world's better results on (1) genuine savings and (2) GDP. Africa scores similarly to the rest of the world on (1) organic farming, (2) employment, (3) and public debt.

Researchers of this study used a series of one-sample t-tests to compare the 114 countries of the world with Africa's value on each of the 21 dimensions. These t-tests disclosed that the average of the world's countries and Africa were the same for only three dimensions: (1) biodiversity, (2) renewable water resources, and (3) public debt. All the other t-tests returned t-values that were statistically significant at $p = 0.05$. In sum, the separations between the points representing Africa and the

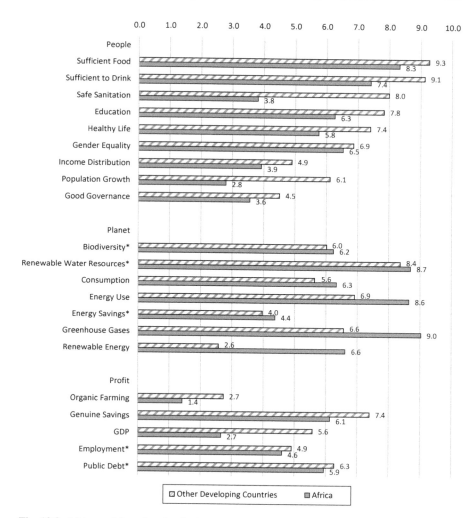

Fig. 13.3 Africa and the other developing countries on the 21 dimensions of the SSI in 2016. * = group means are statistically the same (others are statistically different at $p = 0.05$)

rest of the world in Fig. 13.2 are meaningful differences—except for the three dimensions just mentioned.

Figure 13.3 depicts the average SSI ratings for the 40 African countries in the analysis (solid bar) and 80 other developing countries (bar with diagonal lines). Again, a scale of 0–10 is used with higher values representing increasingly favorable ratings for sustainability. As with the comparisons of Africa to the rest of the world (Fig. 13.2), Africa tends to do comparatively better on most of the environmental dimensions (planet) but lags the other developing countries on the human dimensions (people) and the economic dimensions (profit).

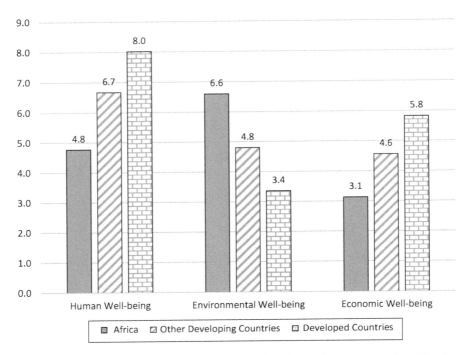

Fig. 13.4 Africa, other developing countries, and developed countries on averages for well-being

Using a grouping variable of African/non-African countries, researchers ran a series of independent sample t-tests across the 21 dimensions of the 2016 SSI. Only five dimensions did not register a statistically significant difference at $p = 0.05$: (1) biodiversity, (2) renewable water resources, (3) energy savings, (4) employment, and (5) public debt.

Comparing Africa to other developing countries, Africa's favorable position on environmental well-being and its unfavorable position on human well-being and economic well-being can be seen in Fig. 13.4. This figure depicts the averages for Africa and the other developing countries, as well as the developed countries on the aggregated dimensions of the SSI that correspond to (1) human well-being, (2) environmental well-being, and (3) economic well-being.

These results resonate with observations about Africa as being a well-endowed continent with mineral and natural resources but in need of development that can only be done through human institutions, such as markets and government, as well as culture that nurtures and reinforces the operation of such institutions (Gane 2014). In fact, the results for Africa and the developed countries are the obverse of each other. Africa has the highest rating on environmental well-being (the developed countries the worst), but Africa has the worst rating on human and economic well-being (the developed countries have the best rating).

Africa's Performance on the Indicators of SSI

Human Well-Being

Africa performs quite low on the human well-being dimension. The SSI scores for the African and other developing countries are 4.8 and 6.7, respectively.

Sufficient Food The SSI score on sufficient food for African countries is 8.3. The corresponding score for other developing countries in the world is 9.3.

Africa has only 8% arable land and only 3.6% of that land is irrigated (Rotberg 2013). By comparison, the average of the world's countries for arable land is 10.0%, while that of the United States is 16.9% (World Bank 2014). In Sub-Saharan Africa, 65% of the arable land is depleted and undernourished making it difficult for the region to meet food security goals (Conway 2014). The poor quality of soil coupled with other environmental shocks (such as poor rainfall, high temperature catalyzing soil demineralization, leaching of essential organic compounds, and soil erosion) exacerbates problems for food production in the region.

Food insecurity is closely related with poverty. The poor and vulnerable sections of African societies rely on subsistence agriculture for their availability of food. The agricultural production is subject to environmental, economic, and social variables such as famine, infestations, governmental policies, and civil wars. Not surprisingly, food consumption across Africa can be highly variable.

The fight against hunger continues, but gains have been made this century. The Global Hunger Index score for the developing world has declined from 30.0 (in 2000) to 21.3 (in 2016) (International Food Policy Research Institute/ Welthungerhilfe/Concern Worldwide 2016). In Sub-Saharan African countries, this has declined from 44.4 to 30.1. While the overall progress in reducing hunger is notable, five out of the seven countries with "alarming" levels of hunger and 28 out of the 43 countries with "serious" levels of hunger are African.

There is a marked difference in the success of hunger mitigation efforts made by African countries. The African Development Bank Group (2017) reports that from 1990 to 2012, three African countries (Ghana, the Democratic Republic of the Congo, and Mauritania) reduced hunger by 50% or more, 19 by 20.0–49.9%, and 13 by 0.0–19.9%. However, five countries (Burundi, Swaziland, Comoros, Cote d'Ivoire, and Botswana) experienced setbacks and chronically suffer from food insecurity. Figure 13.5 depicts the countries of Africa.

Sufficient to Drink The mean score of Africa on this indicator, measured as the number of people with sustainable access to an improved water source, is 7.4. It is lower than the score for the other developing countries score, which is 9.1.

The World Health Organization defines an improved drinking water source as a source that by nature of its construction adequately protects the water from outside contamination, in particular from fecal matter. Piped household water connections, protected wells, and springs qualify as improved drinking water sources.

Fig. 13.5 Political map of Africa (GeoCurrents 2017)

Despite an abundance of water on planet Earth, around 1.2 billion people grapple with the problem of scarcity of water (United Nations Department of Economic and Social Affairs 2014). The number of people facing absolute water scarcity is expected to go up to 1.8 billion by 2025—an increase of 50%. Although water is a renewable resource, its availability for drinking use is limited by freshwater resources which are unevenly distributed across the world. In Sub-Saharan Africa, the Democratic Republic of the Congo has an abundance of water that far exceeds what the inhabitants require. However, there are also countries such as Kenya, Malawi, and South Africa that struggle to secure adequate freshwater and are chronically stressed for water (United Nations Development Program 2006).

The United Nations' seventh Millennium Development Goal (7c) committed to reducing by half the proportion of people without sustainable access to safe drinking water and sanitation in the world. The target had to be achieved by the end of 2015. While the goal has been met globally (World Health Organization 2015), African countries are still making progress toward achieving it. Most North African countries (Algeria, Egypt, Morocco, and Tunisia) have met this target in urban areas (Mutasa and Paterson 2015). In Sub-Saharan Africa, the proportion of people with access to clean drinking water has increased.

Regarding the availability of clean drinking water, a wide disparity exits across the African regions. The safe water coverage is as high as 92% in North Africa and as low as 61% in Sub-Saharan Africa. Presently, the Sub-Saharan Africa alone has around 783 million people without access to safe drinking water (United Nations 2016).

Safe Sanitation Access to safe drinking water and availability of safe sanitation are closely related. The mean SSI score for safe sanitation for African nations is 3.8, which is less than half of the other developing countries' mean score of 8.0. Clearly, the availability of safe sanitation facilities remains a huge challenge for Africa.

The WHO/UNICEF Joint Monitoring program for water supply and sanitation takes into account improved sanitation facilities to assess the availability of safe sanitation. An improved sanitation facility is defined as one that prevents human excreta from coming into contact with humans. Shared sanitation facilities may have a number of persons using them. It may not be an adequately safe facility because such a facility would not prevent air or water borne diseases arising out of lack of hygiene. Therefore, they do not qualify as improved sanitation. According to the WHO/UNICEF 2015 update and Millennium Development Goal (MDG) assessment, 68% of people have access to improved sanitation facilities around the world. In Africa, the northern region has met sanitation targets set by MDGs for the year 2015. Sub-Saharan Africa lags far behind. Only 30% of persons living in Sub-Saharan Africa have access to improved sanitation. The lack of proper sanitation is related to the outbreak of diseases (such as diarrhea, malaria, dengue, and cholera) that claim millions of lives.

The overall progress of Africa on safe sanitation has been sluggish due to the high costs of building sanitation infrastructure and the relatively low returns on such investments for the private sector (Onyeiwu 2015). Open dumping of rubbish can result in fly infestation and rapid spread of disease. Even large dumping sites near urban areas in Africa are typically oversized and become the source of disease to those living (in the dump sites) or near them (Vidal 2014).

Education African countries lag their developing counterparts across the world as shown by the SSI score for education (measured as combined enrollment into primary, secondary, and tertiary education). The mean score for African region is 6.3 as compared to 7.8 for other developing countries.

Africa's public education expenditure is 5% of its total GDP making its share of GDP spending on education the second highest among all continents in the world. The global public expenditure on education is 4.7% of the world's GDP per capita (Africa-America Institute 2015). Despite the African governments devoting relatively large proportion of their resources on education, the continent has not been able to reap the benefits of human development. The education sector requires more funding to overcome the challenges posed by (1) population growth, (2) the need to maintain quality standards, and (3) ensuring equity in access to education services.

Yet, compared to where it was, Africa has made remarkable progress in education in the last two decades. The net primary enrollment increased by 14% since 1999 and reached 76% in 2008 (Bright and Hruby 2015). Secondary school enrollment rose by 10% in a period of two decades since 1999 and stood at 35% in 2008. Exceptional progress in primary school enrollment was seen in the Sub-Saharan Africa, which was the highest for any world region between 2000 and 2012. However, a simultaneous increase in population meant similar growth in school facilities (including both the construction and staffing of such schools) did not keep pace with population growth. This shortfall resulted in many children not having access to schools in many parts of Africa. Also, due to financial constraints or for not meeting the eligibility requirements for secondary and tertiary education, only a small percentage of students enroll in colleges or universities.

Education is emerging as one of the fastest and promising sectors in Africa as many countries on the continent are now attracting investment by private organizations. Tertiary school enrollments have surged with the growing education opportunities. The need for establishing a sound and sustainable education is also pressing as Africa's population is increasing, and the population must be equipped with the required knowledge and skillsets to be able to create a productive workforce. For harnessing the potential of African youth, it is important that the education system be structured to provide for the holistic development of students and offer them vocational skills for future jobs.

Healthy Life The Social Sustainability Index assesses healthy life in terms of life expectancy at birth in number of healthy life years—defined as the number of years that a newborn is expected to live minus the number of years spent in poor health.

Africa needs much improvement on this front. Its mean SSI score is 5.8 versus 7.4 for other developing non-African nations. WHO's conceptualization of health goes beyond mere absence of disease or infirmity. The state of being healthy means presence of complete physical, mental, and social well-being.

Sadly, Africa has the highest incidence of undernourishment in the world. More than one quarter of persons living in Sub-Saharan Africa are undernourished, and the number of those who experience hunger has been rising by 2% per year since 2007 (World Hunger Education Service 2016). Today, Africa is home to more than a quarter of the total number of undernourished people in the world (Mutasa and Paterson 2015). Child-maternal health in many parts of Africa needs much improvement. Half of the world's child deaths under the age of 5 years are in Africa (United Nations Children's Fund 2013). Due to malnutrition, at least one in every three African children under the age of 5 years was estimated to be stunted in 2011. South Sudan, Nigeria, Chad, Mali, and Sudan had more than 5% of its children showing evidence of severe wasting. Sadly, around 3.1 million children under the age of five were infected with HIV in Africa according to 2011 statistics.

Niger was declared as the "worst place to be a mother" in 2012 by Save the Children's thirteenth annual mother index after it replaced Afghanistan at the bottom of this ranking (BBC News, 2012). Seventy-four percent of AIDS-related deaths reported globally in 2013 came from the Sub-Saharan Africa. Thankfully, this number has declined between 2005 and 2013 with the increased access to antiretroviral coverage (UNAIDS 2014). Africa has seen a significant decline in new HIV infection, as well. This has led to stabilized rates of HIV infection in many African countries.

Malaria caused by *P. falciparum*, particularly rampant in tropical Africa, accounts for 91% of deaths due to malaria around the world (World Health Organization 2012). Encouragingly, governments in Africa are committed to combat the disease and have pledged 15% of their budgets, under the Abuja Declaration (World Health Organization 2011).

Gender Equality   There is the least disparity on gender equality indicator between African and non-African developing countries than on any other indicator of human well-being. The mean SSI scores are 6.5 and 6.9, respectively. SSI measures gender equality in terms of the Global Gender Index published annually by the World Economic Forum (WEF).

In 2015, Rwanda made it to the 6th place on global rankings in the Global Gender Gap Report outperforming developed countries like the United Kingdom (which ranked 18th), the United States (28th), France (15th), and Canada (30th) which did not even make it to the top 10 (World Economic Forum 2016). Rwanda's fresh entry to the list in 2014 at rank number 7 was surprising because the country had never made it previously onto the list. It is likely that the efforts made by the country to boost equal rights for women after the 1994 Rwanda genocide have begun to take effect. (A painful memory for the country associated with the trauma of this upheaval in the country is the rape of an estimated one quarter million to half a million women who experienced rape.) Today, women comprise 64% of Rwanda's parliament—the highest in the world (World Economic Forum 2016). Other African countries that appearing in the top 30 of the Global Gender Gap are Namibia (which ranked 16th), South Africa (17th), Burundi (23rd), and Mozambique (27th).

The United Nation's Millennium Development Goal 3 (MDG 3) focuses on gender equality and the empowerment of women. At primary school level, the enrollment of women increased from 72% to 96% from 1999 to 2010 in Sub-Saharan Africa (United Nations 2012). Comparatively, the progress has been slower in enrollment in the secondary level of education and the slowest for enrollment in tertiary education. The representation of women in nonagricultural wage employment in the Sub-Saharan Africa is markedly below the global average. Gender inequality is also reflected in terms of the pay disparity between male and female employees, the female-to-male pay ratio being higher than 0.70 in countries like Egypt, Gambia, Ghana, Malawi, Nigeria, Uganda, and Malawi (Mutasa and Paterson 2015). By comparison, the female-to-male ratio for pay in the United States in 2015 was .80 (Swartz and Jones 2017). Notably, female representation in African parliaments has improved substantially because of legal policies that ensure seats for women (United Nations Economic Commission for Africa 2015).

Income Distribution SSI considers the ratio of income of the richest 10% to the poorest 10% of persons in a country as a measure to assess income distribution. The mean SSI score of the African countries for this indicator is 3.9 as compared to a 4.9 score for other developing countries of the world.

Although six out of the world's ten fastest-growing economies were in Africa in the 2000s, the gap between the rich and the poor as far as income distribution is concerned has not been bridged (African Development Bank Group 2012). In 2010, six of the ten countries worldwide, with the most uneven concentration of wealth between the rich and the poor, were in the Sub-Saharan African region. In 2011, 60.8% of the African population lived on less than USD 2 per day and held 36.5% of the total income. On the other hand, the nonpoor living on more than USD 20 per day (amounting to 4.8% of the total population) held 18.8% of the total income.

As of 2012, South Africa had the most unequal income distribution in the world. The Gini coefficient for the country has remained consistently high between 1990 and 2011 (Euromonitor International 2012). After the end of the Apartheid era in 1990, the inequality between racial groups in South Africa narrowed. However, the income inequality within the racial groups became wider (Whiteford and van Seventer 2000). The result of this can be seen in a relatively high Gini coefficient of 0.69 meaning that 69% of wealth would have to be reallocated to have everyone in the country have equal wealth (Forslund 2016). By comparison, the United States posts a Gini coefficient of 0.39 (OECD 2017).

Population Growth The mean SSI score of the African countries for the population growth indicator is 2.8 as compared to the world's other developing countries' average of 6.1.

Population growth makes Africa attractive for firms around the world for future marketing efforts. However, it also stresses many countries' weak infrastructure such as schools, hospitals, and safe water and sanitation facilities required for human development.

While most of the developed countries of the world have been seeing a drop in fertility rates since the 1960s (South China Morning Post 2014), Africa as a region has undergone a population explosion. While only one African country (Nigeria) is included among the top 10 most populous countries of the world, the continual population growth will likely lead to 40% of the world's population being African by the end of this century. According to some estimates, the continent might quadruple its numbers by 2100 (African Globe 2014). These are astounding predictions.

On the way to becoming the most populous continent by 2050, it is and will remain the youngest of all continents in the coming decades. By 2050, 1.3 billion people will be added in Africa—which will double the African population (United Nations 2015). Five African countries (Congo, Egypt, Uganda, Nigeria, and Ethiopia) will be among the top 15 most populous countries of the world (Population Reference Bureau 2016). However, Africa has not been able to harness its demographic dividend, yet. Its population could prove to be a significant asset or a liability that worsens the effect of persistent poverty. Currently, there is a pressing need to develop institutional and infrastructural capacity to keep pace with the burgeoning population.

Good Governance The World Bank's six indicators of good governance are (1) voice and accountability, (2) political stability and absence of violence, (3) government effectiveness, (4) regulatory quality, (5) rule of law, and (6) control of corruption (World Bank Group 2015). The Sustainable Society Index (SSI) considers the sum of these indicators as a measure to assess good governance. The mean SSI score of African countries is 3.6, while the corresponding score for the other developing countries in the world is 4.5, suggesting another dimension for improvement for African countries.

Africa's journey to democracy has been difficult. The transitions to more democratic societies have improved over the past two decades when authoritarian regimes began to be overthrown. Good governance is more than just democracy, but democracy is an important and integral part of good governance. Encouragingly, the continent has made significant advancements in the way of institutionalizing democracy (CNN 2013). The World Bank attributes recent improvements in economic performance to better governance.

Botswana, Namibia, and Ghana are consistently well-governed countries. Good governance in these countries is evidenced by (1) low crime rates, (2) relatively high GDPs, (3) a fair distribution of wealth compared to other African countries, (4) a good network of transport facilities, (5) an exemplary law enforcement system, (6) comparatively lower corruption rates, and (7) respect for human rights (Rotberg 2013). These three countries bring some hope for other countries across the Sub-Saharan African region to improve on this important dimension of human well-being.

On the other hand, countries like Somalia, Sudan, Guinea Bissau, and the Democratic Republic of the Congo represent the worst cases of governance in Africa mostly because of the persistent civil wars there. Guinea Bissau has not been able to have an elected president finish a 5-year term since its independence from Portugal in 1974. Such instability contributes to the poor governance in the country.

Overall, there has been a reduction in the prevalence of violent conflicts across the continent. The number of countries that experienced violence and conflict declined to five in 2007 (compared to 26 in the 1990s) (Dowden 2009).

Environmental Well-Being

As can be seen in Fig. 13.4, African countries lead other developing countries in the environmental well-being category comprising seven dimensions of the SSI. As depicted in Fig. 13.4, the mean rating on environmental well-being dimension for Africa is 6.6, while the average for the other developing countries is 4.8.

Biodiversity This indicator has two components: (1) biodiversity forest area (measured as a 10-year change in forest area) and (2) biodiversity protected area (measured as the size of protected land area) (in percent total land area). SSI utilizes statistical data from the Protected Planet Report 2016 for computing the score of this indicator. The International Union for Conservation of Nature (IUCN) defines protected area as "a clearly defined geographical space, recognized, dedicated, and managed through legal or other effective means, to achieve long-term conservation of nature with associated ecosystem services and cultural values." The mean SSI scores for African countries and the other developing countries of the world are 6.2 and 6.0, respectively. Hence, Africa posts a slight advantage.

In April 2002, as a part of the Convention on Biological Diversity's (CBD) action plan, a significant reduction in biodiversity loss had to be achieved. The Aichi Biodiversity targets of the strategic plan 2011–2020 were adopted to address the causes of biodiversity. UN researchers note that biodiversity in Africa continues to decline because of human intervention in nature (UNEP 2010).

According to those UN researchers, deforestation and threat to biodiversity are the top environmental issues in Africa. Nearly 1% of Africa's tree cover is lost each year due to (1) population increase and (2) climatic factors, such as low rainfall and the effects of global warming. The conversion of forests into pasturelands is the main reason for tree loss in the Sub-Saharan Africa. Disturbingly, it is estimated that by 2025 the wide savannah belt from Mauritania in West Africa to Ethiopia in East Africa will turn treeless (Rotberg 2013).

Land and coastal water protected areas, on the other hand, are being increased in number and size. For example, protected areas now account for substantial portions of African regions (14.6% of the Eastern and the Southern African regions, 10.5% of the Western and the Central African regions, and 7% of the North African regions) (United Nations Environment Programme 2010). Transboundary protected areas that span the boundary of more than one country are becoming susceptible to illegal activities like poaching that endanger the sustainability of these areas. There is a pressing need for multinational collaborative efforts to tackle such threats.

Renewable Water Resources The Sustainable Society Index measures renewable water resources as the annual water withdrawals (m^3 per capita) as a percent of total available renewable water resources. Africa's mean SSI score is 8.7 compared to 8.4 for the other developing countries.

Aquastat, a global information system on water and agriculture of the Food and Agriculture Organization (FAO), considers inland waters renewed by the global water cycle as a renewable water resource. This is the main source of available water to people. In Africa, the renewable water resources are 3930 km^3, that is, 9% of the global renewable water resources (Food and Agriculture Organization of the United Nations 2016). While the Democratic Republic of the Congo and countries along the Gulf of Guinea from Gabon north to Cameroon and across to Liberia are well supplied with water, the North African region is the most disadvantaged (UN Water/Africa 2009).

In Africa, 85% of water withdrawals is for agriculture, 9% for community use, and 6% for industry (UN Water/Africa 2009). The withdrawal of water is significantly lower than would be expected given the higher rainfall amounts outside desert areas. This suggests a low level of development and use of water resources on the African continent.

The water-related issues in Africa are either due to supply and demand for water. Low incidence of rainfall and poor management of water resources are two leading problems of supply. Competing demands for water lead to demand-side issues (UN Water/Africa 2009).

Consumption Ecological footprint (measured in global hectare) is a metric of human impact on Earth's ecosystems. Carbon footprint is the total set of greenhouse gas emissions caused by an individual, an organization, or a product that is expressed as a carbon dioxide equivalent. SSI calculates consumption as the difference between ecological and carbon footprints. The SSI score for African consumption is 6.3, while the score for developing countries is 5.6.

Africa's ecological footprint is almost equal to its bio-capacity (World Economic Forum 2015). This means the continent is neither ecologically deficient nor in surplus. However, some countries cannot make this claim. Some North African countries (such as Libya, Egypt, and Algeria) and some Sub-Saharan countries (such as Burundi, Djibouti, Swaziland, Tunisia, South Africa, Kenya, and Uganda) are in ecological deficit. This means that these societies are exerting more pressure on nature than nature can bear.

Some countries are not stressing nature. Gabon's ecological surplus is the highest in the continent. It is using only one-tenth of its bio-capacity. Three other countries with an economic surplus are (1) the Democratic Republic of the Congo, (2) the Central African Republic, and (3) the Republic of the Congo.

Although Africa's consumption is significantly lower as compared to other countries in the world, the growing African population will increase ecological degradation. This underscores the need to adopt sustainable ways to utilize the demand for natural resources.

Energy Use SSI assesses energy use in tons of oil equivalent per capita, a unit of energy. The mean SSI scores for African and other developing countries are 8.6 and 6.9, respectively. Hence, Africa performs well most likely because of the lack of economic development across much of Africa.

Sub-Saharan Africa, despite having 15% of the world's population, uses only 3% of the world's energy output (Anyaogu 2016). With recent discoveries of 64 oil and natural gas fields and with growing economies, Africa's energy consumption is growing faster than anywhere in the world (Pflanz 2013).

Electricity consumption in the Sub-Saharan Africa (except for South Africa) is a fraction of electricity consumption rates in Brazil, India, and South Africa. Forty-eight percent of the global population without access to electricity lives in Sub-Saharan Africa (McKinsey & Company 2015). It is estimated that this region's demand in 2040 will be the same as what India and Latin America's combined demand was in 2010. A capital investment of $ 835 billion will be required to meet this demand. Regarding energy resources, the Sub-Saharan region has a rich potential for coal, gas, geothermal, hydro, solar, and wind resources to deliver more than 12 terawatts of energy.

Energy Savings The SSI index assesses energy savings by change in energy use over 4 years in percentage terms. The score for African countries is 4.4 and that for developing countries is 4.0.

Because of recent economic development in these countries, neither of these scores is favorable. One African country is attempting to address this deficient performance in energy savings. The Department of Minerals and Energy for the Republic of South Africa has recognized the physical and economic benefits of sustainable energy sources. This ministry drafted an energy efficiency strategy for the country. This initiative represents governmental concern, but time will tell if such guidance for the country proves effective.

As of 2012, only 35% of Africa had the access to electricity (World Bank Group 2016). However, deliberate attempts to save energy are being taken in Africa by encouraging sustainable consumption through replacement of traditional fuels with alternative renewable resources.

Greenhouse Gases To represent greenhouse gases, SSI uses CO_2 emissions per person per year. The mean score of African countries for this indicator is 9.0—an excellent score. For the other developing countries, it is 6.6. In the period between 1990 and 2012, the Sub-Saharan Africa was responsible for only 1.8% of the total CO_2 emission, a third of which was contributed by South Africa (International Energy Agency 2014). However, temperatures across the continent are expected to rise faster than the global average in coming years (James and Washington 2012).

In 2012, 28 billion cubic meters of natural gas (mainly consisting of methane, a greenhouse gas) was vented without producing power in Sub-Saharan Africa. Out of this amount, Nigeria accounted for 60%, with the remaining 40% accounted for by Angola, Congo, and Gabon (Organization for Economic Co-Operation and Development/International Energy Agency 2014). In sum, Africa wastefully flares and vents gas equal to half its power consumption. Better practices in oil and gas extraction could drastically reduce such waste and such potent greenhouse gas emissions. The Global Gas Flaring Reduction (GGFR) program that supports national efforts is expected to reduce vented gas in the Sub-Saharan Africa.

Renewable Energy The SSI uses renewable energy as a percentage of total energy consumption. The mean scores for the African nations and the other developing countries are 6.6 and 2.6, respectively. The wide gap in the SSI scores shows that the African countries are far ahead of their developing country counterparts in the application of renewable energy technology. As the world moves toward green energy consumption, Africa shall benefit economically, ecologically, and biologically.

South Africa (although now also dependent on coal) has been making remarkable progress toward incorporating alternative energy systems such as solar, biomass, and wind. South Africa has become a success model by adding 4322 MW of renewable energy generation capacity from 2011 to 2015 (Barbee 2015).

Following the rise in oil prices in the first years of the twenty-first century and the subsequent power crises in many African countries, alternative sources of energy were explored by African countries. The most promising sources of renewable energy in Sub-Saharan Africa are (1) biomass energy (sugarcane residue having the potential to meet significant power requirements), (2) geothermal energy (first harnessed in Kenya significantly, followed by Ethiopia), and (3) hydropower (massive hydropower potential, more evident in eastern and southern parts of the continent) (Karekezi and Kithyoma 2003).

Economic Well-Being

The composite mean SSI score for African nations is the lowest of the three well-being dimensions. Africa posts a low score of 3.1 compared to a 4.6 average for the other developing world countries.

Organic Farming This indicator is measured as the area for organic farming as a percent of the total agricultural area of the country. The mean scores of the African countries and the other developing countries are 1.4 and 2.7, respectively. No African countries score well on this dimension. Egypt posts the highest score of 5.0 followed by Uganda with 4.0 and Tunisia with 3.6. The other African countries score 2.1 or below.

According to the World of Organic Agriculture 2009 report, Uganda and Ethiopia are among the countries with the highest number of producers. About half of the world's organic producers are in Africa. Compared to 2006, organically measured land increased by 27% (0.18 million hectares) in Africa. Almost 900,000 ha of land that constitutes 3% of the global organic agricultural land was certified as organic. Despite having a major proportion of organic producers, the domestic organic products' market is very small in Africa. Thus, the organic produce from Africa must find markets in industrial economies (International Federation of Organic Agriculture Movements 2009).

Genuine Savings Genuine savings or adjusted net savings (ANS) measure the true rate of savings in an economy after taking into account investments in human capital, depletion of natural resources, and damage control caused by pollution (Sustainable Society Foundation 2017). For the calculation of SSI, genuine savings or adjusted net savings are measured as a percent of gross national income (GNI). The SSI scores for the African countries and the other developing countries are 6.1 and 7.4, respectively.

The adjusted net savings (in percent of GNI) inclusive of particulate emission damage for the world in 2015 were 11.67. Two African countries—Algeria and Botswana—occupied ranks 9 and 10 in the top 10 countries with highest adjusted net savings (as percent of GNI) (World Bank 2016). Tanzania, Morocco, and Botswana's adjusted net savings were higher than the world average. Angola, the Democratic Republic of the Congo, Zimbabwe, Malawi, Ghana, and Mauritius featured in the list of bottom ten countries with the lowest adjusted net savings. Their adjusted net savings for these countries were in negative numbers indicating that their spending is more than the available resources. This implies that the economic growth in these countries is not sustainable (World Bank 2013). The Sub-Saharan region saw positive genuine saving rates in most years from 1990 to 1999. However, it has been negative for the most part in the twenty-first century.

GDP The mean scores of African countries and the other developing countries are 2.7 and 5.6, respectively. The SSI uses GDP per capita based on purchasing power parity (PPP) published by the International Monetary Fund to calculate SSI scores. According to the International Monetary Fund (2017), the ten African countries with the highest GDP (PPP) occupy ranks within top hundred countries in the world. In order of decreasing GDP within Africa, these are Equatorial Guinea, Seychelles, Mauritius, Gabon, Botswana, Algeria, Libya, South Africa, Egypt, and Namibia.

The World Bank reports that the Sub-Saharan African region's GDP growth has shrunk from 4.5% in 2014 to 3% in 2015 because of the fall in commodity prices, rise in borrowing costs, weak growth in trading partners, and unfavorable developments in many countries (World Bank Group 2015). This is particularly painful for the region as commodities (such as oil and metal) comprise about 60% of the region's exports. Countries such as Nigeria, Equatorial Guinea, the Republic of the Congo, South Sudan, Cameroon, Chad, Botswana, South Africa, and Zambia are witnessing a deceleration in GDP growth owing to various reasons (such as the fluctuations in commodity prices, political instability, and natural disasters).

Employment SSI uses the number of unemployed people as a percent of the total labor force to gauge employment. The mean SSI score for the African developing countries is 4.6, while for the other developing countries, it is 4.9.

The average unemployment rate for the world from 2010 to 2016 was 5.89% (World Bank 2017). Fourteen Sub-Saharan countries (including Benin, Madagascar, Uganda, Niger, Tanzania, Sierra Leone, Rwanda, and Burkina Faso) had lower unemployment rates than the world average during this period. For the majority of countries in the Sub-Saharan region, the mean unemployment rates have been consistently higher than the world average. For Gambia, Swaziland, Namibia, Lesotho, South Africa, and Mozambique, unemployment rates are the worst, that is, more than 20%. These statistics present an extremely challenging situation for the continent as population growth has created a youth bulge that calls for a commensurate increase in job opportunities in the near future. Africa's unemployment is a consequence of factors (such as many seasonal jobs in agriculture and lack of vocational skills/industrial experience among the youth).

Public Debt This dimension of the SSI is measured as the level of public debt of a country as a percent of its GDP. The mean SSI score is 5.9 for African countries and 6.3 for other developing countries in the world. When measured in relation to the GDP, public debt indicates the capacity of a country to repay its creditors. Although a low debt to GDP ratio is preferred, it may not necessarily mean a good economy (World Atlas 2017). Developed countries can better handle a higher debt as a percent of its GDP, while developing countries with debt more than 60% of GDP can expect growth rates to be reduced by half of what they would be without such debt loads for the government (Reinhart and Rogoff 2010).

Historically, Senegal, South Sudan, Republic of the Congo, and Equatorial Guinea have had very low national debts (International Monetary Fund 2015).

Three African countries with the highest public debt as a percent of GDP in decreasing order are Eritrea (137.6%), Gambia (107.7%), and Egypt (90%). These countries are among the top 25 countries in terms of the national debt.

Analysis of Africa's Five Regions

Comparing Africa's Five Regions

The United Nations' classification of African countries into five regions is presented in Fig. 13.6. This geoscheme of five regions will be used to analyze the different geographical grouping of countries in Africa.

Figure 13.7 depicts the change in the 21 SSI dimensions for the five regions of Africa from 2006 to 2016. The changes in Fig. 13.6 range from more than 4 points on a 10-point scale to −3 points. Moving from the top in a clockwise direction, the region of the South African countries posts a noticeably lower change score than the other regions on the education dimension but posts higher change scores for biodiversity and renewable water resources. Both the South and the North regions post an almost 3.0 change score on energy savings. The West region spikes out more than 4 change points on genuine savings. Finally, near the top again, the Central region posts an improvement of 3 change points on the dimension of public debt, while the South registers a negative movement during the same period of −2 points on public debt.

Figure 13.8 is a radar chart depicting the 2016 SSI ratings for all the regions of the world on the three dimensions of well-being: (1) human well-being, (2) environmental well-being, and (3) economic well-being. The five African regions are located on the left side of the radar chart. At the top of the chart is the composite of all the non-African countries. Here, one can see that generally, the African regions underperform the other regions on human well-being (with the exception of the North African region) and economic well-being. However, the African regions do better than the other regions on environmental well-being. The story emerging from an analysis of Fig. 13.8 is one of African being an underdeveloped continent (in

Fig. 13.6 United Nations Statistics Division's geoscheme for Africa's five regions

human and economic terms) with abundant natural resources that have not yet been spoiled (which is evident in the above average scores for the African regions on the environmental dimension).

Figure 13.9 depicts the regions ranked on the combination of the average scores for the three well-being dimensions. While the African regions can be seen in the bottom of the figure as solid bars, some African regions (such as East, West, and North Africa) outperform the North American region. This comparison suggests that despite challenges in developing the human-made dimensions of sustainability (human and economic), some regions in Africa can be said to have better ratings of sustainability than a developed region of the world, such as North America. This should be encouraging to those who live in Africa or seek to preserve or to improve Africa's sustainability.

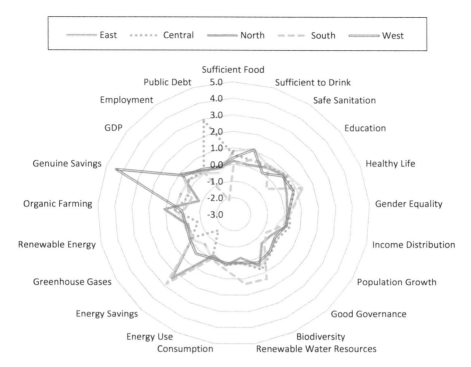

Fig. 13.7 2006–2016 change in 21 SSI dimensions for the 5 regions of Africa

Discussion

Four research questions about sustainable development shaped the analysis in this study comparing (1) Africa to the rest of the world, (2) Africa to other developing countries, (3) Africa's regions on changes over a 10-year period, as well as (4) Africa's regions to the other regions of the world. By answering these research questions, one can better understand how global marketing strategies for firms and the perspectives of those in the media and public sector might need to change because of new realizations about sustainable development in Africa.

For the first two research questions, a general pattern characterizing Africa's performance on the three dimensions for well-being is that Africa lags the rest of the world and the other developing countries in human well-being and economic well-being, but Africa compares favorably in environmental well-being. With the exception of gender equality, Africa lags the rest of the world and other developing countries in terms of human well-being. This can be seen by the separation of the two lines in Fig. 13.2 on the right side of this figure. The widest separations can be seen for (1) sufficient drinking water, (2) safe sanitation, (3) education, (4) healthy life, and (5) population growth. When comparing Africa to other developing countries, a similar pattern can be discerned. In Fig. 13.3, one can see that Africa posts

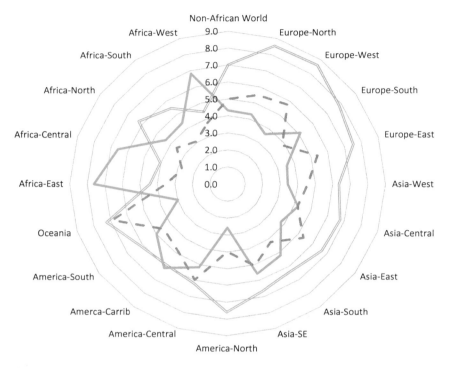

Fig. 13.8 2016 SSI ratings on three dimensions of well-being for UN regions of the world

better scores on each of the seven dimensions for environmental well-being (planet) than the other developing countries. Four of these differences are statistically significant at $p = 0.05$.

To close the gaps Africa has with the rest of the world and with other developing countries, hard infrastructure needs to be developed for assets, such as water treatment plants and delivery systems, schools, and hospitals (Shultz et al. 2012). Additionally, cultural change is needed in the form of (1) respect for the rule of law and governance, (2) adoption of healthy living practices in households, (3) development of public sanitation practices, (4) increased commitment to keeping children in school, and (5) appreciating the beauty of smaller families. In these ways, African countries can make needed gains in human well-being.

Regarding the rule of law and governance, the independent watchdog organization Freedom House reports that 12% of Africa's 1.02 billion persons live in countries Freedom House rates as free, 49% live in partially free countries, and 39% live in countries rated "not free" (Freedom House 2017). A comparison of the average for Africa's countries in 1977 and those in 2017 for political rights, as well as civil

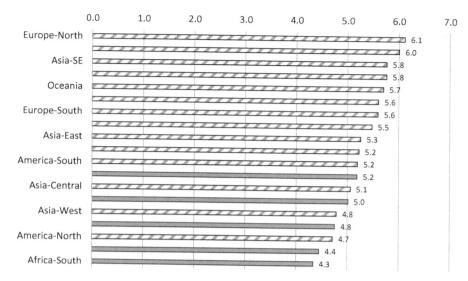

Fig. 13.9 Average of three well-being dimensions for UN regions of the world

liberties, shows that both groups of countries improved 1.1 and 0.8, respectively, on these dimensions using Freedom House's 7-point scale (with 1 representing most free and 7 the least free). This is the identical amount that other countries of the world improved on these dimensions over the same time period. This suggests that Africa is improving on political rights and civil liberties at the same rate as the rest of the world. This is good news. However, the bad news is that Africa remains noticeably behind the rest of the world's countries in the 2017 data (in political rights, other countries of the world have an average score of 3.1 compared to a worse score for Africa's countries of 4.9; and in civil liberties other countries earn an average score of 3.1 compared to a lower score for Africa's countries of 4.6).

At the same time as human well-being gains are made, African countries must protect the natural environment from overdevelopment while encouraging the development of sustainably minded businesses. Of course, tension typically characterizes a society's conservation efforts when these imply changes for its economic development. Sheth (1992) has proposed an important idea of macromarketing as the harmonization between society's interests and business' interests. According to Sheth, the objective for these three sectors should be goal convergence through a process of (1) win-win value creation, (2) mutual interdependence, (3) networked structure, (4) mutually accepted practices, and (5) frontline information systems (which today might be in the form of mobile phone technology). African leaders in business, government, and civil society would do well to focus on these in order to realize important benefits from such a macromarketing approach to country development.

For the last two research questions about the regions of Africa, regions have changed from 2006 to 2016 only slightly on most of the 21 dimensions, while (with

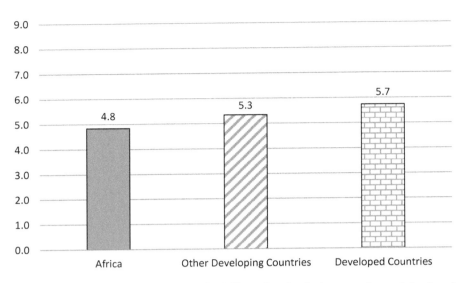

Fig. 13.10 Overall sustainability scores for Africa, other developing countries, and developed countries

notable exceptions) Africa's regions underperform on human and economic well-being but perform better than the rest of the world on environmental well-being. The notable exceptions are (1) North Africa's better performance than the average for the rest of the world on human well-being, (2) the regions of North and South Africa's worse performance than the average for the rest of the world on environmental well-being, and (3) East Africa's better performance than the average for the rest of the world on economic well-being.

These findings highlight the heterogeneity across regions of Africa for well-being. North African countries can offer some best practices for developing human well-being to other regions of Africa. Some African regions, such as North Africa and South Africa, need to improve in terms of environmental well-being and can look to East Africa, West Africa, and Central Africa for insights on how to do this. While no African region clearly eclipses other regions in terms of economic well-being, some are edging ahead, such as East Africa, North Africa, and West Africa.

When combining the average scores for the three well-being dimensions, comparisons can be made across Africa, the other developing countries, as well as developed countries. Figure 13.10 depicts these results which should be sobering to those who read and hear hype about Africa and its development prospects. Such prospects could be favorable, but the current position overall for sustainable development is lower than in other developing countries and the developed countries. This view should be valuable for marketers in African-based and non-African-based firms, as well as for those in the media, the public sector, and academia who study Africa.

A Macromarketing Assessment of Africa's Future Development

Macromarketing researchers have noted that economic development is likely to occur under certain conditions. Such conditions would include (1) natural resources, (2) transportation and communications infrastructure, (3) institutions to protect individual property rights, (4) stable and business-friendly political environment, (5) educational resources, and (6) a cultural ethos that values work, entrepreneurship, and material progress (Klein and Nason 2000, p. 288).

Regarding the first condition for economic development, Africa boasts abundant mineral resources and is a leading supplier of crucial commodities for the global economy, such as oil, cobalt, copper, diamonds, gold, platinum, titanium, and coltan (used in manufacturing electronic capacitors) (Carmody 2016). Regarding the next four conditions for economic development, both physical and institutional infrastructure in Africa have markedly improved this century (Berman 2013). Although Africa still lags in income growth, it has made marked improvement in health, education, gender equality, security, and human rights (Kenny 2011, p. 4). Regarding the final condition for economic development, reinforcing cultural values (that esteem work, entrepreneurship, and material progress) remains a challenge across Africa (Gane 2014).

The Importance of Values Values, beliefs, and attitudes are commonly shared by members of a cultural group (Harrison 2006, p. 6). These can support and promote prosperity because they strongly affect perceptions of individuals and organizations about the way to win (Porter 2000). In 2009, Zambian economist Dambisa Moyo asserted that foreign aid has undermined the mindset of too many in Africa (Solomon 2009). "I believe it's largely aid," Moyo said. "You get the corruption—historically, leaders have stolen the money without penalty—and you get the dependency, which kills entrepreneurship."

Table 13.3 presents the framework proposed by (Grondona 2000) to explain the differences between progress-prone cultures and progress-resistant cultures. For Africa to develop economically, more in Africa will need to embrace values that encourage and nurture societal progress (the left column of Table 13.3). A worldview of progress-prone cultures includes personal agency for the individual, as compared to fatalism for the progress-resistant culture. The expandability of wealth characterizes progress-prone cultures, as opposed to a peasant mentality that wealth is finite (if someone gains, someone else must lose). In terms of values and virtues, progress-prone cultures reinforce trust in public or commercial activities with lesser values like punctuality being important. By comparison, progress-resistant cultures reinforce mistrust and give little emphasis to lesser values, such as punctuality.

Economic behavior in progress-prone cultures is influenced by regard given to entrepreneurial effort in competitive markets. Progress-resistant cultures see rent seeking (taking advantage of what their position allows for self-gain) by cultural elites in government as the privilege granted to those who attain power.

Table 13.3 Typology of progress-prone and progress-resistant cultures (Grondona 2000)

Dimension	Progress-prone culture	Progress-resistant culture
World view		
Destiny	I can influence my destiny for the better	Fatalism, resignation, sorcery
Wealth	Product of human creativity is wealth expandable (positive sum)	What exists (zero-sum) is wealth; not expandable
Values, virtues		
Ethical code	Rigorous within realistic norms; feeds trust	Elastic, wide gap twixt utopian norms and behavior. Mistrust reinforced
The lesser values	A job well done, tidiness, and punctuality matter	Lesser virtues unimportant
Economic behavior		
Entrepreneurship	Investment and creativity	Rent seeking: income derives from government connections
Competition	Leads to excellence	Is a sign of aggression and a threat to equality—and privilege
Advancement	Based on merit, connections	Based on family and/or patron connections
Social behavior		
Rule of law/corruption	Reasonably law abiding; corruption is prosecuted	Money, connections matter; corruption is tolerated
Family	The idea of "family" extends to the broader society	The family is a fortress against the broader society
Gender relationships	If gender equality not a reality, at least not inconsistent with value system	Women subordinate to men in most dimensions of life

Social behavior in progress-prone cultures can be characterized by a self-governing citizenry in which half the population (women) are able to function as the equals of the other half (men). Progress-resistant cultures tend to carry patriarchal hierarchy in which male chiefs or strong men dominate others because of their place in the tribe or kinship group. Women might run the home, but usually not business, government, or civic organizations.

Guarded Optimism While daunting challenges remain for development in Africa, these challenges can focus the efforts of firms—both foreign-based and local—and provide some of the most meaningful and exciting advances. For example, one of the most acute challenges faced by the continent is the education and training of its ever increasing youth population. In the period from 1990 to 2007, the number of public universities in the Sub-Saharan Africa doubled from 100 to 200, while the increase in private universities was about 20 times (from 24 to 468) (World Bank 2009). Pearson Education has expanded its Affordable Learning Fund (for schools and material providers) in African countries such as Ghana, Kenya, and South Africa (Mance 2015). In January 2016, the entire preprimary and primary education system in Liberia was announced to be outsourced to Bridge International Academies, a private American firm (Mungai 2016).

In the healthcare sector, multinational corporations have made collaborative efforts in combating life-threatening diseases such as HIV/AIDS, malaria, and Ebola. In South Africa, leading automotive manufacturers, such as General Motors, Volkswagen Group, Mercedes-Benz, BMW, Toyota, and Nissan, are making continuous efforts to fight HIV/AIDS (Müller-Debus and Thauer 2013). Additionally, firms such as Chevron, Marathon Oil, and ExxonMobil have developed effective initiatives to reduce the incidence of malaria (Ollong 2016). Spurred by the 2014 outbreak of Ebola in West Africa, IBM committed to employ big data analytics to identify Ebola virus-infected carriers (Monegain 2017).

In the telecommunications sector, Kuwait-based Zain became one of the world's largest telecommunication firms by targeting developing countries, such as those in Africa (Khanna and Palepu 2010, p. 170). When operating in Sub-Saharan African countries, Zain discovered that it needed to fill voids in the infrastructure by generating its own power with thousands of small generators. With such agility, Zain went from a government-controlled monopoly with just 600,000 customers in Kuwait in 2002 to becoming the world's fastest-growing telecommunications provider with 42 million customers in 15 countries of Africa in 2008. In 2010, Zain sold its African operations—then in 15 African countries—to Bharti Airtel of India for $10.7 billion, posting a $3.3 billion profit on the sale (Daily Nation 2010). Zain's story in Africa highlights the potential rewards for firms committed to success in African infrastructure development.

In a similar way, quality and quantity gaps in public goods (such as roads and railways, electricity grids, and water systems) offer firms opportunities to join in African development and to benefit themselves, as well. For example, electrification in rural parts of Sub-Saharan Africa is only 14% (Lindermann 2015). Firms can also play a major role in reducing unemployment by moving young Africans from the self-employed, informal sector (subsistence agriculture, small household enterprises, and street vending) to formal sectors such as skill-based jobs in the public and private sectors. To attract such firms that will assist in this movement of Africans into the formal sector, countries in Africa must provide improved access to finance and easy entrance to foreign businesses (McKinsey 2012).

Political Risk Political risk is a factor that threatens sustainable development in Africa more than any other. One political risk report asserts that only nine African countries can be classified as "moderately unstable" (Marsh 2017). These are Egypt, Tunisia, Algeria, Morocco, Senegal, Ghana, Namibia, Botswana, and South Africa. The rest are classified as "unstable" which means that business conditions in these countries could markedly change in the event of a shock, such as an economic crisis or a sudden change in the political environment within the country. To put this into perspective, the only countries rated as "stable" in this report are the developed countries of Northern Europe, Australia, New Zealand, Japan, Malaysia, United Arab Emirates, Chile, South Korea, Taiwan, Canada, and the United States. This suggests that firms wishing to do business outside these countries rated as "stable" take on a measure of political risk when they do so.

Government corruption contributes to political risk in many ways. It diverts resources from their best use for a community or society and exacerbates poverty, as the most marginalized in a society lose access to health, education, sanitation, and water resources they would have had without the diversion of resources. Additionally, corruption foments resentment among citizens who would later agitate for regime change or energetically pursue such change in order that they themselves or their group should enjoy the financial gains associated with the rents imposed by corrupt governments (Burgis 2016). José Ugaz, the Chairman of Transparency International asserts that "With corruption, there's no sustainable development" (Transparency International 2017).

Transparency International generates its Corruption Perceptions Index (CPI) by using 13 different data sources from 12 different institutions that capture perceptions of corruption for a country within the past 2 years. It uses a 0–100 scale (with higher numbers representing less corruption). The CPI is moderately and positively correlated with the SSI which supports the assertion of Ugaz—the Chairman of Transparency International—that corruption harms sustainable development for a country (Simkins and Peterson 2016).

In the 2016 CPI, African countries posted a median value of 30 with Botswana and Rwanda having the most favorable ratings (60 and 54, respectively). South Sudan and Somalia received the worst ratings in Africa on the CPI (11 and 10, respectively). By comparison, the OECD countries had a median value of 72 on the CPI. These findings suggest that non-African firms will likely find themselves in a different context for corruption when operating in Africa. Such firms need to make sure their employees understand and follow the policies of the firm when conducting business in Africa. Encouragingly, Berman (2013) reports that improvement in good governance in Africa is the trend, rather than the exception across the continent. However, firms developing their entry strategies for Africa would do well to consult the CPI and the historical trend of the CPI in countries being considered for their new operations.

Conclusion

In the African context, macromarketing has relevance for practitioners because marketing and society can be seen to influence each other in clear ways. Such a macromarketing view can help visionary leaders of firms develop their own vision of success in Africa and realize the commitment needed to realize such success.

This study has provided evidence for Africa's lagging economic development relative to other regions of the world that has resulted in less environmental degradation in Africa. Fewer factories, roads, and industrial areas mean less harm to the environment. But those new to Africa should remember that economic activity is lively in many parts of Africa. Arnould (2001) presented evidence of this in his ethnographic study of onion marketing in the West African countries of Niger, Benin, Togo, Ghana, and the Ivory Coast. Here, entrepreneurs—many of them women—grew a large regional consumer market over the years, fueled local development, and increased nonfarm incomes.

In the manufacturing sector, foreign-based businesses, such as China's C&H Garments, have established successful factories in Africa. C&H Garments located its factories in Ethiopia, Kenya, Senegal, and Rwanda (Manson 2015). Helen Hai, one of the founders of C&H Garments, has become the goodwill ambassador for the United Nations Industrial Development Organization and CEO of the Made in Africa Initiative. "Every country has its own comparative advantage—you just need to find it," Hai said.

Hai believes that because of rising wages in China, firms will be seeking lower-wage countries like those in Africa to establish new manufacturing facilities. She predicts that firms will move 85 million jobs from China to Africa by 2015. In this way, Africa's need to develop economically can become an attractive aspect to firms in the future. This is part of the global shift that forward-looking and savvy business leaders, such as Hai, envision. These firm-level global/regional strategies may not be focused on sustainable business practices (Peterson 2013), but they could help Africa develop along all three of the sustainability dimensions (people, planet, and profit).

Based on Africa's history after colonialism in the last 70 years, one could expect that the business activity will be uneven across the countries of Africa because of the heterogeneity of markets and cultures across Africa (Shultz et al. 2012; Hosley and Wee 1988). A study of the top African brands found that of the top 25 brands, all but one—Kenya's Safaricom—came from Nigeria or South Africa. Seven of the top 10 brands came from South Africa (Kulish 2014).

The titans of the consumer products field, Unilever and Procter & Gamble, have shifted their geographic priorities to include Africa (Reingold 2011) because of the population growth forecasted for the continent. By 2040, Africa's current population of more than one billion will surpass that of India and China (Figueiredo et al. 2015). With this knowledge of the future in mind, one can understand the shift in attitude of business leaders around the world to target Africa for their future operations. Non-African firms such as Zain of Kuwait earned billions in profits from its 10 years in the African telecommunications market. Kenya's Safaricom developed M-PESA the "mobile wallet" that has become enormously successful because of the scarce banking services in many parts of Africa (Eyring et al. 2011).

No doubt, African-based firms will emerge to lead Africa's economic development. Such firms have to become resilient and develop the know-how needed to succeed in the demanding conditions of African markets characterized by a lack of infrastructure, by extreme weather, and by customers constrained by poverty.

Whit Alexander, from Seattle, Washington, came to Ghana and launched his for-profit firm Burro in order to serve the poor by selling rechargeable AA batteries to off-grid villagers (half of Ghana's population) (Alexander 2012). Over 3 years, Alexander had to become not only an expert on the technology of his product but also to be alert and flexible enough to pivot toward new products, such as a lantern with four lighting levels and cell phone chargers, that his poor consumers wanted enough to buy.

However, as electrification unfolds across Ghana, Burro's customers will no longer need the Burro products that are suitable for those living off the electrical grid. In this way, one can glimpse how markets can lead the way to economic development (consumers can create value in better lit dwellings and with charged cell phones) and then how such development can change markets (governments and public utilities gain the revenue to build electrical grids). This interaction is the kind of phenomenon macromarketing scholars seeks to explain. Africa will offer rich opportunities for studying such macromarketing phenomena far into the future.

References

Africa-America Institute (AAI). 2015. State of education in Africa report 2015. http://www. aaionline.org/wp-content/uploads/2015/09/AAI-SOE-report-2015-final.pdf. Accessed 11 June 2017.

African Development Bank Group. 2012. Briefing notes to ADB's long-term strategy. https://www. afdb.org/fileadmin/uploads/afdb/Documents/Policy-Documents/FINALper cent20Briefingper cent20Noteper cent205per cent20Incomeper cent20Inequalityper cent20inper cent20Africa. pdf. Accessed 29 June 2017.

———. 2017. Millennium development goals. https://www.afdb.org/en/topics-and-sectors/topics/millennium-development-goals-mdgs/goal-1-eradicate-extreme-poverty-and-hunger. Accessed 29 June 2017.

African Globe. 2014. Africa's population will quadruple by 2100. What does that mean for its cities? https://www.africanglobe.net/africa/africas-population-quadruple-2100-cities/. Accessed 9 June 2017.

Alexander, M. 2012. *Bright lights, no city: An African adventure on bad roads with a brother and a very weird business plan.* Hyperion: New York.

Anyaogu, I. 2016. Energy efficient solutions can assuage sub-Saharan Africa's energy challenge. https://asokoinsight.com/news/energy-efficient-solutions-can-assuage-sub-saharan-africas-energy-challenge. Accessed 29 June 2017.

Arnould, E.J. 2001. Ethnography, export marketing policy, and economic development in Niger. *Journal of Public Policy & Marketing* 20 (2): 151–169.

Barbee, J. 2015. How renewable energy in South Africa is quietly stealing a march on coal. *The Guardian.* https://www.theguardian.com/environment/2015/jun/01/how-renewable-energy-in-south-africa-is-quietly-stealing-a-march-on-coal. Accessed 9 June 2017.

BBC News. 2012. Niger worst place to be mother – Save the children. http://www.bbc.com/news/world-africa-17984899. Accessed 9 June 2017.

Berman, J.E. 2013. *Success in Africa: CEO insights from a continent on the rise.* Brookline: Bibliomotion.

Bright, J., and A. Hruby. 2015. *The next Africa: An emerging continent becomes a global powerhouse.* New York: Thomas Dunne Books/St. Martin's Press.

Burgis, T. 2016. *The looting machine: Warlords, oligarchs, corporations, smugglers, and the theft of Africa's wealth.* New York: Public Affairs.

Carmody, P.R. 2016. *The new scramble for Africa.* Cambridge: Polity Press UK.

Chitonge, H. 2015. *Economic growth and development in Africa: Understanding trends and prospects.* Oxon: Routledge/Taylor & Francis Group.

CNN. 2013. Africa's rocky road to democracy. http://www.cnn.com/2013/03/01/opinion/africa-democracy-mbaku/index.html. Accessed 9 June 2017.

Conway, G. 2014. Soil isn't sexy – But it could explain hunger in Africa. https://www.theguardian. com/global-development/2014/dec/04/soil-sexy-hunger-africa-food-security. Accessed 9 June 2017.

Daily Nation. 2010. Kuwait's Zain closes African sale to India's Bhartihttp. *Daily Nation* (Kenya). July 20, 2010. http://www.nation.co.ke/business/Kuwaits-Zain-closes-African sale-to-India's-Bharti/996-961048-15p7co0/index.html.

Dowden, R. 2009. *Africa: Altered states, ordinary miracles.* London: Portobello Books.

Eccles, R.G., and M.P. Krzus. 2015. *The integrated reporting movement: Meaning, momentum, motives, and materiality.* New York: Wiley.

Euromonitor International. 2012. South Africa- the most unequal income distribution in the world. http://blog.euromonitor.com/2012/06/south-africa-the-most-unequal-income-distribution-in-the-world.html. Accessed 11 June 2017.

Eyring, M.J., M.W. Johnson, and H. Nair. 2011. New business models in emerging markets. *Harvard Business Review* 89 (1–2): 88–95.

Figueiredo, B., J. Chelekis, B. DeBerry-Spence, A.F. Fırat, G. Ger, D. Godefroit-Winkel, O. Kravets, J. Moisander, K. Nuttavuthisit, L. Peñaloza, and M. Tadajewski. 2015. Developing markets? Understanding the role of markets and development at the intersection of macro-marketing and transformative consumer research (TCR). *Journal of Macromarketing* 35 (2): 257–271.

Fisk, G. 1981. An invitation to participate in affairs of the journal of macromarketing. *Journal of Macromarketing* 1 (1): 3–6.

Food and Agriculture Organization of the United Nations (FAO). 2016. Food and Agriculture Organization of the United Nations. http://www.fao.org/nr/water/aquastat/countries_regions/profile_segments/africa-WR_eng.stm. Accessed 11 June 2017.

Forslund, D.. 2016. World Bank finds itself in a Gini fix. *Mail & Guardian*, March 18, 2016. https://mg.co.za/article/2016-03-17-world-bank-finds-itself-in-a-gini-fix.

Freedom House. 2017. Freedom in the world today. https://freedomhouse.org/report/freedom-world/freedom-world-2017.

Gane, M.K. 2014. *Is this why Africa is?* London: MarrickeGane Publishing.

GeoCurrents. 2017. Africa conventional political map. http://www.geocurrents.info/geographical-education/free-customizable-map-of-africa-for-download.

Grondona, M. 2000. A cultural typology of economic development. In *Culture matters: How values shape human progress*, ed. L.E. Harrison and S.P. Huntington, 44–55. New York: Basic Books.

Harrison, L.E. 2006. *The central liberal truth: How politics can change a culture and save it from itself.* New York: Oxford University Press.

Hosley, S., and C.H. Wee. 1988. Marketing and economic development: Focusing on the less developed countries. *Journal of Macromarketing* 8 (1): 43–53.

International Energy Agency (IEA). 2014. *Africa energy outlook*. http://www.iea.org/publications/freepublications/publication/WEO2014_AfricaEnergyOutlook.pdf. Accessed 29 June 2017.

International Federation of Organic Agriculture Movements (IFOAM). 2009. The world of organic agriculture, statistics & emerging trends 2009. http://orgprints.org/15575/3/willer-kilcher-2009-1-26.pdf. Accessed 9 June 2017.

International Food Policy Research Institute (IFPRI)/ Welthungerhilfe/ Concern Worldwide 2016. 2016. Global hunger index getting to zero hunger. http://www.ifpri.org/publication/2016-global-hunger-index-getting-zero-hunger. Accessed 29 June 2017.

International Monetary Fund (IMF). 2015. Africa-public debt (per cent of GDP). https://en.actualitix.com/country/afri/africa-public-debt-per-gdp.php. Accessed 9 June 2017.

———. 2017. List of African countries by GDP per capita. http://statisticstimes.com/economy/african-countries-by-gdp-per-capita.php. Accessed 9 June 2017.

James, R., and R. Washington. 2012. Changes in African temperature and precipitation associated with degrees of global warming. *Climate Change* 117 (4): 859–872.

Karekezi, S., and W. Kithyoma. 2003. Renewable energy in Africa: Prospects and limits. https://sustainabledevelopment.un.org/content/documents/nepadkarekezi.pdf. Accessed 9 June 2017.

Kenny, C. 2011. *Getting better: Why global development is succeeding—and how we can improve the world even more.* New York: Basic Books.

Khanna, T., and K.G. Palepu. 2010. *Winning in emerging markets: A road map for strategy and execution.* Boston: Harvard Business Press.

Klein, T.A., and R.W. Nason. 2000. Marketing and development: Macromarketing perspectives. In *Handbook of marketing and society*, ed. P.N. Bloom and G.T. Gundlach, 263–297. Thousand Oaks: Sage Publications.

Kulish, N. 2014. Africans open fuller wallets to the future. *New York Times A*, 1.

Lindermann, T. (2015). 1.3 Billion are living in the Dark. *The Washington Post.* https://www.washingtonpost.com/graphics/world/world-without-power/. Accessed 24 July 2017.

Mahajan, V. 2009. *Africa rising: How 900 million African consumers offer more than you think.* New Jersey: Pearson Prentice Hall.

Mance, H. 2015. Pearson expands education venture fund. *Financial Times.* https://www.ft.com/content/1f4338ea-9fef-11e4-9a74-00144feab7de. Accessed 24 July 2017.

Manson, K. 2015. Chinese manufacturers look to Rwanda. *Financial Times.* May 6, 2015. https://www.ft.com/content/8c3b27ec-e8e1-11e4-87fe-00144feab7de.

Marsh. 2017. Political risk map 2017, https://www.marsh.com/us/campaigns/political-risk-map-2017.html.

McKinsey. 2012. Africa at work: Job creation and inclusive growth. http://www.mckinsey.com/global-themes/middle-east-and-africa/africa-at-work. Accessed 24 July 2017.

McKinsey & Company. 2015. Powering Africa. http://www.mckinsey.com/industries/electric-power-and-natural-gas/our-insights/powering-africa. Accessed 9 June 2017.

Monegain, B. 2017. IBM says big data has provided new insight into how Ebola spread. *Healthcare IT News.* http://www.healthcareitnews.com/news/ibm-using-big-data-take-aim-ebola. Accessed 24 July 2017.

Müller-Debus, A.K. and Thauer, C.R., 2013. HIV/AIDS in South Africa. Business and Governance in South Africa:Racing to the Top?, p.41.

Mungai, C. 2016. An Africa first! Liberia outsources entire education system to a private American firm. Why all should pay attention. http://mgafrica.com/article/2016-03-31-liberia-plans-to-outsource-its-entire-education-system-to-a-private-company-why-this-is-a-very-big-deal-and-africa-should-pay-attention. Accessed 24 July 2017.

Mutasa, C., and M. Paterson. 2015. *Africa and the millennium development goals: Progress, problems, and prospects.* Lanham: Rowman & Littlefield.

OECD. 2017. Income inequality. OECD Data. https://data.oecd.org/inequality/income-inequality.htm.

Ollong, K.A. 2016. Multinational corporations and the fight against malaria in Africa. *Journal of Pan African Studies* 9 (4): 318–341.

Onyeiwu, S. 2015. *Emerging issues in contemporary African economies: Structure, policy, and sustainability.* New York: Palgrave Macmillan.

Organization for Economic Co-operation and Development (OECD)/ International Energy Agency (IEA). 2014. Africa energy outlook. http://www.iea.org/publications/freepublications/publication/WEO2014_AfricaEnergyOutlook.pdf. Accessed 9 June 2017.

Oxford Business Law Blog (OBLB). 2017. Heralds new non-financial reporting requirements across Europe. https://www.law.ox.ac.uk/business-law-blog/blog/2017/03/2017-heralds-new-non-financial-reporting-requirements-across-europe. Accessed 10 June 2017.

Peterson, M. 2013. *Sustainable enterprise: A macromarketing approach.* Thousand Oaks: SAGE.

Pflanz. 2013. Africa's energy consumption growing fastest in the world. *The Christian Science Monitor.* https://www.csmonitor.com/World/Africa/2013/0101/Africa-s-energy-consumption-growing-fastest-in-world. Accessed 29 June 2017.

Population Reference Bureau. 2016. World population data sheet with a special focus on human needs and sustainable resources. http://www.prb.org/Publications/DataSheets/2016/2016-world-population-data-sheet.aspx. Accessed 29 June 2017.

Porter, M. 2000. Attitudes, values, beliefs, and the microeconomics of prosperity. In *Culture matters: How values shape human progress*, ed. L.E. Harrison and S.P. Huntington, 14–28. New York: Basic Books.

Reingold, J. 2011. Can P&G make money in places where people earn $2 a day? *Fortune* 163 (1): 86–91.

Reinhart, Carmen M, and Kenneth S Rogoff. 2010. Growth in a time of debt. *American Economic Review* 100, no 2: 573–578.

Rotberg, R.I. 2013. *Africa emerges: Consummate challenges, abundant opportunities*. Cambridge: Polity Press.

Sheth, J.N. 1992. Toward a theory of macromarketing. *Canadian Journal of Administrative Sciences/ Revue Canadienne des Sciences de l'administration* 9 (2): 154–161.

———. 2017. The African awakening: When will the giant wake up? https://www.youtube.com/watch?v=ZIomNXAwGc4. Accessed 29 June 2017.

Shultz, C.J., R. Deshpandé, T.B. Cornwell, A. Ekici, P. Kothandaraman, M. Peterson, S. Shapiro, D. Talukdar, and A. Veeck. 2012. Marketing and public policy: Transformative research in developing markets. *Journal of Public Policy & Marketing* 31 (2): 178–184.

Simkins, T.J., and M. Peterson. 2016. Assessing the value of a societal-level sustainability index for macromarketing research. *Journal of Macromarketing* 36 (1): 78–95.

Solomon, D. 2009. The anti-Bono. *The New York Times Magazine*, February 9, 2009. http://www.nytimes.com/2009/02/22/magazine/22wwln-q4t.html?mcubz=1. Accessed 26 July 2017.

South China Morning Post. 2014. Economists fear low birth rates in developed world will choke growth. http://www.scmp.com/business/economy/article/1510742/economists-fear-low-birth-rates-developed-world-will-choke-growth. Accessed 11 June 2017.

Sustainable Society Foundation. 2017. Indicator 18 – Genuine savings. http://www.ssfindex.com/ssi2016/wp-content/uploads/pdf/indicator18-2016.pdf. Accessed 11 June 2017.

Swartz, J., and C. Jones. 2017. The pay gap could vanish for all women – Sometime in the 23rd century. *USA Today*. https://www.usatoday.com/story/tech/2017/03/13/womens-pay-gap-23rd-century/97901550/. Accessed 11 June 2017.

Transparency International. 2017. No sustainable development without tackling corruption: The importance of tracking SDG 16. https://www.transparency.org/news/feature / no_sustainable_development_without_tackling_corruption_SDG_16.

UN Water/Africa. 2009. The Africa water vision for 2025: Equitable and sustainable use of water for socioeconomic development. https://www.afdb.org/fileadmin/uploads/afdb/Documents/Generic-Documents/africanper cent20waterper cent20visionper cent202025per cent20toper cent20beper cent20sentper cent20toper cent20wwf5.pdf. Accessed 9 June 2017.

UNAIDS. 2014. The gap report. http://files.unaids.org/en/media/unaids/contentassets/documents/unaidspublication/2014/UNAIDS_Gap_report_en.pdf. Accessed 9 June 2017.

United Nations. 2017. Sustainable development goals: 17 goals to transform our world. http://www.un.org/sustainabledevelopment/sustainable-development-goals/. Accessed 31 May 2017.

United Nations (UN). 2012. The millennium development goals report. http://www.un.org/millenniumgoals/pdf/MDGper cent20Reportper cent202012.pdf. Accessed 9 June 2017.

———. 2015. World population prospects https://esa.un.org/unpd/wpp/ Publications/Files/Key_Findings_WPP_2015.pdf. Accessed 11 June 2017.

———. 2016. Water for life decade. http://www.un.org/waterforlifedecade/africa.shtml. Accessed 9 June 2017.

United Nations Children's Fund (UNICEF). 2013. Child malnutrition in Africa. https://data.unicef.org/wp-content/uploads/2015/12/Africa_Brochure_2013_158.pdf. Accessed 9 June 2017.

United Nations Department of Economic and Social Affairs (UNDESA). 2014. International decade for action 'water for life' 2005–2015. http://www.un.org/waterforlifedecade/scarcity.shtml. Accessed 29 June 2017.

United Nations Development Programme (UNDP) 2006. Human development report, 2006. http://
hdr.undp.org/sites/default/files/reports/267/hdr06-complete.pdf. Accessed 9 June 2017.
United Nations Economic Commission for Africa (UNECA). 2015. MDG report 2015 lessons
learned in implementing the MDGS. https://www.afdb.org/fileadmin/uploads/afdb/Documents/
Publications/MDG_Report_2015.pdf. Accessed 9 June 2017.
United Nations Environment Programme (UNEP). 2010. State of biodiversity in Africa. https://
www.cbd.int/iyb/doc/celebrations/iyb-egypt-state-of-biodiversity-in-africa.pdf. Accessed 9
June 2017.
Van de Kerk, G., and A.R. Manuel. 2013. Sustainable society foundation. http://www.ssfindex.
com. Accessed 27 Mar 2015.
Vidal, J. 2014. Smelly, contaminated, full of disease: The world's open dumps are growing. *The
Guardian*.   https://www.theguardian.com/global-development/2014/oct/06/smelly-contami-
nated-disease-worlds-open-dumps. Accessed 11 June 2017.
Whiteford, A., and D.E. van Seventer. 2000. South Africa's changing income distribution in the
1990s. *Journal for Studies in Economic and Econometrics* 24 (3): 7–30.
World Atlas. 2017. Countries with the biggest public debt. http://www.worldatlas.com/articles/
top-20-countries-with-the-biggest-public-debt.html. Accessed 9 June 2017.
World Bank. 2009. Accelerating catch-up: Tertiary education for growth in Sub-Saharan Africa.
http://siteresources.worldbank.org/INTAFRICA/Resources/e-book_ACU.pdf.   Accessed   24
July 2017.
———. 2013. A more accurate pulse on sustainability. http://www.worldbank.org/en/news/fea-
ture/2013/06/05/accurate-pulse-sustainability. Accessed 11 June 2017.
———. 2014. Arable land (per cent of land area). http://data.worldbank.org/indicator/AG.LND.
ARBL.ZS.
———. 2016. Adjusted net savings, including particulate emission damage (per cent of GNI).
http://data.worldbank.org/indicator/NY.ADJ.SVNG.GN.ZS?end=2015&start=2014&year_
high_desc=true. Accessed 11 June 2017.
———. 2017. Unemployment, total (per cent of total labor force). http://data.worldbank.org/indi-
cator/SL.UEM.TOTL.ZS.
World Bank Group (WBG). 2015. Worldwide governance indicators. http://info.worldbank.org/
governance/wgi/index.aspx#home. Accessed 9 June 2017.
———. 2016. Africa's pulse – An analysis of issues shaping Africa's economic future.
https://openknowledge.worldbank.org/bitstream/handle/10986/24033/9781464809187.
pdf?sequence=5&isAllowed=y. Accessed 9 June 2017.
World Economic Forum (WEF). 2015. Which countries are in ecological debt? https://www.wefo-
rum.org/agenda/2015/08/which-countries-are-in-ecological-debt/. Accessed 9 June 2017.
———. 2016. The global gender gap report. http://www3.weforum.org/docs/GGGR16/WEF_
Global_Gender_Gap_Report_2016.pdf. Accessed 9 June 2017.
World Health Organization (WHO). 2011. The Abuja declaration: Ten years on. http://www.who.
int/healthsystems/publications/abuja_report_aug_2011.pdf?ua=1. Accessed 9 June 2017.
———. 2012. World malaria report. http://www.who.int/malaria/publications/world_malaria_
report_2012/en/. Accessed 9 June 2017.
———. 2015. Millennium development goals (MDGs). http://www.who.int/mediacentre/fact-
sheets/fs290/en/. Accessed 11 June 2017.
World Health Organization (WHO)/The United Nations Children's Fund (UNICEF). 2015.
Progress on sanitation and drinking water 2015 update and MDG assessment. http://apps.who.
int/iris/bitstream/10665/177752/1/9789241509145_eng.pdf?ua=1. Accessed 11 July 2017.
World Hunger Education Service. 2016. World hunger and poverty facts and statistics. http://www.
worldhunger.org/2015-world-hunger-and-poverty-facts-and-statistics/. Accessed 11 June 2017.

Index

A
Africa, 333, 336–364
Anti-counterfeiting, 180, 186, 187, 191,
    194–197, 199
Automated content analysis, 31–33, 35, 55
Average variance extracted (AVE), 164

B
Brand, 149–174
Brand awareness, 150, 152, 154, 155,
    157–162, 164–173
Brand centrality, 130, 146
Brand distinctiveness, 124, 130

C
CBEC pilot cities, 102, 104, 105, 115
Collaborative projects, 150, 172
Conceptualization, 149–174
Consumer behavior, 330
Corporate social responsibility (CSR),
    257–282, 291–306
Counterfeiting, 180, 183–187, 189–191,
    193–199
Country development, 333–364
Country of origin (COO), 156–159, 161, 162,
    164, 166–168
Cronbach alpha, 164
Cross-border e-commerce (CBEC), 93–115
Cross-cultural model, 65–67, 69, 70, 74, 77,
    78, 80, 84
Cross-national model, 67, 69, 70, 77
Culture, 61–86

D
Developed-market multinationals, 245–247
Digital managers, 150
Digital marketing, 153, 169, 171
Discriminant validity, 164

E
E-commerce, 93–115, 169, 231–249
Electronic word-of-mouth (eWOM), 150, 154
Emerging economies, 231–249
Emerging market multinationals, 247–248
Emerging markets, 205–225
Emerging trends in global marketing, 4–6
Entertainment, 150, 154
Etic *vs.* emic framework, 83
Exploratory factor analysis (EFA), 18, 20–22,
    25, 27–33, 54

F
Facebook, 149, 151, 159, 162, 169, 170
Fakes, 180, 182, 184, 185, 189–195, 197, 198,
    200
Firm performance, 293, 294, 299, 302, 305,
    306
Flickr, 151

G
Global brand mapping, 122, 124–126
Global brand positioning, 122, 145, 146
Global brands performance, 126
Global CSR, sustainability, 6, 9

Global firm strategies, 231–249
Global market, 150, 152, 156, 169–171
Global marketing scholarship, 15–56
Global marketing strategies, 6, 7, 11
Global trade, 93–115

H
Higher-order, 157, 165–167
Hypothesis, 167, 168

I
I-based N-OLI framework, 96–98
Information, 150–154, 157–159, 161, 163,
        168, 170–172
Instagram, 149, 151
Institutional distance, 205–225
Integrate marketing communication, 152
Intention, 155–162, 164–172
Interactions, 150, 151, 153–155, 158, 159,
        161, 163
Interactivity, 151, 152, 154
International, 152, 169
International Country Risk Guide (ICRG)
        political risk data, 17–22, 24, 27,
        29, 30, 33, 35–37, 39, 42–43,
        45–47, 49, 51–56
Internationalization, 257–282
International marketing, 121, 122, 125,
        126, 133, 134, 145, 147, 259, 262,
        279, 281

J
Japan, 293–302, 304, 306

K
Knowledge, 150–155, 157–162, 164–173

L
LinkedIn, 149, 151
Luxury, 311–330

M
Macromarketing, 6, 9, 10, 333–364
Market entry strategy, 205–225
Marketing mix, 179–200
Micro-blogs, 150, 172
Model fit, 165

Multinational enterprises (MNEs), 205–225
Musical.ly, 149

N
Nigeria, 206, 208, 210–215, 217–225

P
Personal computers, 150, 162, 163,
        169, 171
Pharmaceutical industry, 293–301, 305, 306
Pinterest, 151
Piracy, 180, 186, 195, 199
Pokémon Go, 149, 171
Purchase, 150, 151, 155–162, 164–171

Q
Qualitative research, 329

R
Reliability, 164, 174

S
Satisfaction, 61–86
Service quality, 61–86
Shifting paradigm, 6, 7, 11
Small-and medium-sized enterprises
        (SMEs), 257–282
Smartphones, 149, 150, 159
Snapchat, 149
Social media, 149–155, 157–159, 161, 162,
        164, 165, 167–173
Social media marketing, 150, 152, 154, 168,
        171, 172
Social media presence, 150, 151, 155, 157,
        158, 161, 162, 164, 165, 167, 168,
        172, 173
Social network brand visibility
        (SNBV), 149, 174
Social networking, 150, 152, 162, 169, 170
Social networking sites (SNS), 150–152, 157,
        159, 162, 163, 169–172
Stakeholder engagement, 206, 207, 215–217,
        219, 220, 224, 225
Sustainability, 334, 335, 337, 339, 344, 348,
        354, 358, 363
Sustainable consumption, 311–330
Sustainable development, 334, 335, 337, 355,
        358, 361, 362

T
Trends in political risk, 15–59
Tumblr, 151
Twitter, 149, 151, 159, 162, 169

V
Validation, 157, 164, 165

Value equity, 154, 155, 157, 158, 160–162,
    164–169, 172, 173
Visibility, 149–174

Y
YouTube, 149, 151, 158, 162, 170

CPSIA information can be obtained
at www.ICGtesting.com
Printed in the USA
LVHW081022241119
638339LV00002B/90/P